EVANGELICALS
AT THE BALLOT BOX
★ ★ ★ ★

EVANGELICALS
AT THE BALLOT BOX

★ ★ ★ ★

ALBERT J. MENENDEZ

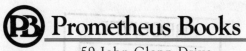

Prometheus Books

59 John Glenn Drive
Amherst, New York 14228-2197

BHW 5993 - 8/3

Published 1996 by Prometheus Books

00 99 98 97 96   5 4 3 2 1

Library of Congress Cataloging-in-Publication Data

Menendez, Albert J.
    Evangelicals at the ballot box / by Albert J. Menendez.
        p.   cm.
    Includes bibliographical references and index.
    ISBN 1–57392–093–2 (cloth : alk. paper)
    1. Evangelicalism—United States. 2. Christian sects—United States—
Political activity. 3. Christianity and politics. I. Title.
BR1642.U5M46   1996
324.973′00882—dc20   96–22931
                                                                                          CIP

Printed in the United States of America on acid-free paper

For Shirley

Contents

Acknowledgments

As always, I appreciate the support and encouragement of my colleagues at Americans for Religious Liberty, Edd Doerr and Marie Gore.

Introduction

Religion clearly affects the outcome of election decisions, depending, of course, on the time and circumstances in which the election is held and the degree to which religious issues are discussed in the campaign. Consider, for example, the following: In 1928 Catholic Alfred E. Smith was the first Democrat ever to carry Massachusetts and Rhode Island, then as now the states in the Union with the largest Catholic percentage of the vote. But Protestant America, especially its evangelical sector, overwhelmingly rejected the New York governor. Republican Herbert Hoover was the first Republican presidential candidate since Reconstruction to carry Virginia, Florida, North Carolina, and Texas. He was the second Republican ever to carry Tennessee, and his margins of victory in Protestant rural areas exceeded those of most other GOP (Grand Old Party) candidates.

In 1960 Democrat John F. Kennedy, the second Catholic candidate to be nominated by a major party, carried Connecticut, New York, New Jersey, and New Mexico largely because of Catholic voting, but he lost Kentucky, Oklahoma, and Tennessee, and very likely Florida, Virginia, Ohio, Wisconsin, Iowa, and California because of anti-Catholic sentiment. In 1976 Jimmy Carter's Baptist connections undoubtedly helped him carry fifteen of the seventeen Southern and Border states. His victory in Ohio and Wisconsin was also largely due to Protestant Republican crossovers. During the 1980s evangelicals cast such heavy votes for Ronald Reagan and George Bush that the Republican candidates had a virtual electoral lock on many states. In 1984 Reagan won over 90 percent of ballots cast at a number of evangelical college precincts.

In 1992 George Bush won a majority only among white evangelicals, thereby securing his Southern victories. Fundamentalists of all stripes supported his candidacy. In Kiryas Joel, a Satmar Hasidic commune in Orange County, New York, Bush received an incredible 94 percent of ballots cast, compared to 5 percent for Clinton and 1 percent for Perot. In Greenville, South Carolina, the mostly student- and faculty-populated precinct surrounding Bob Jones University gave Bush 86 percent, Clinton 9 percent, and Perot 5 percent. The evangelical vote (Bush 61 percent, Clinton 23 percent, Perot 16 percent) represented a long-term Republican gain, because Carter had received almost half of their votes in 1976. The Catholic vote remained unchanged from 1976 to 1992 (moderately Democratic by about 10 points), while Clinton did better than Carter among mainline Protestants, Jews, and the religiously unaffiliated. The Republican vote plunged among Jews and secular voters from about 35 percent for Ford in 1976 to under 15 percent for Bush in 1992.

As this book will demonstrate, religious convictions and attitudes play a major role in forming opinions that have political significance. These influences vary from faith group to faith group and from region to region. Some religious groups are more comfortable in discussing public policy questions and in attempting to influence governmental policies. Others are more reticent. Religion exercises both visible and subliminal influences. Its impact can be charted empirically on the popular vote, the electoral college vote, and congressional decisions.

Finding the precise number of evangelicals is difficult. It is not so easy a task as locating the Roman Catholic population, or the Presbyterian church membership. Evangelicals exist in most Protestant denominations, and even some Catholics call themselves evangelicals. The term "born again Christian" is fairly synonymous with "evangelical," but it is a broader term also accepted by those who are not Protestants. "Conservative Protestant" is a somewhat broader term than evangelical, because it includes fundamentalists and others who may not be comfortable with the designation evangelical.

For the purposes of this book, which is about politics and political coalitions, the term evangelical will refer to those Protestants who believe in a theological rebirth through faith in Jesus Christ and who accept the Bible as the only and the authoritative rule of faith and practice. This rebirth is generally said to have occurred at a particular time; hence, the phrase "born again." The Bible is also generally held to be in some ways inerrant, inspired, infallible, and trustworthy. Evangelicals also emphasize proselytism, evangelism, and missionary efforts to win others to their viewpoint. Fundamentalists are even stricter in their interpretations and their convictions are often accompanied with a degree of separatism and anti-intellectualism not found among evangelicals. Worship is often subjective and emotional, and less attention is given to historical forms of worship and belief such as sacraments and creeds.

I've tried to make this definition as inclusive as possible in order to treat evangelicals or conservative Protestants as a large, relatively cohesive but still diverse community that has had and will continue to have a major impact on U.S. political life. Ideas have consequences, and evangelical values and beliefs have taken on political and social dimensions in recent years. Indeed, they have always had political connotations.

This analysis will concentrate on white Protestant evangelicals, not to slight the many black evangelicals or the few but interesting Catholic evangelicals, but because white evangelicals are becoming a cohesive political bloc that differs markedly from other Protestants and other Christians. Black evangelicals generally hold to a very different Social Gospel orientation and hold political beliefs that do not make them differ from other black voters. They should be considered as a discrete political bloc, as are Catholics, Jews, mainline Protestants, and the religiously nonaffiliated community.

Because of these definitional problems, estimating the total evangelical community and locating it by states takes ingenuity and interpretation. Thus, polling data, research by leading scholars of religion and politics, religious identification surveys, and church membership data have all been utilized to prepare this portrait.

This book attempts to answer some basic questions. Who are evangelicals and how do they vote? What is their impact on the electoral process? Can they substantially influence the outcome of upcoming national elections? Where is their impact greatest in geographical terms? Do they control the Republican party, its platform, and apparatus? Why do they vote as they do? What issues resonate with them? Are they capable of forming alliances with those of other religious traditions for the purpose of achieving political goals? What influence do they have on Congress, the state legislatures, and school boards?

Other questions immediately come to mind. Does America face renewed religious conflict as religious groups vie for political power and control? Do evangelicals have the answers to the nation's social, moral, and cultural problems? Are the regions where their influence is paramount worthy of emulation by the rest of the country? This book attempts to offer reasonable and credible answers to these and related questions.

1

Where Evangelicals Live

Evangelicalism in the United States has a distinct Southern flavor. Evangelicals form the highest percentage of the population in the eleven Southern (Old Confederacy) states and the six Border states, where Southern cultural patterns are influential. According to the National Survey of Religious Identification (NSRI) conducted by City University of New York Graduate School in 1990, these states, plus Indiana and Kansas, are the heartland of evangelical America. Of these states, Alabama, Arkansas, Georgia, Kentucky, Mississippi, Oklahoma, South Carolina, and Tennessee are, for all practical purposes, evangelical majority states, i.e., states where a majority of the entire population is affiliated with evangelical churches. The other states in the region have an above average evangelical percentage of the population. (See map 1.1.)

To be sure, not all of the South is overwhelmingly evangelical. There are strong Catholic communities in southern Louisiana, where a unique French Cajun culture has flourished for two centuries. Spanish-flavored Catholicism dominates South Texas and, to an extent, parts of South Florida. Historic Catholic and Episcopalian communities trace their heritage to colonial days in the coastal regions of the South, from Norfolk, Virginia, to the Texas Gulf Coast. Towns like Charleston, Savannah, St. Augustine, and Biloxi have long had large Catholic, Episcopalian, and Jewish populations in a region largely populated by Baptists, Methodists, Presbyterians, Disciples of Christ, and the smaller evangelical fundamentalist communities. It is the interior South, which stretches culturally as far north as the southern portions of Illinois,

15

Map 1.1. NSRI Survey of Evangelical Strength

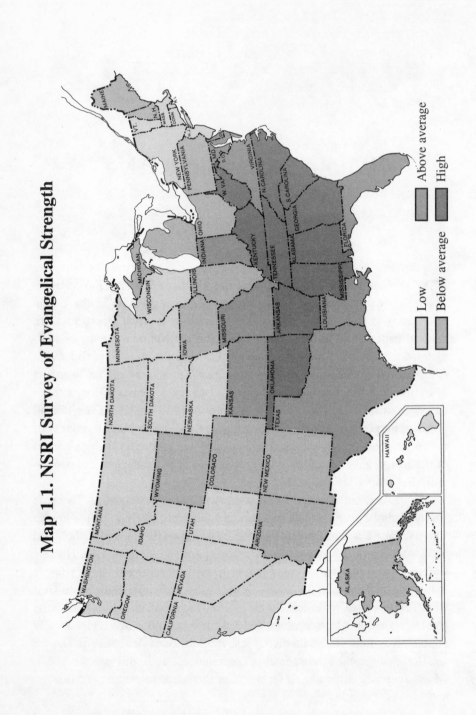

Low

Below average

Above average

High

Indiana, and Ohio, that is the heartland of evangelical religion. As a consequence, the political life of these areas has been shaped by evangelical values. These were the historic strongholds of Prohibition, revivalism, Sunday closing laws, antigambling statutes, and prayer in public schools. (Parts of the rural North shared these sentiments.)

There are also pockets of evangelical strength in the North and West. Indiana and Kansas are the two non-Southern states where a larger-than-average evangelical population is found. The rural areas of the North are still somewhat inclined toward evangelicalism, at least outside of New England and the Northeast. The Pennsylvania Dutch country, southern Illinois, the Dutch areas of Michigan and Iowa, the "Little Dixie" area of eastern New Mexico, eastern Colorado, and portions of Iowa are still influenced by larger-than-average evangelical populations.

During the nineteenth century, rural New England and upstate New York were strongly evangelical, as were areas of the Midwest settled by New Englanders. But an increasing religious liberalism has become dominant in these areas, and evangelicalism's weakest region is the Northeast, along with the always secular and pluralistic West.

The variable definitions of evangelicalism lend themselves to various interpretations. Are Methodists evangelicals? What about Presbyterians? Are the Evangelical Lutherans evangelicals in the American usage of the term? These questions make a definitive location of evangelical political influence somewhat difficult to define with absolute precision.

Therefore, using Glenmary Research Center data reveals a slightly different geographic pattern. (See map 1.2.) The South remains the dominant evangelical region, when denominational membership becomes the criterion for inclusion, as it is in the NSRI study. But the Dakotas, Missouri, and New Mexico fall in the above-average category, largely because of the Missouri Synod Lutherans and smaller denominational families. Delaware, Maryland, and Florida fall away from the above-average evangelical states, primarily because of their large and hard-to-classify Methodist populations, and, in the case of Florida, because of its relatively low church membership. In Florida more people identify with evangelical religion than actually join evangelical churches, a factor, perhaps, of the state's high mobility and population growth. The Northeast from Maryland to Maine is the least evangelical region, along with parts of the Pacific West. For purposes of political analysis, I am inclined to use the NSRI data for the states. There is little significant difference between the two surveys, except in three or four states. Glenmary data are excellent for county election returns.

Another phenomenon of evangelicalism is its rural location. In every

Map 1.2. Glenmary Survey of Evangelical Strength

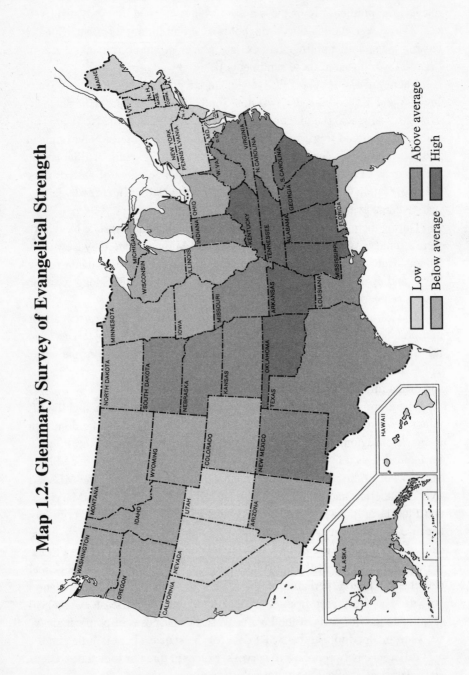

Low

Below average

Above average

High

state, evangelicals are a higher percentage of the population in nonmetropolitan areas than in metropolitan areas. Sociologists and geographers have long noted this pattern without ever being quite able to explain the reasons for it. Missionary and evangelism activity, the appeal of emotionalism and traditionalism in areas where change comes slowly, perhaps even the preference for rural living imbedded in certain religious traditions have all been advanced as explanations for this phenomenon.

Protestantism has always had a considerable rural character in the United States in comparison with Roman Catholicism, Eastern Orthodox Christianity, and Judaism. (Episcopalians and Unitarians are also urban in their membership.)

Evangelicals are more rural in membership than nonevangelicals. In the last U.S. Census of Religious Bodies, taken in 1936, 62 percent of Southern Baptists lived in rural areas, double the percentage of all U.S. church members. A majority of Mennonites, United Brethren, and Church of Christ members lived in rural areas. Nearly half of Methodists, Mormons, Lutherans, and members of the Evangelical Church resided in rural areas. (See table 1.1.)

The general and prevailing pattern of the rural orientation of evangelical Christians was revealed in the religious reports of the 1890 census and in the special religious censuses conducted in 1906, 1916, and 1926. The 1936 religious census was the last comprehensive one undertaken by the Census Bureau, and all information had been provided by the religious bodies themselves in order to protect individual privacy in religious matters.

Opposition was widespread when the Census Bureau included religion in its 1957 sample. The constitutional protection of separation of church and state was invoked by many individuals and church groups who questioned the appropriateness of any survey on religion. Thus, the National Council of Churches (NCC) collected and published statistics of church membership by county and denomination for 1952, and the material was published between 1956 and 1958. Unfortunately, it was not as comprehensive as the 1926 and 1936 reports, nor was it widely disseminated. It reported that 49.2 percent of U.S. adults were church members, though surveys showed about 60 percent of respondents claimed to be members of a religious group. The predominantly African-American churches and the Eastern Orthodox were undercounted. Still, the results of the National Council of Churches report reiterate the basic patterns of U.S. religious geography.

Using a slightly different definition of nonmetropolitan versus metropolitan, the 1952 NCC data show the same pattern of residence revealed in previous surveys. (See table 1.2) A majority of Protestants (54.4 percent) resided in nonmetropolitan counties compared to only a fourth of Catholics (25.5

Table 1.1

1936 U.S. Census of Religious Bodies*
Urban vs. Rural

Religion	% of Members in Rural Areas
All Protestant	42.6
Roman Catholic	19.4
Eastern Orthodox	5.4
Jewish	0.9
All	30.6
Mennonites	85.4
Southern Baptist	62.1
Brethren	61.0
Friends	57.4
Church of Christ	57.3
United Brethren	53.3
All Baptist	52.2
Latter Day Saints	49.7
Churches of God	46.7
Methodist	46.7
Evangelical	44.3
Lutheran	43.5
Reformed	40.1
Disciples of Christ	37.9
Evangelical & Reformed	37.8
Congregationalist	35.0
Presbyterian	29.0
Unitarian Universalist	16.2
Episcopalian	15.5

*This table is based on information in *Religious Bodies: 1936 Volume 1* (Washington, D.C.: U.S. Government Printing Office, 1941), pp. 86–97.

percent) and a tiny proportion of Jews (2.5 percent). Fully 65 percent of Baptists and 60 percent of Methodists were nonmetropolitan dwellers, as were substantial numbers of other evangelicals.

After studying the 1952 data, religious geographer Wilbur Zelinsky developed the thesis that America can be divided into seven major religious regions and five subregions. New England is the Catholic and mainline Protestant region, while the Midland includes New York, New Jersey, and most of the area from Pennsylvania to Colorado and Wyoming. This is the

Table 1.2

1952 Churches and Church Membership Data*
Urban vs. Rural

Religion	% of Members in Nonmetropolitan counties
All Protestant	54.4
Roman Catholic	25.5
Eastern Orthodox	N/A
Jewish	2.5
All	39.2
Major Churches	
Southern Baptist	75.0
Churches of God	65.4
All Baptist	65.1
Brethren	64.3
Disciples of Christ	64.0
Mennonite	62.1
Methodist	59.9
Evangelical United Brethren	58.0
Church of the Nazarene	56.2
Friends	55.2
Latter Day Saints	54.2
Lutheran	48.9
Adventist	47.9
Reformed	45.1
Presbyterian	41.9
Evangelical & Reformed	40.5
Congregationalist	40.1
Episcopalian	27.2
Unitarian Universalist	25.6

*National Council of Churches 1956–58, *Churches and Church Membership in the United States*, Series D., Nos. 3 to 6, Tables 136 to 139; and Series E., No. 1., Table 140.

most pluralistic area, with Methodism particularly strong. But many smaller evangelical groups, often of German and Dutch origin, are strong here, as are Presbyterians and Catholics. A subregion of the Midland is the Pennsylvania Dutch country, a German Protestant and evangelical bastion that has preserved a unique identity into the 1990s.

The Upper Middle Western region is Lutheran territory, with a strong

Catholic contingent. Scandinavian and German subcultures abound in this area, stretching from Montana to Minnesota.

The South is the fourth region, the Baptist-Methodist area so reviled by H. L. Mencken that he called it "the Sahara of the Bozart."[1] Zelinsky identified four subregions in the South: the Carolina Piedmont, where Lutherans and Presbyterians were numerous; Peninsular Florida, where Catholics, Jews, and Episcopalians challenged the religious culture of the region; the French Catholic area of Louisiana; and the Texas German region, the Hill Country of South Central Texas, where Lutherans, Catholics, and Moravians added to the religious mix.

A fifth region, labeled Spanish Catholic, ranged from South Texas through New Mexico, southern Colorado, southern Arizona, and the California coast; its heritage can be gleaned by the Spanish Mission trail.

A sixth area he labeled the Mormon region, while the seventh region was the Western, traditionally individualistic, secular, and given to experimentation with new religious movements.[2]

Zelinsky, professor emeritus of geography at Pennsylvania State University, wrote his seminal essay in 1961, and it retains its validity today. His pattern is again revealed in 1971, 1980, and 1990 data compiled by the National Council of Churches and published by the Glenmary Research Center.

The largest evangelical group is the Southern Baptist Convention, a loosely linked confederation of about 38,000 churches claiming nineteen million adherents, most of them residing in fourteen Southern and Border states. These white Baptists dominate the region to some degree, and their impact is most pronounced in rural areas and in the small towns of the region. Zelinsky commented on this fact more than three decades ago: "One of the most provocative questions confronting the student of American cultural geography is the close affinity between Baptists and Southern culture during the past several decades."[3]

The rural tilt of the Baptist cultural influence still holds true, even though millions of Baptists have moved to suburbs and cities during the past three or four decades. Of the ninety-six Baptist-majority counties, all are rural or non-metropolitan. An additional forty-four counties where Baptists of smaller or independent denominations added to the Southern Baptists to constitute a majority are also rural. Of the counties containing over 100,000 population, only two are 40 percent or more Baptist: Calhoun County, Alabama, and Anderson County, South Carolina. The small cities of Anniston and Anderson are the county seats. Seventeen other counties with a population exceeding 100,000 are 30 percent to 40 percent Baptist. These include counties containing some fairly large cities such as Birmingham, Knoxville, Greenville, Jackson, and Spartanburg.

Table 1.3

Strongest Southern Baptist Counties with
Populations Exceeding 100,000 (1990)

% Baptist	County	State	Major City	Population
42.5	Calhoun	AL	Anniston	116,000
40.5	Anderson	SC	Anderson	145,000
38.7	Spartanburg	SC	Spartanburg	226,000
37.9	Morgan	AL	Decatur	100,000
37.3	Knox	TN	Knoxville	335,000
36.9	Comanche	OK	Lawton	111,000
36.3	Taylor	TX	Abilene	119,000
34.7	McLennan	TX	Waco	189,000
34.7	Wichita	TX	Wichita Falls	122,000
34.3	Ouachita	LA	Monroe	142,000
33.9	Greenville	SC	Greenville	320,000
33.6	Rapides	LA	Alexandria	131,000
33.1	Aiken	SC	Aiken	120,000
32.8	Smith	TX	Tyler	151,000
31.5	Gregory	TX	Longview	105,000
31.1	Hinds	MS	Jackson	254,000
30.9	Buncombe	NC	Asheville	175,000
30.8	Jefferson	AL	Birmingham	651,000
30.5	Gaston	NC	Gastonia	175,000
29.7	Caddo	LA	Shreveport	248,000
29.7	Robeson	NC	Lumberton	105,000
29.0	Oklahoma	OK	Oklahoma City	599,000
28.8	Tuscaloosa	AL	Tuscaloosa	150,000
27.6	Jackson	MS	Pascagoula	115,000
27.5	Bibb	GA	Macon	150,000
26.6	Mobile	AL	Mobile	378,000
26.4	Ector	TX	Odessa	119,000
25.7	Muscogee	GA	Columbus	179,000

Other good-sized towns with large Baptist percentages of the population include Shreveport, Oklahoma City, Mobile, Macon, and Columbus (Georgia). Waco, Texas, site of Baptist-related Baylor University, is among the top-ten Baptist counties with populations exceeding 100,000. (See table 1.3.)

In every Southern and Border state where Baptists are strong, their percentage of the population is greater in nonmetropolitan counties than in met-

Table 1.4

Southern Baptists in Metropolitan* and Nonmetropolitan Areas (1990)

| | Southern Baptists in | |
State	Metropolitan Counties %	Nonmetropolitan Counties %
AL	28.6	35.8
AR	23.8	26.9
FL	8.0	18.9
GA	18.4	29.3
KY	15.9	30.1
LA	14.9	21.6
MS	27.1	35.6
MO	9.7	22.8
NC	16.7	27.5
OK	25.9	34.4
SC	24.8	27.0
TN	22.9	32.1
TX	15.7	28.8
VA	9.0	15.0

*Metropolitan counties are those with over 100,000 residents.

ropolitan counties. (See table 1.4) The gap is particularly large in Kentucky, Missouri, Texas, Florida, and North Carolina; it is less pronounced in South Carolina and Arkansas.

The changing demography of the South has also begun to weaken, if slightly, Baptist strength in its traditional strongholds. Of the ninety-six Baptist majority counties, eighty had a lower Baptist percentage of the population in 1980 and 1990 than in 1971.

In their fourteen strongest states Baptists have declined as a percentage of the population in seven states (Florida, Georgia, North Carolina, South Carolina, Tennessee, Texas, and Virginia), while they are stronger in seven states (Alabama, Arkansas, Kentucky, Louisiana, Mississippi, Missouri, and Oklahoma). (See table 1.5)

Methodists are the second largest Protestant religious family in America, and they tend to skirt the divide between evangelicals and mainliners. They are clearly a mainline church with a considerable influence on the body politic. But they would have been classified as an evangelical church until the 1960s. In many of the great political crusades of the nineteenth and early twentieth centuries that involved religious issues, Methodists were often the

Table 1.5

Southern Baptists in Total Population of Fourteen Strongest States

State	1971 %	1990 %	% Change 1971–1990
AL	30.6	32.5	+1.9
AR	22.6	26.3	+3.7
FL	11.9	9.0	–2.9
GA	27.8	24.4	–3.4
KY	25.5	26.1	+0.6
LA	16.6	18.0	+1.4
MS	30.7	33.8	+3.1
MO	13.4	15.4	+2.0
NC	24.8	21.8	–3.0
OK	26.3	30.7	+4.4
SC	28.4	25.7	–2.7
TN	27.9	27.5	–0.4
TX	21.1	19.2	–1.9
VA	13.8	12.0	–1.8

leaders of the evangelical party. Methodists, even more than Baptists, led the Prohibitionist movement. Their Washington office, formerly called the Methodist Board of Temperance and Public Morals, was set up to lobby for Prohibition enforcement in the 1920s. Their leaders were resolutely opposed to Gov. Alfred E. Smith's presidential campaign in 1928, and on the local level they formed a conservative presence.

While this posture has changed greatly during the past three decades, and the leadership of the United Methodist Church (formed in 1968 as a merger between the Methodists and the much smaller German-oriented Evangelical United Brethren Church) has espoused political and social liberalism, many Methodists remain conservative and evangelical in orientation. Especially in the South and Midwest Methodists are relatively evangelical at the grassroots level. Many Southern politicians on the right, including Alabama's former governor and presidential candidate George Wallace and present Mississippi governor Kirk Fordice, are Methodists. So is the Reverend Donald Wildmon of Mississippi, the founder of the American Family Association, a procensorship lobby.

So there is some logic in including Methodists as a potential or at least partially evangelical group, keeping in mind that many Methodists are ardent foes of the religious and political right.

Table 1.6

The Top Ten Methodist States

NSRI Survey	% Methodist	Glenmary/NCC Data	% Methodist
DE	26.5	OK	10.4
IA	15.7	WV	10.2
SC	15.6	IA	9.8
WV	14.9	MS	9.3
KS	14.7	DE	9.2
MD	13.8	NE	9.2
VA	13.1	NC	9.1
NC	12.7	SC	8.9
GA	11.5	AR	8.4
MS	11.4	AL	8.2
		GA	8.2

Zelinsky wrote that "Methodists more closely approach the status of a national denomination in a geographical and statistical sense than any other group."[4] Their strength has always been in the upper South states (Virginia, North Carolina, West Virginia, Maryland, Delaware) and the lower North states (Iowa, Kansas, Nebraska, Ohio), though they also have a strong following in parts of the Deep South (South Carolina, Georgia, Mississippi). (See table 1.6)

There are some discrepancies between official church membership data and religious preference surveys. Oklahoma ranked first in the Glenmary survey but is not on the top ten in the NSRI survey. Most other states are relatively comparable, but statistical differences like this point up the division between how people define themselves religiously and their specific denominational ties.

Like Baptists, Methodists are more likely to dominate rural areas than large metropolitan counties. The twenty most heavily Methodist counties are all rural. (See table 1.7.) Eight are in Kansas, six in Nebraska, and three in Oklahoma, though the nation's most Methodist county is in the mountains of Virginia, Highland County. Of the nation's metropolitan counties only ten have a Methodist share of the population exceeding 10 percent. Four are in Pennsylvania, including Cumberland County, which is the most Methodist metropolitan county in the United States. Cumberland is a relatively prosperous area, partly rural, partly suburban, in the Dutch country. Nearby Dauphin County (Harrisburg) and York County are also Pennsylvania Dutch

Table 1.7

The 20 Strongest Methodist Counties (1990)

County	State	% Methodist
Highland	VA	39.3
Kiowa	KS	36.6
Deuel	NE	36.3
Ness	KS	36.2
Jewell	KS	33.2
Faulk	SD	32.6
Hooker	NE	32.5
Hitchcock	NE	32.4
Grant	OK	32.0
Cimarron	OK	31.2
Clark	KS	31.0
Chase	KS	30.6
Perkins	NE	30.5
Greene	IA	30.0
Cheyenne	KS	29.3
Lane	KS	29.3
Webster	NE	28.8
Furnas	NE	28.6
Harper	OK	28.5
Stanton	KS	28.0

areas where most Methodists are probably of German or German-English ancestry. Cambria County (Johnstown), a mostly Catholic area of western Pennsylvania, also has a strong Methodist community.

Two North Carolina counties, Forsyth (Winston Salem) and Guilford (High Point) have strong Methodist communities. In 1936 High Point had the highest Methodist percentage of the population of any town in the country. It remains the second most Methodist metropolitan county. Oklahoma City and Tulsa are also Methodist strongholds, as are Little Rock, Arkansas (Pulaski County) and Montgomery, Alabama. (See table 1.8.)

The NSRI survey also found that "Methodists are most likely to be found east of the Mississippi River, particularly in rural areas,"[5] and that they are "proportionately almost twice as common in the countryside (11.5 percent) as in the cities (6.5 percent) and suburbs (7.4 percent)."[6]

Lutherans are in some instances also regarded as evangelicals, in terms of their historic theology, though the term evangelical as used in the United

Table 1.8

Ten Strongest Methodist Counties with More Than 100,000 Population

County	State	% Methodist
Cumberland	PA	12.3
Guilford	NC	12.1
Tulsa	OK	12.0
Cambria	PA	11.7
Pulaski	AR	10.6
Dauphin	PA	10.5
Forsyth	NC	10.3
Oklahoma	OK	10.2
York	PA	10.1
Montgomery	AL	9.8

States has tended not to include Lutherans. This may stem from Lutheranism's strong German and Scandinavian roots, as opposed to the strong Anglo-Saxon character of American evangelicalism.

Lutherans also have tended to oppose church involvement in politics and frowned on the Prohibition movement and other crusades to regulate public moral behavior, unlike other evangelicals. Still, there is a sense in which Lutherans should be considered in any study of evangelical voting behavior, if only because many remain Democrats and liberals in politics, again setting them apart from the evangelical mainstream.

The Evangelical Lutheran Church in America, which claims more than five million members, is, despite its name, less evangelical than other Lutheran sects in terms of its ecumenical involvements and its inclusion of women in major church offices. The Lutheran Church–Missouri Synod, however, is a conservative evangelical group with a distinctive character and anti-ecumenical posture. The Missouri Synod, claiming two million members, was one of the last churches to establish a Washington-based lobby, which allies itself with the Religious Right on most issues. The tiny Wisconsin Synod is separatist and fundamentalist.

Lutheranism is anchored in the Midwest. It is the largest single religion in Minnesota and the Dakotas, with strong representations in Wisconsin, Montana, Nebraska, and Iowa. There are pockets of Lutheran strength in the West and in Pennsylvania and Maryland, but Lutheranism has little strength south of the Mason-Dixon line, except in the historically German counties of Texas, Virginia, and the Carolinas.

Table 1.9

Top-Ten Lutheran States

	NSRI Survey			Glenmary/NCCI Data	
Rank	State	% Lutheran	Rank	State	% Lutheran
1	ND	36.5	1	ND	33.5
2	MN	33.9	2	MN	25.5
3	SD	30.3	3	SD	22.8
4	WI	26.2	4	WI	19.1
5	NE	16.3	5	NE	15.9
6	IA	15.4	6	IA	14.4
7	MT	12.2	7	MT	8.2
8	PA	8.6	8	PA	5.9
9	MI	8.3	9	IL	5.2
10	WA	7.8	10	MI	5.0

There is not a wide discrepancy between Lutheran self-identification and Lutheran church membership. The eight top Lutheran states are in exactly the same place in both the NSRI and Glenmary studies. (See table 1.9.)

The strongest Lutheran counties are in rural areas of the Midwest. About three dozen counties in this region have Lutheran majorities and another several dozen have Lutheran populations of 40 percent to 50 percent of the population.

Lutherans are also strong in some metropolitan counties. Six Wisconsin and Pennsylvania counties are metropolitan counties containing 100,000 or more people, as are five Minnesota counties, two in Illinois, and one each in Indiana, Nebraska, and Michigan. (See table 1.10.)

The most Lutheran county in this population range is Outagamie, Wisconsin, anchored by the small city of Appleton, the home of the late Senator Joseph McCarthy. (The county is actually more Catholic than Lutheran, which is generally true of the urban Midwest.) Other metropolitan areas with substantial Lutheran percentages of the population include Minneapolis-St. Paul and its suburbs and Duluth, Minnesota; Reading, Allentown, York, and Bethlehem, Pennsylvania; Racine, Green Bay, Madison, and Milwaukee, Wisconsin; Saginaw, Michigan; Fort Wayne, Indiana; and Rockford, Illinois.

The Mennonite, Brethren, and Amish communities represent the historic German Anabaptist peace churches, whose unique brand of evangelical theology espouses pacifism and nonmaterialistic life stances. They tend to congregate in farming communities in rural America from Pennsylvania to Kansas. (See table 1.11.) Although only a small percentage of the evangeli-

Table 1.10

The Most Lutheran Counties with Populations Exceeding 100,000

County	State	% Lutheran
Outagamie	WI	22.8
Anoka	MN	19.2
Hennepin	MN	18.9
Dakota	MN	18.1
Waukesha	WI	17.5
Ramsey	MN	16.8
St. Louis	MN	16.7
Racine	WI	16.6
Berks	PA	16.3
Saginaw	MI	15.0
Dane	WI	14.8
Schuykill	PA	14.6
Lehigh	PA	14.1
York	PA	13.4
Brown	WI	13.3
Northampton	PA	13.2
Allen	IN	13.1
McHenry	IL	12.2
Cumberland	PA	11.5
Winnebago	IL	11.3
Lancaster	NE	11.3
Milwaukee	WI	11.3

cal community, they add a unique perspective that is politically and socially noteworthy.

Presbyterians are clearly a mainline denomination, but many of their adherents are committed evangelicals. Some of the Religious Right leadership are Presbyterian, including D. James Kennedy, pastor of Coral Ridge Presbyterian Church in South Florida. Bill Bright of the Campus Crusade for Christ was once a member of Hollywood Presbyterian Church in California. A century ago a fundamentalist Presbyterian was the Democratic candidate for president, William Jennings Bryan.

The historic Presbyterian stronghold is Pennsylvania, though Wyoming has more Presbyterian identifiers as a percentage of the population. Presbyterian areas of influence extend from Virginia, West Virginia, and Tennessee to Iowa and the West (Washington, Oregon, Colorado, and Nebraska). (See table 1.12.)

Table 1.11

Top Dozen Amish-Brethren-Mennonite Counties

County	State	% Amish-Brethren-Mennonite
Holmes	OH	40.1
Marion	KS	32.3
LaGrange	IN	30.3
McPherson	KS	20.2
Turner	SD	18.8
Harvey	KS	18.2
Floyd	VA	16.1
Adams	IN	15.4
York	NE	14.4
Rockingham	VA	14.2
Harrisonburg*	VA	14.2
Bedford	PA	12.2

*Harrisonburg is an independent city considered a county equivalent by the U.S. Census Bureau.

Table 1.12

Top Ten Presbyterian States

State	% Presbyterian
WY	8.7
PA	5.3
WA	4.6
IA	4.5
CO	4.4
NE	4.4
TN	4.3
WV	4.3
OR	4.2
VA	4.1

Pentecostals are a fast-growing segment of evangelical Christianity, especially in Latin America and South Asia. In the United States Pentecostalism has always been a religion of the downtrodden and marginalized and has a strong appeal to blacks and Hispanics. Many of its adherents have

Table 1.13

Top-Ten Pentecostal States

State	% Pentecostal
AR	5.9
MS	3.9
DE	3.4
WV	3.2
OK	2.9
TX	2.9
AL	2.6
TN	2.6
KS	2.5
MO & FL	2.4

moved from blue-collar to white-collar status in recent years, and its theology has influenced Catholicism and Mainline Protestantism.

The strongest Pentecostal states are all in the South and the Border South, especially in Arkansas and Mississippi. (See table 1.13.)

Another strongly evangelical or fundamentalist community is the membership of the Churches of Christ. This group is probably more fundamentalist than evangelical in character, and its members, like the Pentecostals, have traditionally been Democrats, though conservative ones. They are strongest in Tennessee, Oklahoma, Arkansas, and other areas of the South. (See table 1.14.)

The Reformed Churches are an ethnic group with a strong evangelical theology and a conservative political orientation. Mostly of Dutch descent, they are strongest in Michigan and Iowa. These middle-class individualists are not only Republicans but also conservative Republicans. They prefer to reside in rural areas and are strongly supportive of parochial schools. The strongest Reformed county in the United States is Sioux County, in Northwest Iowa. This county also has the second highest percentage of private school students in the nation. (See table 1.15.)

An intriguing subject for future inquiry will surely be the political habits of the growing Hispanic Protestant minority, most of whom are Pentecostals or evangelicals. Most are originally from Catholic backgrounds, and many are intense in their rejection of their former religion. Latin Protestants tend to emphasize what separates them from Catholics, and their explanations often appear anti-Catholic. In Latin America evangelical Protestantism is growing

Table 1.14

Top-Ten Church of Christ States

State	% Church of Christ
TN	5.4
OK	4.7
AR	4.5
AL	3.4
KY	2.1
TX	2.1
OH	1.9
IN	1.8
MS	1.8
WV	1.6

Table 1.15

Top-Eight Dutch Reformed Church Counties

County	State	%Dutch Reformed
Sioux	IA	62.4
Douglas	SD	47.1
Ottawa	MI	27.2
O'Brien	IA	26.8
Pipestone	MN	24.3
Marion	IA	23.6
Missaukee	MI	20.3
Rock	MN	17.4

by leaps and bounds, and more than a quarter of the population of Guatemala and Chile are practicing Protestants. Clashes between Catholics and Protestants are increasing in Brazil and Mexico. Politically, Latin American Protestants tend to support right wing military dictatorships, especially when a Protestant is the dictator, as in the case of General Rios-Montt in Guatemala, who is also admired by Pat Robertson. Robertson effusively praised the Chilean military dictator, General Pinochet, for allegedly aiding Christianity in Chile. "General Pinochet clearly fostered the growth of Christianity in Chile," wrote Robertson.[7]

Hence, there is a possibility that Hispanic Protestants in the United

States may be inclined toward the political and Religious Right. As yet there is little hard data, since Hispanics, Catholic or Protestant, tend to be under-represented in exit polls. What little data are available suggest that Hispanic Protestants are more Republican and conservative than Hispanic Catholics but less conservative and less Republican than non-Hispanic Protestants. The NSRI data found "no statistically significant social class differences between Hispanic Catholics and Protestants."[8] The same survey found that 66 percent of Hispanic Americans are Catholic and 25 percent are Protestant[9]—a con-siderable Protestant gain over the past few decades. Gallup data show figures of 72 percent Catholic and 18 percent Protestant for the Hispanic community. About 10 percent are nonaffiliated. Protestants are strongest among Puerto Rican and Central American subgroups and are weakest among Cubans and among Mexicans except in Texas.[10] Kosmin and Lachman suggest that this trend is likely to continue because "Only 23 percent of Hispanic Catholics are practicing" and "About three times as many Hispanics are enrolled in Protestant seminaries and schools of theology as in Catholic seminaries."[11] The Gallup Youth Survey, 1994–95, revealed that only 46 percent of His-panic teenagers are Catholic, while 37 percent are Protestant, and 17 percent hold no religious preference. The trend is clearly away from Catholic iden-tity among America's growing Hispanic community.[12]

The only Hispanic Protestant in Congress is Henry Bonilla, a Republi-can from Texas and a Southern Baptist.

The religious configuration of a state clearly has some impact on the social and cultural life of the state. David Fairbanks studied the influence of religion on liquor and gambling legislation in the states. Even when control-ling for economic and income levels, he found that the percentage of evan-gelical and fundamentalist Protestants in the population was the most signif-icant relationship between a state and its restrictions on drinking and gam-bling. The initial prohibitionist legislation was most likely to be enacted in the evangelical states, and repeal of restrictions was difficult to achieve in these states.[13] Fairbanks also found that the strictness of contraception and marriage laws and a relatively low divorce rate varied directly with the pro-portion of Catholics in the population.[14] Fairbanks's research was published in 1977, before the widespread popularity of state lotteries, but his observa-tions are valid for the preceding decades.

Daniel J. Elazar discovered that the fundamentalist proportion of the state population was associated with a high teacher-pupil ratio in the public schools and a low level of state taxation.[15]

Evangelicalism's impact on Southern religiosity is apparent from Gallup polling data. Although a substantial majority of all Americans say they believe in God and heaven, far more Southerners believe in the devil (77 percent compared to 65 percent for all Americans) and hell (81 percent compared to 73 percent of all Americans, and just 60 percent of Westerners). Southerners believe in angels more than all Americans (84 percent compared to 72 percent).

Residents of the South are 12 percent more likely than all Americans, and 25 percent more likely than residents of the West, to believe that religion can answer all or most of today's problems. And 68 percent of Southerners say religion is very important in their lives, while only 58 percent of all Americans and 48 percent of Westerners agree.

Church affiliation and attendance are a bit higher in the South: 75 percent of Southerners say they are church members compared to 69 percent of all Americans, and 47 percent report weekly church attendance compared to 42 percent of the nation.

Evangelicals are much stronger in the South than elsewhere, as 49 percent of Southerners call themselves "born again or evangelical" compared to 36 percent of all U.S. residents.

Finally, the Religious Right movement receives the support of 26 percent of Southerners, only 18 percent of all Americans, and just 12 percent of Westerners.[16]

Are rural areas really more religious? Yes, say the Gallup organization's pollsters. Rural religiousness is a fact of life borne out repeatedly in surveys. The differences are stronger in churchgoing and preference patterns than in basic beliefs, however. Rural dwellers are only 3–4 percentage points more likely than urban or suburban residents to believe in heaven, hell, miracles, and angels.

But 51 percent of all rural and small town residents call themselves "born again or evangelical Christian" compared to 32 percent of city dwellers and 31 percent of suburban residents.

About 75 percent of rural folks are church members, compared to 69 percent of all Americans, and 48 percent claim to be weekly churchgoers, compared to 42 percent of all U.S. residents. The difference widens to 53 percent in rural areas and 45 percent in all areas when "almost weekly" attendance is considered. Sixty-five percent of rural residents say religion is very important in their lives, more than the 58 percent of all Americans who feel that way. Seventy-two percent of rural and small-town residents believe that religion can answer all or most of today's problems, while only 62 percent of all Americans believe that it can.

Rural Americans are far more likely to be Protestant (69 percent) than Catholic (16 percent), while the Protestant edge over Catholics is only 50

Table 1.16

Religious Strengths in Rural Areas

	% More Religious in Rural Areas Than among All Americans
Born again or evangelical	+15
Protestant preference	+10
Religion can answer all or most questions	+10
Religion is very important	+ 7
Southern Baptist identification	+ 7
Church member	+ 6
Weekly church attendance	+ 6
Believe in miracles	+ 4
Believe in heaven	+ 4
Believe in angels	+ 3
Believe in hell	+ 2

Source: Princeton Religion Research Center, *Religion in America, 1995 Supplement.*

percent-30 percent in the cities, and 60 percent-24 percent in the suburbs. There are, however, almost as many nonreligious identifiers (7 percent) in rural areas as elsewhere (8 percent). "Other religions," including Jews, Mormons, and Eastern Orthodox Christians, are less likely to be found in rural areas than elsewhere.

The major evangelical Protestant churches claim 48 percent of rural residents as members, compared to 33 percent of suburbanites and 26 percent of city folk. Among Protestants, rural dwellers are nearly 70 percent evangelical, compared to 55 percent in the suburbs and 52 percent in the cities.[17] (See table 1.16.)

Notes

1. Mencken, Maryland's own iconoclast, attended Methodist and Lutheran Sunday Schools before becoming an agnostic, and once wrote that one could determine the low cultural level of a state by merely combining the Baptist and Methodist percentages of the population.

2. Wilbur Zelinsky, "An Approach to the Religious Geography of the United States," in his *Exploring the Beloved Country* (Iowa City: University of Iowa Press, 1994), pp. 63–131.

3. Ibid., p. 87.

4. Ibid., p. 81.

5. Barry A. Kosmin and Seymour P. Lachman, *One Nation Under God: Religion in Contemporary American Society* (New York: Harmony Books, 1993), p. 64.

6. Ibid., p. 71.

7. Pat Robertson, *The Turning Tide* (Dallas: Word Publishing, 1993), p. 48.

8. Kosmin and Lachman, *One Nation Under God,* p. 141.

9. Ibid., p. 137.

10. Ibid., p. 138.

11. Ibid., p. 139.

12. Princeton Religion Research Center (PRRC), *PRRC Emerging Trends* 18 (January 1996): 5.

13. David Fairbanks, "Religious Forces and 'Morality' Policies in the American States," *Western Political Quarterly* 30 (September 1977): 411–17.

14. David Fairbanks, "Politics, Economics and the Public Morality: Why Some States are More 'Moral' than Others," *Policy Studies Journal* 7 (1979): 714–20.

15. Daniel J. Elazar, *American Federalism: A View from the States* (New York: Harper & Row, 1984).

16. Princeton Religion Research Center, *Religion in America, 1995 Supplement.*

17. Ibid.

2

Evangelical Subcultures

A t least seven evangelical subcultures exist, and their political nuances
and religious lifestyles help to explain the diversity of the evangelical
community. Four of the subcultures are defined by the religious community
and three are geographic subregions that reflect an intermingling of religious
and ethnic distinctives.

Dutch Reformed America

An evangelical subregion that combines ethnicity, religion, and conservative
small town values can be found primarily in portions of Michigan, Iowa, and
Wisconsin, where cohesive communities of Dutch Reformed Christians live.
These areas are relatively prosperous, clannish, and supportive of parochial
education. Sioux County, Iowa, which ranks first in the nation in percentage
of individuals of Dutch ancestry and membership in the Dutch Reformed
Church, ranks second in percentage of students attending private schools
(nearly 38 percent). All the other Dutch-oriented counties rank well above
the national average in private school enrollment. Apparently these individuals have no objections to public funding for nonpublic schools, since voters
in Dutch communities supported parochial school aid in a 1970 referendum
in Michigan.

There are two brands of Reformed Christians, the very conservative
Christian Reformed Church and the more moderate Reformed Church in

America, but both tend to be politically conservative. (Norman Vincent Peale, who was a partisan Republican, was a member of the Reformed Church in America.)

Several towns in the Dutch belt reflect the flavor of a religion-absorbed community. Zeeland, Michigan, write Mary and Don Hunt, is "a most distinctive town that bans the sale of liquor, shuts down on Sunday, is still almost entirely Dutch, and is dominated by huge Dutch Reformed churches."[1] Continuing, the Hunts observe, "Nowhere is the vaunted Dutch-American work ethic more pronounced than in Zeeland, the headquarters of three large and famous home-grown industries. The town has an air of well-build solidity which suggests the Calvinist attitude that worldly prosperity is a natural sign of devout Christian faith."[2] There is little wonder that Zeeland, the birthplace of author Paul de Kruif, of *Microbe Hunters* fame, often votes 90 percent Republican. In 1992 Bush received 77.2 percent of Zeeland's ballots, while Perot received 11.5 percent and Clinton 11.3 percent.

The larger town of Holland, Michigan, is a historic center of Dutch culture, though its population is changing, with 15 percent of residents of Hispanic descent and 5 percent of Asian ancestry. Founded by Dutch Separatists, who wanted a more conservative church than the state-controlled one in the Netherlands, the town of Holland, Michigan, became a homogeneous 90 percent Dutch city for more than a century.

The phone book is full of Dutch names, 6 percent of them with the prefix "Van." There are fifty-four Reformed churches in Holland and only a handful belonging to other denominations. Hope College, established in 1866, is an important cultural resource and a moderating influence. "Catholic students are said to outnumber Reformed Church members,"[3] write the Hunts about the school's appeal beyond the Reformed community.

Still, the area retains strong Dutch Reformed influences. Write the Hunts, "The Dutch have given the region a unique social and political coloring and a strong non-union work ethic."[4] Sabbatarianism and prohibition were commonplace until only a few years ago. "Until recent years the effects of this deeply religious community were conspicuous to outsiders. Virtually everything shut down on Sundays. Holland was a place where there were few taverns or restaurants serving alcohol. Even today, there are a few neighborhoods in Holland where the elderly residents frown on outside Sunday activities. When the local newspaper, the *Holland Sentinel*, began a Sunday edition several years ago, dozens of subscribers cancelled in protest."[5]

Holland, which attracts thousands of visitors for Tulip Time in May, remains Republican but is less so than smaller, more homogenous communities. "Virtually all the Dutch vote Republican, except for very few renegade intellectuals—it's one of those natural political affinities that goes back to the Civil War,"[6] commented Mary and Don Hunt. The Dutch vote is also strong in parts of Grand Rapids, Muskegon, Kalamazoo, and in rural Missaukee County.

Berton Roueché found a similar Sabbatarianism in the town of Pella, Iowa, which is 90 percent Dutch. In 1982 he wrote:

> Sunday in Pella is a difficult day for a visitor. The town observes the Sabbath with an almost Puritan rigidity. . . . With certain humanitarian exceptions, no places of business—not even chain stores—are open on Sunday. It is generally considered reprehensible to wash one's car or mow one's lawn on Sunday. . . . Pellans observe the Sabbath in church, and many of these church-goers attend both morning and evening services. The only Sunday-morning sound in Pella is the sound of church bells, and the only stir of life is the bumper-to-bumper crawl of church-bound traffic.[7]

America's two strongest Dutch Reformed counties in Iowa and Michigan are bedrock Republican areas. In the past ten presidential elections, every GOP nominee has carried them easily; only one Democrat, Lyndon B. Johnson in 1964, was able to secure more than 40 percent of the votes. Most Democrats have been stuck at the 25 percent level.

President Eisenhower easily won 76 percent of the vote in 1956, and Richard Nixon, buoyed by anti-Catholic sentiments, increased that margin a half point in 1960. Turnout was a factor that year, since Nixon gained 4,700 votes over Ike, while Kennedy added only 1,200 votes to Stevenson's total. Barry Goldwater still won by a comfortable 57–43 percent margin in the following election, and Richard Nixon easily won in 1968 and 1972.

While voter shifts here were tiny, it is of some significance that George McGovern's voter support in 1972 was higher than that of Humphrey, Carter, Stevenson, or Kennedy. In 1976, contrary to national trends, that quintessential Midwesterner, Gerald Ford, ran 1 percent stronger than Nixon in these Dutch areas, where Ford was personally well known.

In 1980 about 7 percent of Dutch-area voters shifted from Ford to Anderson, leaving Reagan weaker than most other Republicans while Carter's vote was unchanged. Dutch voters soon warmed to "Dutch" Reagan, however, and gave him 80 percent of their 1984 ballots, an all time record high. In 1988 George Bush dropped 7 points here, and, though he easily won, his Democratic opponent, Michael Dukakis, received the second highest modern vote support for a Democrat.

In 1992 Bush dropped 12 points, which was less than his national

Table 2.1

**Presidential Voting 1956–1992 in Dutch Counties
Sioux (Iowa) and Ottawa (Michigan)**

Year	% Republican	% Democrat	% Other
1956	75.9	24.1	
1960	76.4	23.6	
1964	57.2	42.8	
1968	70.2	23.7	6.1
1972	74.6	25.4	
1976	75.8	24.2	
1980	69.1	23.6	7.3
1984	80.3	19.7	
1988	72.8	27.2	
1992	61.1	22.1	16.8

decline. Sioux County, Iowa, where Bush won 72 percent, was Bush's second strongest county in the nation. (Only Jackson County, Kentucky, where Civil War memories contribute to never-ending Republican victories, was higher.) Clinton received only 22 percent in Dutch counties, the second lowest modern Democratic support level. Ross Perot won 17 percent of the Dutch ballots—a bit below his national support, but still impressive for an independent in a staunchly Republican area. Voter turnout increased 20 percent over 1988, due almost entirely to the Perot candidacy. (See table 2.1.)

The higher the Dutch percentage of the population, the higher the Republican vote usually goes. In six almost entirely Dutch communities in Iowa, Michigan, and Wisconsin, Bush received 73 percent of the votes cast, Clinton 16 percent, and Perot 11 percent. (See table 2.2.)

Even in Pella, Iowa, which had been a Democratic enclave until Eisenhower captured it in 1952, the Republicans regularly win by 2–1 margins or better.

Mennonites and the German Peace Churches

Mennonites have long been Republican voters despite their peace and justice orientation, which would seem more compatible with the modern Democrats. This Republicanism may have originated as part of the socialization process of Mennonites, who reside mostly in the rural North where the GOP has long

Table 2.2

1992 Presidential Vote in Six Heavily Dutch Reformed Towns

Town	State	% Bush	% Clinton	% Perot
Orange City	Iowa	78.4	12.6	9.0
Oostburg	Wisconsin	78.4	10.8	10.8
Zeeland	Michigan	77.2	11.3	11.5
Alto	Wisconsin	73.1	10.1	16.8
Cedar Grove	Wisconsin	72.9	15.4	11.7
Pella	Iowa	62.8	27.5	9.7
ALL		73.1	16.2	10.7

been the dominant and almost unchallenged party of choice. Republicans were seen as more responsive to Protestant sectarians, while Democrats were viewed as too inclined toward urban and labor interests and to Catholic cultural concerns. These concerns may have reinforced the Mennonite-Republican connection.

With the exception of Barry Goldwater, who lost 52 to 48 percent in 1964, the dozen most heavily Mennonite counties have supported all other Republican presidential candidates, usually by wide margins, since 1940.

During the 1920s about 35 percent voted Democratic in Mennonite areas, but support for Al Smith fell off to 27 percent in 1928 because of Smith's Catholicism and his opposition to Prohibition. Economic hard times produced two Roosevelt victories in 1932 and 1936, though FDR lost a couple of points in 1936. Only about 40 percent supported FDR and Truman during the three elections in the 1940s, and Adlai Stevenson fell below 30 percent in the 1950s. John F. Kennedy gained only one point over Stevenson in 1960, and Hubert Humphrey and George McGovern received fewer than 1 in 3 Mennonite votes, which remains the Democratic norm. Jimmy Carter did relatively well for a Democrat, winning 41 percent in 1976.

In 1992 George Bush eked out a bare majority, the second lowest GOP support level in half a century. Bill Clinton received 29.1 percent and Ross Perot 20.4 percent. The high Perot vote probably reflects the independent-minded character of Mennonite voters who, in some areas, gave strong support to Robert LaFollette in 1924 and Theodore Roosevelt in 1912, both of whom ran on the Progressive Party ticket.

Mennonites are not avid voters. A study published in 1975 found that 46 percent of Mennonites vote in most elections, but 39 percent never vote.[8] Those who do participate in the political process are Republicans. The same survey found that 74 percent of Mennonites are Republicans, compared to 14 percent Democrats and 12 percent Independents.[9]

Calvin Redekop writes that "Very few Mennonites have participated at all levels of the political spectrum."[10] Redekop explains the Mennonites' political orientation: "United States Mennonites have tended to vote conservative in most elections, thus indicating their economic and political loyalties. . . . There are indications that Mennonites have identified with the politics of the far right. Thus, for example, in Kansas between 1928 and the later 1940s, during the heyday of Gerald Winrod, Mennonites supported his anticommunist, anti-liberal campaigns. But in general, Mennonites did not become heavily involved in the religious far right."[11]

The first Mennonite elected to the U.S. Congress was E. W. Ramseyer, who held an Iowa seat from 1915 to 1933. Ohio's B. F. Welty served from 1917 to 1921, while Edward C. Eicher was elected in Iowa in 1933 and served until 1939.[12]

James C. Jahnke studied a number of homogeneous Mennonite communities in Kansas and offered this explanation for their loyal Republicanism: "Given the ascendancy of the Republican Party in the Mennonite area and given the fact that Mennonites had received their introduction to America from Republican-oriented railroads, it was natural for Mennonites to vote Republican. Good citizenship in central Kansas entailed Republican politics. To vote Republican was to certify the authenticity of one's naturalization."[13]

Jahnke discovered that Mennonites occasionally defected to protest movement–third parties such as the Greenbacks, the Populists, and the Progressives, when they were dissatisfied with Republicans. But the GOP almost always won, except in 1912 when popular former President Theodore Roosevelt won the Mennonite vote as a Progressive.

In 1924 a third of Kansas Mennonites defected to Robert LaFollette, a Progressive, while 52 percent backed Republican President Calvin Coolidge and 15 percent supported Democrat John Davis. In 1928 anti-Catholic sentiments caused the Mennonite vote to go 84 percent to 16 percent for Herbert Hoover over Al Smith. Apparently, the entire Mennonite LaFollette vote shifted to Hoover, while nationally a majority of LaFollette voters supported Smith.

Franklin Roosevelt won a majority in 1932, the first and only Democratic victory among Kansas Mennonites in this century. Alf Landon, the state's governor and the 1936 GOP nominee, was the victor in that election, and Wendell Wilkie crushed FDR 81 percent to 18 percent in 1940.

In 1956 Stevenson received the support of only 13 percent of Kansas Mennonites, and John F. Kennedy fell to 12 percent in 1960. Fear of Kennedy's Catholicism seems to have increased the voter turnout in Men-

Table 2.3

Presidential Voting 1956–1992 in the Strongest Mennonite Counties

Year	% Republican		% Democrat		% Other	
1956	Eisenhower	70.8	Stevenson	29.2		
1960	Nixon	69.6	Kennedy	30.4		
1964	Goldwater	48.1	Johnson	51.9		
1968	Nixon	63.3	Humphrey	28.5	Wallace	8.2
1972	Nixon	73.2	McGovern	26.8		
1976	Ford	58.6	Carter	41.4		
1980	Reagan	61.6	Carter	30.6	Anderson	7.8
1984	Reagan	71.4	Mondale	28.6		
1988	Bush	66.0	Dukakis	34.0		
1992	Bush	50.5	Clinton	29.1	Perot	20.4

nonite areas. Nixon received 4,091 votes in these precincts compared to Eisenhower's 3,493. Even in 1964, Republican Barry Goldwater received 58 percent of the Kansas Mennonite vote, suggesting that this state's Mennonites are even more conservative than their counterparts in other states.

This is borne out by Mennonite voter conservatism on social issues. In 1934 the Mennonite communities were 75 percent in favor of Prohibition. In the early 1930s they favored an independent candidate for governor, Dr. John Brinkley, a notorious quack and political extremist. In 1938 Mennonites supported an extreme right-wing fundamentalist preacher, Gerald Winrod, in the Republican primary for U.S. senator. Winrod's campaign attacked an alleged Jewish-communist conspiracy against the United States.

This picture of Mennonite voting behavior seems to contradict their image as a peace-oriented community dedicated to social justice. Jahnke comments on this in the context of why Mennonites did not support "peace" candidates like William Jennings Bryan in 1900, Woodrow Wilson in 1916, or George McGovern in 1972. He says, "The lack of a strong Mennonite peace vote suggested that Mennonites were not anxious to let their religious doctrines get in the way of their growing confidence in and commitment to America.[14] . . . Mennonites expressed little discomfiture at the lack of a bridge between religious doctrine and political behavior. Religion and politics were completely compartmentalized."[15]

Jahnke also points out that "The Kansas Mennonite's attraction to Gerald Winrod in 1938 is part of a broader picture of Mennonite susceptibility to right-wing political nationalism in the twentieth century."[16] (See table 2.3.)

Seventh-day Adventists: Dissenters in the Heartland

One conservative religious group has been moving away from the Republicans just as other evangelicals are embracing the GOP. Adventists combine a conservative life style, a disdain for labor unions, distrust of Catholicism, and a separatism that allowed them to pursue their culture and Saturday worship unimpeded by hostile forces. These factors conspired to create a historic loyalty to the Republican party through good times and bad.

In 1932, for example, the then heavily Adventist community of Takoma Park, Maryland, was one of only two precincts in Montgomery County to stick with Herbert Hoover against Franklin Roosevelt. (The other was the WASPish upper-class enclave of Chevy Chase.) In a 1933 referendum, Adventist Takoma Park joined Methodist Damascus as the only Montgomery County precincts to support Prohibition, which was unpopular in Maryland.

Adventist preference for living in homogeneous communities is remarkable and has attracted attention. Kosmin and Lachman write, "A prime example of a closed community is the Seventh-day Adventists. Its members can be born in an Adventist hospital, educated in Adventist schools from kindergarten to university, work in Adventist institutions, buy Adventist food, live in Adventist communities, and end their days in Adventist retirement centers."[17]

Adventists are relatively well educated, with about 18 percent holding college degrees. They are strongly committed to a parochial school system, which educates a higher percentage of their members than that of any other religious group except possibly the Mennonites and Amish. According to NSRI data, their median household income is slightly below the national average, as is their percentage of college graduates, but they are ahead of most other evangelical groups. Interestingly, only 46 percent of Adventists work full time, the third lowest percentage for all religious groups. And their divorce rate is the second highest, ranking just behind Unitarians.

Consequently, political analysts have identified five overwhelmingly Adventist communities where long-term voting trends can be ascertained: Loma Linda, California; Keene, Texas; Berrien Springs, Michigan; College Station, Washington; and Collegedale, Tennessee. All are anchored by small Adventist colleges.

These towns routinely gave Republican candidates 90 percent or more of their presidential vote. Even Barry Goldwater won easily in 1964, and Richard Nixon received 85 percent in 1968 and 1972, as did Gerald Ford in 1976. But then the Religious Right emerged as a powerful new force in GOP life, and Adventists expressed growing concern for policies that they feared might erode the cherished principle of separation of church and state and lead to majoritarian persecution. As a minority acutely aware of religious intolerance, Adventists fear that religious majoritarianism of any kind, even from conservative Protestants, may harm their ability to practice their faith freely, especially the Saturday worship, the day Adventists regard as the genuine Sabbath.

This concern has been frequently enunciated in the glossy, well-written bimonthly *Liberty* magazine, which has consistently criticized the Religious Right.

Ronald Reagan remained personally popular among Adventists but his vote support was only around 65 percent to 70 percent in 1980 and 1984. George Bush received about the same level of support in 1988. Adventists have still been unable, it seems, to back the Democratic candidate because of the weight of history, but their Republicanism has grown lukewarm. The Adventist's Washington area office, located at the denomination's world headquarters in the Maryland suburb of Silver Spring, has been outspoken in its criticism of Religious Right–Republican proposals on school prayer. Many Adventists express disdain that a Republican-dominated Supreme Court issued a series of rulings sharply reducing the free exercise of religion and allowing more religious cooperation or accommodation with government. While other evangelicals applauded, Adventists stood firmly opposed.

In 1992 George Bush received the lowest support ever given to a Republican presidential candidate by Adventists: 48 percent to Bill Clinton's 31 percent and Ross Perot's 21 percent. For the first time a majority of Adventists in the most heavily Adventist towns voted against a Republican nominee for the White House. As the party drifts further to the Right, this trend may intensify.

It should be noted that a substantial portion of the Adventist community nationally is African American, and they are Democrats. One of the more interesting new members of Congress elected in 1994 was Sheila Jackson Lee, a Texas Democrat and Adventist, who represents Barbara Jordan's old Houston district. The two other Adventists in Congress are white Republicans of a conservative bent.

One survey of Adventist political attitudes during the 1980s was published in 1992. It found that Adventists held liberal positions on issues concerning world peace, gun control, and race relations, but conservative views on crime and economic issues. Politically, they favor the Republicans 2 to 1 over the Democrats. In the 1984 presidential election, only 61 percent of Adventists voted; those who did supported Reagan over Mondale 3 to 1. In political orientation Adventists were divided between moderate and conservative, with only 5 percent calling themselves liberal.

Table 2.4

1992 Presidential Vote in Five Seventh-day Adventist Towns

Town	State	% Clinton	% Bush	% Perot
Loma Linda	California	34.2	46.1	19.7
Keene	Texas	24.2	48.6	27.2
College Place	Washington	32.8	47.0	20.2
Berrien Springs	Michigan	32.2	45.9	21.9
Collegedale	Tennessee	23.8	57.7	18.8
ALL		31.4	47.6	21.0

On one issue Adventists differed markedly from other conservative Christians. They opposed a school prayer amendment by 47 percent to 38 percent at a time when more than 80 percent of other evangelicals endorsed the idea.[18] (See table 2.4.)

The Southern Baptist Empire

The Southern Baptist subculture represents an increasingly conservative, Republican-trending region of the South, where religion influences political belief more strongly than perhaps anywhere else in the United States. After having supported all Democratic presidential candidates from Andrew Jackson to Franklin Roosevelt (except for Al Smith, whose Catholicism and opposition to Prohibition doomed his candidacy in Baptist areas), Baptists grew increasingly restive toward the Truman administration. As the most Southern-oriented denomination in the South, the Southern Baptists reflected "traditional values," which meant segregation and opposition to civil rights, more convincingly than other groups, though all shared in the segregationist way of life to some degree. While Truman won a slim majority among his fellow Baptists, many defected to Dixiecrat Strom Thurmond, a Southern Baptist who claimed to represent the historic states rights philosophy of government. Republican Thomas Dewey won the usual Baptist mountain Republicans and some city dwellers.

During the 1950s Baptists split their votes about equally between Republican Dwight Eisenhower and Democrat Adlai Stevenson. In 1960 anti-Catholic voting reduced Kennedy's support 2 percentage points throughout the Baptist region, but was particularly severe—often 10 points or more—in Kentucky, Tennessee, Oklahoma, Arkansas, and Missouri. In 1964 the kind of conservatism represented by Barry Goldwater won a small majority among Baptists, the only major religious group to give the Arizona senator a majority. In 1968 George Wallace and Richard Nixon split the Baptist vote, with Hubert Humphrey running a poor third. The Baptist vote split along economic lines, with the blue-collar voters going to Wallace and middle-income voters favoring Nixon.

After Nixon swept the Baptist vote 3–1 over George McGovern in 1972, a swing to the Democrats occurred when fellow believer Jimmy Carter won 58 percent of the rural and small-town Baptists in 1976. (Even in that year, however, Carter may have lost narrowly to Ford among suburban Baptists.)

Ronald Reagan took the Baptist vote away from Carter in 1980 and won two-thirds or more against Walter Mondale in 1984. George Bush did nearly as well against Michael Dukakis in 1988. In 1992 Baptists voted against the all-Baptist Democratic ticket of Bill Clinton and Al Gore by 46 percent to 40 percent, with 14 percent for Perot. In the suburbs and cities, Bush did even better.

All during this period, Baptist presidential Republicanism did not quite extend to the congressional or state-level races, though GOP sentiment was rising sharply. By 1994 the conversion to Republican voting at the lower levels accelerated. Republican identification and registration are now strong among Baptist elite groups such as the clergy and among younger Baptists and those who are prosperous.

This dramatic shift, occurring as it has over one generation, is largely a result of the ingrained religious, moral, and political conservatism of the Baptist community. Every social science survey for the past three decades, including the pioneering studies of Charles Glock and Rodney Stark, has revealed that Baptists are probably the most conservative major religious group in the country on questions involving religious doctrine, social life, military and defense issues, and religion's role in public life. Not only do Baptists now prefer Republican candidates, but they also prefer conservative Republicans and often Religious Right conservatives, many of whom are themselves Baptists.

Baptists in South Carolina gave a majority to Republican and fellow Baptist David Beasley in the 1994 governor's race. Beasley ran a thoroughly sectarian campaign and was the Religious Right's poster boy in 1994. His relatively narrow majority came from white Baptists.

In Mississippi, the Southern Baptists were drawn to Kirk Fordice, an ultraconservative Republican (and a Methodist) who called the U.S. "a Christian nation,"[19] much to the discomfiture of many Republicans nationwide. The Baptist vote was essential to Fordice's three-percentage-point margin in 1991.

He won 66 percent of the votes in the strongest Baptist counties. Fordice was even more popular among Baptists than was President George Bush, who carried Mississippi by 9 points, but won by a smaller margin than Fordice in Baptist counties. Fordice carried the strongest Baptist counties by 31 points; Bush won them by 20 points. (By contrast, predominantly Catholic Hancock County went for Bush by 13 points but voted against Fordice by 29 points.)

Another way of looking at the Mississippi results is to focus on fourteen counties where Fordice ran significantly better than Bush. Those counties had a Southern Baptist population that was 50 percent higher than statewide. They were 53.1 percent Southern Baptist, compared to 35.4 percent for Mississippi as a whole. One of these pro-Fordice counties was Pontotoc County, scene of a nasty religion-in-the-schools dispute while Fordice was governor. The controversial governor was reelected in 1995 by a larger margin than in his first election.

Baptists have trended Republican more than any other group when comparing the 1976 and 1992 presidential elections. Bill Clinton was 11 points weaker than Jimmy Carter among Baptists, though he ran stronger than Carter among mainline Protestants, Jews, and the religiously nonaffiliated, and evenly with Carter among Catholics, Lutherans, and Mormons. (Only among the smaller sectarian evangelicals did Clinton lose more ground compared to Carter than among Southern Baptists.) That is why Clinton lost, but Carter won, such Baptist strongholds as Mississippi, Alabama, South Carolina, and North Carolina.

Baptist conservatism is the best explanation for this turn of events. Catholic priest-sociologist Andrew Greeley is one of the few observers of religion to study the Southern Baptists as a separate and unique religious community. Using the National Opinion Research Center (NORC) General Social Survey data from 1983 to 1991, Greeley constructed a portrait of the social, cultural, and political attitudes that define the Southern Baptists.

Greeley found that while "there is considerable de facto pluralism within the Southern Baptist community,"[20] the faith itself is a living incarnation of evangelical Reformation Protestantism. Southern Baptists, Greeley discovered, "are more conservative on family values than other Protestants and Catholics but differ very little from other Christians in their attitudes toward abortion" (243).

Baptists scored higher on scales of racism and militarism and lower on feminism and support for civil liberties than other Protestants, and both Protestant groups were more conservative than Catholics. Baptists were twice as likely as Catholics to own guns and to believe that premarital sex was always wrong. Other Protestants were midpoint between Baptists and

Catholics. Of all religious groups, Baptists were the most critical of homosexuality, were more likely than others to favor corporal punishment for children, and were most likely to favor legal bans on pornography. Their religious orientation was responsible for these differences, according to Greeley, who wrote, "Differences in religious imagery, differences that date at least to the Reformation, account not only for the different religious styles but even for the different cultural values of Catholics and Southern Baptists" (248). Baptists scored highest on a scale measuring religious dogmatism and antiscientific views and lowest on a scale measuring religious flexibility (236, 238).

In family-income demographics Baptists were about 4 percent lower than other Protestants and 17 percent lower than Catholics. About 12 percent of Baptists were college graduates compared to 17 percent of other Protestants and 18 percent of Catholics during the 1984–91 time frame. About 47 percent held white-collar jobs, compared to 53 percent of other Protestants and 38 percent of Catholics. About 19 percent lived in rural areas, compared to 17 percent of other Protestants, but only 29 percent lived in large cities or suburbs compared to 33 percent of other Protestants and 44 percent of Catholics.

Baptists were still predominantly Democratic in these NORC surveys, which may have failed to reflect the Republican trends of the 1990s. About half of Southern Baptists were married to fellow believers, and 20 percent of Southern Baptists were converts. However, 22 percent of those raised as Southern Baptist had defected to other religions (233). And despite their strong heritage of religious liberty, only 22 percent of Baptists scored high on a scale measuring support for religious freedom, compared to 37 percent of other Protestants and 54 percent of Catholics (238).

Greeley concluded, "Baptists who identify with the Southern Baptist Convention are a more complex and pluralistic group than one might have anticipated. . . . Positions taken by the leadership and by the resolutions at the annual Convention are no more likely to represent the sentiments of many Southern Baptists than are the statements of the Catholic hierarchy reflective of the positions of ordinary Catholics" (252).

Greeley adds, "Their religious style, however, is both devout and profoundly Reformation, even though only three out of five of their members believe in the literal interpretation, word for word, of the Bible. They are more likely to be suspicious of science, moralistic, dogmatically rigid, and, despite their doctrines of 'soul freedom,' dependent on the leadership of their church than are Catholics and other Protestants" (252).

Not all is well with Southern Baptists, however. Intense intradenominational animosity between fundamentalists and moderates has taken a toll on church morale. Internal divisions always produce some shuffling among members, reducing the commitment and support of dissenters and those who perceive themselves on the losing end of ecclesiastical struggles. Annual conventions have been rancorous since the 1980s, and seminaries and colleges have been riveted by turmoil.

While Southern Baptists continue to grow in membership, their annual growth rate is much lower than it was during the 1950s and 1960s. Internal church surveys and research papers show that Baptists lose more members to other denominations than they gain; their growth rate, such as it is, comes from the ranks of the unchurched. Many Baptists are inactive. Gallup polls show church attendance among Baptists to be moderate. Nearly a third of Baptists never attend church during an average year. Some surveys suggest that the annual "growth rate" might actually be negative were it not for converts among Hispanics.

Greeley also concluded, "The period of their recent spectacular growth seems to be over, and a period of slight decline may have set in" (252).

Heavily Southern Baptist counties are often battlegrounds over religious expression in the public schools. Some of the major legal conflicts have originated in counties where Baptists are the dominant religious tradition.

In Okaloosa County, Florida, the most Baptist county in the state with a population exceeding 100,000, conflicts have been numerous. In the 1970s a public school teacher, who also taught Sunday School at a Methodist church, was fired and driven out of the county after she protested against the mandatory prayer and religious exercises existing in the school in clear violation of a U.S. Supreme Court ruling. In the late 1980s a Jewish family was harassed when they opposed the practice of beginning all high school football games with public prayer. The local ministerial association, all of whose members were Protestant, determined which pastor would deliver the invocations. This led to a nasty community dispute and a court decision.

Similar problems have occurred in other Baptist areas, like Lubbock, Texas, and Douglas, Georgia. In 1984 ABC television portrayed schools in Nassau County, Florida, where formalized school prayers continued twenty years after being declared unconstitutional by the nation's high court.

In Hawkins County, Tennessee, a Baptist majority county, a bitter dispute arose when fundamentalist parents tried to have their children exempted from reading books with which the parents disagreed. Eventually, they sought removal of all offending books from the school system. This case became a cause celebré for the Religious Right and for church-state separationists. Its study was admirably recounted by Stephen Bates in *Battleground* (New York: Henry Holt, 1993).

An ugly dispute in another Baptist majority county, Pontotoc County, Mississippi, arose in 1995 when a parent from a Lutheran-Christian Science background objected to the heavy-handed evangelical religious activities in her children's school. She filed suit in federal court, and the federal district court ruled in her favor in June 1996. Denounced from the pulpit at the county's powerful First Baptist Church, Lisa Herdahl waged a lonely fight typical of the fate of religious outsiders in a majoritarian society.

She told the press:

> I personally have received a death threat in the mail and my family has received bomb threats. For several months I was afraid to start my car in the morning, and my husband did the shopping so I wouldn't have to go into the stores. My family believes deeply in God, and our religious faith is important to us. But because our religious beliefs are different from those of others in the community, and because of organized religious practices in our public school, we had been harassed and stigmatized. . . . My children are learning . . . about real religious liberty.[21]

In her testimony before a House Judiciary Subcommittee on July 10, 1995, Mrs. Herdahl explained her position.

> I learned that vocal prayers were broadcast over the school intercom and recited in classrooms during the school day, and that students at the school attended religious Bible instruction as part of the school curriculum. I stated that I did not want my children to attend the Bible classes or to participate in the prayers. I am a Christian and I am raising my children as Christians. . . . I was particularly concerned because the intercom prayers were in the name of Jesus, and I teach my children to pray directly to God. My ability as a parent to teach my children to pray and our religious freedom was being undermined. Because I requested that my children not participate in the religious instruction at the school, my children have been ridiculed and harassed by teachers and classmates, and falsely called "devil worshippers" and "atheists." . . . I had many conversations with the superintendent of schools and with the principal and assistant principal of North Pontotoc Attendance Center to request that the school stop the unconstitutional Bible classes and prayers, but was told that this is the way things were done in Pontotoc. . . . In order to protect my children, I had no choice but to file a lawsuit in federal court to stop the school's unconstitutional practices. As a result, the harassment of my family got even worse. Signs appeared all over town in support of the school's practices. I personally have received a death threat in the mail and my family has received bomb threats. Fortunately, the First Amendment protected us in court.[22]

Many Baptists retort that they have an absolute right to proclaim the gospel any time, any place, regardless of how it impacts the community. Local supporters of school prayer in Pontotoc County organized a "religious liberty" campaign, claiming that their rights to religious freedom were being violated by the Herdahl lawsuit and the temporary injunction against the school's practices issued by the courts.

Given the intensity of feelings surrounding religious activities in schools, disputes like these are likely to intensify, and not just in Baptist-oriented communities.

The most recent (1994) Gallup survey data confirm that Southern Baptists are heavily Southern, middle class, white, and likely to reside in small towns and rural areas.

Seventy-six percent of Baptists live in the South, 11 percent in the Midwest, 7 percent in the East, and 6 percent in the West. Fifty-two percent reside in small towns and rural areas, while 26 percent live in urban areas and 22 percent are suburbanites. Baptists are still far more rural (16 percentage points) than Lutherans and Presbyterians, less urban (6–8 points) and less suburban (10 points).

Baptist household income is 45 percent middle income, 32 percent lower income, and 17 percent upper or upper middle income. In comparison with Presbyterians, Baptists are one-third more likely to live in households making under $20,000 a year, but only half as likely to live in households where the annual income exceeds $50,000. This disparity holds true for education. Only 40 percent of Baptists attended college compared to 72 percent of Presbyterians. (About half or a little less than half of Americans who attend college actually graduate, according to U.S. Census Bureau data.)

Baptists are relatively younger than most other Protestants. About 58 percent are younger than 50, compared to 45 percent of Presbyterians.

These Baptist demographic findings influence national polling data, since 16 percent of all Americans who live in rural or small-town communities are Baptists, compared to only 7 percent of suburbanites and 6 percent of city dwellers.[23]

The Shenandoah Valley

Virginia's Shenandoah Valley is a fabled land, a place of early migrations by English, Scotch Irish, and German settlers, and a primary battleground in the U.S. Civil War. Part of the Appalachian Mountain chain, the Valley, which stretches from the West Virginia and Maryland borders to the Roanoke area, forms a subregion of conservative Protestant culture that offers many features of interest to political commentary.

Unlike much of the South, where only a few religious denominations are dominant, churches of many persuasions dot the Valley's landscape. It is an ecumenical Protestant area. Its Catholic population has always been tiny, totaling 3 percent of residents in 1990 and 2 percent in 1980. Jewish residents are fewer still.

Historically Methodist, the Valley's Baptist population surpassed the Methodists in 1990, largely because of Baptist strength in the Roanoke area at the southern end of the region. Baptists outnumber Methodists 47,000 to 18,000 in Roanoke, but Methodists lead 60,000 to 35,000 in the rest of the Valley. The nation's most Methodist county, Highland, lies nestled in the Valley.

Presbyterians (33,000 strong) are most numerous in the Lexington-Rockbridge County area, where the Presbyterian military hero, Gen. Stonewall Jackson, lies buried. Presbyterians are also strong in Augusta County, which has been called the most Scotch-Irish county in the U.S. (though several other counties make the same claim).

About 29,000 Valley residents belong to the Mennonite or Brethren traditions. These German peace churches are strongest in Rockingham County and in Harrisonburg, where Eastern Mennonite College is located. The 19,000 Lutherans are scattered throughout the Valley, and they are the strongest religious community in Shenandoah County.

Episcopalians (10,000 Valley members) are not as numerous here as in the Richmond-Williamsburg area and in Northern Virginia's metropolitan region. Those who do reside here are most numerous in Clarke County, in the northern part of the Valley, and in nearby locations. The northern Valley lies just west of the Virginia Hunt Country, where Episcopalians are historically influential.

Not all Valley members are religious, by any means. About 54 percent were church members according to the 1990 Glenmary Research Center survey, which matches the national average and exceeds the state average. But cultural and social conservatism, much of it rooted in religion, dominates the Valley and influences the political culture.

Historically Democratic, the Valley rebelled in 1948 when Republican Tom Dewey beat President Truman by ten percentage points. And with the solitary exception of Barry Goldwater in 1964, the Valley has loyally supported the GOP's presidential candidates. By the late 1970s this Republican orientation extended to state candidates as well. The region is moderately prosperous, for a rural area, and counties like Clarke and Roanoke, and the cities of Salem and Winchester are near the state average in per capita income. The college towns of Lexington and Harrisonburg have high rates of college-educated adults, of course, and counties like Roanoke and Clarke and the cities of Staunton and Waynesboro are near the state average in the percentage of college-educated adults.

Presidents Eisenhower and Nixon were easy Valley winners. And while Nixon defeated Kennedy in 1960 by 63 percent to 37 percent, Kennedy ran 6 points better than Stevenson, which would indicate a relative absence of anti-Catholicism.

In 1964 Lyndon Johnson edged Barry Goldwater 51 percent to 49 percent, which suggested that there were limits to the Valley's conservatism. George Wallace won only 20 percent in 1968, to Humphrey's 25 percent and Nixon's 55 percent, indicating that the kind of hard-edged racism found farther south was not strong in the Valley.

Jimmy Carter won a respectable 47 percent in 1976 and carried the Roanoke area by 5,500 votes. Heavily Baptist Roanoke voted much like other Baptist-oriented regions, since LBJ had won Roanoke by only 200 votes. But the Methodist-Lutheran-Presbyterian areas liked Carter a good deal less than Johnson.

Ronald Reagan and George Bush were victorious during the 1980s, as the Valley became ever more conservative. In 1992 George Bush defeated Bill Clinton by 14 percentage points, winning exactly half the Valley vote to Clinton's 36 percent and Perot's 14 percent. Fiercely conservative Augusta County gave Bush 60 percent, one of his highest national levels of support. The Mennonite areas in Rockingham County supported the President with 62 percent, though he barely topped 50 percent in Harrisonburg, where the student and academic vote serves as a brake on the area's Republican habits.

The hotly contested state elections of 1993 and 1994 reinforced the Valley's reputation as a conservative stronghold. Voting 2 to 1 for Republican George Allen for governor in 1993, the Valley also remained loyal to Michael Farris, the far-right fundamentalist, by 52 percent to 48 percent in the lieutenant governor's contest. Farris lost among his fellow Baptists in Roanoke, but won among other groups—one of the many ironies in this election.

In 1994 Valley voters registered strong support for Republican U.S. Senate nominee Oliver North, who defeated Senator Charles Robb by 13 points in the area. North ran as well as Bush, indicating no serious loss of support for North because of his ultraright stance. Valley Republicans did not defect from North, as many suburban and academic area Republicans did in other parts of the state. North, who lives in Clarke County, even captured Allegheny County, a swing county that supported Clinton. Independent candidate Marshall Coleman, who grew up in the Valley in the Staunton-Waynesboro area, received only average support. The Valley remains 5 per-

Table 2.5

Presidential Voting 1956–1992 in Virginia's Shenandoah Valley

Year	% Republican		%Democrat		% Other	
1956	Eisenhower	68.7	Stevenson	31.3		
1960	Nixon	62.7	Kennedy	37.3		
1964	Goldwater	48.9	Johnson	51.1		
1968	Nixon	55.5	Humphrey	24.6	Wallace	19.9
1972	Nixon	75.6	McGovern	24.4		
1976	Ford	52.7	Carter	47.3		
1980	Reagan	55.7	Carter	38.9	Anderson	5.4
1984	Reagan	67.8	Mondale	32.2		
1988	Bush	63.3	Dukakis	36.7		
1992	Bush	50.0	Clinton	35.9	Perot	14.1

cent to 10 percent more Republican than Virginia as a whole, a state that clearly favors the GOP most of the time.

Social, cultural, and religious conservatism have united to produce a faithfully Republican bailiwick in this scenic, historic, and tradition-conscious subregion of America. (See table 2.5)

The Southern Highlands: Appalachia to the Ozarks

One of the most enduring subcultures in the United States is that of the mountain or Upland South, the residents of the Appalachian Mountain chain, including the Blue Ridge, and extending across the northern regions of Georgia, Alabama, and Mississippi, and concluding, culturally, in the Ozark region of southwestern Missouri and northwest Arkansas.

This is one of the oldest inhabited areas of the United States and its residents are almost entirely white Protestants of Anglo-Saxon ancestry. This is Scotch-Irish America, the area where immigration from the British Isles first laid strong roots and where the immigrants and their descendants shaped a frontier culture based on individualism and a rigorous kind of Calvinistic Protestantism.

The area has undergone repeated economic hardship, and its geographic isolation has produced a kind of cultural and psychic isolation from the mainstream of American economic and political life.

Bypassed by the Industrial Revolution, this region is hardscrabble and still poorer than most other regions of the country. Dozens of counties, especially in eastern Kentucky and Tennessee, have the lowest incomes and lowest educational levels in the nation. It is not uncommon to find counties where the majority of adults have not completed high school.

Most residents are of English, Scottish, or Irish ancestry, and many refuse to claim any ethnic ancestry or identity, claiming to be "just plain Americans." Most of the counties with the highest percentage of residents who claim no ethnic ancestry are in the Highland-Appalachia area. So are most of the counties with high percentages of British ancestry. These factors of lower education and income and high Anglo Saxonism combine with religious fundamentalism to produce a strange kind of politics, with equal mixtures of populism, nativism, and ultraconservatism.

Political loyalties, though, are partially based on Civil War memories. Pockets of long time Republican support are found even in the poorest counties, where the ancestors of today's residents wore the Union blue rather than the Confederate gray, even though many of them resided in the Confederate States of America. Jackson County, Kentucky, for example, was George Bush's strongest county among America's 3,100 counties in 1992. Bush won 75 percent of the votes cast in a county where per capita income was $7,097 (compared to the U.S. $14,420) and where only 4.9 percent of adults were college graduates (U.S. 20.3 percent), and only 38.3 percent of adults are high school graduates (U.S. 75.2 percent). Obviously, something other than income and education has affected the politics of places like Jackson County.

This region has produced a unique folk culture, with distinctive musical idioms, speech patterns, and preservations of early English ballads and folklore. Berea College in Kentucky, Appalachian State University in North Carolina, and the College of the Ozarks in Missouri have all devoted research centers to the study of the region.

The religious life of this subculture is influenced more by fundamentalism than by evangelicalism, though large regions retain such an individualistic character that church membership is low. However, those areas that are religious are very religious, and tend toward small fundamentalist denominations. Even the mainline churches are conservative. Revivals and religious radio stations are common religious phenomena.

In 1921 the Russell Sage Foundation published a detailed study of the Mountain South that has become a classic blend of sociology and history. Entitled *The Southern Highlander and His Homeland*,[24] it was written by John C. Campbell, a Presbyterian educator from the North who spent his adult life in the region. His attention to religious cultures and ethnicity serves to this day as an essential place of departure for modern research.

Campbell found that just over a third of the residents were church members in 1916. Of these, 90 percent were Protestant. "It may be stated almost without qualification that the rural Highlander is a Protestant,"[25] he observed. Of the nearly two million church members, 40 percent were Baptist, 31 percent Methodist, and 6 percent Presbyterian.

While Baptists, Methodists, and Presbyterians are still strong in the Highlands, other denominations are highly competitive in numbers. The Primitive Baptists, Free Will Baptists, Old Regular Baptists, United Baptists, Duck River Baptists, Enterprise Baptists, and similar groups have their most loyal followings in Appalachia. The Pentecostal Holiness Church and the Church of God are strong in these parts, as are the Cumberland Presbyterians, the Church of the Brethren, and the Associate Reformed Presbyterians. Most of these groups have a majority of their national membership in the Highlands of the South, giving the subregion a different religious stamp. The Church of God, which has about 700,000 members, was founded in 1903 in Bradley County, Tennessee, where it is still influential.

Observers have long noted the staunch religious fervor found in much of this subregion. To them this is the land of "Holy Rollers," camp meetings, snake handlers, and the 1925 Scopes trial about the teaching of evolution in the schools. Folks in this area did not take much to Clarence Darrow, scientists, or intellectuals. In 1930 Dayton, Tennessee, fundamentalists established a new Christian college and named it for Williams Jennings Bryan.[26] The college, now known as Bryan University, is still going strong, and its location in Rhea County perhaps symbolizes the changing politics of the region. Rhea County has supported every Republican presidential candidate in modern times except in 1976, when it went for Jimmy Carter.

H. C. Nixon once wrote, "The rural hill country has been fed Protestant orthodoxy more exclusively than any other part of America. It has had a minimum exposure to Episcopalian and Roman Catholic influences, being different in this respect from people in other regions of the South. It has had no contact with Unitarianism. It has had doctrinal controversies, between Methodists and Baptists, or between Baptists and Baptists."[27] Nixon argued that this kind of religion had educational and political consequences. "The rural and small-town orthodoxy has tended to neglect or oppose scientific thought. The ministers of the hills have been deeply concerned with the spiritual life of individuals. Aside from the anti-liquor crusade, these orthodox ministers have, with striking exceptions, viewed the social scene with relative unconcern. Personal soul-salvation for the other world takes precedence over working for community salvation and social justice in this one."[28]

Erskine Caldwell, a once popular novelist, was also a seasoned journalist who grew up in rural Georgia and South Carolina, the son of a rather liberal minister of the Associate Reformed Presbyterian Church. (His father subsequently left the ministry.) Late in his life, he wrote a superb study of Southern religion entitled *Deep South*. Caldwell's analysis, written during the 1960s, was first published in England with the title *In the Shadow of the Steeple*, a far more perceptive title than the one given to the American edition. Caldwell's observations are among the most sentient and balanced and illuminate the religious ethos of this unusual subregion. He wrote, "Like the coming of the circus, revival meetings conducted by evangelists with well-known reputations attract large crowds in cities once or twice a year. It is here, usually in the low-rent residential districts of towns or in impoverished rural areas, that evangelical religion thrives best."[29]

He notes that the purest strain of fundamentalism still exists in the Highland South. "The major source of elemental evangelicalism continues after nearly two hundred years to be those portions of Virginia, Kentucky and Tennessee in the Cumberland and Blue Ridge Mountains of Appalachia. While the effervescent source in this mountain region continues after all this time to be constant and undiminished, its evangelicalism loses some of its primitivism and tends to become less exuberant and more sophisticated when it gravitates southward from the mountains to the Piedmont of the Carolinas, Georgia, Alabama, and Mississippi" (39).

Caldwell believed that the region's "fundamentalistic religious beliefs have already begun to influence a trend towards social and political reactionism (51). . . . The precept of fundamentalism leads inevitably to reactionary and ultraconservative principles and conduct in secular life. A Cumberland religious zealot is a prime prospect for membership, and often leadership, in segregationalist and similar extremist organizations (26–27). In such an environment of unyielding traditions and steadfast fundamentalism, it is to be expected that the social and political changes that have been commonplace elsewhere in the U.S. in recent years should be resisted in the Cumberlands" (27).

Caldwell's interviews throughout the region convinced him that "excessive emotionalism" had "debased and perverted" religious faith and practice and that "the ethical values inherent in the Bible were ignored and replaced by the theatrical antics of evangelism and the mesmerizing promises of spirituality and immortality" (164).

Whether or not one agrees with Caldwell's observations or his interpretations, one can hardly argue with one of his conclusions: "The white Southern Protestant, saint or sinner, clings to his religious convictions with unshakable tenacity" (185).

The Ozarks are to some extent the southwesterly cultural extension of Appalachia. Straddling two states, Missouri and Arkansas, they represent a strong Scotch-Irish, Anglo Saxon region noted for the persistence of subcultural identity, right-wing politics, and fundamentalist religious expressions. W. K. McNeil, a folklorist at the Ozark Folk Center in Mountain View, Arkansas, explains that "Traditional Ozarkers hold to fundamentalist religious beliefs and belong to such churches as Church of Christ, Assembly of God, and various Pentecostal churches that feature highly emotional services."[30]

This area exemplifies a hardy and individualistic strain of religious and social conservatism. Found in southwestern Missouri and northwestern Arkansas, it roughly corresponds to the Third Congressional District in Arkansas and the Seventh Congressional District in Missouri. This economically depressed but highly individualist area is typified by religious camp meetings, denominational rivalries, and fundamentalist theology. There are virtually no Catholics, Jews, Episcopalians, or religious liberals here, which is why Al Smith and John Kennedy ran so poorly in the Ozarks in 1928 and 1960. The most famous anti-Catholic magazine in U.S. history, a monthly called *The Menace*, was published in Aurora, Missouri, from 1911 to 1931. (At one time its circulation exceeded one million readers.) This is the land of television's "The Beverly Hillbillies," the "Christ of the Ozarks" monument in Eureka Springs, Passion plays, Bible colleges, and the headquarters of the fast-growing Assemblies of God denomination. The region's best interpreter, Vance Randolph, described the area where he lived and about which he wrote many books as "The most deliberately unprogressive people in the United States."[31]

The Ozarks area has a per capita income of $10,953, 25 percent lower than the nation; it is almost entirely white (96.5 percent), and nearly half of its residents live in rural areas. About five in eight residents reside in married-couple families and one in six residents is over age sixty-five. Most residents are of Anglo-Saxon ancestry.

The population has grown considerably since the 1970s, and parts of the region are retirement meccas, which may eventually change the area's character somewhat. Service industries abound. Vigorous folk music and arts-and-crafts traditions also flavor the area.

A kind of ultraconservatism, or conservative populism, pervades the Ozarks. One of its congressmen, Republican Mel Hancock, was among the handful of members who voted against the Hate Crimes Act a few years ago. (He apparently saw nothing wrong with ignoring the verbal and physical abuse of people because of their race, religion, or ancestry.) In 1979 then-Congressman Gene Taylor vociferously opposed the Martin Luther King national holiday bill.

Despite low income, the Ozarks have leaned Republican since the 1960s, due in large part to cultural conservatism. Although Barry Goldwater lost in 1964, most Republicans since Eisenhower have won here. One exception came in 1976, when Jimmy Carter edged Gerald Ford by 51 percent to 49 percent. Carter was more adept at appealing to evangelical voters than any recent Democrat. Reagan won 70 percent in 1984 and Bush secured 64 percent in 1988.

In 1992 Bill Clinton lost the Ozarks 44 percent to 40 percent (16 percent voted for Perot), despite the fact that he was the well-known governor of about half the area. The Republicans won both congressional seats, with 57 percent of the vote. Arkansas's Third District elected Tim Hutchinson, a Baptist preacher and Christian radio-station owner who is a graduate of Bob Jones University, a fiercely fundamentalist school in South Carolina.

Given this cultural scenario, it was not surprising that George Bush chose Branson, Missouri, a fast-growing mecca for country and western music, as the place to kick off his fall campaign. Immediately after the Houston convention, Bush went to Branson, where he received an enthusiastic welcome and was serenaded by Glen Campbell, Loretta Lynn, Boxcar Willie, Jim Stafford, and Missouri's gospel-singing Governor John Ashcroft, who won a U.S. Senate seat in 1994.

Journalist Bruce Cook thought Bush picked the right place. "After all, these were his people. They stood foursquare for the 'family values' that had been extolled so fervently during the course of the convention. This is, as I had been told often, the buckle on the Bible Belt."[32] Bush easily won in Branson and surrounding Taney County on election day. Country music star Roy Clark echoes this sentiment in his autobiography *My Life*. Now a resident of Branson, he trumpeted the town as "America's capital of family values."[33]

Political differences are influenced by religious participation in the Appalachian Highlands subregion. There are even differences *within* the subregion. The Virginia mountains, for example, the twenty or so counties southwest of Roanoke that border West Virginia, Kentucky, and Tennessee, are a long-time political battleground, traditionally called the "Fighting Ninth" congressional district. Politics is a blood sport here, and Democrats and Republicans have been closely contesting this part of southwest Virginia for many decades. There are some Civil War Republican counties here, and some staunch Democratic bastions in the coal mining region, where voters are National Democrats, i.e., pro-labor liberals. This is therefore a divided region. In the 1920s GOP presidential candidates won half of the votes here, and Hoover won 57 percent in 1928, though the anti-Smith vote was mild compared to the rest of Appalachia. Quirky Buchanan County, a coal mining area with a low church-membership, went for Coolidge in 1924 and then Smith in 1928, the only Southern county outside of Louisiana to *counter* the Southern backlash against Smith. In 1960 John F. Kennedy did better than Stevenson in the Virginia mountains, running nearly even with Nixon, and easily carrying Buchanan County and its neighbors. The Democrats still did relatively well from the 1960s through the 1980s in the Fighting Ninth, and Bill Clinton edged out George Bush in 1992, doing much better in the low church-membership counties, while Bush won in areas of high evangelical/fundamentalist support. In 1993–94, however, cultural backlash politics, only partially related to religion, hurt the Democrats here. Ollie North ran stronger than George Bush, and Michael Farris ran surprisingly well in the 1993 lieutenant governor's race.

In Kentucky's depressed Cumberland Plateau region, the Republicans have generally won, though the Democratic vote has been rising as some of the Great Society legislation has taken hold and made an impact on people's lives. The Democrats, from Kennedy to Clinton, have done better in those Cumberland counties where religious identification is less intense.

In 1992 Clinton defeated Bush 64 percent to 27 percent in the "unchurched" counties of the Cumberland Plateau. In the heavily Baptist counties, however, Bush won 50 percent to 38 percent over Clinton. Thus, Clinton won by 37 percentage points in the low church-membership counties but lost by 12 percentage points in counties where Baptists are a majority of the population. Four years before, Dukakis received 63 percent support in the unchurched counties and 35 percent support in the Baptist counties.

This political difference was also true in 1960, when John Kennedy won 57 percent among the unchurched and 31 percent among Baptists. Back in 1928 Al Smith received 47 percent in the unchurched areas and 18 percent in Baptist strongholds.

The Cumberland Plateau counties are distinctive in many demographic variables. The average per capita income is only two-thirds of the Kentucky average and half of the national average. The educational attainment level is 60 percent of the state average and 40 percent of the national average. But 61 percent of residents claim English or "American only" ancestry, compared to 40 percent of all Kentuckians and about 20 percent of all U.S. residents.

A similar political orientation can be found in West Virginia, where in 1960 JFK won 62 percent of the votes in the Appalachian counties with the lowest church membership but only 44 percent in the heavily evangelical counties, where Methodists and Baptists are dominant. That pattern remains today.

Anti-intellectualism and nativism may have combined in 1988 to hurt

Democrat Michael Dukakis in this region. There were seven counties in Tennessee, Georgia, and South Carolina that supported Democrat Walter Mondale in 1984 but switched to Republican George Bush in 1988. In all of these counties, JFK fared worse in 1960 than Stevenson did in 1956. There were 125 other counties in Tennessee and Georgia where Dukakis ran more weakly than Mondale. Kennedy ran weaker than Stevenson in 80 percent of them. All of the counties share several characteristics: (1) a low level of educational attainment; (2) low income; (3) residents that are mostly white Protestants of English ancestry. Though these connections may be tenuous, it seems odd that counties that did not particularly like a Catholic candidate for president in 1960 were also reluctant to support a Greek-American in 1988. Since most of the counties that shared this sentiment were in the highland or Piedmont South, there was clearly a reluctance among many voters to support candidates who did not fit the voter's image of what a president should be, an image rooted in religion and ethnicity.

Republican politics tends toward the ultraconservative in the Mountain South. This is not a region where conservative GOP candidates run worse than moderates; the opposite is more likely to be true.

Independent right-of-center candidates often do better here than in the lowlands if they emphasize cultural issues. Ed McAteer, a former Colgate Palmolive salesman who founded the Religious Roundtable, received on average about twice as many votes in Republican east Tennessee as elsewhere in the state when he sought a seat in the U.S. Senate in 1984. Running as an independent rather than as a Republican, he siphoned off 10 percent of the ballots in east Tennessee, reaching 14 percent in Greene County (where Ross Perot also did well in 1992).

Anti-Catholicism has always been rife in this region. Fundamentalist preachers have regularly regaled audiences with diatribes against the old Whore of Babylon, and anti-Catholic political movements had a receptive ready-made audience. Al Smith was slaughtered at the polls here in 1928, having been pulverized by sermons, broadsides, and roadside advertisements warning of a Catholic plot to seize America. In 1960, anti-Catholic agitators and propagandists blanketed the region, causing Kennedy to drop several percentage points behind Stevenson, especially in Kentucky and Missouri. Dozens of counties from Appalachia to the Ozarks switched from Stevenson to Nixon.

These attitudes also affected city dwellers in the region. Springfield, Missouri, the capital of the Ozarks, gave Nixon a 16,000-vote majority over Kennedy, well above Eisenhower's margin of 9,000 votes.

One of the region's finest interpreters, a journalist and onetime member of the Kennedy legislature, Harry Caudill, explains the religious psyche in this passage from his 1962 classic, *Night Comes to the Cumberlands*: "The well-spring of these folk churches was a stern Calvinism which the Scotch element of the population had carried with it from the dour highlands. Without competition from other religious ideas or doctrines, it slowly pervaded the whole populace, and eventually became deeply rooted in their mores, so widely and unquestionably accepted as to constitute unwritten law. And while its adherents might split into a myriad of disputing minor sects, they were to remain steadfastly loyal to its basic tenets. One of these was a hatred for the Roman Catholic Church and the Pope as nothing less than the arms of Satan."[34]

Antipopery even raised its head at the 1964 Republican National Convention, when several delegates from east Tennessee refused to vote to confirm Sen. Barry Goldwater's running mate, New York Congressman William Miller, because Miller was a Catholic. In the early 1960s fundamentalists strenuously opposed the opening of a Catholic hospital in Rowan County, Kentucky, an area desperately short of adequate medical care and ravaged by disease, low life expectancy, and malnutrition. After officials of the Baptist and Methodist churches refused to participate, the Sisters of Notre Dame proceeded to fund and staff a hospital that opened in June 1963. Local Protestant opposition slowly softened, and pastors from the Church of God and the Disciples of Christ participated in the dedication ceremonies. However, "Baptist clergymen seem to have been absent from the ceremony, as they were from the one for the groundbreaking,"[35] according to historian James McConkey.

Pennsylvania Dutch Country

The term "Pennsylvania Dutch Country" (PDC) is a misnomer; this region was settled early in American history not by immigrants from the Netherlands, but by immigrants from Germany. The term "Dutch" in popular parlance is a corruption of the German word *Deutsch,* which means German. Though some linguists challenge this explanation, it is the popular one used to describe this part of southeastern Pennsylvania, where a unique subculture of German Protestantism has flourished for over two centuries.

In nine Pennsylvania counties more than 30 percent of residents claim single German ancestry. Including multiple ancestry, probably a majority are of German descent. These counties are the big three (Lancaster, Berks, and York) and nearby Lebanon and Adams. In the north lie Union, Snyder, and Juniata, while Bedford lies to the west along the Maryland border. This analysis will primarily focus on these counties. There are, it should be noted, substantial German communities in neighboring counties (Franklin, Perry,

Cumberland, Mifflin, and Lehigh), and there are townships in Dauphin and Schuykill Counties that belong to the PDC ethnographically. House Speaker Newt Gingrich, for example, is a Pennsylvania Dutchman, who grew up in Hummelstown in Dauphin County, and his parents live in Dauphin Borough. Both are solid Dutch towns. In Schuykill County, towns like Hegins and Pine Grove are extensions of the Dutch Country. Even in the Philadelphia suburbs, outlying districts in Bucks County (Haycock, Trumbauersville, Richland-town, Springfield, and East Rockhill) and Montgomery County (Red Hill, Douglass, East Greenville, Pennsburg, and Upper Hanover) belong to the PDC culturally. In Montgomery County, Souderton is a strong Mennonite town, and many Schwenkfelders live in the Perkiomen area. (Former Republican U.S. Senator Richard Schweiker was a Schwenkfelder from this area.)

A substantial Amish and Mennonite community resides in Somerset County. The towns on the fringes of the PDC share similar political and religious outlooks. A good clue to locating them is to look for areas where John F. Kennedy did particularly poorly in 1960, and especially where a majority of registered Democrats defected to Nixon. This pivotal election was shaped by longstanding fears of Catholicism that were ingrained from generation to generation by the evangelical religious groups that remembered centuries-old religious persecutions in the Old Country.

The PDC is a strongly Protestant area, where both evangelical and confessional principles shaped a strong religious fellowship that has influenced social mores and community life. The term "PDC" has been corrupted by tourism promoters in recent decades to suggest that the entire region consists solely of Amish and/or Mennonite farm communities noted for their quaint customs and peaceful ways.

The reality, however, is a good deal more complex. The Amish and Mennonites are strong in Lancaster County, primarily in the northern and eastern precincts, but collectively they represent only about 14 percent of religiously affiliated people in Lancaster County, and fewer than 5 percent throughout the nine-county PDC. In popular terminology, the Amish, Mennonites, and their first cousins, the Brethren, constitute the "Plain Dutch," those who eschew many of the accoutrements of material success and worldly ambition. Their personal lives, like their clothing and homes, are unpretentious. They often prefer parochial schools, of which there are many in Lancaster County. The "Fancy Dutch" are the far more numerous Lutherans, Methodists, and Reformed communities. The German Reformed faith was strong in Revolutionary and pre–Civil War times. It became the Evangelical and Reformed Church and was reborn as the United Church of Christ (UCC) in 1957. The UCC represents the liberal wing of evangelicalism in Pennsylvania, and its members still tend to vote Republican. Nationally, it has become a liberal mainline church, and many of its adherents vote Democratic. United Methodists are numerous in the region, particularly because they absorbed the Evangelical United Brethren (the German Methodists) in 1968. But Lutherans remain the largest faith group in the PDC. Large and impressive Lutheran churches resembling cathedrals dot the countryside. Numerous church-related colleges are found in the region, including Juniata College, founded by the Brethren, and Ursinus College in Collegeville, established by the German Reformed community. Ursinus for many years maintained a center for the study of the Pennsylvania Dutch culture. Historical and folklore societies also try to keep the area's artistic and literary traditions alive.

Among Protestants, 32 percent are Lutheran, 19 percent are Methodist, 18 percent are United Church of Christ, 6 percent are Mennonite or Amish, and 4 percent are Brethren.

The German Protestant culture has had strong political implications, owing to the central role that religion has played in the area's life.

In 1942 historian Ralph Wood made a number of trenchant observations about Pennsylvania German culture. He concluded: "In spite of the competition of Grange events, the automobile and the small-town movie, the church has remained the center of community life in the Pennsylvania German countryside. What the New England town meeting was to the Yankee, the church was to the Pennsylvania German."[36]

This sentiment is echoed by recent observers writing in the late 1970s. Noel Bausher Szundy writes:

> Today the Lutheran and Reformed churches are still the cornerstone of Pennsylvania Dutch religion. . . . Ours is a heartwarming and healthy stew of many sects, well balanced and integrated. The Pennsylvania Bible Belt comes honestly by its name, and not only do we have numerous churches of all flavors, but they are thriving. The "Dumb Dutchman" has not forgotten his Reformation roots, nor will he ever turn his back on the God who guided his ancestors to these shores.[37]

Mildred Jordan concurs. "Today our area is filled with churches of various sects, old and new. For many a Dutchman his church is the social center of his life."[38]

The Pennsylvania Dutch are also distinctly conservative. Earl Robacher argues that "the strongest single tradition in the Dutch Country is what it always has been—maintaining tradition."[39]

Historian William T. Parsons maintains that the Pennsylvania Dutch "fit very well into the isolationist mood of the twenties and early thirties,"[40] and "remain committed to a system of private volunteer charities and distrust impersonal government."[41]

Few PDC residents are Catholics, who comprise 11 percent of the population, compared to nearly 33 percent statewide. Most live in the cities of Reading and Lancaster. Lancaster's Eighth Ward contains the historic German Catholic Cabbage Hill neighborhood. A few rural towns like Bally are Catholic, as are some townships in eastern Adams County, in whose rolling hills can be found Conewago Chapel. The "Chapel" is an unpretentious, deliberately low-key name for a majestic baroque Basilica of the Sacred Heart of Jesus, which may remind some of the churches of the Austrian or Bavarian countryside.

But the predominant culture of the PDC is, has always been, and will likely always remain Protestant and evangelical, with a distinct coloration that makes the subregion unique. It is of some significance that a Roman Catholic publisher, Paulist Press, devoted a major volume in its American spirituality series to the remarkable religious ethos of the PDC.

Politically, the Dutch Country has leaned Republican since the party's early days, though deep pockets of Democratic sentiments lingered in Berks and York Counties for a century later. The elections were closely contested after the Civil War, and Democrats like William Jennings Bryan and Woodrow Wilson did relatively well in the region, especially among country folk.

But as the Democratic party became more liberal and more multicultural, the PDC became more Republican. In 1928 Herbert Hoover decimated Al Smith 83 percent to 17 percent, carrying dozens of towns in rural Berks and York Counties that had never voted Republican before. Anti-Catholicism united all of the disparate Protestant groups. Many rural areas gave Hoover 90 percent support. Hoover's landslide was fueled by the turnout of voters who had previously shunned politics as worldly and irrelevant. The Church of the Brethren actually encouraged its members to register and vote for Hoover. Donald Fitzkee explains why this happened: "As the 1920s progressed, more Pennsylvania Brethren were voting, lobbying, and cooperating with other groups to ensure that the 18th Amendment remained the law of the land. As the 1928 presidential election approached, the fate of Prohibition hung in the balance. Faced with a clear choice between a dry Republican and a woefully wet Roman Catholic Democrat, Brethren who thus far had resisted the temptation to vote found it difficult to shun the ballot box yet another time. While just 20 years earlier Annual Conference had strongly discouraged voting, by 1928 the church's *Gospel Messenger* editors were exhorting Brethren to do their Christian duty by voting against Smith."[42]

Within a couple of elections, the Democrats were competitive again. Both Franklin Roosevelt and Harry Truman ran relatively well in the PDC.

Fellow German-American Dwight Eisenhower, whose ancestors had grown up in this area, swept the PDC by a 2-to-1 landslide over Adlai Stevenson in 1952. Since Ike every Republican except Goldwater has carried the area. Ike repeated his sweep in 1956 and Richard Nixon, again benefiting from anti-Catholic voting, equaled the Eisenhower vote in 1960.

In the region's cities, Lancaster, York, and Reading, Kennedy was popular and won a majority of the cities' ballots, especially among Catholics and liberals. But in rural areas he ran weaker than Stevenson and lost two dozen rural communities that had voted for the Stevenson-Kefauver ticket in 1956. Kennedy's vote plummeted in southern and western York County and in northern and eastern Lancaster County. Stevenson carried eighteen townships in York County; Kennedy, only seven. In Manheim Stevenson received 59 percent and Kennedy only 36 percent. In the hamlet of Railroad Stevenson's vote was 67 percent and Kennedy's 45 percent. In the heavily Dutch town of Spring Grove, Stevenson won 60 percent and Kennedy 47 percent.

The same was true in much of rural Berks County. The Democratic Dutch deserted Kennedy in droves. Only 15.6 percent of Democratic precincts in rural Berks were carried by Kennedy. Party registration figures meant little, since the Democrats still enjoyed a large margin in registration in Berks and York Counties, while Kennedy's vote was just over 40 percent.

In Lenhartsville Democratic registration was 67 percent but Kennedy received only 16 percent. In Centerpoint it was 82 percent Democratic but Kennedy could only manage 35 percent. In Richmond 75 percent of the voters were Democrats but only 35 percent voted for JFK. In the nine-county area that comprises the heart of the Dutch Country, Kennedy received 37 percent but Democratic registration was 47 percent.

While Lyndon Johnson carried the Dutch Country in 1964, Barry Goldwater still received 42 percent of the vote and carried three counties. Richard Nixon easily won in 1968 and 1972, though his 1968 margin was lower than in 1960, since his vote was not enhanced by religious animosity. Jimmy Carter received 40 percent in 1976, but he did not come even near Truman's 1948 vote level.

The Democrats of the 1980s had little support in this cultural bastion of the older America, where voters are mostly white, Protestant, and German. The modern Democratic Party, once the party of many Dutch voters, had seemed to have taken on an exotic cast and emphasized issues and concerns of little interest to Dutch Country residents. This can be seen in the steady Republican registration gains of the past three decades. In 1972, for example,

Table 2.6

Presidential Voting 1956–1992 in the Pennsylvania Dutch Country

Year	% Republican		% Democrat		% Other	
1956	Eisenhower	63.5	Stevenson	36.5		
1960	Nixon	63.3	Kennedy	36.7		
1964	Goldwater	42.1	Johnson	57.9		
1968	Nixon	57.6	Humphrey	34.6	Wallace	7.8
1972	Nixon	71.6	McGovern	28.4		
1976	Ford	59.6	Carter	40.4		
1980	Reagan	62.6	Carter	29.8	Anderson	7.6
1984	Reagan	71.0	Mondale	29.0		
1988	Bush	67.2	Dukakis	32.8		
1992	Bush	48.0	Clinton	31.6	Perot	20.4

while Democrats had gained 5 percentage points statewide since 1960, they lost 5 points in the PDC. In York County, Republicans moved ahead of Democrats in registration during the middle of the Reagan presidency, after more than a century of Democratic predominance.

Ronald Reagan was immensely popular in the Dutch Country, and this rubbed off on George Bush in 1988, who won a higher percentage of the vote than Eisenhower in 1956. Bush's 160,000-vote margin in the Dutch Country was instrumental in his statewide victory over Michael Dukakis, since he ran behind Dukakis by 53,000 votes in the rest of the state.

But in 1992 there was considerable disaffection and disenchantment with the Republicans, even though George Bush managed to win 55 percent in Lancaster County, his highest county percentage in the state. The Mennonite precincts were especially loyal to the GOP, but Ross Perot took a solid 20 percent among the Dutch, the highest support for a third-party candidate since Teddy Roosevelt in 1912. Perot did especially well in rural precincts that had been Democratic but had moved toward the Republicans in recent years. These Democrats-turned-Republicans gave Perot 25 percent to 30 percent levels of support.

Bill Clinton won easily in the region's three cities and made an occasional breakthrough in the countryside. He carried Kutztown, a college town where the Pennsylvania Dutch Folk Festival was born in 1952. Clinton carried Bechtelsville and Longswamp, which Kennedy had lost, and captured Spring Grove in York County. But his overall support was just 32 percent compared to Bush's 48 percent and Perot's 20 percent.

Perot clearly hurt Bush in the Dutch Country. His entire vote had gone for Bush in 1988, while in some cities in western areas of the state a large chunk of the Perot vote had come from the Democrats. Bush's plurality represented the poorest GOP showing in modern times except for Goldwater. But Clinton received a lower percentage of the total vote than had Stevenson, Kennedy, or Humphrey.

In state races the PDC invariably favors the Republican candidate, except for Governor Robert Casey, who won a landslide in 1990. Even in 1991 Democrat Harris Wofford was unable to win the region in his U.S. Senate race despite winning a comfortable 55 percent statewide. The last Pennsylvania Dutchman to win the governorship was George Leader, a Lutheran farmer from York County, who was elected in 1954 with considerable support for a Democrat in the Dutch Country.

Notes

1. Mary Hunt and Don Hunt, *Hunt's Highlights of Michigan* (Waterloo, Mich.: Midwestern Guides, 1991), p. 320.

2. Ibid.

3. Mary Hunt and Don Hunt, *Hunt's Guide to West Michigan* (Waterloo, Mich.: Midwestern Guides, 1990), p. 129.

4. Ibid., 120.

5. Ibid.

6. Ibid., p. 122.

7. Berton Roueché, *Special Places: In Search of Small Town America* (Boston: Little, Brown, 1982), pp. 181–82.

8. J. Howard Kauffman and Leland Harder, *Anabaptists Four Centuries Later* (Scottdale, Pa.: Herald Press, 1975), p. 161.

9. Ibid., p. 165.

10. Calvin Redekop, *Mennonite Society* (Baltimore: Johns Hopkins University Press, 1989), p. 219.

11. Ibid., pp. 226–27.

12. John Redekop, "Mennonites and Politics in Canada and the United States," *Journal of Mennonite Studies* 1 (1983): 79–105.

13. James C. Jahnke, *A People of Two Kingdoms: The Political Acculturation of Kansas Mennonites* (Newton, Kans.: Faith and Life Press, 1975), pp. 41–42.

14. Ibid., p. 61.

15. Ibid., p. 94.

16. Ibid., p. 142.

17. Barry A. Kosmin and Seymour P. Lachman, *One Nation Under God: Religion in Contemporary American Society* (New York: Harmony Books, 1993), p. 264.

18. Roger L. Dudley, Edwin I. Hernandez, and Sara M. K. Terian, "Religiosity and Public Issues Among Seventh-day Adventists," *Review of Religious Research* 33 (June 1992): 330–48.

19. David S. Broder and Thomas B. Edsall, "Mississippian Speaks His Mind," *Washington Post,* May 28, 1995.

20. Andrew M. Greeley, *Religion as Poetry* (New Brunswick, N.J.: Transaction Publishers, 1995), p. 230. Additional references to this work appear in parentheses following the cited material.

21. *The Churchman's Human Quest* 192 (November–December 1995), pp. 23–24.

22. Ibid.

23. Princeton Religion Research Center, *Religion in America, 1995 Supplement.*

24. A modern reprint was issued by the University Press of Kentucky in 1969.

25. John C. Campbell, *The Southern Highlander and His Homeland* (Russell Sage Foundation, 1921; University Press of Kentucky, 1969), p. 169.

26. North Callahan, *Smoky Mountain Country* (New York: Duell, Sloan and Pearce, 1952), p. 157.

27. H. C. Nixon, *Lower Piedmont County* (New York: Duell, Sloan and Pearce, 1946), p. 91.

28. Ibid., p. 92.

29. Erskine Caldwell, *Deep South* (Athens, Ga.: University of Georgia Press, 1995 edition), p. 41. Further page references to this work appear in parentheses following the cited material.

30. W. K. McNeil, *Ozark Country* (Jackson, Miss.: University Press of Mississippi, 1995), p. 20.

31. Vance Randolph, *Ozark Superstitions* (New York: Columbia University Press, 1947), p. 3.

32. Bruce Cook, *The Town That Country Built* (New York: Avon Books, 1993), p. 246.

33. Roy Clark, *My Life* (New York: Simon & Schuster, 1994).

34. Harry M. Caudill, *Night Comes to the Cumberlands* (Boston: Little, Brown and Co., 1962), p. 132.

35. James McConkey, *Rowan's Progress* (New York: Pantheon, 1992), p. 186.

36. Ralph Wood, *The Pennsylvania Germans* (Princeton: Princeton University Press, 1942), pp. 14, 87.

37. Mildred Jordan, introduction to *The Distelfink Country of the Pennsylvania Dutch* (New York: Crown, 1978), p. xxiii.

38. Ibid., p. 4.

39. Quoted in Jordan, *Distelfink County,* p. 13.

40. William T. Parsons, *The Pennsylvania Dutch* (Boston: Twayne, 1976), p. 237.

41. Ibid., p. 249.

42. Donald R. Fitzkee, *Moving Toward the Mainstream: 20th Century Change Among the Brethren of Eastern Pennsylvania* (Intercourse, Pa.: Good Books, 1995), pp. 182–83.

3

Evangelicals:
True-Blue Conservatives

A 1987 survey[1] by Gallup for the Times Mirror Study of the American Electorate discovered that white evangelicals were decidedly more conservative than any other religious community. Dividing Americans into seven religious categories, pollsters found that of all religious groups evangelicals were the most anticommunist, the most supportive of the antiabortion movement, and by far the most sympathetic to the National Rifle Association. They were the most opposed to the gay rights and women's movements, had the lowest support for labor unions (along with Jews, surprisingly), were second to white Catholics in their support for business interests, and were the most pro-Israel group among Christians. They also had the lowest support for civil rights and were average in their support for environmental causes.[2]

On issues related to tolerance and intolerance, the "Moralists," as they were dubbed by the Times Mirror surveyors, proved to be the least tolerant group. Fully 77 percent of Moralists said that books containing dangerous ideas should be banned from public school libraries, and 88 percent favored a constitutional amendment to permit organized prayer in public schools. Eighty percent favored mandatory drug testing for government employees, 78 percent said school boards should be able to fire homosexual teachers, and 61 percent said "AIDS might be God's punishment for immoral sexual behavior."[3] Sixty percent favored changing laws to make it more difficult for a woman to get an abortion, and 47 percent said that "Women should return to a traditional role in society."[4]

On racial issues Moralists proved to be unsympathetic to civil rights and

Table 3.1

Political Views of "Moralists"

Issue	% Moralists	% All Americans
Favor banning library books	77	51
Favor school prayer	88	71
Favor firing gay teachers	78	52
Agree that AIDS must be God's punishment	61	44
Favor mandatory drug testing	80	65
Favor restricting abortion	60	41
Favor women in traditional roles	47	30
Favor interracial dating	25	48
Favor spending on minorities	21	36

*Table based on data contained in the Times Mirror Survey, Ornstein et al., *People, Press and Politics,* pp. 36-39.

related issues. Only 21 percent favored increased spending on programs that assist minorities, and only 25 percent said that it is acceptable for whites and blacks to date each other.

On social justice questions Moralists were only slightly more conservative than all Americans, but they were still 11 percent less likely than all Americans to favor programs to aid the unemployed and 7 percent less likely to favor Social Security increases. But they were strongly pro-military. (See table 3.1.)

The Times Mirror study, based on 4,244 interviews, defined Moralists as follows: "Middle-aged, middle income with a heavy concentration of Southerners, this group forms the second bedrock of the Republican Party. Moralists hold strong and very conservative views on social and foreign policy. They are 94 percent white, live in suburbs, small cities and rural areas, are regular church-goers with a large number of born-again Christians. Their information level is average and their voting likelihood is high."[5] About 14 percent of the American electorate are Moralists. Thirteen percent of Moralists are college graduates, compared to 18 percent of all Americans in 1987. Nineteen percent of Moralists are Catholic and 81 percent are Protestant Evangelical.

The Times Mirror Center for The People and The Press updated its 1987 national survey with a telephone interview opinion survey of 3,800 adults in 1994. Released on September 21, 1994, and called "The New Political Landscape," it revealed escalating strength for the Moralist category of voters.[6]

The Moralists are now 18 percent of the adult population and 20 percent of registered voters. They are overwhelmingly Republican and voted for Bush, and among the Moralist category independents and Perot voters outnumbered Democrats and Clinton voters. They are white, middle-aged, married, and most numerous in the South, the Midwest, and rural America.

This group almost doubled in size since 1987. The Times Mirror report wrote that:

> Religious and cultural conservatives—many of them former Democrats— have identified with the GOP and are drawn to the party as a defender of traditional moral values. They are socially intolerant, opposed to social welfare, militaristic and xenophobic, and critical of big business as well as big government. They strongly favor a constitutional amendment to permit prayer in the schools, mandatory sentencing for violent criminals and disapproval of permitting gays to serve openly in the military and using government funds to pay for abortions.

This group attends Bible study and prayer group meetings regularly and exhibits a moderately high attentiveness to political issues. Among all voters they are most opposed to, fearful of, and critical of homosexuality. Fully 79 percent say that "homosexuality is a way of life that should be discouraged by society," compared to 49 percent of all voters who feel that way.

This survey indicated a rise in the intensity of religious feelings since 1987. There was a 12-point gain in the percentage of those who said they have never doubted the existence of God, an 11-point gain in the percentage of those who believe that God works miracles today, an 11-point gain in those who pray daily, and a 9-point increase in those who believe that "we will all be called before God at the Judgment Day to answer for our sins." Overwhelming majorities of all Americans—78 percent to 88 percent— expressed agreement with the preceding four premises. This increase in religious fervor may have led to an increase in the percentage of voters who now see the Republican Party as the party better able "to protect traditional American values and to promote morality and personal responsibility." Voters gave the GOP a 12-point edge over the Democrats on these two points.

The number of voters who said that family/morality issues were the most important facing the country went up from 3 percent to 10 percent, though they still placed fourth behind crime, health care, and unemployment.

Generational gains now help Republicans, according to the survey, since 15 percent of voters said they were Republicans although their parents had voted Democratic, while only 8 percent were Democrats whose parents had been Republicans. The greatest Republican gains came among white evan-gelical Protestants, white Catholics, men over age 50, and all voters whose family income is between $50,000 and $75,000 per annum.

The survey also found that 27 percent of Americans attend church every week, which is lower than the Gallup poll's consistent finding of 40 percent. However, 12 percent said they attended "almost every week," which translates into 39 percent, a comparable figure. But 45 percent of Americans attended worship services only a few times a year or never. And 30 percent of those sur-veyed said religious leaders "had too much say in the way the government in Washington is run," which suggests that a vigorous backlash could develop if the Religious Right leadership pushes its agenda too far, too fast.

On the issues of school prayer and abortion, evangelicals are clearly more conservative than other religious groups. The 1984 American National Election Study found that 85 percent of Southern Baptists, 83 percent of fun-damentalists, and 83 percent of all born-again Christians favored school prayer. This compared to 66 percent of all Americans, 64 percent of Catholics and 14 percent of Jews.[7]

On abortion 63 percent of fundamentalists and 60 percent of Southern Baptists either opposed all abortions or would allow them only in rare cir-cumstances. Forty-eight percent of Lutherans and Catholics held that view but only around 15 percent of Jews, Presbyterians, and Episcopalians. Methodists were in the middle on the abortion question.[8]

Kenneth D. Wald's study, utilizing the General Social Surveys, suggests that evangelical Protestants may be as much as 33 percent of the population, compared to 25 percent for Catholic, 23 percent mainline Protestant, 9 per-cent black Protestant, and 2.5 percent Jewish. About 7.5 percent have no affiliation.[9]

Wald found that evangelicals were much more conservative than other groups on social issues like sexuality, pornography, and abortion. On issues like government spending for health, education, and the environment, and support for racial integration, evangelicals and mainline Protestants held the most conservative attitudes. Jews, Catholics, and the nonaffiliated were much more liberal in their political and social attitudes.[10]

Surveys going back as far as Samuel Stouffer's classic 1955 study, *Com-munism, Conformity and Civil Liberties*, showed that conservative Protes-tants, especially in the South, held the least tolerant political views and were less inclined to allow freedom of speech for atheists, socialists, and commu-nists. Jews and the religiously nonobservant were the most tolerant.

Kenneth Wald replicated this study three decades later, using the General Social Surveys, which asked questions regarding civil liberties for racists, communists, atheists, militarists, and gays, all said to be unpopular groups. Wald discovered that little had changed.

> Religious group differences during the 1980s produced essentially the same patterns observed in 1954. The nonaffiliated were substantially more likely than persons attached to religion to score high on a scale of support for civil liberties. Among religious groups, the same ordering reported by Stouffer was in evidence: low tolerance among evangelical Protestants (black and white alike), intermediate support for civil liberties by Catholics and main-line Protestants, the highest commitment to Democratic norms among Jews.[11]

This lack of tolerance shows up in other polls, including the one commissioned by the Williamsburg Charter Foundation. Wald says that "researchers have found that hostility to blacks, Jews and other minority groups has most often been expressed by adherents of theologically conservative churches and has been least common in persons outside the churches."[12]

Rigney and Hoffman found that fundamentalist Protestants were significantly less positive in their attitude toward intellectual orientation, the priority of education, freedom of scientific inquiry, and the value of thinking for oneself. Only 43 percent of fundamentalists consider thinking for oneself an important value, compared to 77 percent of Jews. Only 55 percent of fundamentalists endorse freedom of scientific inquiry compared to 79 percent of Jews and 66 percent of Catholics.[13]

Studies conducted during the 1980s on evangelical-fundamentalist politics concentrated on the Moral Majority. Clyde Wilcox, a professor of government at Georgetown University, found that "support for the Moral Majority is greatest among those who are fundamentalist or evangelicals, among those who hold conservative positions on social issues, among those who believe that religion should be involved in politics, and among those who spend a good deal of time watching televangelists."[14] In addition, he found "supporters were conservative Republicans who took anti-feminist positions and were conservative on foreign policy issues."[15] Anti-Catholicism was also a strong factor in Moral Majority support. "One in four evangelicals supported the Moral Majority in 1983,"[16] said Wilcox, and this support rose to 40 percent among the best informed. There were denominational variables. "There were significant differences between Moral Majority supporters and other evangelicals. Support was highest among Baptists, Methodists, fundamentalist and pentecostal denominations, and was lowest among Lutherans and Catholics."[17]

In a study of tolerance toward unpopular minorities, Gay and Ellison found significant denominational differences in the development of tolerant or intolerant attitudes. Jews, Episcopalians, and the religiously nonaffiliated exhibited the highest overall tolerance of dissidents. Methodists, Lutherans, and Presbyterians fell into the moderately tolerant category while Baptists and other conservative Protestants were the least tolerant. Conservative Protestants varied widely in their attitudes toward dissenters, exhibiting less homogeneity than some other studies have found.[18]

There is clear evidence that those evangelicals and fundamentalists who joined the Moral Majority exhibited the most extreme political and social views. A study of Indiana and Arkansas Moral Majority members in 1983 found that 97 percent favored firing gay school teachers, 93 percent wanted creationism taught in public schools, 83 percent wanted to ban the mentioning of evolution in biology classes, and 96 percent supported school prayer. Among them 93 percent favored the death penalty, 90 percent endorsed a "male-dominated" family, and 55 percent were opposed to abortion even in cases of rape. Racism was also prominent: 53 percent said the civil rights movement was unnecessary, 58 percent opposed racial integration in schools, and 90 percent disapproved of school busing to achieve integration.[19]

Robert Young found that religion was a major factor in support for or opposition to capital punishment. Young, a professor of sociology and director of the Criminal Justice Program at the University of Texas-Arlington, concluded: "The association of fundamentalism with high levels of support for the death penalty was not surprising. The absolutism of a fundamentalist orientation appears to eliminate some of the uncertainty which others experience in considering the appropriateness of this punishment. . . . Support for the death penalty is likely to be increased by the belief in individual free will and responsibility that characterizes fundamentalism. It is important to note that these inclinations are apparently nurtured only in white fundamentalist churches, since affiliation with fundamentalist churches had no significant influence on the death penalty attitudes of blacks."[20]

Conservative Protestants are also less enamored of scientific inquiry than those of other religious traditions. Ellison and Musick concluded in their study, "The members of Conservative Protestant groups are more skeptical of the fruits of scientific progress than other persons. . . . Consistent with the apprehensions of many observers, the members of conservative Protestant denominations generally express more negative views of the scientific community than other Americans. Three aspects of conservative evangelical theology—biblical literalism, theological orthodoxy, and beliefs about the ubiquity of sin—are also associated with these negative views of science."[21]

Dixon, Lowery, and Jones discovered that born-again Christian voters were far more likely than others to support legal restrictions on activities they considered sinful or to hold negative views toward practices that most others do not reject. A majority of the born-again believe that homosexuality should be against the law, that abortion should not be legal, and that unmarried couples should not be legally allowed to live together. The born again were 22 to 32 points more likely to hold such views than those who said they were not born again. About 40 percent of the born again even thought that local government should be allowed to ban harmful books and movies.[22]

While the sociopolitical differences between conservative and religious positions have been well established, there remains the intriguing question of causation. Why, in other words, is this so? Why are religious conservatives more often than not political conservatives?

Several political scientists and sociologists have wrestled with this question. Writing in 1967 Michael Parenti postulated four defining differences between conservative and liberal religious value systems, all of which affected political decision-making. They are

a. The extent to which divine teaching is considered fixed, final, and unchallengeable, as opposed to being susceptible to rational investigation and modification; and consequently, the extent to which intellectualism and many of the values associated with it are opposed or welcomed.

b. The extent to which the drama of redemption and atonement is defined as a personal battle waged for one's soul for the sake of eternal salvation, rather than as a moral commitment to a worldly social betterment of mankind.

c. The extent to which sin and evil are defined as inherent in human nature (e.g., original sin) and inevitable in human behavior (e.g., concupiscence), rather than as social effects of widespread environmental causes.

d. The extent to which human well-being and natural pleasures are manifestations of a lower, corrupting realm of nature—something to be repressed as the contamination of the spiritual, rather than responsibly cultivated as the fulfillment of God's beneficence.[23]

Benson and Williams argued that religious conservatives see God as an omnipotent, strict deity who has a plan for all individuals. Salvation is a personal matter and the path to salvation consists of the avoidance of evil. Conservatives believe that God protects social institutions and is a causal agent in individual lives. Conservatives also emphasize self-restraint and believe that God has chosen America for a special purpose and that He has uniquely blessed America.

Religious liberals believe passionately in social justice, see love as a path to salvation, which itself has corporate dimensions. In the liberal value system, religion must address corporate life in order to be meaningful.[24]

Sociologist Lawrence Kersten outlined a number of major differences between conservative and liberal theology that have political salience. Theological liberals, he says, emphasize social reform to make the human condition more reflective of God's will, hold positive attitudes toward science and civil liberties, believe in social activism and ecumenism, and favor equal treatment of women in all areas of life. Liberals believe in intellectual freedom and relative standards of morality and ethics, oppose harsh methods of punishing deviants, stress group action rather than individual responsibility, and believe that most events can be explained by human causes. Liberals see the clergy as ethical and prophetic leaders, reject the literal interpretation of the Bible, and respect the insights of other religions.

Theological conservatives advocate the literal interpretation of the Scriptures, hold to an otherworldly spiritual emphasis with personal salvation as the center, believe that many events can be explained as the will of God, and see clergy as spiritual leaders and servants. Conservatives stress the necessity of obedience to authority and believe in absolute standards of morality and unchanging religious doctrines and beliefs. They hold negative attitudes toward science, favor a subservient role for women, and are intolerant of religious and cultural minorities. They are lukewarm on civil liberties and favor harsh methods of punishing deviants. They stress individual responsibility to improve life and tend to oppose governmental solutions to problems they believe are rooted in individual action.[25]

Andrew Greeley has suggested that individual concepts of God lead to certain political orientations. Greeley says belief in a warm, caring God who loves the world tends to increase commitment to social justice and welfare, while an image of a cold, harsh, impersonal God leads to greater support for government repression of violence and support for law and order.[26]

Kenneth Wald cautions that the interpretations do not always agree on why certain religious traditions operate in certain ways politically. This is because "most religious traditions are elastic enough to support very different political applications."[27] He writes, "It should be emphasized that links between political attitudes and religious orientations have been more often asserted than proven. Attempts to assess direct connections between religious belief and political outlook have yielded mixed results."[28]

Sexuality and family life have become political issues in recent decades. Thus, religious attitudes are affecting political behavior and public policy more and more. It is therefore understandable that adherents of those religions that advocate traditional avenues of sexual expression will gravitate toward political movements or parties that comport with their views.

It is not quite certain whether political parties have adopted platform positions as a result of the religious orientation of their members and leaders, or whether they have consciously adopted positions in an effort to curry political favor with members of certain religious traditions or communities. It is probable that both statements are true. There was a time in U.S. history when the two major parties would not have adopted hard line positions on issues like abortion and family planning or religious activities in public schools, but both parties now do so routinely. Some state Republican parties have even endorsed the teaching of creationism in public education and have expressed their belief that the United States is a Christian nation in law as well as custom. While calculated to win the votes of certain kinds of Christians, adoption of sectarian-slanted positions will alienate non-Christians and Christians who disagree with such concepts.

According to the Janus Report sexual attitudes and practices strongly relate to religious beliefs, political attitudes, educational attainment, and even regional location. The researchers found "a very strong correlation between religiosity and attitudes about abortion: the more religious respondents were, the more they believed that abortion was murder."[29] The researchers classified respondents to their national survey as very religious (9.8 percent), religious (31.6 percent), slightly religious (36.0 percent), and not religious (22.6 percent). The two "religious" categories correspond roughly to that percentage of the U.S. population that claims to attend church weekly or more. The "not religious" category was a good deal higher than the secular or nonaffiliated categories in other surveys, but may reflect the nonpracticing or rarely observant members of all faith traditions.

Among the very religious, 61 percent said abortion was murder, compared to 40 percent of the religious, 24 percent of the slightly religious, and 12 percent of the nonreligious. Very religious women were slightly more likely to agree with that statement than very religious men.

Religion had some impact on the practice of abortion but not as heavy a one as some might think: 18 percent of very religious women had had an abortion, compared to 32 percent of the nonreligious. Increasing religiosity had a small effect on reducing the incidence of abortion. Denominational differences were surprising: 32 percent of Protestants, 29 percent of Catholics, 22 percent of the nonaffiliated, 18 percent of other religions, and 11 percent of Jews had reported an abortion. Attitudes toward contraception, sex education, and premarital sex did not vary as widely between religious groups as might be anticipated. Commented the researchers: "Recent trends in American society have reduced the amount of guilt feelings, allowing all Americans of all religious persuasions to function sexually in strikingly similar ways, even as they support extremes of opinion regarding the most intensely debated issues of abortion, contraception and sex education in the schools" (260--61).

Classifying respondents politically as independent, ultraconservative, and ultraliberal, which is not really a very satisfactory scale, the researchers found that 40 percent of ultraconservatives, 31 percent of independents, and 10 percent of ultraliberals considered abortion murder. But the practices did not vary much: 27 percent of ultraconservatives, 22 percent of independents and 30 percent of ultraliberals had had an abortion. Those on the political right were three times more likely than those on the left to support traditional sex roles, but were more likely than the others to have engaged in premarital or extramarital sex. (Twenty-three percent of the ultraconservatives admitted to frequent extramarital affairs, compared to 16 percent of ultraliberals and 8 percent of independents.) Write the Januses, "Ultraconservatives show a distinct separation between theory and practice. While professing stability, ultraconservatives have been modifying their behavior to accommodate to the contemporary world. They are having abortions, including repeat abortions, just like everyone else" (294).

Higher education correlates with more liberal attitudes toward sexuality and family life. Only 16 percent of those holding postgraduate degrees held abortion to be murder, compared to 38 percent of those with a high school education or less. Among college graduates with one degree, 22 percent thought abortion was murder, as did 28 percent of those who had attended college but did not graduate. On the subject of divorce, the best educated did not think that divorce laws were too easy now: only 32 percent of the postgraduates agreed, compared to 63 percent of those who did not attend college at all. The researchers concluded, "Education tends to be a liberating force that enables people to evaluate the social and sexual values with which they were raised and to accept or reject them, as seems appropriate. Education provides the basis for making the choices that meet individual needs, avoiding mere conformity to social values. From many perspectives, the responses to the questions in our study demonstrated clear indications that an individual's sexuality was clearly influenced by the educational level he or she had achieved" (321).

Finally, regionalism plays a strong role in attitudes toward sex and family life. The evangelical South and somewhat evangelical Midwest were only slightly more anti-abortion than the West and Northeast: 34 percent in the South, 33 percent in the Midwest, 27 percent in the West, and 23 percent in the Northeast considered abortion murder. The incidence of abortion was higher in the Northeast (36 percent) and West (33 percent) than in the South (19 percent) or Midwest (18 percent).

However, the South was the region with the earliest ages of sexual initiation and the highest incidence of reported premarital sex. The Midwest was the true morality belt, with the lowest reported incidence of premarital and extramarital sex. The researchers did not control for such factors as urbanization, divorce, or migration and they noted that "a great diversity of cultures exists in each region, and their constant interaction continues to be influential in mutual effect and change" (352).

The Janus researchers had this to say about the South:

> The New South, as many Southerners like to call it, has gone through tremendous changes, but has still managed to retain its charm and warmth as well as many of the values that made the South such a popular region in past decades. Much of the South is bound by the Bible Belt of religious fundamentalism, but its sex life in many ways reflects the serious contradictions of the televangelists who were caught practicing the opposite of what they were preaching. The South is at the same time frantic and denying; its passion is directed as much at the body as at the spirit, which may very well confuse its residents and lead to what appear to be contradictions between their stated beliefs and their actual behavior. (373)

The Northeast and West are "the pacesetters of sexual America" (373), while "the Midwest stolidly follows several paces back, seeming to be the most content with itself" (374).

The 1987 Times Mirror Study of the American Electorate concluded that "religion plays an important and surprising role in American politics, both in its presence and absence in crucial voting blocs."[30]

The evangelical contribution to the Republican party is a mixed blessing. According to the survey "while the movement of white evangelical Protestants into the party has added to GOP strength, it has also introduced some division into the Republican ranks. Religion itself divides the solidly Republican ranks more than any other political value. Identification of the party with the social agenda of the Christian right may also hurt the GOP among key swing groups" (77).

The religious impact on Republican primaries is maximized by the evangelical groups' newfound enthusiasm for politics and by their location in the South. While 18 percent of the total population are white evangelicals, they are 25 percent of the Republican identifiers and 42 percent of Republican primary voters in the South. By contrast only 14 percent of Democrats are white evangelicals, though 26 percent of Democratic primary voters in the South are white evangelicals (87, 92).

Another finding is that 31 percent of Southern white males are "Moralists" while only 12 percent of white males in the North and West hold similarly conservative politico-religious views. More white males than females in the South have switched from Democrat to Republican in the past decade, and white evangelical Protestants under age 30 frequently come from Democratic families, though they are now Republicans (100, 101).

This survey confirms other evidence that women and Southerners are more religious than men and non-Southerners. Nearly half of females (47 percent) compared to one-third of males (32 percent) are "deeply religious." "Those who reside in the South are more likely to be religious than people living elsewhere (49 percent vs. 36 percent)" (110).

A number of political scientists and sociologists have studied the impact of religious activities, beliefs, and affiliations on elections and politics during the past decade or so. Their insights have helped to expand our general understanding of the currents and trends in this field.

Paul Lopatto used election survey data compiled by the University of Michigan from 1960 to 1980 to chart religious factors on the six presidential elections of that period.[31] He subdivided Protestants into three categories: conservatives, who are essentially evangelicals and include Southern Baptists, Missouri Synod Lutherans, Mormons, Churches of Christ, Pentecostals, Nazarenes, Seventh-day Adventists, Independent Baptists, and Mennonites; the moderate Protestants, who are Presbyterians, Lutherans, Disciples of Christ, and Northern Baptists; and liberal Protestants, in which group he included Unitarians, Methodists, Episcopalians, and members of the United Church of Christ. While some may quibble with his categorizations, they represent a reasonable way of looking at demographic, cultural, and political differences among Protestants.

He found that the conservative Protestants had moved steadily in a Republican direction even before the Reagan presidency. This was especially true of the young and middle-aged cohorts. Among conservative Protestants under age 36, Democratic affiliation fell from 64 percent in 1960 to 41 percent in 1980, while Republican identification quadrupled, from 8 percent to 32 percent. The Independent category remained static. In the age group 36 to 55, Democratic support fell from 62 percent to 38 percent, while both the Republican and Independent categories increased. Only among those aged 56 or over did the party preferences remain mostly the same.

In presidential voting conservative Protestants gave Kennedy 48 percent in 1960, down from Stevenson's 50 percent in 1956. Still, conservative Protestants gave Kennedy higher support than moderates (32 percent) or liberals (28 percent). This is undoubtedly due to socioeconomic differences and to the regional, Southern Democratic traditions of many conservatives, half of whom reside in the South. The conservative Protestants voted 2 to 1 for Johnson over Goldwater in 1964, again surpassing other Protestants, but turned against Hubert Humphrey in 1968. Nixon received 46 percent of their support, compared to Wallace's 32 percent and Humphrey's 22 percent. Wallace received a third or more of his support from the low income, low education, Democratic and independent sectors of the conservative Protestant community. In 1968 conservative Protestants were less likely to support the Democratic nominee than moderate or liberal ones. In 1972 only 20 percent of conservative Protestants supported McGovern, giving him the lowest percentage of any religious group in the electorate. Only one-third of Democrats among conservative Protestants supported the South Dakota senator.

Jimmy Carter brought the Democratic support up to 50 percent in 1976, more than the 40 percent he won among moderates and 36 percent among liberals. In 1980 Carter dropped to 40 percent among conservatives, which was still higher than his support among moderate or liberal Protestants. Carter's support fell 14 points among moderates but only 4 points among liberals (55). It should be noted, in passing, that the Michigan Survey data tends to be skewed somewhat toward Republicans, in comparison to network exit polling data and Gallup data.

Demographically, conservative Protestants were less likely than moderates or liberals to have attended or graduated from college and were more likely to have lower incomes. The gap narrowed between 1960 and 1988, especially in education; 37 percent of conservative Protestants had attended college in 1980, compared to 16 percent in 1960, an increase of 21 points. College attendance for moderates increased 17 points and liberals 13 points, but they were still well ahead of conservatives (143).

Between 1960 and 1980 conservative Protestants also increased their proportion of the electorate from 14 percent to 16 percent, while liberals plunged 7 points and moderates declined 4 points—a harbinger of an even greater change in the future (140).

It was on issues that the gap between conservative Protestants and other Protestants was most pronounced. They were more conservative on virtually all issues, from school prayer to military spending. And this cost the Democrats dearly, especially among their younger adherents. Writes Lopatto, "The notion that young conservative Protestants were moving away from the Democratic party because of their relatively conservative stands on religion-related issues is supported by the fact that among conservative Protestants under 36, both independents and Republicans were more conservative than Democrats on most issues" (168).

Why should conservative Protestants have turned against the Democratic Party? Lopatto suggests a variant on the status politics theory that Seymour Martin Lipset and other scholars advanced to explain right-wing extremism. It is not so much a loss of status experienced by these individuals, who, after all, have improved their socioeconomic status in recent decades and who largely shape the values of one large region of the nation. It is, Lopatto suggests, a lifestyle threat or a perception of a declining national appreciation for their values that motivates this shift of allegiance to a party (the GOP) seen as more receptive. He writes, "The conservative Protestants are clearly more likely than members of the other religious groups to bemoan the moral changes that have taken place in American society in the last 20 years. . . . The latest threat to the conservative Protestant style of life seems to have resulted from the process of modernization and the emergence of what are often referred to as postindustrial values" (147, 150).

Writing in 1985, Lopatto did not believe that the Religious Right had yet convinced substantial numbers of conservative Protestants to join their crusade. "It may be that the majority of conservative Protestants have not reached a level of lifestyle threat that would make them ripe for mobilization by the religious right elites" (150). He also predicted that economic issues would slow down the rightward shift. "Finally, the modern religious right elites have had the misfortune of having to compete with other, nonreligious concerns that have dominated the recent political agenda. Specifically, the economic downturns of the 1980s have created severe economic hardships for many conservative Protestant voters. It should be remembered that in spite of the economic gains that they have made in recent decades, the conservative Protestants are still the poorest of the major American religious groups. Thus, economic recessions are likely to hit hard, causing many of them to put aside cultural or lifestyle concerns and concentrate instead on bread and butter issues" (151).

Lopatto reached one conclusion that is held by many observers. "Under the right circumstances religious beliefs can come to play a critically important role in determining the outcome of a given presidential race" (130).

Green and Guth have documented how different the Republican and Democratic parties have become in terms of class, social and cultural structures, and internal dynamics. The Republicans are increasingly seen favorably by the Protestant clergy and religious activists. As a consequence, the Republican party has a much higher percentage of evangelicals among its state and national convention delegates, its major campaign contributors, and its activist cadres. Twice as many evangelicals serve as Republican activists than serve as Democratic activists. This difference is true also for mainline Protestants, making the Republican activists and donor lists overwhelmingly Protestant (76 percent of Republican activists are Protestants, but only 33 percent of their Democratic counterparts are). On the other hand, nearly half (48 percent) of Democratic activists are Jews, religious liberals, or religiously unaffiliated compared to just one in eight (12.6 percent) Republicans.[32] Republican activists attend church more often and consider themselves religious persons more often than the Democrats.

The authors comment: "The GOP's attractions for the orthodox and the Democrats' evident appeal to the 'Nones' suggests that a new cleavage based on religious traditionalism, or perhaps simple religiosity, may be supplementing or even supplanting older confessional attachments. . . . The organizational aspects of religious identity also reveal distinctive partisan patterns. Republicans are regular church attenders, while a majority of Democrats seldom or never darken the door" (118). About the Democrats the authors write, "Their historic identity as the refuge of religious minorities is still secure" (117).

Republican activists, say the authors, "are much closer than Democrats to the American public," but "on such issues as life after death and Biblical authority, they tend to hold beliefs characteristic of upscale educated Americans (which they are) rather than the general public. Democrats, on the other hand, tend to represent minority positions on religious practice and beliefs as well as denomination" (120).

Republican activists are well-to-do, with income levels well above that of the Democratic activists. But the Democrats are much better educated: two-thirds of Democrats but only 45 percent of Republicans hold postgraduate degrees. Interestingly, the wealthiest subgroup—and the one with the highest percentage of people who are divorced or single are secular Republicans—is the small number (7 percent) of Republican activists who have no religious connections (121).

The most religious Republican activists tend to reside in rural areas and small cities, and have modest incomes and less education than other activists. They also are more likely to be married (121). On an ideological scale, they are the most conservative subgroup: 81 percent are opposed to abortion, 97 percent favor school prayer, 83 percent want stricter censorship laws (124). Religious Democratic activists are also much more conservative than less-religious Democrats on the social issues, which suggests that adherence to conservative religious values is becoming an independent variable affecting political attitude formation across party lines.

Kellstedt and Smidt have researched the impact of religious commitment on partisan political behavior. They write, "Recent research has shown that religious salience correlates highly with various social and political attitudes and behaviors, including attitudes toward abortion, racial relations, partisanship, voting turnout, and vote choice" (143).

As they explain it, "If religion truly does matter politically, then those voters who are religiously committed should exhibit different political characteristics than those voters who are relatively uncommitted" (149–50).

Church attendance is frequently used as the best measure of religious involvement. Data increasingly show that regular attenders are more conservative on almost all issues, especially social issues, than those whose church attendance is occasional, sporadic, or nonexistent. This is especially true for Protestants in general and for evangelicals in particular. The 1988 American National Election Study found that 74 percent of "committed evangelicals" (the term used by Kellstedt and Smidt) were ideological conservatives, compared to 43 percent of evangelicals whose commitment level was low. On social issues highly committed evangelicals were 72 percent conservative, while the less committed were only 28 percent conservative. The committed called themselves pro-life on abortion more often (87 percent) than the less committed (55 percent) (154).

As expected, 78 percent of highly involved evangelicals voted for Bush compared to 65 percent of those who attended church less often. Interestingly, among Southern Baptists, there was a reverse factor: 69 percent of the less committed and 67 percent of the highly committed supported Bush. Also, 61 percent of Southern Baptists—the highest among evangelicals—had a low religious commitment (153).

Church attendance clearly affected the vote. Among evangelicals, 74 percent of those who attended church more than once a week voted for Bush, but those who attended once a month or less gave Bush only 57 percent (152).

Among mainline Protestants a similar pattern prevailed: 75 percent of the highly committed voted for Bush, while 63 percent of the less committed voted for him (153).

For Catholics the pattern is more complex. Say Guth and Green, "Although Catholics increasingly resemble Protestants in religious observance, they showed a different political pattern: those less religious and more liberal on social issues are most likely to vote Republican, while the more religious and socially conservative still vote democratic" (215) On the other hand, they found that among political activists, "Catholics involved in the Republican party are more observant than their Democratic counterparts" (216). The

1992 and 1994 exit polls show that Catholics are moving in the Protestant direction. That is, the more religiously involved are voting Republican more frequently.

This correlation between church attendance and Republican support is a recent phenomenon. It began about 1980, according to Petrocik and Steeper,[33] and has intensified.

Writes Allen D. Hertzke, "Church attendance is itself correlated with opposition to abortion. . . . In each denomination frequent attenders are less supportive of the prochoice position than infrequent attendees, and only among Episcopalians are the majority of those actively attending church supportive of unconditional choice on abortion. Lutheran and fundamentalist frequent attenders are the two groups least supportive of unconditional choice."[34] Catholics who attend church infrequently are twice as supportive of the prochoice position as frequent churchgoers.

Hertzke also found that individual views on the origin, authorship, and authority of the Bible are closely related to opinion formation on school prayer and abortion. Of those who hold that "the Bible is the inerrant word of God," 79 percent favor school prayer and 77 percent oppose abortion in most circumstances. Of those who believe the Bible "was written by men and inspired by God," 57 percent favored school prayer and 55 percent generally opposed abortion. Among those who believed "God had nothing to do with the authorship of the Bible," 27 percent favored school prayer and 31 percent opposed abortion.[35]

The Barna Research Group Ltd., a marketing research firm in Glendale, California, was established in 1984 and specializes in studying the evangelical community. Its standard annual surveys since 1991 have provided a great deal of useful information relevant to the study of religion and politics.

Barna's eight-point definition of evangelicalism, however, tends to limit the community to the most conservative individuals and is probably closer to the definition of a fundamentalist in comparable surveys. He also separates evangelicals from born-again Christians, which no other surveyors do. He also insists on classifying people who do not meet his narrow definition of born-again as non-Christian, which is insulting to millions of individuals who call themselves Christians (the vast majority of the Christian community in fact).[36] His methodology, while sound, raises questions about his objectivity as a social scientist. Nevertheless, the data appearing in his four volumes help to fill out a portrait of evangelicals as the most politically and socially conservative religious community in America.

On some issues the differences are astounding and reveal an intense Puritanism among evangelicals and a desire by them to use the government

Table 3.2

Contrasting Views of Evangelicals and Nonevangelicals from Barna Reports

	% Agree	
	Evangelicals	All Others
Doctors performing abortion should be imprisoned	57	20[a]
Euthanasia should never be allowed	58	17[a]
Pornography should be made illegal	59	38[a]
All casinos should be made illegal	54	8[a]
Abortions should never be legal	35	13[b]
Sex education should not be taught in schools	35	15[b]
If family unit falls apart, America will collapse	81	48[c]
All religions teach similar lessons about life	11	62[d]
Religious views have greatest influence on life	78	41[e]
Mass media are biased against Christian beliefs	89	38[f]
Agree strongly that mass media should report moral behavior of candidates	71	39[g]
Homosexuality is immoral	92	55[h]
Homosexuality is a private matter	30	61[i]

Sources:

a. George Barna, *Virtual America: The Barna Report 1994–1995* (Ventura, Calif.: Regal Books, 1994), p. 127

b. Ibid., pp. 292, 293, 296.

c. George Barna, *Absolute Confusion: The Barna Report 1993–1994* (Ventura, Calif.: Regal Books, 1993), p. 184

d. Ibid., p. 207

e. Ibid., p. 247

f. Ibid., p. 254

g. Ibid., p. 256

h. Ibid., p. 268

i. Ibid., p. 267

to enforce their vision of morality on all Americans. For example, a Barna survey in 1993 found that 57 percent of evangelicals favored imprisoning doctors for performing abortions—a legal procedure in the U.S.—compared to 26 percent of all those surveyed. A majority of evangelicals opposed euthanasia, and wanted all pornography made illegal.

More than 80 percent of evangelicals believe that America would collapse if the family unit falls apart, believe that the media are biased against Christians, and say that homosexuality is always immoral. Twice as many evangelicals as nonevangelicals support the media's investigation of the personal life of candidates for public office, and only half as many believe homosexuality to be a private matter. Only about one in nine evangelicals believe that all religions teach similar principles about life, while 62 percent of nonevangelicals believe so. (See table 3.2.)

It is important to note that there are evangelicals who are political liberals or moderates. Individuals like Jim Wallis, Tony Campolo, and Ronald Sider are representative of this tradition. But they have attained only a limited influence among the evangelical community at large.[37]

Notes

1. Norman Ornstein, Andrew Kohut, and Larry McCarthy, *The People, the Press and Politics* (Reading, Mass.: Addison-Wesley Publishing Co., Inc., 1988).

2. Ibid., p. 126.

3. Ibid., pp. 35–38.

4. Ibid., p. 36.

5. Ibid., p. 13.

6. The following paragraphs are based on this unpublished report, which is available from the Times Mirror Center, 1875 Eye St., NW, Suite 1110, Washington, D.C. 20006.

7. Allen D. Hertzke, *Representing God in Washington* (Knoxville: University of Tennessee Press, 1988), p. 120.

8. Ibid., p. 124.

9. Kenneth D. Wald, *Religion and Politics in the United States* (New York: St. Martin's Press, 1987), p. 65.

10. Ibid., pp. 71–77.

11. Ibid., p. 271.

12. Ibid.

13. Daniel Rigney and Thomas J. Hoffman, "Is American Catholicism Anti-intellectual?" *Journal for the Scientific Study of Religion* 32 (1993): 211–22.

14. Clyde Wilcox, "Evangelicals and the Moral Majority," *Journal for the Scientific Study of Religion* 28 (1984): 400–14 at 400.

15. Ibid., 407.

16. Ibid., 410.

17. Ibid., 405.

18. David A. Gay and Christopher G. Ellison, "Religious Subcultures and Political Tolerance: Do Denominations Still Matter?" *Review of Religious Research* 34 (1993): 311–32.

19. Clyde Wilcox, Ted Gelen, and Sharon Linzey, "Rethinking the Reasonableness of the Religious Right," *Review of Religious Research* 36 (1995): 263–76.

20. Robert L. Young, "Religious Orientation, Race and Support for the Death Penalty," *Journal for the Scientific Study of Religion* 31 (1992): 76–87.

21. Christopher G. Ellison and Marc A. Musick, "Conservative Protestantism and Public Opinion Toward Science," *Review of Religious Research* 36 (1995): 245–59.

22. Richard D. Dixon, Roger C. Lowery, and Lloyd P. Jones, "The Fact and Form of Born Again Religious Conversions and Sociopolitical Conservatism," *Review of Religious Research* 34 (1992): 117–31.

23. Michael Parenti, "Political Values and Religious Cultures: Jews, Catholic and Protestants," *Journal for the Scientific Study of Religion* 6 (1967): 259–69.

24. Peter L. Benson and Dorothy L. William, *Religion on Capitol Hill* (San Francisco: Harper & Row, 1982), p. 146.

25. Lawrence K. Kersten, *The Lutheran Ethic* (Detroit: Wayne State University Press, 1970), pp. 219–20.

26. Andrew M. Greeley, *Religion: A Secular Theory* (New York: Free Press, 1982).

27. Wald, *Religion and Politics in the United States,* p. 87.

28. Ibid., p. 85.

29. Samuel S. Janus and Cynthia L. Janus, *The Janus Report on Sexual Behavior* (New York: John Wiley and Sons, Inc., 1993), p. 230. Additional references to this work appear in parentheses following the quoted material.

30. Ornstein, *People, Press and Politics,* p. 3. Additional references to this work are in parentheses following the quoted material.

31. Paul Lopatto, *Religion and the Presidential Election* (New York: Praeger, 1985). Additional references to this work will appear in parentheses following the quoted material.

32. James L. Guth and John C. Green, *The Bible and the Ballot Box: Religion and Politics in the 1988 Election* (Boulder, Colo.: Westview Press, 1991), p. 117. Additional page references to this work will be found in parentheses following the cited material.

33. J. R. Petrocik and F. T. Steeper, "The Political Landscape in 1988," *Public Opinion* 10 (1987): 41–44.

34. Hertzke, *Representing God in Washington,* p. 126.

35. Ibid., pp. 122, 128.

36. George Barna, *Virtual America: The Barna Report 1994–95* (Ventura, Calif.: Regal, 1994), pp. 17–18.

37. Two stimulating books from this tradition are: Jim Wallis, *The Soul of Politics* (Maryknoll, N.Y.: Orbis Books, 1994), and Tom Sine, *Cease Fire* (Grand Rapids, Mich.: Eerdmans, 1995).

4

Evangelicals and Presidential Politics from Thomas Jefferson to Richard Nixon

Evangelicals divided their political loyalties during the early-nineteenth-century elections involving such titanic figures as Thomas Jefferson, John Adams, and Andrew Jackson. Much of their allegiance depended on the religious culture of the state in which they resided and on the challenges they felt from other religious groups.

Congregationalists in New England, who were then orthodox evangelicals, were the backbone of the Federalist party of George Washington, Alexander Hamilton, and John Adams. They dominated New England life and even retained state establishments for their religion in Connecticut and Massachusetts until the 1820s and 1830s. As a consequence, Baptists, Quakers, and Episcopalians in those states gravitated toward the party of Jefferson. Baptists and Episcopalians—mortal enemies in Virginia and the South —were allies in the struggle to disestablish the Congregationalists in New England.

Methodists, Presbyterians, and the Reformed Dutch and German churches favored the Democrats in most areas. Presbyterians carried Pennsylvania for fellow Presbyterian Andrew Jackson during his three campaigns for the White House. The Quakers in the middle colonies supported the Federalists because of the Presbyterian influence in the Democratic party. Evangelicals, then, were found in both parties during the early national period of U.S. history, and they differed among themselves on the proper role that religion should play in political life.

Baptists were strong Democrats everywhere and generally opposed government efforts to bring about moral reform. Presbyterians, on the other hand, launched a movement to stop delivery of the mail on Sundays during the second and third decades of the nineteenth century. They wanted rigid limitations on all Sunday activities enforced by the government. Presbyterian Andrew Jackson, however, opposed presidential declarations of prayer and fasting days, opposed religious tests for public office, and appointed Catholics to the Supreme Court and to his cabinet, for which he was denounced by many Protestant clergy. Jackson opposed any shades of religious establishment even though as territorial governor of Florida he did enforce Sabbath-breaking laws.

After the breakup of the Federalist party, the Whigs became the main conservative opposition party to the Democrats. They began to speak for the native-born Protestant working class that was increasingly terrified of Catholic immigration and the growing Catholic population from Ireland and Germany. While the country was still overwhelmingly Protestant, the Catholic community had grown, especially in the Eastern Seaboard cities. Economic rivalry joined historic doctrinal controversies to heighten religious conflict. Numerous anti-Catholic periodicals sprang up during the 1830s, and a nativist American political movement began to take hold and catch the imagination of the frightened Protestant masses. Violence erupted in several communities, as mobs burned a convent in Charlestown, Massachusetts, in 1833, and communal conflict over school prayer and Bible reading in the public schools of Philadelphia in 1844 resulted in days of rioting, killing, and the torching of several Catholic churches. Philadelphia's Catholics had asked that their children be excused from reading Protestant versions of the Bible and reciting Protestant prayers in public schools. Protestant nativists saw this as a threat to their established values and way of life. Conflict was inevitable and Philadelphia's streets resembled Belfast, where interfaith violence has erupted every thirty or forty years since the nineteenth century.

James Reichley writes of this era, "Anti-Catholicism is a recurring theme in American history from earliest colonial times. In part, this sentiment was undoubtedly an expression of simple bigotry: primordial fear and hatred of insiders toward outsiders. In part, too, it sprang from economic concern among working-class Protestants over the competition of low-wage immigrant labor."[1]

The Whigs soon benefited from the religious conflicts and disorders. The party was seen as the party of order while the Democrats, who welcomed Catholic immigration and participation in politics, were the party of equality. Reichley continues on this theme. "Anti-Catholicism undoubtedly helped move some of the Protestant groups that had supported the party of equality under the first party system to the side of the party of order under the second. . . . The Whigs appealed for Protestant support not only through the negative appeal of nativism but also through positive backing from much of the program for moral reform promoted by the activist wing of evangelical Protestantism."[2]

Most Methodists and Baptists still remained Democrats, as did Lutherans and Episcopalians, but Presbyterians and Congregationalists shifted to the Whigs. The Whigs supported temperance and immigration restrictions and their 1844 vice presidential candidate, Senator Theodore Frelinghuysen of New Jersey, was a Bible Society evangelical and a strong anti-Catholic. The Whigs were soon seen as the more "religious" party. Says Reichley, "It is probably significant that groups that resisted applying religious values directly to politics showed less tendency to shift to the Whigs."[3]

Most Catholics voted Democratic, especially those of Irish and German descent. But economic considerations made Whig supporters of some of the older, earlier-arrived Catholics of English and French ancestry. This was true in Maryland and Louisiana. Many Protestants of the planter aristocracy in the South also favored the Whigs.

Increasing religious animosity led to the formation of the Know-Nothing party in the 1850s. The Know-Nothing, or American, party was a transitional party, as the Whigs collapsed over the slavery issue. The Know-Nothings were frankly anti-Catholic and anti-immigrant and prohibited Catholics or those Protestants married to Catholics from being party members or from receiving support at the polls. They swept local elections in Massachusetts, Delaware, and Pennsylvania in 1854 and captured numerous congressional seats. Clergy were strong in its ranks, and twenty-four Know-Nothing members of the Massachusetts legislature were Protestant pastors. In 1855 the Know-Nothings added Connecticut, Rhode Island, New Hampshire, Maryland, and Kentucky to their victory lists, though they lost bitterly contested elections in the South. Hardly a state escaped the wrath of this new political movement.

But the Know-Nothing hysteria, and the inability of its politically naive and unsophisticated leaders to govern effectively, led to the party's speedy demise. The Know-Nothings, like the Whigs and the Democrats, were themselves divided over the burning issue of slavery in the South and in the territories seeking statehood.

The American party made a last gasp in the 1856 presidential election but its candidate, former Whig President Millard Fillmore, a Unitarian, ran third with about 20 percent of the vote. The Know-Nothing party carried only Maryland, ironically originally the most Catholic state and a state that had pioneered religious freedom. Religious conflicts had engulfed Maryland, and the evangelical Protestant working class in Baltimore and in rural areas carried the day. Fillmore carried many of the old Whig counties in the Upper South states and did well in areas where religious conflict was rampant, such as Philadelphia.

The Know-Nothing (American) vote was clearly an evangelical vote. Studies in Ohio, Indiana, and Illinois found that Baptists were the strongest supporters (47 percent in Illinois and 40 percent in Indiana), followed by Methodists and Presbyterians. In New York, the virulently anti-Catholic Dutch Reformed and Presbyterian voters gave a majority of their ballots to Fillmore.[4] Counties that favored Prohibition in referenda during the 1850s also shifted either to the Republicans or to the American party in 1856.

But the newly established Republican party, which was anti-slavery and pro-economic growth, swept the North, especially New England, and did well among Northern evangelicals. In many Northern states, the evangelical vote was split three ways. In the South, the Democrats won most of the evangelical vote, with some going to Fillmore. The Republicans were kept off the ballot in the South. The 1856 election inaugurated some religious realignment, especially among Northern Protestants. Many Baptists, Methodists, and Presbyterians in northern Pennsylvania and southern New York, in the "tier" counties between the states, switched from Democrat to Republican in 1856. Venango County, Pennsylvania, for example, became the most Republican county in the state and has remained a GOP stronghold for 140 years. Catholics in southern Maryland's St. Mary's County moved in the opposite direction. Fearing both Republicans and Know-Nothings, they shifted heavily from Whig to Democrat.

The four-way battle of 1860 pushed the realignment further along religious and sectional lines. The Know-Nothings split four ways. Most still supported the Constitutional Union ticket, the heirs of the old compromising Whig tradition. A few quirky upstate New York counties switched to Douglas and the Northern Democrats in a desperate attempt to save the Union. Some diehard Southern nativists from Maryland to Louisiana went with the Southern Democrats. But a major chunk of the nativist vote merged with the GOP that, says Reichley, "converted nativism into pan-Protestantism, which attracted much of the former Know-Nothing vote while drawing in many German Lutherans and Reformeds who had felt threatened by Know-Nothingism in its rawer form."[5] Catholics and immigrant voters strongly favored Stephen Douglas while native-born Protestants in the North went heavily for Lincoln, who emerged victorious.

For the next thirty years this pattern remained. All Southerners, including evangelicals, were Democrats and most Northern Protestants were Republicans. Catholics were the backbone of the Democratic party in the North. The small Jewish community favored the Republicans because of the moral idealism they saw in some GOP positions.

The Republicans catered to their Protestant constituency by opposing public aid to parochial schools in their platforms from 1876 to 1892 and by being relatively open to moralizing influences in education. Republican-dominated states were more likely to support temperance legislation and strict Sabbath observances.

There were some interesting differences among Protestant groups, according to historians like Kleppner and Jensen. Kleppner argued that "pietistic" Protestants, with their constant emphasis on moral perfection and reform, sought to use government to compel morality. They linked their moral vision to the GOP. Hence, 75 percent-85 percent of Methodists, Baptists, Presbyterians, Norwegian Lutherans, and other evangelicals voted Republican. So did most Congregationalists and Quakers, who shared some of the pietist predilections. "Liturgical" and "ritualistic" groups that emphasized the corporate dimension of religion and were less concerned about moral reform tended to support the Democrats, the party of individual freedom. German Lutherans and Catholics in the North were generally Democrats. German Lutheran behavior varied, depending on who dominated the local culture. If Catholics were seen as too strong, German Lutherans voted Republican. If pietistic evangelicals were dominant, Lutherans voted Democratic to protest what they saw as insufferable self-righteousness. Episcopalians are clearly on the liturgical side but their high status made them less Democratic than other ritualist groups. Even in the North, however, they were often moderate Democrats or liberal Republicans.

A study of Indiana politics confirms this interpretation. Indiana was a closely divided state in nineteenth-century elections and religion was a major factor in voting behavior. Hammarberg found that Republicans could usually count on support from 98 percent of Quakers, 80 percent of Presbyterians, 74 percent of the United Brethren, 73 percent of Wesleyans, 62 percent of Methodists, 56 percent of the Disciples of Christ, and 53 percent of German Baptists. But only 35 percent of Baptists, 22 percent of Lutherans, and 7 percent of Catholics supported the GOP. Only a third of religiously nonaffiliated voters were Republicans. Native-born voters were far more likely to be Republican than immigrants or families of immigrants. Active church membership also increased Republican support.[6]

Some evangelicals, while remaining Republican, moved into other quasi-religious movements. Some supported the National Reform Association that lobbied for a "Christian Amendment" to the U.S. Constitution, which would have made the United States an officially Christian state, thereby nullifying and negating the First Amendment. The National Reform Association was founded in 1863.

The amendment, if passed, would have "humbly acknowledged Almighty God as the source of all authority and power in civil government and The Lord Jesus Christ as the Governor Among the Nations, and His revealed will as supreme authority."[7] The government was to be called "a Christian government" if this statement were adopted. The General Assembly of the Presbyterian Church endorsed it, as did many evangelicals. This campaign "to put Christ in the Constitution" lasted until 1954 and has been supported by a segment of evangelicals for nearly a century.

Many, if not most, evangelicals supported the temperance and prohibition movements, and some actually voted for its party candidates for president and governor, particularly in rural areas of Alabama and Pennsylvania.

Many evangelicals flocked to a new anti-Catholic banner and joined the American Protective Association (APA), founded in rural Iowa in 1887. The APA was strong in the Midwest and won considerable working-class Protestant evangelical support. It endorsed candidates for Congress (usually Republicans) and achieved a measure of support in places like Saginaw, Michigan, and Akron, Ohio. It pledged its members to vote against all Catholic candidates, to favor restrictive immigration legislation, and to reduce or remove all Catholic influences on public life. Some of its leaders warned of a Catholic plot to massacre Protestants but when the day of the planned Holocaust came and went without incident, the APA scrambled to manufacture a credible response. Its decline began in the 1896 election when many of its leaders—who were often Orangemen from Northern Irish and Scottish descent—supported the Democratic candidate for president.

The 1896 presidential election was one of America's most exciting. Historians generally regard it as a realigning election because substantial numbers of voters switched party lines. Others argue that it was more of a reinforcing election, which made the dominant Republican party a true majority party for the next thirty-six to forty years.

The Democrats nominated William Jennings Bryan, an orator of monumental dimensions, a former Nebraska congressman, and a devout fundamentalist Presbyterian. His campaign, combining economic radicalism and social conservatism, threatened to dislodge the Republicans from their almost three-decade-long domination of the White House. (Except for Grover Cleveland's two nonconsecutive terms, the GOP had won most of the elections since Lincoln's 1860 victory.)

Says Reichley, "Bryan wrapped himself in religious imagery and strove to bring back to the Democratic party the evangelical groups that had shifted to the Republicans at the time of the Civil War."[8] The panicked Republicans nominated a moderate Ohioan, William McKinley, a Civil War veteran (naturally) who had served as governor and U.S. congressman. McKinley and his advisers, led by industrialist Mark Hanna, perceived (even in an era with no polls!) that the liturgical groups (Catholics, Episcopalians, Lutherans) were turned off by Bryan's excessive rhetoric and almost exclusive appeal to rural values. The Republicans proceeded to milk those subliminal emotional and economic issues among city dwellers and among moderate Democrats who opposed many of Bryan's proposals. Bryan's nomination had alienated President Grover Cleveland, and many conservative Democrats, who remained neutral, supported a minor party, or defected to McKinley.

The results in a sharply contested election revealed deep regional and religious differences. Bryan swept the economically depressed West but was stopped in California. He held the South but many city folk and high-status Southerners balked and voted for McKinley, especially in the nonevangelical coastal areas. In the North and Midwest, Catholic voters shifted to McKinley in large numbers. McKinley's vote in strongly Catholic counties nationwide was 43 percent, almost double the usual GOP vote. "Many urban Catholics on election day cast their first Republican ballots,"[9] says Reichley.

In the Midwest Catholics were also reluctant to back Bryan. McKinley's vote doubled in Polish and Czech Catholic precincts in Chicago. Bryan's support plunged 33 points in German Catholic Kewaunee County, Wisconsin, and 26 points in two German Lutheran counties in Wisconsin, Shawano and Dodge.

Bryan's share of the total vote declined 24 points in Louisville, Kentucky (Jefferson County), giving McKinley a 12,400-vote victory, enough to move Kentucky into the Republican column for the first time in history. A stunning McKinley victory in Baltimore helped give Maryland to the GOP for the first time since 1864. McKinley carried every New England county, and virtually every county in New York and New Jersey. Even Boston, New York City, and Jersey City went Republican. The cities became Republican strongholds, which lasted until 1928. Nationwide, Bryan ran better in rural areas, where he won 48 percent of the votes, than in cities, where he received 40 percent.[10]

But evangelicals moved against the national trend, as they so often do. Bryan ran stronger in evangelical rural areas in the North than Cleveland had four years before. Bryan carried fifteen counties in Michigan, including the old APA stronghold of Saginaw. He also won the small fundamentalist city of Springfield, Missouri, in the heart of the Ozarks.

Two additional sources of political strength helped Bryan. He carried about two-thirds of the counties that four years before had supported a third party, the Populist or People's party movement of farmers and laborers who ran General James Weaver for president. While Weaver won only 8 percent of the national votes, he carried several western states and about three hundred counties in the agrarian West and South. Bryan's capture of the Democrats brought most of the Populists, who had voted Republican in the 1880s, into the Democratic ranks. Many were evangelicals.

Bryan also ran strongly where Prohibition sentiment was strong. He carried forty-three of the seventy-one counties where the Prohibitionists had captured a significant vote in state referenda and in state and local races.

Nationally, Bryan won 57 percent to 43 percent in the most evangelical states and carried them by a margin of 637,000 votes, but he was unable to exceed 45 percent even in the most pietistic Northern counties. And he lost a greater percentage of Lutherans, Catholics, and secular voters than he gained among evangelicals. He lost the less evangelical states by 1,205,000 votes, losing 57 percent to 43 percent.

This remained the normal pattern of presidential voting until Al Smith captured the cities and lost the countryside in 1928. Bryan himself ran twice more for the presidency, in 1900 and 1908. In 1900 he gained a few points among Catholics and lost a few among Protestants because of his opposition to U.S. colonialist policies during the Spanish-American War and the U.S. occupation of the Philippines. Catholics saw U.S. intervention as a cultural attack on Catholic educational institutions while Protestants saw the U.S. role as strengthening their desire to penetrate Latin Catholic cultures. McKinley's comment that he intended "to Christianize" the Filipinos offended Catholics and delighted Protestants, as did U.S. support for a nonsectarian public school system in U.S. territories. Bryan gained some evangelicals in 1908 because his Republican opponent, William Howard Taft, was a Unitarian, an offense some evangelical Republicans could not countenance. Woodrow Wilson, a scholarly Presbyterian minister's son, ran well among evangelicals North and South because he spoke their language and his moralism was appealing. Among "Yankee" Protestants, Wilson won a respectable 40 percent of the vote, a figure never surpassed until Lyndon Johnson in 1964.

The old "battler for the Lord," William Jennings Bryan spent his last decade fighting evolution in the schools, supporting Prohibition, and teaching Bible classes as an itinerant preacher in a public park in Miami, Florida. He was a pathetic figure to many Americans, though much admired by conservative Protestants.

From 1896 to 1928 evangelicals voted largely because of regionalism and Civil War memories, with those in the North and West favoring the GOP and those in the South supporting the Democrats for historical reasons, though some convergence occurred around the Prohibition issue.

The growing temperance movement was overwhelmingly evangelical in inspiration and in support mechanisms. Methodists and Baptists played leading roles, though sympathy came from most other evangelical groups, especially those whose constituency was native born and Anglo Saxon in ancestry. Some supported Prohibition from progressive motives, believing the ban on the sale and distribution of all alcoholic beverages would reduce crime, poverty, family disintegration, child abuse, and assorted social ills. Others saw it as a way to reassert evangelical Protestant morality in a changing, more pluralistic society. Others saw it as a way to preserve their status in the culture and to repress the more cosmopolitan Catholic, Jewish, Orthodox, Anglican, and Lutheran communities, which were seen as "alien" by many evangelicals.

Prohibition was highly controversial and was opposed by religious and secular liberals who saw it as a violation of personal liberty and unenforceable. Hypocrisy would be institutionalized by law, said the liberals, and the social ills supposedly cured by Prohibition would grow worse rather than be ameliorated.

Prohibition achieved its greatest political success in those states that were dominated by evangelical religions and by a compliant political culture controlled by rural legislatures. In the early decades of this century and until the 1962 U.S. Supreme Court decision in *Baker* v. *Carr*, rural Americans held disproportionate power in state legislatures. Their vote was worth three or four times that of urban residents, who were unsympathetic to Prohibition. Referenda revealed widespread opposition to Prohibition. New York, Ohio, and even Iowa rejected Prohibition. But America's rural-dominated rotten-borough legislatures and a malapportioned Congress eventually passed a constitutional amendment that went into effect in 1919.

The U.S. House vote on the Prohibition Amendment on December 17, 1917, set in motion America's experience with the "noble experiment." The 282-128 vote sent the amendment to the states for ratification. Within a year Nebraska became the thirty-sixth state to ratify, on January 13, 1919, and on January 16, 1920, the Eighteenth Amendment to the Constitution became the law of the land.

The vote in both Congress and the state legislatures showed how powerful evangelicalism was in the political process. Religion and region overshadowed partisanship in the House vote. Democrats and Republicans both voted yes by 69 percent to 31 percent. But the similarities end there. Representatives from the most evangelical states supported Prohibition 137-30, or by 82 percent to 18 percent. The states with a lower evangelical population gave only 59.7 percent support. Southern and Border State Democrats gave 82 percent support to Prohibition, while only 47 percent of their Northern and Western colleagues did so, an early example of sharp social issue divisions among the Democrats. Southern and Border Republicans (they were few in number in those days) were 76 percent for Prohibition, as were 68 percent of Northern and Western Republicans.

All twenty-one House members from Indiana and Kansas were solid for Prohibition. (If Indiana was the Klan Valhalla, Kansas was the Prohibitionist Citadel.) All House members from Virginia, Georgia, Florida, Mississippi, Arkansas, West Virginia, Tennessee, Delaware, and Oklahoma voted yes. Among the evangelical states, only in Maryland did the noes win.[11]

The state legislatures were even more avid in their support of the amendment, voting 4,284 to 1,363 in favor of it. In the forty-six states that ratified, almost 76 percent of the legislators supported Prohibition. Only Connecticut and Rhode Island refused to ratify (175).

The state legislatures were even more malapportioned than the federal Congress. Rural dwellers were disproportionately represented, and religious minorities were largely excluded from the political process during this era of evangelical domination.

The primary group lobbying for a Prohibition amendment was the Anti-Saloon League, which worked almost entirely through evangelical churches, 5,000 in Pennsylvania alone. Headquartered in Westerville, Ohio, the league set up a publishing empire and a political machine with national clout. Its historian Peter Odegard wrote, "The Anti-Saloon League had received no appreciable support from the Catholics or the Jews. The fact that the Episcopal and Lutheran churches do not as a rule admit the League speakers seems to justify a statement that it is a league of Methodist, Baptist, and Presbyterian and Congregational churches, although it is not by any means limited to these denominations" (18). He also admitted, "It is true that the Anti-Saloon League, being a league of Protestant churches, appeals to essentially the same constituency as the Ku Klux Klan" (29). Thanks to league efforts, nine Southern states adopted Prohibition prior to 1916. White native-born voters were its logical supporters because "the constituency to which the League appeals is suspicious of aliens" (31).

The league was frankly political. When all thirteen of Indiana's congressmen voted against a Prohibition amendment in 1914, the league, writes Odegard, "promptly declared war on them and all but three were retired at the next election. These three joined with the new ten in 1917 and voted solidly for the submission of the prohibition amendment" (98).

The league targeted legislatures and Congress. When the electorate had a chance to vote directly on Prohibition itself, they frequently rejected it, as in California, Colorado, Ohio, Wisconsin, New York, and Iowa. Pressure tactics were most effective on compliant legislators from malapportioned, politically unrepresentative districts.

Opposition to immigration already caused Northern and Southern evangelicals to move closer together. Anti-Catholic and nativist sentiments, coupled with the economic argument of preserving jobs for those already resident in the country, combined to create a movement to restrict immigration. By 1924 Congress had acceded to these demands, reducing legal immigration to a trickle and restricting the immigration to those from Protestant nations in northern Europe. It was a triumph for nativism that received considerable evangelical support.

These social issues produced higher Republican majorities among evangelicals during the 1920s, though Southern evangelicals still preferred the Democrats. Tennessee and Oklahoma bolted to Republican Warren Harding in 1920. Harding, who won a nationwide landslide, promised a "return to normalcy," which to many evangelicals symbolized a rebirth of their political and cultural domination. Harding was a genuine scalawag, a perfect symbol of the hypocrisy and corruption of the 1920s. The first Baptist president, Harding supported Prohibition as a U.S. senator from Ohio and promised strict enforcement of the law. But he smuggled bootleg whiskey into the White House, stayed up all night gambling, and sneaked a mistress, Nan Britton, into the presidential quarters. He joined the Ku Klux Klan secretly while serving as Chief Executive.[12] His scandal-ridden presidency ended when he died mysteriously in San Francisco in 1923. Rumors immediately circulated that he was murdered by his wife, though most historians suggest that poor medical care, possibly even malpractice, was probably the proximate cause of his demise.

Harding was succeeded by Calvin Coolidge, a dour New England Congregationalist, whose personal rectitude and laissez-faire attitudes toward business kept the White House in Republican hands. Economic advances and prosperity (for some) went hand in hand with changes in morality in the "Roaring Twenties."

It was also a decade of religious bigotry, an era of flamboyant evangelists like Billy Sunday and Aimee Semple McPherson. Religious intolerance went hand in hand with political oppression. The engine that united the two forces was the second Ku Klux Klan.

What makes the Klan era important for this story is that it reveals how a large segment of the evangelical community turned toward political extremism and terrorism to fight their enemies on the left. Many had apparently lost faith in conventional political channels and sought an outlet for their political, religious, social, and cultural frustrations. What resulted was a decades-long religious and cultural war that poisoned relations between conservative Protestant evangelicals and the rest of the religious community.

The Ku Klux Klan was reborn on Stone Mountain, Georgia, in 1915, with the backdrop of Confederate heroes adorning the South's version of Mount Rushmore. Building on such movements as Georgia demagogue Tom Watson's anti-Catholic diatribes and coalescing with the Guardians of Liberty and the Knights of Luther, the new Klan had for its central goal the moral reformation of the United States.

The movement tapped into wellsprings of fear and anger among those in the Protestant working class and Protestant rural areas who saw their country drifting away from sound, sober, Bible-based education, entertainment, and community life toward a religiously pluralistic, multicultural, cosmopolitan lifestyle that reflected the values of the growing community of Roman Catholics, Jews, liberals, European immigrants, and others who were different. The cities were seen as moral cesspools, places of danger and corruption to the values and predilections of the native-born American Protestant countryside.

The Klan articulated these fears and resentments and gave an explanation for the changes in American life (too many Catholics and foreigners) and a way to fight and reverse these changes (repress the enemy and drive them into oblivion).

In the decade 1910–19, terrorists had lynched a Jewish businessman who was unjustly convicted of murder and whose sentence of death was commuted by the governor of Georgia. Within a few years, Catholic schoolteachers, policemen and civil servants were dismissed from jobs in Birmingham, Atlanta, and Ft. Lauderdale under pressure from anti-Catholic and pro-Klan elements. A priest, Father James Coyle, was brutally murdered in broad daylight in 1921 on the front porch of his rectory in Birmingham by a crazed evangelist, Rev. Edwin Stephenson, but his murderer was acquitted by an all-white Protestant male jury. For the defense, the Klan hired the best lawyer in the state, one Hugo Black, whose anti-Catholic oratory was legendary. Reverend Stephenson had murdered Father Coyle because Coyle had married Stephenson's daughter, a Catholic convert, to a fellow parishioner, who was of Puerto Rican ancestry. The Klan, whose activities had made Birmingham "the American hot bed of anti-Catholic fanaticism and a cesspool of racial and religious hatred,"[13] controlled the defense team and secured lists of potential jurors. Writes Hugo Black's preeminent biographer, Roger K. Newman, "The majority of jurors were Klansmen, and the foreman was a field organizer for the Klan. Members in the courtroom used hand gestures to the jury during the trial. The judge, William E. Fort, was a Klan member."[14]

After Black browbeat witnesses, singling out Catholics for ridicule and appealing directly to racial and religious fears and prejudices, the jury took only one vote and acquitted the itinerant evangelist on the grounds of self-defense. Jurors prayed and read the Bible while deliberating. Newman says Black "gave to Stephenson's defense his professional devotion" because "he disliked the Catholic Church as an institution and treated prosecution witnesses not just as adversaries but virtually as mortal enemies."[15]

Newman adds a chilling footnote: "No public record of the trial survives. Only one of a stenographer's transcript survives. There is no record of the case in the Jefferson County criminal courts. The *State* v. *Stephenson* case record was apparently destroyed, long ago and almost certainly by the Klan."[16] (Black later reversed course and distinguished himself as a great civil libertarian in a long and illustrious career on the U.S. Supreme Court. But he lied about his Klan affiliation in order to win U.S. Senate confirmation.)

Catholics who owned shops were soon boycotted and Catholic schoolteachers and principals faced intense pressures to resign. The Klan had become a national force to be reckoned with by 1924. Its legions marched down Pennsylvania Avenue in Washington, D.C., and its political power extended from Maine to Oregon. It had strength in both parties and its supporters, estimated at 5 million or more, crossed party lines to vote for Klan-backed candidates.

Religion became a major national political issue when the Democrats nominated New York Governor Alfred E. Smith, a Catholic, for president in 1928. The 1928 presidential election results revealed a deep divide within the American electorate, primarily along religious lines, but also encompassing some urban versus rural antagonisms. There were numerous switchers between 1924 and 1928. Nationally, 520 counties in 24 states supported Democrat John Davis—the weakest candidate the party ever nominated—in 1924 but bolted to Republican Herbert Hoover in 1928. The evangelical connection is strong since 486 of these counties were in the strongly evangelical states, including 14 in Indiana. The largest number (129) were in Texas, followed by Virginia (54), Georgia (43), North Carolina (42), Florida (39), Kentucky (38), and Oklahoma (37). (See map 4.1.)

Evangelicalism was the dominant religious tradition in almost all of these counties. Baptists were the largest religious group in these counties, followed by Methodists, according to the 1926 U.S. Census data for religious bodies.

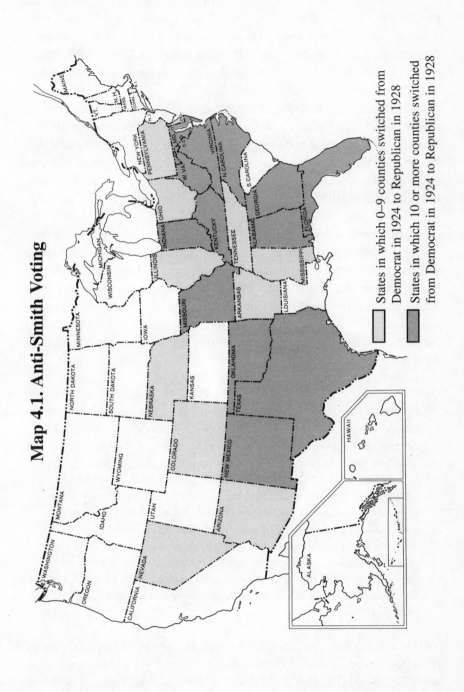

Map 4.1. Anti-Smith Voting

States in which 0–9 counties switched from Democrat in 1924 to Republican in 1928

States in which 10 or more counties switched from Democrat in 1924 to Republican in 1928

As a result of this voter rejection of the Democratic candidate, the Republicans captured Florida, Virginia, North Carolina, and Texas for the first time since Reconstruction. Hoover was only the second Republican to carry Tennessee, Kentucky, and Oklahoma since 1900. And even in the North, Democratic evangelicals defected in Ohio, Pennsylvania, and Illinois, breaking generations of party loyalty.

Smith was also the first Democrat ever to carry Massachusetts and Rhode Island and 15 predominantly Catholic counties in the North. He also carried 115 counties that had supported either Republican Calvin Coolidge or Progressive Robert LaFollette in the previous election. Of these 115 pro-Smith counties, Catholics were the strongest religious group in 83, Lutherans in 17, seculars in 10, Mormons in 3, and Baptists in 2. But the pro-Smith voting paled in comparison with the anti-Smith deluge.

To what extent was Smith's loss due to voter resistance to his religion? An early group of scholars tried to minimize the religious factor by suggesting that a combination of prosperity, Prohibition, and religion resulted in Smith's defeat. But one scholar, Allan J. Lichtman, professor of history at American University, tested previous theories and used quantitative analysis of statistical data for every county. He found conclusively that religion was the primary salient factor in how people voted and is the best explanation for the massive voter shifts between 1924 and 1928.

Lichtman's conclusion is compelling:

Of all possible explanations for the distinctive political alignments of 1928, religion is the best. A bitter conflict between Catholics and Protestants emerged in the presidential election of 1928: religious considerations preoccupied the public, commanded the attention of political leaders, and sharply skewed the behavior of voters. Regardless of their ethnic background, their stand on prohibition, their economic status and other politically salient attributes, Catholics and Protestants split far more decisively in 1928 than in either previous or subsequent elections. No other division of the electorate stands out so distinctively in that presidential year. This cleft between Catholics and Protestants was not confined to particular regions of the nation, to either city or country, to either church members or nominal Protestants. Both Protestants and Catholics responded to the religious tensions of 1928.[17]

Lichtman's study found that Smith's vote declined by 11 percentage points from the combined votes for Davis and LaFollette among Protestants and increased 28 points among Catholics (42). He found that "women opted for Herbert Hoover in greater proportion than their male counterparts" (238), probably because of their higher religious participation and because "The Republican presidential campaign of 1928 relied upon moralistic appeals to the mass of American voters" (244). Lichtman says the GOP "exploited Protestant fears about the consequences of electing a Catholic president" (245).

Says Lichtman, "The evidence suggests that both the local and national leadership of the Republican party was heavily implicated in the effort to incite religious opposition against Al Smith" (233).

Herbert Hoover and the Republican establishment cannot escape complicity with the bigotry of the election. Hoover's failure to denounce the Klan or to speak out against intolerance is evidence enough.

Evangelical voters probably joined the majority of Americans in supporting FDR and Truman during the five New Deal–Fair Deal elections of the 1930s and 1940s, largely because of their Southern orientation and low socio-economic status. Even in the North they were more Democratic than the more prosperous mainline Protestants. Most historians have argued that evangelicals, and perhaps more particularly fundamentalists, withdrew from political activity after Prohibition was repealed in 1933 and after their anti-evolution campaigns failed dismally, even in most Southern states.

Jorstad and Ribuffo argue that some fundamentalists drifted into the far reaches of the political extremism on the Right, supporting anti-Semitic candidates like Gerald L. K. Smith in Michigan and Gerald Winrod in Kansas. Old Right isolationism and postwar anti-communism received disproportionate support from fundamentalists. Billy James Hargis and his Christian Anti-Communist Crusade and the John Birch Society received considerable support from conservative Protestants.

A certain romance has attached itself to the campaign of Sen. John F. Kennedy for the presidency in 1960. His election, we are told, proved how tolerant Americans are, thus breaking the unwritten rule that all presidents had to be Protestants. The true story, however, is quite different.

Even after Kennedy's declaration of independence in his Houston address, Protestant leaders furiously opposed his candidacy. Protestant leaders, evangelical and nonevangelical alike, engaged in a frantic and often mean-spirited attempt to deny the presidency to JFK, not because of his fourteen-year record as senator and representative from Massachusetts, or because he was too liberal, but because he was a member of the Roman Catholic Church. The evidence remains clear, and no amount of whitewash can remove it.

Some revisionist historians, especially apologists for Richard M. Nixon, have even taken to claiming that JFK benefited from Catholic bloc voting, and that he manipulated the electorate to make Protestants feel sorry or ashamed if they did not vote for him. Several recent Nixon biographers and Nixon's daughter Julie have made these absurd claims in the face of clear and compelling evidence to the contrary. In a television interview following Nixon's 1994 state funeral, Charles Colson, Nixon's born-again hatchet man, resurrected the canard that Kennedy stole the 1960 election.

A review of the evidence is sobering, especially in the light of a growing Catholic-evangelical alliance that threatens to upset the balance of political power in the U.S. in the near future.

Kennedy's overall Protestant vote, according to Gallup, was 38 percent, only 1 point higher than Stevenson's 1956 vote. Since this included black voters, who liked JFK much more than Adlai, the white Protestant vote for Kennedy was actually *lower* than the vote for Stevenson. Detailed survey data, county and precinct vote studies, confirm this. Kennedy's victory was due to solid Jewish, Catholic, black Protestant, and secular support, not to white Protestant tolerance. Also, since 65 percent of the electorate was white Protestant in 1960, Kennedy would have been defeated without the solid 75 percent to 80 percent support from the 35 percent non-white Protestant communities. Compared to 1928, Kennedy ran 9 points ahead of Al Smith, and this was due to increased support among all voting groups except, ironically, Catholics. The non-white Protestant percentage of the voting population increased 10 or 12 points by 1960, since few blacks voted in 1928, and virtually none in the South.

Looking at the structure of the 1960 vote reveals the religious cleavages and the correlation between religious preference and the presidential vote that year. The changes in the vote between 1956 and 1960 are the key to understanding the religious factor. Kennedy ran behind Stevenson in six strongly evangelical states: Alabama, Georgia, Mississippi, Oklahoma, South Carolina, and Tennessee. He made minimal gains in other evangelical states (Arkansas, Kentucky, Missouri, North Carolina) and in South Dakota, a moderately evangelical state where Lutheran and Dutch Reformed defections were high. Kennedy made below-average gains in the remaining evangelical states, in Iowa, where there is a strong Methodist and Lutheran vote, and in Oregon and Washington, where secular and nativist traditions are strong. (See map 4.2.)

The correlation between the Catholic percentage of the population and Kennedy's gains or losses compared to Stevenson is high. In the top quartile (the twelve most heavily Catholic states) Kennedy gained 14.4 percent over Stevenson. In the second quartile he gained 6.9 percent, and in the third quartile his gain was only 3.8 percent. In the bottom quartile, i.e., the dozen states with the lowest Catholic percentage of the population, Kennedy lost .4 per-

Map 4.2. Kennedy's Gains and Losses in 1960 Compared to the Stevenson Vote in 1956

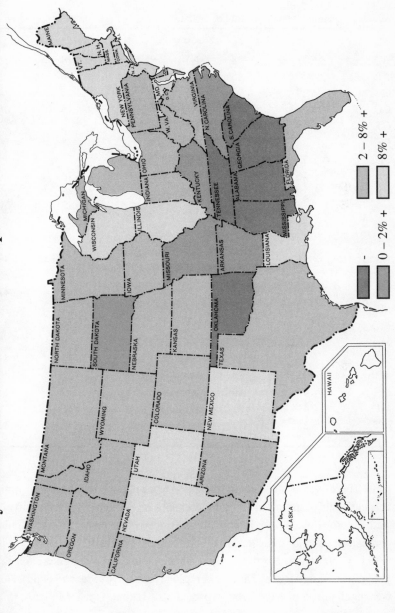

- −
- 0 – 2% +
- 2 – 8% +
- 8% +

Table 4.1

Ranking of States by Kennedy Gain over Stevenson, and Percentage Catholic

State	Kennedy Gain/Losses	% Catholic	State	Kennedy Gain/Losses	% Catholic
AL	43	46	NE	34	23
AZ	28	18	NV	14	25
AR	40	45	NH	10	5
CA	29	22	NJ	5	4
CO	27	29	NM	15	6
CT	4	3	NY	6	7
DE	24	26	NC	38	50
FL	25	35	ND	22	13
GA	46	48	OH	16	19
ID	18	39	OK	45	43
IL	13	12	OR	36	38
IN	32	32	PA	16	11
IA	37	26	RI	1	1
KS	31	32	SC	48	49
KY	39	37	SD	41	20
LA	2	8	TN	44	47
ME	6	14	TX	21	28
MD	8	21	UT	12	42
MA	3	2	VT	8	10
MI	19	15	VA	22	41
MN	33	15	WA	35	36
MS	47	44	WV	19	40
MO	41	31	WI	11	9
MT	25	24	WY	30	34

cent. There was a close relationship between Kennedy's loss/gain ranking and the state's ranking in Catholic population (See table 4.1.). In thirty-four states there was a strong relationship. Kennedy ran better than the Catholic percentage would indicate in a number of Southern, or Border, states (Florida, Maryland, North Carolina, Virginia, and West Virginia) and in the Mormon-oriented Rocky Mountain region (Idaho, Nevada, and Utah). He ran weaker than might have been expected in Arizona, Iowa, Minnesota, Missouri, Nebraska, and South Dakota.

The state results obscure the intensity of anti-Catholic voting in 1960. Rural America was distinctly unfavorable to the idea of a Catholic president,

Table 4.2

Number of Anti-Kennedy Counties by State

State	Number of Anti-Kennedy Counties	State	Number of Anti-Kennedy Counties
AL	41	NE	28
AR	33	NM	6
CA	5	NC	43
CO	5	ND	4
FL	28	OH	4
GA	111	OK	69
IL	12	OR	3
IN	20	PA	16
IA	28	SC	41
KS	3	SD	37
KY	85	TN	73
LA	18	TX	57
MI	2	VA	6
MN	16	WA	6
MS	73	WV	1
MO	92	WI	5
MT	6	Total	977

as county results show. *Almost 1 out of 3 counties in the United States gave Kennedy a lower percentage of their vote than they gave Stevenson in the previous election. Altogether, there were 977 counties in 33 states where Kennedy ran behind Stevenson. Amazingly, 127 counties were carried by Stevenson in 1956 but by Nixon in 1960.* The strongest evangelical states contributed 794 of these counties. (See map 4.3.)

Only fifteen states (mostly in New England, the Rocky Mountains, and the Mid-Atlantic region) had no anti-Kennedy counties. In nine states (Alabama, Georgia, Kentucky, Mississippi, Missouri, Oklahoma, South Carolina, South Dakota, and Tennessee) the majority of counties were anti-Kennedy. (See table 4.2 and map 4.4.)

Most of the strongest anti-Catholic voting was found in rural counties in the Border South (See table 4.3.) or in the Deep South states of Mississippi and South Carolina (See table 4.4.). Baptists were the dominant religious group in these counties, followed by Methodists, pentecostals, and other fundamentalists and evangelicals. This anti-Catholic belt in Oklahoma, Missouri, Kentucky, and Tennessee has shown a strong continuity since the Al Smith

Map 4.3. Anti-Kennedy Voting

States Containing at Least 1 County Supporting Stevenson in 1956 and Nixon in 1960

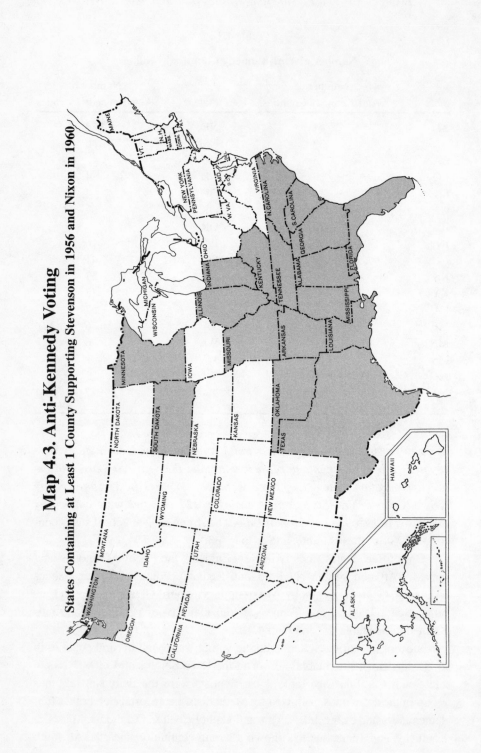

Map 4.4. Extent of Anti-Kennedy Voting in 1960

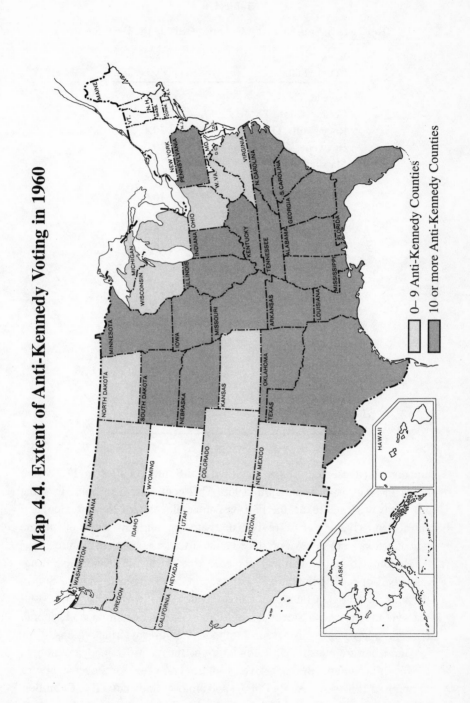

0– 9 Anti-Kennedy Counties

10 or more Anti-Kennedy Counties

Table 4.3

Top Twenty Anti-Kennedy Counties Outside the Deep South

Rank County/State	% Kennedy Decline
Fayette, TN	24.7
Collingsworth, TX	21.2
Roger Mills, OK	20.4
Haywood, TN	20.0
Marshall, KY	17.7
Parmer, TX	17.6
Gibson, TN	16.6
Hardeman, TN	16.5
Moore, TX	16.3
Crockett, TN	16.2
Fulton, AR	16.1
Obion, TN	16.0
Reynolds, MO	15.7
Tipton, TN	15.3
Clay, AR	15.2
Harman, OK	15.0
Roosevelt, NM	14.9
Jackson, AR	14.7
Calloway, KY	14.6
Tillman, OK	14.5

campaign. In these four states the most anti-Smith counties in 1928 were among the most anti-Kennedy in 1960. This continuity also holds in some rural areas of North Texas, the Florida Panhandle, eastern New Mexico, and central Pennsylvania, where revivalism, nativism, and low levels of income and education seem to have produced an anti-Catholic political culture.

Denominational attachment played a role in the anti-Kennedy voting. Kennedy dropped 2 points in key Baptist counties and ran slightly behind in Disciples of Christ, Church of Christ, Dutch Reformed, and pentecostal areas. He ran even with Stevenson in Mennonite and Scandinavian Lutheran areas and a few points stronger in Methodist and Presbyterian regions.

Baptists were unusually prominent in the most anti-Kennedy counties.

Taken as a whole, the fifty-seven counties that voted for Stevenson twice but opposed JFK were heavily Baptist and almost totally devoid of Catholics. The overall church membership was only slightly higher than the U.S. total,

Table 4.4

Top-Ten Anti-Kennedy Counties in the Deep South

Rank County/State	% Kennedy Decline
Barnwell, SC	36.7
Calhoun, SC	31.4
Clarendon, SC	30.7
Montgomery, MS	28.7
Sunflower, MS	28.6
Williamsburg, SC	28.0
Lowndes, MS	27.5
Lee, SC	26.6
Grenada, MS	26.3
Monroe, MS	26.1

but that may have been a result of the failure of many fundamentalist churches, including the large and numerous Churches of Christ, to participate in the 1971 and 1952 surveys.

Nationally, only 7.1 percent of Americans were white Southern Baptists in 1970. In the states where the 57 counties were located, Baptists constituted 19.6 percent of the population. In the fifty-seven anti-Kennedy counties, 33.0 percent were Baptists. The corresponding Catholic percentages were 22.1 percent, 10.0 percent, and 2.2 percent.

The Baptist percentage of the population is a strong explanation for anti-Catholic voting in the 1928 and 1960 presidential elections, especially in Southern Baptist Democratic strongholds that had favored every other Democratic candidate from 1900 to 1960.

In the twenty-eight counties in eight states (see table 4.5) that favored all Democrats except Smith and Kennedy, the Catholic percentage of the population was below the national average (22.1 percent) in *all* of them, while the Baptist percentage of the population exceeded its national average (7.1 percent) in *all* of them. Baptists were the largest religious group in 26 of the counties. (Methodists were in first place in Sullivan County, Indiana, while the Church of God dominated Powell County, Kentucky.) Furthermore, the percentage of the population who were members of all religious groups exceeded the national average in twenty-one of the twenty-eight counties. In other words, these counties were very "churchy" and most church people were white Southern Baptists.

There was almost an absence of Catholics in these counties. In eight of them

Table 4.5

Anti-Catholic Democrats
Twenty-eight Counties Supporting All Democrats 1920–1960
Except Smith and Kennedy

State	County	State	County
FL	De Soto	MO	Iron
	Hardee		Pulaski
GA	Union	NC	Haywood
	Whitfield		Jackson
IN	Sullivan	OK	Grady
KY	Barren		Green
	Boyle		Hughes
	Bullitt		McClain
	Clark		McIntosh
	Grant		Pontotoc
	Livingston		Stephens
	McLean	TX	Gaines
	Powell		Wise
	Spencer		Yoakum

fewer than 1 percent of the population was Catholic. In only three of the twenty-eight did Catholics exceed 10 percent, and the average number of Catholics was a pitiful 2.7 percent. Most people had literally never met a Catholic, which may have increased fears and uncertainties about voting for a Catholic president. Ignorance, prejudice, and religious homogeneity are usually linked.

The Baptist factor was paramount. Even if we compare these counties only to the 8 states in which they are located, the Baptist percentage is twice as high (39.1 percent compared to 19.6 percent). These counties had more church members (60.3 percent compared to 50.0 percent) than their states. But Baptists stand out as the dominant religious influence. In these 8 states, 39 percent of all church members were Baptist. In the anti-Smith, anti-Kennedy counties, 65 percent of all church members were Baptists.

Of the 127 counties in 18 states that switched from Stevenson in 1956 to Nixon in 1960, 117 were in the South and Border states, and 118 (including 1 from Indiana) were found in the 19 strongly evangelical states (see table 4.6). Baptists were the largest religious group in 108 of these counties, Methodists in 8, Catholics in 4, Lutherans in 3, while 1 each were dominated by the Church of Christ, Church of God, Christian Church, Christian Methodist Episcopal Church, and Episcopal Church.

Table 4.6

Number of Counties Supporting Stevenson in 1956 and Nixon in 1960

State	Number of Counties
AL	1
AR	8
FL	2
GA	2
IL	1
IN	1
KY	10
LA	4
MN	2
MS	9
MO	15
NC	3
OK	22
SC	15
SD	3
TN	7
TX	19
WA	3
Total	127

The five counties where Catholics and Episcopalians were strong do not fit the pattern of religious voting in 1960. But all five were highly secular counties, with fewer than 30 percent of voters being members of any church. Perhaps cultural Protestantism was the dominant philosophy in these sparsely populated counties in Washington and South Dakota. Todd County, South Dakota, is a predominantly American Indian area, where Episcopalians and Catholics were traditional rivals.

There is even some indication that anti-Catholicism was a stronger political factor in certain counties in 1960 than it was in 1928. There were fifteen counties in five states (Arkansas, Missouri, Oklahoma, Tennessee, and Texas) that supported Al Smith in 1928 and all other Democrats in this century until 1960. These counties bolted to Nixon. There is simply no explanation other than anti-Catholic prejudice, especially since most of these counties supported Humphrey or Wallace, not Nixon, in 1968. These counties also have a scant number of Catholics (2 percent), a large Baptist population, and an above-average number of other evangelical residents. (See table 4.7.)

Table 4.7

Fifteen Counties Where Kennedy Was First Democrat to Lose since 1920*

State	County	State	County
AR	Clay	OK	Atoka
	Craighead		Garvin
	Fulton	TN	Dyer
	Marion		Madison
	Randolph	TX	Moore
	Sharp		
MO	Dunklin		
	Oregon		
	Reynolds		
	Shannon		

*Indicative of anti-Catholic strength in 1960.

One other group of counties exemplifies a reluctance to support Kennedy among some voters. There were 425 counties in 33 states that supported FDR and Truman five times in a row but rejected JFK. They supported all the winning Democrats from 1932 to 1948 but rejected the next victorious Democrat, John F. Kennedy. Texas was the location of 74 of these counties, followed by Virginia (34), Kentucky (33), Oklahoma (32), Iowa (26), North Carolina (22), and Missouri (20). Lutherans and Methodists predominated in the Midwestern counties, while Baptists and other evangelicals were strong in the Southern and Border counties. But some relatively secular areas in the West were found in this category, including Multnomah County, Oregon (Portland).

Ethnic factors were influential in anti-Kennedy voting. Kennedy ran almost 6 percentage points weaker than Stevenson in the thirty-five most heavily Scotch-Irish counties in eleven Southern and Border states. He ran about even with Stevenson in Scandinavian counties, slightly better in German Protestant strongholds, and a bit weaker in regions where the Dutch and Swiss are prominent. These same areas were relentlessly anti-Smith in 1928.

Many Baptist and some Methodist state conventions went on record in opposition to any Catholic president. So did many church-related newspapers. In her study McCleren concluded, "During the 1928 and 1960 campaigns the Southern Baptists opposed the election of a Roman Catholic to the presidency of the United States. The Southern Baptists used their state newspapers as the main organs of opposition to the presidential candidates of the Catholic faith. The Southern Baptist state papers, the official voice of Southern Baptists on the religious issues in 17 states during 1928 and 28 states during 1960, devoted much space (477 pages in 1928, 485 pages in 1960) to editorials, articles and speeches dealing with the religious issue."[18]

America's largest Pentecostal church, the Assemblies of God, formally and officially opposed JFK's election. Writes Edith Blumhofer, "Protestants in general and Pentecostals in particular harbored deep suspicions about Roman Catholic intrigue. . . . During the campaign for the 1960 presidential election, Assemblies of God anti-Catholicism had become unusually focused."[19] The group's leader, Thomas F. Zimmerman, wrote an article for the *Pentecostal Evangel*, the church's official newspaper, warning, "we must not now let down the guard and lose our time-honored and sacred position by giving the highest position in the land to the Roman Catholic Church. We must take a positive stand with others at the polls in November. Every Roman Catholic is completely under the control of his church, mind, soul and body. A Roman Catholic cannot make a decision on any level which runs counter to the thinking and expressed policy of papal authority."[20]

America's two most famous Protestant clergymen were also involved in the anti-Kennedy movement. World-renowned evangelist Billy Graham worked quietly and surreptitiously for Nixon. He saw no problem in using and inflaming the religious issue to defeat Kennedy. Graham was an old friend of Nixon's and had worked behind the scenes for the Eisenhower-Nixon ticket in 1956. Nixon had attended Graham's 1957 New York crusade. In early 1960 Graham mentioned Nixon favorably several times on his *Hour of Decision* radio broadcasts.

Graham urged Nixon to attend church more faithfully and to weave religious themes into his speeches to shore up the Protestant vote. He even urged Nixon to pick Dr. Walter Judd, a former evangelical missionary then serving as a Republican congressman from Minnesota, as his running mate. Graham told Nixon, "It is imperative for you to have as your running mate someone in the Protestant church, someone the Protestant church can rally behind enthusiastically. . . . With Dr. Judd, I believe the two of you could present a picture to America that would put much of the South and border states in the Republican column and bring about a dedicated Protestant vote to counteract the Catholic vote."[21]

Graham's biographer, William Martin, says that "Graham and Nixon apparently decided that something less than a flat-out endorsement would better serve the interests of both men, at least for the time being" (270).

Graham continued his pro-Nixon maneuverings throughout the year. He refused to sign a pledge against using the religious issue in the campaign, as requested by some in the Kennedy camp, and was obsessed by a fear that

Kennedy would receive the entire Catholic vote. He tried to prevent an endorsement of Kennedy by Martin Luther King, Jr., and wrote to those on his two-million-family mailing list urging them to vote. He encouraged other religious organizations to work quietly for Nixon and asked President Eisenhower to campaign for Nixon in the South (270–73). In his letter to Eisenhower, Graham warned that Kennedy's election would elevate Montana Senator Mike Mansfield to majority leader. Mansfield and House leader John McCormack were both Catholics, and Graham told Eisenhower, "The Roman Catholic Church will take advantage of this" (quoted, 276). It was a blatant appeal to religious prejudice.

Graham then told the press that religion was a legitimate issue. "I have been informed by political experts that it will be deeper than in 1928 because people are better informed. Some Protestants are hesitant about voting for a Catholic because the Catholic Church is not only a religious, but a secular institution which sends and receives ambassadors from secular states" (quoted, 276). Graham then tried to backtrack. Writes Martin, "Graham quickly sent statements to both *Time* and *Newsweek* denying he had John Kennedy in mind when he made these observations about religion and politics. Despite this waffling, Graham's interest in the religion issue stemmed less from fear of Kennedy's Catholicism than from awareness that raising the specter of religious bigotry could help Kennedy's campaign" (quoted, 276).

Graham still declined to endorse Nixon openly because it might hurt the evangelist's carefully calculated public image of fairmindedness and tolerance. Graham told Nixon that the press would "crucify" the religious leader if he made his preference official, so he "avoided the press like a plague." Graham added, "I will make statements that will by implication be interpreted as favorable to you without getting directly involved" (quoted, 277).

As Graham's fears of a Kennedy victory mounted, he penned a favorable, glowing article on Nixon that Henry Luce promised to run in *Life* magazine a week before the election. However, Graham and Luce now had misgivings that the article would be construed—rightly—as an appeal for Protestants to vote against Kennedy. The article never appeared.

But Graham's partisanship and religious bias remained unabated. In a letter to Nixon, he accused Democrats of printing and distributing anti-Catholic literature in Catholic areas, which is nonsense and completely unsupported by factual evidence. He flew to South Carolina to give the invocation at a Nixon rally a few days before the election, pleading in private with the vice president to emphasize religion more in the closing days of the campaign.

In another letter to Nixon, Graham urged the vice president to refer to God and prayer in his speeches, once again accused the Democrats of stirring up the religious issue, and closed with these words, "Thousands of prayer meetings have been organized across America to pray about this election. I am certain that during the next few days you are going to sense supernatural wisdom in answer to prayer. I have a sneaking suspicion that by midnight on November 8, we are all going to be rejoicing. In the meantime, a great deal of hard work and praying needs to be done" (quoted, 278).

After Nixon's defeat, Kennedy's aides asked Graham to visit with the president-elect. Now, Graham could move to rehabilitate his image and rewrite history. He declared, said the *New York Times*, that "the election of John F. Kennedy, a Roman Catholic, had promoted a better understanding between the Protestant and Catholic Churches in the United States. Kennedy's victory had proved there was not as much religious prejudice as many had feared, and had probably reduced forever the importance of the religious issue in American elections" (quoted, 282). Graham also commended Nixon for not bringing up the religious issue and praised Kennedy for facing the issues directly and reducing Protestant misgivings.

It was altogether an extraordinary and skillful rewriting of history.

Norman Vincent Peale was another icon of American popular religion. The pastor of the Marble Collegiate Church on New York City's Fifth Avenue and author of the 1952 bestseller *The Power of Positive Thinking*, Peale was a household name. He had also long been associated with extreme right-wing causes, serving from 1942 to 1945 as Chairman of the Committee for Constitutional Government, an isolationist, America First, anti-New Deal organization established in 1937. Peale was involved with H. L. Hunt's Facts Forum and the National Association of Evangelicals, both Old Right groups. Peale, as a young Methodist minister, "fiercely supported Prohibition from a sense of tribal loyalty"[22] to Protestant group identity, claims his biographer Carol George. George labels Peale a conservative populist who supported a kind of conservative civil religion. "For the first three years of his ministry in Syracuse, the fight over Prohibition consumed much of his energy and politicized his ministry, until ultimately his Prohibition sympathies were transformed into anti-New Dealism" (63), she writes. Peale blasted the Pope in a 1929 sermon and called on Prohibition supporters to support a third party, the Law Preservation Ticket, in Syracuse in 1931 when the local Republicans refused to enforce Prohibition as avidly as he wanted. He still adhered to "the Victorian evangelical-Whig synthesis, the belief in the identity between Protestant values and bourgeois culture" (64), says George. After moving to New York's Marble Collegiate Church in 1932, he transferred to the Reformed Church and "actively supported all the anti-New Deal candidates from Hoover to Dewey" (193). Dewey was Peale's neighbor in the fashionable Quaker Hill section of Pawling, New York, a rich Republican town in Dutchess County. Peale also campaigned actively for the Eisenhower-Nixon ticket in 1952 and 1956 and frequently endorsed candidates because of their compatible conservative Protestant religious views.

So a convergence of political conservatism and dislike of Catholicism, both culturally and religiously, led Peale to open warfare against Senator John F. Kennedy in 1960. Writes Carol George, "Events during the summer and fall of 1960 persuaded Peale to abandon his pledge to stay aloof from partisan activity, and he entered into the thick of the political fray. Evangelicals who opposed Kennedy's impending candidacy attempted to ground their challenge in terms of church-state principles, but few people were seriously misled by the strategy" (194).

In the spring of 1960, Peale gave a speech in Charleston, West Virginia, a month before that state's pivotal Democratic primary contest between Senators Kennedy and Humphrey. Peale said it was essential to consider the religious upbringing of the candidates and questioned whether JFK would be "as free as any other American to give his first loyalty to the United States" (quoted, 195).

In a letter to Dean Francis Sayre of Washington's Episcopal Cathedral of St. Peter and St. Paul, who admired Kennedy, Peale said he had "gotten very tired of the power hungry and contemptuous attitude of the Roman Catholic Church and think[s] it time to restrengthen the oldtime, if somewhat narrow, loyalties of Protestantism, or else we shall deteriorate" (quoted, 196).

Peale and his wife thought a Catholic bloc vote, as well as Kennedy glamour and money, would carry the day unless there was an aroused Protestant electorate. Peale not only hated and feared Catholicism, which he thought culturally incompatible with Protestant virtues and values, but he also despised liberal Protestantism, too. In a May 10, 1960, sermon he called liberal Protestantism a blend of "humanitarianism and socialism," urged the return of an "old, strong, narrow Protestantism that made the United States strong," and asserted that "the only true Protestants left in the United States are those who believe in the Bible and Jesus Christ the Savior and in salvation from sin" (quoted, 197).

As his concerns deepened, Peale lent his name to an extremist group called "Citizens for Religious Freedom," set up by the National Association of Evangelicals to mobilize conservative Protestant activity against Kennedy. The group was funded by right-wing evangelical industrialists such as J. Howard Pew of the Sun Oil Company.

In a sermon that he decided not to deliver, Peale claimed that "Protestantism and freedom were married in Geneva and John Calvin performed the marriage ceremony. . . . America was founded by Calvinistic Christians" (quoted, 198, 196). Peale said nothing about Calvin's approval of burning heretics at the stake, as his government did to the Unitarian Michael Servetus.

Peale and other evangelicals had attended a summit conference in Montreux, Switzerland, where fear of a Kennedy victory in the coming election was topic number one. They then headed for the nation's capital, to a September press conference attacking the Kennedy candidacy. The group claimed that "the nature of the Roman Catholic Church created the religious issue in the present campaign," and argued "it is inconceivable that a Roman Catholic president would not be under extreme pressure by the hierarchy of his church to accede to its policies."[23]

The prominent liberal Protestant theologian Reinhold Niebuhr dismissed the Peale group, saying "It combines piety with right-wing Republicanism in a most remarkable way."[24]

Peale's poor performance at the conference and his identification with the forces of bigotry caused dozens of newspapers and radio stations to cancel his columns and sermons. Wounded and resentful, he removed himself from the remainder of the campaign. Peale's reputation would never fully recover from his embrace of what Union Theological Seminary dean John Bennett called "The Protestant underworld—a religious opposition that expresses itself in unsigned manifestoes and stirring up undisguised hatred of Catholics."[25]

Peale's bitterness was undiminished. After the election he commented to friends, "I think Kennedy is a jerk. Protestant America got its death blow on November 8th."[26]

Adlai Stevenson undoubtedly contributed the best line to the Peale incident, when he told a Minneapolis audience, "I find St. Paul appealing and St. Peale appalling."

Both Graham and Peale remained close friends and supporters of Richard Nixon and were delighted when he finally won the presidency in 1968. The Nixons often attended Peale's church when they lived in New York from 1963 to 1969, and Peale married David Eisenhower and Julie Nixon a month after Nixon's election. During Watergate, Peale was part of a pro-Nixon group called "Americans for the Presidency," which encouraged Nixon to hang tough and not resign.

Graham remained a Nixon confidant and supporter and openly endorsed his reelection in 1972. Nixon attended a Graham crusade in Knoxville, Tennessee, as president, in 1970.

Ironically, both Peale and Graham admired Pope John Paul II and visited the pontiff at the Vatican, Peale in 1979 and Graham in 1984.

The opposition to Kennedy by the Protestant establishment clearly seems to have hurt his candidacy among the rank and file. Gilbert's study[27] indicated that 44 percent of evangelical Protestants and 34 percent of mainline Protestants voted for Kennedy, compared to 80 percent of Catholics. This analysis, based on the 1960 National Election Study, is similar to the Gallup poll's results.

While this may appear surprising in the context of three decades later, when evangelicals are the most Republican voting group, it must be remembered that evangelicals are strongly Southern and working class, more so in 1960 than today. In elections prior to 1960 evangelicals were often 20-30 percentage points more Democratic than the more Northern, middle class mainline Protestants. That the difference narrowed to 10 points in 1960 actually indicates more anti-Kennedy voting among evangelicals than mainliners. Gilbert also found "a strong connection between increasing church attendance and Republican voting among evangelicals in 1960; they were the only group to show an effect from church exposure, leading to speculation that perhaps some direct proscriptions were emanating from the pulpit against the Kennedy candidacy."[28]

The real 1960 "swing" voters were those who broke with their party to support or oppose Kennedy. Gilbert discovered that 28 percent of evangelical Protestant Democrats and 20 percent of mainline Protestant Democrats voted for Nixon, compared to 21 percent of Catholic Republicans who supported Kennedy. The defection rate was not terribly different for these three groups, but one important variable is often ignored by political historians: *the number of Protestant Democrats who defected to Nixon was more than seven times the number of Catholic Republicans who defected to Kennedy.* This, in a nutshell, was why JFK nearly lost in 1960. Among all Americans surveyed in the 1960 National Election Study, 27 percent were Protestant Democrats and fewer than 4 percent were Catholic Republicans. It is also significant that 74 percent of evangelical Protestant independents and 63 percent of mainline Protestant independents voted for Nixon.[29]

Barry Goldwater's capture of the GOP nomination in 1964 pushed the party to the right and toward a Southern base. While Goldwater's later career exemplified a libertarian posture toward abortion, gay rights, and school prayer (he was the only "conservative" Republican to oppose Reagan's school prayer amendment in 1984), his campaign for the White House emphasized social and cultural issues. While opposing all federal aid to education, he said he would include private and parochial schools if Congress overwhelmingly approved federal assistance. He endorsed school prayer and hammered hard at crime and racial issues, as well as anti-communism.

Evangelicals were much less impressed with Goldwater than they had been with Nixon, their real first choice. Goldwater lost 60 percent–40 percent to Johnson in a representative sample of evangelical counties outside the Deep South. In key evangelical precincts in Pennsylvania, Johnson won 61 percent compared to Kennedy's 33 percent.

But fundamentalists seem to have been more attracted to Goldwater, as were Southern conservative Protestants in general. Goldwater carried five Deep South states and won about half of the Southern white Protestant vote, compared to 39 percent support nationwide.

In 1968 Nixon won the bulk of northern evangelical votes but had to fight third-party candidate George Wallace for support in the South. Heavily Southern Baptist counties voted 38 percent to 37 percent for Wallace over Nixon with Hubert Humphrey a poor third. Of the 127 anti-Catholic swing counties from 1960 (almost all of them dominated by evangelicals or fundamentalists), only 59 supported Nixon, while 40 went to Humphrey (mostly in the Border states) and 28 to Wallace.

Wallace clearly played well among fundamentalists, North and South, and for many reasons. Wallace's cultural and economic populism appealed to the class resentments and social fears of many fundamentalist voters. Wallace voters had a low educational level and lived disproportionately in rural areas or in blue-collar city districts.

In Atlanta, Houston, Memphis, and Richmond, Wallace ran strongly in precincts where voters opposed liquor by the drink. Hixson writes, "Though the survey data indicated that the Wallace supporters were less likely to attend churches than were others in the sample, they were indeed more likely to be affiliated with pietistic denominations such as the Methodists and the Baptists or with the smaller neofundamentalist sects."[30]

Hixson, drawing upon the work of sociologist Anthony M. Orum, also argued, "The widely noted affinity of fundamentalists for Wallace was not simply an artifact of their church affiliations. Within each denomination, those with fundamentalist attitudes were more likely to have voted for Wallace. At all levels of education, the correlation between fundamentalist attitudes and voting for Wallace held."[31] Orum himself concluded that "Wallace appealed to a very definite and clear segment of the religious community."[32]

Wallace also won the Goldwater vote in the South, carrying 221 of the 235 counties that voted Republican for the first time in their history for Goldwater in 1964. In the North and West, Goldwaterites remained loyal to Nixon.

Nationally in 1968, Nixon gained among Catholics, compared to 1960, though still losing 59 percent-33 percent, and lost ground to Humphrey among mainline Protestants. Jews and blacks voted overwhelmingly for Humphrey. Among evangelicals and fundamentalists both Nixon and Humphrey lost ground to Wallace.

In 1972 Richard Nixon won a smashing 80 percent victory among evangelicals over George McGovern. In the South Nixon won majorities among whites of every religion. Nationally, 53 percent of Catholics and 35 percent of Jews voted for Nixon, the highest GOP support among these groups since the early 1920s. McGovern did well among the nonreligious and won a respectable vote among Lutherans and some mainline Protestants. He also did well on evangelical college campuses, winning 35 percent at Wheaton and 37 percent at Calvin College, revealing a generation gap between young and not-so-young evangelicals. Campuses everywhere were pro-McGovern. He carried the precinct surrounding Luther College in Decorah, Iowa, where Nixon had beaten Kennedy 85 percent to 15 percent twelve years before.

As the Nixon presidency ended in disgrace after Watergate and the first presidential resignation in U.S. history, a heretofore obscure governor of Georgia, who was also a peanut farmer and a Baptist Sunday school teacher, emerged as the central figure in U.S. politics.

Notes

1. A. James Reichley, *Religion in American Public Life* (Washington, D.C.: Brookings Institution, 1985), p. 185.

2. Ibid., p. 186.

3. Ibid., p. 187.

4. William E. Gienapp, *The Origins of the Republican Party 1852-1856* (New York: Oxford University Press, 1987), pp. 540–42.

5. Reichley, *Religion in American Public Life,* p. 193.

6. Melvyn Hammarberg, *The Indiana Voter* (Chicago: University of Chicago Press, 1977), p. 111.

7. Quoted in Isaac Kramnick and R. Laurence Moore, *The Godless Constitution* (New York: Norton, 1996), p. 146.

8. Reichley, *Religion in American Public Life,* p. 210.

9. Ibid., p. 211.

10. Paul W. Glad, *McKinley, Bryan and the People* (Philadelphia: Lippincott, 1964), p. 203; and William Diamond, "Urban and Rural Voting in 1896," *American Historical Review* 46 (1941): 281–305.

11. Peter H. Odegard, *Pressure Politics* (New York: Columbia University Press, 1928), p. 269. Additional page references to the work appear in parentheses following the cited material.

12. For the story on Harding's induction into the Klan in the Green Room of the White House, see Wyn Craig Wade, *The Fiery Cross: The Ku Klux Klan in America* (New York: Simon & Schuster, 1987), p. 165.

13. Charles Sweeney, "Bigotry Turns to Murder," *Nation,* August 31, 1921.

14. Roger K. Newman, *Hugo Black* (New York: Pantheon, 1994), p. 86.

15. Ibid., p. 87.

16. Ibid.

17. Allan J. Lichtman, *Prejudice and the Old Politics: The Presidential Election of 1928* (Chapel Hill: University of North Carolina Press, 1979), p. 231. Additional page references to this work will appear in parentheses following the cited material.

18. Beryl F. McCleren, "The Southern Baptist State Newspapers and the Religious Issue During the Presidential Campaigns of 1928 and 1960," Ph.D. diss., Southern Illinois University, 1963, pp. 18, 343.

19. Edith L. Blumhofer, *Restoring the Faith: The Assemblies of God, Pentecostalism, and American Culture* (Urbana: University of Illinois Press, 1993), p. 235.

20. Quoted in Blumhofer, *Restoring the Faith,* p. 235.

21. Quoted in William Martin, *A Prophet with Honor: The Billy Graham Story* (New York: Morrow, 1991), p. 271. Additional page references to this work will appear in parentheses following the cited material.

22. Carol George, *God's Salesman: Norman Vincent Peale and the Power of Positive Thinking* (New York: Oxford University Press, 1993), p. 190. Additional page references to this work appear in parentheses following the cited material.

23. Patricia Barrett, *Religious Liberty and the American Presidency* (New York: Herder & Herder, Inc., 1963), pp. 149–52.

24. Quoted in George, *God's Salesman,* p. 206.

25. Quoted in ibid., p. 204.

26. Quoted in ibid., p. 208.

27. Christopher P. Gilbert, *The Impact of Churches on Political Behavior* (Westport, Conn.: Greenwood, 1993), pp. 43–50.

28. Ibid., p. 46.

29. Ibid., p. 44.

30. William B. Hixson, Jr., *Search for the American Right Wing* (Princeton, N.J.: Princeton University Press, 1991), p. 132.

31. Ibid., pp. 132–33.

32. Anthony M. Orum, "Religion and the Rise of the Radical White: The Case of Southern Wallace Support in 1968," *Social Science Quarterly* 51 (1970): 674–88.

5

Evangelicals and
Presidential Politics, 1976–1992

1976

The election of Jimmy Carter in 1976 inaugurated the series of modern elections in which religion has played an increasingly prominent role. Both *Newsweek* and George Gallup dubbed 1976 the "year of the Evangelical." The Gallup poll revealed that one-third of adult Americans, or about 50 million people, said they had had a "born again" religious conversion. This figure includes 51 percent of the Protestants and 18 percent of the Roman Catholics. The political impact of this growing religious force was on the minds of pollsters, politicians, and preachers as election day came around.

Jimmy Carter clearly did better among evangelicals than Democratic presidential candidates normally do, though probably falling short of a majority. A Wheaton College (sometimes called the evangelical Harvard) poll just before election day found students and faculty for Ford by about 67 percent to 30 percent. However, since only 10 percent called themselves Democrats (versus 50 percent Republicans and 40 percent Independents), Carter's showing is quite respectable, indeed about double the McGovern support.

Fifty key evangelical counties gave Carter 49.4 percent, a 20 percent increase over McGovern. Assuming that he won 40 percent of all evangelicals, Carter received at least 6.4 million of the 16 million evangelical votes. Ford's 9.6 million, or 3.2 million majority, was not enough to overcome the Catholic, Jewish, other Protestant, and nonaffiliated majority for Carter. In addition to his 92 percent landslide among black voters, who are not included in the white evangelical category, this was how Carter won.

The decisiveness of the black vote for Jimmy Carter may have been partially related to a comfortable feeling among black voters, most of whom are evangelicals, with Mr. Carter's religion. However, there is no real evidence to suggest that black Catholics, for example, voted any differently from black Baptists. In southern Louisiana black parishes, where there are many black Catholic voters, Carter won with incredible 97 percent or higher majorities. It is true that Carter frequently spoke at black churches and received the support of black ministers in his campaign, but it is likely that this was due to his support for issues that the black community regarded as vital to the survival and prosperity of its people.

In 1968 Nixon had a 7.2-million-vote majority over Humphrey among evangelicals, which just overcame the 6.7-million lead for Humphrey among Catholics, Jews, and "others." In 1976 Carter dropped to about a 5-million edge over Ford among nonevangelicals, but cut Ford's evangelical majority to only 3.2 million. The result? Almost a 2-million-vote victory and the presidency for James Earl Carter, Jr.

Carter's stunning evangelical reversal was the decisive factor in his Missouri, Ohio, Tennessee, Kentucky, and Pennsylvania victories, and his near-miss in Oklahoma. In ten heavily evangelical counties in Missouri, for example, where Kennedy won 38 percent, Carter won 55 percent. With this electoral shift, Carter was unbeatable.

Jimmy Carter's Baptist coreligionists gave him a majority of their votes, and the first time since Truman in 1948 that a Democrat won. ABC/Louis Harris claimed a 57 percent to 43 percent edge for the Sunday school teacher/deacon/missionary whose religious views provoked so much speculation.

Time called the Baptist vote 56 percent for Carter. The ninety-six Baptist strongholds gave Carter an unprecedented 58 percent, a gain of 33 percent over McGovern and Humphrey. Carter swept counties that haven't gone Democratic since Franklin Roosevelt. Carter even carried two rock-ribbed Baptist Republican mountain counties that remained loyal to Barry Goldwater and Alfred Landon: Winston County, Alabama, and Fannin County, Georgia. He piled up record votes in East Tennessee, carrying several long-time Republican areas.

(The Baptist press, incidentally, was as impartial in this campaign as the Catholic press in 1960, probably not wanting to be accused of partisanship toward a fellow believer. This contrasted sharply with 1960 and 1928 when, as Beryl F. McClerren discovered, Baptists "used their state newspapers as the main organs of opposition to the presidential candidates of the Catholic faith."[1])

Protestants of all stripes clearly gave Carter a substantially higher-than-usual vote for a Democrat. Though much of it was cultural, regional, and economic, some must have been related to his willingness to stand up and be counted religiously. Even in counties not recognizably evangelical or denominationally homogeneous, Carter did quite well.

This was true in upstate New York, far away from any Southern migratory patterns that may have intermingled with religion to give Carter a solid showing in Ohio, Pennsylvania, Illinois, and Indiana. In thirteen predominantly Protestant counties, Carter ran better than Kennedy in all, and better than Humphrey in all but one. In the five heaviest Protestant strongholds, Carter ran 8 percent to 11 percent ahead of Kennedy and 5 percent to 7 percent better than Humphrey. The total Democratic share of the vote in these historic Republican bailiwicks was Carter 39.7 percent, Humphrey 36.7 percent, Kennedy 32.8 percent. In some other mostly Protestant counties, Carter almost won an upset. In Orange County, which Kennedy and Humphrey had lost by 17,000, Carter lost by less than 9,000. In Ulster County, Humphrey lost by 14,000, Kennedy by 13,000, and Carter by less than 5,000. Carter made similar gains in five Protestant strongholds in Vermont, Maine, and New Hampshire, winning 36 percent to Kennedy's 22 percent and Humphrey's 32 percent. In seven Iowa WASP (white, Anglo Saxon Protestant) counties, Carter carried six and won 55 percent of the vote. None of these counties voted for McGovern, Humphrey, Kennedy, or Stevenson. Carter ran 18 percent ahead of McGovern and 13 percent to 14 percent ahead of Kennedy and Humphrey.

In six precincts in Baltimore's Thirteenth Ward live many blue-collar Protestant voters. Rejecting George McGovern 79 percent to 21 percent, they gave Jimmy Carter 54 percent. One-third of these white Protestants switched to the man from Plains.

The researchers for the Gallup Opinion Index, in the Introduction to *Religion in America 1976,* made a statement that seems almost prophetic as we examine the 1976 election returns. They said: "Social commentators have expressed surprise that so many people in what they describe as a 'secularized and largely agnostic nation' have supported a devout evangelical Southern Baptist Jimmy Carter. Yet the fact is Americans are extraordinarily religious people. . . . Not only are levels of religious belief and practice extremely high in this country, but an estimated two-thirds of Protestants are evangelicals. Thus, the type of religion of Mr. Carter, a 'born again Christian,' sits well with most Protestants and his public professions of personal piety are not found offensive." That is without a doubt one clue to his strong Protestant vote.

Carter won an impressive and perhaps unexpected 52 percent victory in the Lutheran counties, a showing far exceeding McGovern, Humphrey, Kennedy, and Stevenson. Carter ran well ahead of Humphrey in Minnesota and better than Johnson in German Lutheran Sibley County. To a very great extent, the Lutheran farm vote was essential to the Carter upset victory in Wisconsin.

The heavily Methodist counties in the Midwest and Border states gave Carter 50 percent, one of the best showings for a Democrat in years. Maryland's Eastern Shore, where Carter did well in the May primary, also split 50-50, hardly 100 votes separating the two candidates. It was a photo finish in several Methodist counties.

Mormon voters intensified their conservative and increasingly Republican reputation, giving Mr. Ford a solid 65 percent in Utah and Idaho counties. The Mormon vote may have been decisive in Ford's narrow edge in Nevada.

Counties populated by descendants of New England Protestants—Congregationalists, American Baptists, Methodists, Presbyterians, and similar groups—continued to move in a Democratic direction, away from their historic Republican moorings. These once-solid GOP areas gave Humphrey and McGovern a higher vote percentage than they gave Franklin Roosevelt in 1940 and 1944. However, theological liberalism and Northern disdain for the South did not make them prime targets for a good Carter vote. Nevertheless, Carter won 42 percent, a gain of 6 percent over McGovern and 4 percent over Humphrey.

Carter hardly gained at all among these staid burghers, winning just 26 percent to Ford's 74 percent. Carter actually ran behind McGovern in Ottawa County, Michigan, where Ford's almost hometown status prevailed. (Ford had scored over 90 percent against Reagan in the primary.)

The towns of Loma Linda, California, and Keene, Texas, are so heavily Adventist that mail is delivered on Sunday, not Saturday. Ford beat Carter by an 85 percent landslide. In 1972 Nixon had won 86.4 percent, so Ford's victory shows the continuing Republican orientation of Seventh-day Adventists.

Catholics were an important part of the Carter-Mondale strategy for reconstructing the Roosevelt coalition. The Democrats were somewhat more successful among other segments of the coalition, but surely would have lost the election without capturing at least a majority of the pivotal Catholic vote. CBS gave Carter 55 percent-45 percent of the Catholics, while NBC gave him 56 percent-41 percent, and ABC's Louis Harris claimed a dead heat. NBC showed Irish Catholics 51 percent-47 percent for Carter and Italian Catholics 57 percent-40 percent for him. Carter's showing was thus 5 percent or 6 percent behind normal. His 10 percent-15 percent majority was less than Humphrey's 25 percent and way behind Kennedy's and Johnson's. He ran a little better than Stevenson and 7 percent ahead of McGovern.

Let us look at the Catholic vote in some detail. Carter recorded impressive gains in several Catholic strongholds. In twenty-nine key Baltimore precincts Carter won a shade under 60 percent, compared to McGovern's 34 percent. He carried all but one precinct, while McGovern lost every one of them. In 17 Philadelphia wards, Carter won almost 57 percent, compared to McGovern's 39 percent. In ten Chicago wards where McGovern won only 35 percent, Carter won 50 percent. (In these Chicago wards, religious influences on voting have always been apparent. In 1972, for example, Catholic Democrat Roman Pucinski carried all ten wards, which McGovern lost, and won a solid 56 percent of the vote. About one-fifth of the Catholics voted for Nixon and Pucinski.) Carter's showing in Baltimore, Philadelphia, and Chicago was about even or slightly better than Humphrey's.

In New York State the pattern was mixed. Carter barely won Democratic Albany, but rolled up an impressive 45 percent on Staten Island—a Republican Catholic stronghold that gave McGovern 26 percent and Humphrey 36 percent. (Carter barely won Albany, by 700 votes compared to Humphrey's 28,000 and Kennedy's 30,000 vote margins.) In Erie County (Greater Buffalo), New York, Carter could only manage a 9,000 majority compared to Humphrey's 82,000. (Carter topped McGovern by only 5 percent to 6 percent in Buffalo and Albany.) In Onondaga (Syracuse), Carter lost by 41,000; Humphrey by only 12,000. In several middle- to upper-middle-income districts in Queens, where McGovern won barely 20 percent, Carter won almost 45 percent—a showing exceeding Humphrey's. In the Bay Ridge area of Brooklyn, Carter won 41 percent, McGovern 23 percent.

The difference among New York City Catholics might be explained by that famous *New York Daily News* headline: "Ford to New York: Drop Dead."

The nation's fifteen heaviest Catholic urban counties gave Carter almost 56 percent, an increase of 15 percent over McGovern, but about 6 percent less than Humphrey. Carter won Jersey City by only 24,000, and lost Manchester, New Hampshire, by 8,000. In ninety-one small-town and rural Catholic bastions Carter received 55 percent, a gain of 3 percent over Humphrey. He carried six of the ten heaviest Catholic states.

Carter swept Hispanic Catholic areas in New Mexico and Texas, piling up impressive majorities in several counties. In southern Louisiana parishes, where Ford was a clear favorite, Carter won 56 percent—a smashing gain of 26 percent over McGovern and Humphrey. He just missed Lyndon Johnson's 58 percent, but understandably ran well behind Kennedy's 78 percent. In several key German-American counties in Iowa, Wisconsin, Minnesota, Illinois, Indiana, Missouri, and North Dakota, Carter generally ran well ahead of Humphrey and McGovern, winning comfortable majorities in Stearns

County, Minnesota, and Dubuque, Iowa, historic strongholds of German Catholicism.

If the national surveys are correct in showing only 55 percent for Carter, it is likely that suburban Catholics gave a majority for Ford. In 31 percent Catholic St. Louis County, for example, Carter lost to Ford by 50,000 votes compared to Humphrey's 15,000 vote loss and Kennedy's 9,000 vote victory margin.

The relative decline in Catholic Democratic vote support in 1976 was probably due to a combination of many factors: distrust that a small-town Southerner could really understand the needs of urban dwellers; traditional Catholic reserve about candidates who emphasize public morality. Many Catholics, in the view of Prof. James M. Powell, felt that Carter's approach to problem solving placed too great an emphasis on subjective factors. Writing in *America* (October 23, 1976), Powell says: "They can share Governor Carter's deep concern about the need for moral revival, but many stop short at his failure to develop programs and query his practicality. The reason for this is that Catholics are accustomed to living within a highly developed institution, and they expect approaches to reform to be cased in institutional and programmatic terms, while the evangelical Carter regards such approaches as secondary to his main thrust for moral reform, the restoration of goodness."

There is no evidence to substantiate earlier fears that abortion, parochiaid (parochial school aid), and anti-Baptist prejudice might significantly influence Catholic voting behavior. The evidence shows incontestably that Carter did well in both Catholic and Baptist areas of New Mexico, Texas, Missouri, Louisiana, and Kentucky.

The Jewish community apparently gave Jimmy Carter a substantial majority, but one that failed to match the Democratic norm. NBC gave Carter 75 percent, CBS 68 percent, but ABC only 54 percent. The last figure is credible only if one believes that Carter ran 12 percent behind McGovern among Jews. Sample precinct data belie that. Nevertheless, Jewish support for Carter may have been the poorest, except for McGovern and possibly Truman (who lost 15 percent or more among Jews to Henry Wallace), among postwar Democratic candidates.

Baltimore's banner Jewish precincts gave Carter 65 percent, a showing quite above McGovern's 50 percent, but below Humphrey's 80 percent. Philadelphia's two predominantly Jewish wards rewarded Carter with 67 percent, again better than McGovern by 11 percent, but 7 percent behind Humphrey. In five heavily Jewish wards of Brooklyn and the Bronx, Carter swept 76 percent, again exceeding McGovern easily and almost equaling Humphrey. In six affluent Montgomery County, Maryland, precincts Jewish voters gave Carter 69 percent, up from McGovern's 62 percent, but below

Table 5.1

Anti-Carter Voting, 1976
(% Rounded off)

Academia	% McGovern 1972	% Carter 1976
State College, PA	54	49
Evanston, IL	52	51
Hanover, NH	60	52
Durham, NH	51	48
Orono, ME	49	46
Amherst, MA	69	68
Liberal Rich		
Chicago Ward Forty-three (Gold Coast)	56	51
Philadelphia Ward Five (Society Hill)	63	60
Boston Ward Five (Beacon Hill)	68	60
Pittsburgh Ward Seven	51	49
Brookline, MA	63	58
Lexington, MA	53	52
Conservative Rich		
Whitefish Bay, WI	34	30
Ben Avon Heights, PA	13	11
Rosslyn Farms, PA	20	15
Wellesley, MA	41	38

Humphrey's 74 percent. In seven heavily Jewish precincts in Miami Beach, Carter won 76 percent, an increase of 8 percent over McGovern.

Five Los Angeles precincts gave Carter a solid 82 percent, a gain of 8 percent over McGovern. These data would suggest at least 75 percent for Carter among all Jews nationally, unless there was a substantial Ford vote in the heterogeneous suburbs, where Jews have blended in the landscape and vote more like their Republican gentile neighbors.

CBS News reported that Carter swept the religiously identified "other" and "none" category by 59 percent to 41 percent. This group tends to be somewhat more liberal and Democratic than the electorate as a whole. Carter may have lost some potential support among this broad group. Survey after survey throughout the campaign found some voters volunteering negative comments about Carter's demonstrative religion. A Buffalo factory worker told reporter Finlay Lewis that religion was one of the reasons he was going to vote for Ford. "The fact that he is a Baptist doesn't bother me. What does bother me is the fact that he's pushing his religion."[2] Haynes Johnson found many Southerners chiding Carter for allegedly "overusing" his religion.[3] As a possible consequence, some of the more fashionable city districts gave Carter a lower vote percentage than McGovern, as did several university areas. (See table 5.1.)

1980

Carter's evangelical strength proved ephemeral. His administration was caught in the rising tide of angry religious conservatives, especially those who patronized private schools. By 1979 animosity over perceptions of unjustified federal intervention into and regulation of religious private schools led to the foundation of the Moral Majority, the Religious Round-table, Christian Voice, and other political interest groups that became known collectively as the Religious Right.

Their disappointment in the way the Carter administration handled these issues, largely a result of his inept religious liaison staff, caused conservatives to look for a new champion of their values. They found one in former California Governor Ronald Reagan, who narrowly lost the GOP nomination to President Gerald Ford in 1976.

Reagan's personal views, the issues he chose to emphasize, and the Republican platform appealed directly to religious conservatives of all faith traditions, though white Protestant evangelicals were the largest segment of the target audience and, ultimately, were the most supportive of Reagan.

In any given election the various exit polls plus data gathered from precincts or counties that are representative of the religious group as a whole can tell us a great deal about the voting patterns of each given group in the population.

In dividing the vote 51 percent–41 percent with President Carter, Governor Reagan made substantial gains throughout the religious spectrum. The Republican's strongest gains came among the three traditionally Democratic groups: Jews, Catholics, and Southern Baptists. All three groups showed a larger trend toward Reagan than the electorate as a whole.

The quarter of the population who are Catholics went for Reagan by 51 percent to 40 percent in the CBS survey and by 47 percent to 42 percent in the comparable ABC poll. Carter had won 57 percent of their votes four years before. The Catholic voter swing turned a close election into a landslide for Reagan in New Jersey, Pennsylvania, Ohio, New Hampshire, and New Mexico, and contributed to Reagan's upset victory in Massachusetts. Louisiana's French Catholics shifted heavily to Reagan, giving him 58 percent–39 percent and a large majority in the French Catholic parishes (counties). Four years ago they had saved the state for Jimmy Carter. In New York City, Catholic voters who narrowly favored Carter four years ago gave Reagan a landslide. Twelve heavily Catholic assembly districts in Queens, Brooklyn, the Bronx, and Staten Island gave Reagan about 65 percent. The one dissenting district was a Polish constituency in Brooklyn where he won only 43 percent. The Polish voters are still heavily Democratic and were one of the few Catholic subgroups to give an edge to President Carter. In ethnic terms Reagan won a 19-point edge among German Catholics, a 12-point edge among Italians, and a 10-point edge among Irish Catholics. He even carried Irish Catholic districts in Boston that had gone for McGovern in 1972. Indeed, the Catholic vote for Reagan was as high as it was for Nixon in 1972 or during the unusual Republican landslide of 1920, while Carter's Catholic vote was the lowest for any Democratic candidate since 1924.

The Catholic defection to Reagan was broad. Although Carter carried 84 of the 105 heaviest Catholic counties in 1976, this time he won only half. Carter was simply out of the running in a dozen states, including Connecticut, New Jersey, Ohio, Pennsylvania, Illinois, and Louisiana, when Catholic voters moved toward Reagan. In Louisiana, a 1976 Carter majority of 56 percent in the French Catholic parishes produced a 60,000-vote majority for Carter, or most of his 75,000 edge in Louisiana. This year a 58 percent Reagan sweep produced a 70,000-vote victory margin for Reagan in a state that he carried by 90,000. In both instances the Cajun vote was decisive.

The results from three other Catholic strongholds tell the story of the successful appeal of the Reagan campaign or relative lack of appeal of the Carter campaign. In Green Bay, Wisconsin, Reagan won a 17,000-vote margin compared to Ford's 4,000. Stearns County, Minnesota, which had gone for McGovern and Carter, switched to Reagan. And that loyal Democratic bastion, Dubuque, Iowa, gave Carter a mere 39-vote edge. The blue-collar, substantially Catholic suburb of Macomb County, Michigan, went for Reagan by 35,000 and Ford by 11,000.

The Jewish vote for the Democratic candidate dipped below 50 percent for the first time in over fifty years. Carter received the lowest Democratic Jewish vote since 1924 and Reagan the highest Republican vote. The CBS survey showed Carter with a 45 percent–40 percent edge among all Jewish voters, with 15 percent for John Anderson. The ABC survey showed roughly similar results, with about 42 percent-37 percent for Carter with 21 percent for Anderson. Four years before Carter won an estimated 70 percent of Jewish votes, so he lost nearly half among this important and historically Democratic voting group. The Jewish swing to Reagan was decisive in New York State's Reagan victory. In Brooklyn, heavily Orthodox Jewish neighborhoods that had voted 2 to 1 for McGovern and 3 to 1 for Carter gave Reagan 63 percent. In the suburbs Reagan carried precincts in Scarsdale, New Rochelle, and Long Island that had gone for Carter and McGovern.

What do the changes in religious voting patterns mean on the practical level? Quite simply, they translate into the voting blocs from which winning coalitions, whether ephemeral or long-lasting, are built. For example: Rockland County, New York, is a Hudson River suburb with a fast-growing Jewish population (22 percent). Ford carried the county by only 3,000, but Reagan took it by 23,000. Sullivan County is a heavily Jewish enclave in the Catskill Mountains resort area of upstate New York. While nearby counties were giving Carter a slightly *better* showing in 1980 than in 1976 (one of the oddities of 1980), Sullivan County went to Reagan 60 percent to 33 percent. In 1976 Carter had carried Sullivan County. In Broward County, Florida, which includes a large Jewish "condominium" community, a 1976 Carter majority of 15,000 became a Reagan sweep by 77,000. Florida's normally Democratic Dade County (Miami), which is heavily Catholic (largely Cuban) and Jewish, shifted from a 92,000 Carter majority in 1976 to a 49,000 Reagan victory in 1980.

Carter's unique appeal to the "born again" vote proved to be a one-time phenomenon. In 1976 he carried 58 of 100 heavily evangelical counties in 12 states. This time he won just 16 of them. Carter's success among evangelicals in 1976 was not confined to the South. He carried 32 of 47 evangelical counties in Illinois, Indiana, Ohio, Iowa, and Missouri in 1976. In 1980 he won 5 of them to Reagan's 42. The CBS exit poll data singled out "born again white Protestants" (17 percent of all voters) as a special category and found that these votes were for Reagan over Carter by 61 percent to 34 percent. Last time they were evenly divided.

Curiously, ABC News found that 8 percent of voters responded favorably to a candidate's personal religious views. (Presumably, this candidate's religious convictions match the individual voters' who said they believed religion to be an important attribute of the candidates they preferred.) Of this tiny sample, 60 percent voted for Carter over Reagan. So, Carter may have done even worse among the evangelicals had he not been prominently identified as a fellow believer. Thus, Carter's "religious style" still proved to be a positive factor in the polling booths, albeit a relatively insignificant one. One reason why this segment of evangelicals may have stayed with the president is that his religiousness is well known to voters. It was an issue in 1976

and remained a visible aspect of his presidency. On the other hand, most voters, according to an early fall Gallup survey, were unaware of Ronald Reagan's personal religious conservatism, his churchgoing habits, and his commitment to evangelical values. The evangelical press, which I judged as pro-
Carter in 1980, simply chose not to inform readers that Reagan shared some
of Carter's religious values. Still, as it turned out, two-thirds or more of evangelical voters felt that Reagan, not Carter, was right on the campaign issues.
And I would suspect that perceived "family/morality" concerns played an
important role in the formation of evangelical opinion.

Two conservative religious groups voted overwhelmingly for Reagan, as
expected. Mormon voters gave him 80 percent, a gain of 15 percent over
Ford's showing. The Mormon vote was certainly a factor in the Reagan landslide in the Mountain States. Christian Reformed voters in Michigan, Wisconsin, and Iowa gave Reagan 70 percent. Methodist voters in southern Delaware
and the Eastern Shore of Maryland also went for Reagan about 3 to 2.

The Lutheran vote was a big surprise. In 1976 Carter carried twenty-five
of the forty-three most heavily Lutheran counties in Wisconsin, Minnesota,
Nebraska, Iowa, and the Dakotas. He carried only five of them against Reagan. His overall Lutheran vote slid from 52 percent to 33 percent. German
Lutherans were the primary defectors. Since they are generally members of
the Lutheran Church-Missouri Synod or the Wisconsin Evangelical Lutheran
Synod, the "family/morality" issue may have played a role. Then, too, these
voters have historically favored "anti-war" candidates such as LaFollette in
1924 and Wilkie in 1940. They went heavily for Nixon in 1968, hoping he
would end the Vietnam War. When he did not, there was a mild McGovern
trend in 1972 in these counties. Carter did better than Democrats usually do
in 1976. But he fell short in 1980, which suggests that the war/peace issue or
the Carter campaign attempt to depict Reagan as a "mad bomber" backfired
and offended these voters. (Many voters in every category felt this way. The
ABC exit poll found that 40 percent of all voters said "Carter's campaign tactics were unfair." Of these, 85 percent voted for Reagan.)

German Catholics, as we have already noted, vote much like German
Lutherans. The war/peace issue backfired in places like Emmons County,
North Dakota, where German Catholics gave Carter 52 percent in 1976 and
17 percent in 1980.

The Lutheran swing to Reagan was not confined to Lutherans of German
descent or to the Midwest. Lutherans of Scandinavian descent gave Carter
the worst vote for a Democrat since Al Smith in 1928. Reagan won a clear
majority, though Anderson's Swedish background helped him win a higher
percentage of Lutheran votes than he won among any other Protestant sub-

group. But far away from the Midwest Lutherans defected from Carter. One has only to look at the Reagan landslides in Lexington County, South Carolina; Rowan County, North Carolina; and Shenandoah County, Virginia, to see that.

Finally, Carter's decline among Southern Baptists, from 58 percent of the vote in 1976 to 40 percent in 1980, was the most significant clue to the surprise Reagan victory in Alabama, Mississippi, Tennessee, Arkansas, and the Carolinas. It contributed to the Reagan win in Missouri and Kentucky. The ABC key precinct data found that, in every Deep South state, the white Baptist swing to Reagan was the highest for any voting group.

It was particularly pronounced in the suburbs and cities of the region, which cost Carter such 1976 strongholds as Jacksonville, Panama City, and Lakeland in Florida; Spartanburg, South Carolina; Greensboro, North Carolina; and Hot Springs, Arkansas.

In addition, about three dozen Baptist "Mountain Republican" counties in Virginia, West Virginia, Tennessee, Arkansas, Alabama, and Georgia trended sharply to Reagan. In 1976 Carter had won a record vote for a Democrat in these historic GOP bailiwicks, even carrying a few of them. He ran stronger than LBJ or FDR. But in 1980 they returned to the GOP banner in a landslide. What was considered a possible realignment in 1976 must now be viewed as an aberration.

The so-called evangelical vote—which includes Baptists, but also includes millions of Christians of other denominations—has always been more difficult to analyze because of the difficulty in precisely defining "evangelical." Nevertheless, there are key counties and precincts that have significant numbers of evangelical or born-again voters. They are less Democratic than Baptists and gave the edge to Ford in 1976, though estimates vary as to what extent. I estimated a 60 percent–40 percent edge for Ford among all evangelicals in 1976, though my estimate may have been a little high on the Ford side. In 1980 CBS included "born again white Protestants" in its religious category and found that 17 percent of all voters classified themselves in this way. These voters chose Reagan by 62 percent–34 percent over Carter, with only 4 percent for Anderson. They were split roughly 50-50 in 1976, so a part of Carter's 1976 coalition slipped away from him when he lost an additional sixth of the born again voters. The shift of some born-again voters to Reagan in southern Ohio, central Pennsylvania, southern Illinois, Indiana, Iowa, Kansas, and throughout the South helped to doom Mr. Carter's chances of a second term.

Among all Protestant voters nationwide ABC showed a 59 percent–33 percent victory for Reagan, while CBS showed a 56 percent–37 percent Reagan lead. Compared to 1976 this represented a decline of 9 percent–14 percent for Carter.

The only group to resist the trend to Reagan somewhat were the "Yankee" Protestants, who can be described as nonevangelical and moderate to liberal in theology but historically supportive of the GOP. Unlike many other religious groups, they have trended Democratic since the 1960s and gave Humphrey, McGovern, and Carter a higher percentage of their votes than they gave FDR, Kennedy, and Truman. In 1980 Anderson polled 10 percent–15 percent in most Yankee Protestant counties, while Carter declined and Reagan ran about even with Ford.

The final segment of the population, religiously speaking, is the 10 percent–12 percent of the electorate that indicates no religious affiliation. In 1976 they favored Carter 59 percent–41 percent, but in 1980 there was a significant swing to John Anderson. ABC found that Carter and Reagan both won 39 percent while Anderson took 17 percent. To a large extent Anderson ran as the anti–clergy-in-politics candidate. His attacks on Boston's Cardinal Humberto Medeiros, Jerry Falwell, and other clerical politicians probably gained him support among voters without religious affiliation.

To what extent was religion a factor in the election, and how important were such issues as abortion, parochiaid, school prayer, gay rights, and a host of other borderline issues?

The ABC exit poll found that 8 percent of the voters were concerned enough about the abortion issue to cast a presidential vote primarily on this issue, and yet the poll did not separate the antis from the pros and the results tended to indicate that the two extremes cancelled one another out. Of this 8 percent constituency who felt strongly about abortion, ABC found, 52 percent voted for Reagan, 35 percent for Carter, 11 percent for Anderson. The CBS/New York Times survey got a different result. When asked, "Which issue was the most important in determining your vote?" the Equal Rights Amendment and abortion issues (lumped together as "ERA/abortion") rated most important with 8 percent of Carter voters, but only 5 percent of Reagan voters. Apparently the abortion issue had little effect upon the election, though it did bring Anderson some votes. Certain groups in the population that are said to be more heavily pro-choice than others, such as the affluent, the young, the well educated, gave Anderson 10 percent–15 percent of their votes.

Economic and foreign policy issues clearly overshadowed the sociocultural or religious issues in this campaign. But religious influences on voting are often subconscious and difficult to interpret precisely.

We do not yet know much about the increase in registration and voter turnout. Certainly the evangelical and fundamentalist New Right are largely responsible for the increase in voter turnout in a number of Southern states, and though we do not have detailed county data as yet, it can be assumed that Governor Reagan at least profited from some of it. In Virginia, for example, the vote increased 150,000 over 1976 and Reagan defeated Carter by 230,000 votes. In Louisiana the vote increased 250,000 and Reagan won by 90,000. In Tennessee the vote increased over 140,000 and Reagan won by 5,000, and so on. In a few states the Moral Majority and allied groups can claim some credit for influencing elections, surely in the U.S. Senate races where they backed conservative Catholic Republicans Jeremiah Denton in Alabama and Don Nickles in Oklahoma. Both Republicans were underdogs but won impressive victories, and, in Denton's case, he ran a bit ahead of the Reagan presidential ticket. But there was also an increase in the black vote in the South, which went overwhelmingly for Carter.

It would appear that economic and foreign policy concerns overshadowed any of the distinctive "family/morality" issues that dominated the campaigns waged by independent political action groups. It is possible that a segment of the Catholic community moved to Reagan because he was perceived as more sympathetic to two of the issues on the "official" Catholic Church agenda: tuition tax credits and a constitutional amendment restricting abortion. The election was the fourth straight time that the Republican platform and campaign sought to dislodge normally Democratic Catholic votes, and the strategy may have added to the Reagan vote. Jewish voters may have perceived Reagan as the better candidate to preserve and strengthen both Israel and U.S. national security. Some evangelicals, according to the respected *Washington World and Religion Report*, were upset at Carter's apparent ignoring of their concerns and failure to appoint a single "known" evangelical to any cabinet position. Others felt that a Reagan Administration would be more open to evangelical influence. Many conservative evangelicals were displeased with the Democratic platform positions on abortion and homosexual rights.

There were seventeen states that supported Jimmy Carter in 1976 but switched to Ronald Reagan in 1980. Nine were in the South, where the electoral vote impact was the greatest, and the symbolism most poignant, since that region rejected its native son's bid for a second term. Three were Border states (Missouri, Kentucky, and Delaware), while the others were Ohio, Pennsylvania, New York, Massachusetts, and Wisconsin.

The election returns show that the shift of white Baptists to Reagan was the single most significant factor in Reagan's victory in Alabama, Florida, Georgia, Kentucky, Mississippi, Missouri, North Carolina, Oklahoma, South Carolina, Tennessee, and Texas. In all of these states, Carter's losses among Baptists, especially in rural areas, exceeded his statewide loss. In the Caroli-

Table 5.2

Baptist Voting Behavior, 1980

State	Rural Baptists	% Reagan Gain 1980 Urban Baptists	Statewide
AL	13.3	3.7	7.4
FL	17.3		11.8
GA	15.0		9.2
KY	8.5		4.5
LA	7.8	4.2	5.8
MS	3.6		1.7
NC	7.8	7.5	6.7
OK	17.8		12.8
SC	6.3	8.4	7.3
TN	10.9		6.7
TX	14.3	8.3	8.8

nas Carter lost and Reagan gained as much among urban Baptists as among rural Baptists. (See table 5.2.)

In Ohio rural Protestant evangelical gains for Reagan were higher than for any other religious group, with Catholics close behind.

In Delaware rural Methodists gave Reagan a 6–7 point gain, which contributed greatly to his victory.

In Florida, the Jewish and Catholic swing to Reagan was almost as great as the Baptist shift, but Baptists were still most responsible for Reagan's win there.

In Louisiana, Wisconsin, and Massachusetts, the Catholic swing to Reagan was greater than the Protestant swing. In New York the Jewish vote shift to Reagan was responsible for his surprise victory in the Empire State. Catholics and Protestants gave Reagan modest gains in New York City and its suburbs, but upstate Catholics and Protestants gave Carter greater support in 1980 than in 1976, one of the year's anomalies.

In Pennsylvania Jews in Philadelphia gave Reagan a 14-point gain, though Reagan gains were smaller among Jewish voters in Pittsburgh and the Philadelphia suburbs. The gain for Reagan was 8 points among Catholics and 7 points among conservative Protestants. So Pennsylvania remains the one state where no one group can be credited with the Reagan victory.

Thus, Baptists and evangelicals were the major factor in twelve of the seventeen states that switched from Carter to Reagan. Catholic voters were largely responsible for the shift in three states, and Jews in one state.

1984

Most polling places in Tulsa, Oklahoma, closed at 7:00 P.M. on November 6, but the precinct near Oral Roberts University (ORU) did not. Lines of voters were still waiting to cast their ballots. Over an hour and a half passed before they finished.

When the votes were counted, more than twice as many people had trooped to the polls than did so in 1980. If GOP registrars had been led to "expect a miracle" at the faith-healing campus, they weren't disappointed. Of the 2,000 votes cast, a phenomenal 92 percent went for Republican Ronald Reagan.

The students at fundamentalist ORU had no doubts about whom they preferred for president and they didn't mind witnessing to it in the voting booth.

The election returns brought "real joy" to the campus, according to Victor Smith, vice president for graduate affairs and himself a second-year law student. He said his fellow students believe the GOP "best reflects their Christian values and beliefs."

The ORU vote is but one example of Ronald Reagan's triumph with an important new electoral constituency, the Christian Right. The Republican candidate's forty-nine-state landslide majority clearly was shaped by the 80 percent support given to him by "white, born-again Christians."

A CBS News survey indicated that Reagan won this segment of the electorate by some eight million votes, a total that represented nearly half of his 17-million vote majority.

The Republican standard-bearer gained almost 20 percentage points over his 1980 showing with these conservative Protestants. What this means in hard political terms is that Walter Mondale was simply out of the running throughout the South, Border states, and parts of the Midwest where evangelicals and other conservative Protestants predominate.

Of 114 representative evangelical counties in states from Colorado to North Carolina, Mondale carried only 9. In contrast, born-again Baptist Jimmy Carter won 54 of these counties in 1976 (though his total fell to 16 in 1980 as evangelicals became disenchanted with one of their own).

Mondale's showing among Southern Baptists, a key element of the conservative Protestant constituency, was nothing short of disastrous. Of 96 representative Southern Baptist counties in rural and small-town areas, Mondale carried only 7. Carter had picked up 80 of these in 1976, hanging on to 49 in 1980.

In the Southern Baptist suburbs and cities Mondale did even worse. Baptist strongholds that stuck with Carter in 1980—Nashville, Tennessee; Colum-

Table 5.3

Baptist Voting Behavior, 1984

State	Rural Baptist	% Reagan Gain 1984 Urban Baptist	Statewide
AL	15.3	8.6	10.6
FL	22.9		6.2
GA	23.5		17.9
KY	11.5		9.6
LA	15.1	6.9	8.6
MS	17.9		11.6
NC	9.4	13.8	10.9
OK	7.8		5.7
SC	18.9	17.2	13.4
TN	3.7		8.1
TX	11.0	9.0	6.6

bus, Georgia; Muskogee, Oklahoma—went to Reagan. While the Plains Sunday school teacher may have held 40 percent of the white Baptist voters in his last campaign, Mondale probably held less than one fourth. (See table 5.3.)

Southern Baptist church colleges were Reagan hotbeds. Students at Baylor University in Waco, Texas, gave more than 82 percent of their vote to the Republican candidate, up from about two thirds last time. Students at Georgetown College in Kentucky went two to one for Reagan, though they had gone four to three for Carter four years ago. (Only the Southern Baptist Seminary in Louisville, Kentucky, resisted the Reagan tide. A seminary-dominated voting precinct gave Mondale 62 percent of its vote, down only slightly from the 69 percent given co-religionist Jimmy Carter.)

Many evangelical colleges were even more one-sided than Southern Baptist schools. Reagan won 90 percent of the vote at Abilene Christian College, a Church of Christ school in Texas.

The Republican candidate netted 82 percent of the vote at Evangel College, an Assemblies of God school in Springfield, Missouri. The vote is a dramatic shift from 1980 when Carter won 44 percent.

How much of the evangelical swing to Reagan was due to the religious and social issue agenda—school prayer, abortion, and "lifestyle" concerns— and how much was due to the economy and national defense will never really be known for sure. Economic issues, according to exit polls by the television networks, seemed to overshadow the religious concerns, but Reagan's religious rhetoric and repeated appearances before evangelical audiences must have had some effect.

The Rev. Jerry Falwell's Moral Majority and other fundamentalist/evangelical political groups made every effort to portray Reagan as a defender of traditional Judeo-Christian values, while the Democrats were depicted as agents of "secular humanism," the sinister cabal supposedly ruining America.

The Presidential Biblical Scorecard, distributed to fundamentalist churches across the country, described Walter Mondale's religion as "Humanist/Presbyterian" and assailed his views on church-state separation and other political concerns. By contrast, Reagan was quoted as saying he had "an experience that could be described as 'born again.'" His views on tuition tax credits, school prayer, abortion, and other issues were praised as "Biblical."

This fervent support for Reagan among fundamentalists remained unchanged even though the candidate became something of a backslider late in the race and tried to play down his religious agenda. During his debate with Mondale, for instance, Reagan disavowed his much-touted "born again" status.

In answer to a question about his faith, the Republican candidate said, "Well, I was raised to have a faith and a belief, and have been a member of a church since I was a small boy. In our particular church we did not use that term, 'born again,' so I don't know whether I would fit that, that particular term. But I have, thanks to my mother—God rest her soul—the firmest possible belief and faith in God."

Reagan's affirmation was no more evangelical than Mondale's. (The Democrat said, "I don't know if I've been born again, but I know I was born into a Christian family.")

Reagan also denied during the debate that he believed in the imminent fulfillment of the biblical prophecies of Armageddon. Despite his sympathetic discussions with fundamentalists preachers about these final-battle theories, Reagan said "no one knows whether those prophecies mean that Armageddon is 1,000 years away or the day after tomorrow. So I have never seriously warned or said we must plan according to Armageddon."

Unconvinced, more than a hundred religious leaders, including Roman Catholic Bishop Thomas Gumbleton, held a press conference a few days later to ask Reagan to repudiate his previously expressed view that a nuclear Armageddon may be at hand. The church coalition said it is "disturbing that any political leaders—especially leaders with the responsibility for decisions affecting war and peace—might identify themselves with extremists who believe that nuclear Armageddon is inevitable and imminent."

In the waning days of the campaign, Reagan even distanced himself from fundamentalist supporters Tim LaHaye and Jimmy Swaggart. In an interview with the Catholic weekly, *Our Sunday Visitor,* the Republican candidate was asked why he did not disassociate himself from such men who have attacked Catholicism as a "false religion."

Reagan responded, "While I have not seen such direct quotes from these individuals, I would certainly disassociate myself from any views such as you've described. Criticism by one person of another's religious beliefs is totally improper and should never be condoned. I can tell you there is no room in our party or our nation for religious intolerance or bigotry of any kind, and I repudiate anyone claiming to be a supporter of mine who engages in that."

If this repudiation of fundamentalist doctrine had any effect on fundamentalist support for Reagan, the returns didn't show it. Perhaps the comment, published in a Catholic newspaper, did not receive any distribution in fundamentalist circles. Or perhaps fundamentalist leaders intentionally ignored it.

During the heat of the presidential campaign when Reagan was under fire for his close ties to fundamentalists, Jerry Falwell urged Reagan to ignore his Christian Right friends for the remainder of the race. We know you're with us, Falwell told Reagan, so shore up other constituencies.

On election night, the Lynchburg evangelist was jubilant. "Praise the Lord," he exulted. "We're very happy. For the first time, religious conservatives and political conservatives have joined forces. Come 1988, we'll be back stronger than ever."

Commenting on the devotion of his fundamentalist forces, Falwell said, "If the snow's up to their hips, they'd have gone to vote, because they're committed."

Though Ronald Reagan may not have commanded that kind of revivalist fervor from Roman Catholic voters, his party's courtship of the nation's largest religious faith also paid off handsomely on November 6. By a 56 percent to 44 percent margin, Catholics favored the Republican candidate. The figure represents a modest gain over Reagan's 1980 total.

But Democratic party leaders had to face the fact that the once solidly Democratic Catholic community voted Republican in three of the last four presidential races.

Regional, cultural, and ethnic factors shaped the Catholic vote. Catholics of Italian, German, and Irish ancestry voted about 60 percent for Reagan, while those of Polish-Slavic descent dropped to the lower fifties.

Mondale swept Boston, but Catholic voters in Philadelphia, New York, and Chicago gave a slight edge to Reagan.

Hispanic Catholic voting varied according to region. Mondale won by two to one among Hispanics in California, and did even better in Texas. He even ran ahead of the Carter totals in parts of Colorado and New Mexico.

But Reagan cut into the Hispanic Catholic constituency enough to carry the Texas cities of Corpus Christi and San Antonio. And the Cuban-Americans of Miami, Florida, gave the Republican a phenomenal 90 percent of their vote.

Even in Mondale's home state of Minnesota, Catholics moved into the Republican column in large numbers. Only in St. Paul did Catholic voters break two to one for Mondale, indicating perhaps a rural/urban split in the Catholic community there.

Public opinion polls across the country indicate that most Catholic voters, like other voting blocs, favored Reagan's reelection drive for nonreligious reasons. The improving economy, the nation's stronger international posture, and that undefined quality "leadership" seemed to move most of those at the polls.

A Harris poll in late September found that Catholics by a two-to-one margin oppose political activity by Catholic bishops and Moral Majority preachers on such issues as school prayer and abortion. By a 69 percent–23 percent margin, Catholics disagreed with new York Archbishop John O'Connor for urging Catholics to vote for antiabortion candidates. A Bannon poll of Massachusetts Catholics showed church members supporting the pro-choice position by 61 percent–30 percent.

Still, the constant Republican wooing of the Catholic community must have made it much easier for some Catholics to break with their traditional Democratic allegiance and vote for Reagan and George Bush. Reagan met with Pope John Paul II, spoke of him often, and became the first president to send a U.S. ambassador to the Holy See. Reagan also curried favor with U.S. bishops, pushing for tuition tax credits and other government aid to parochial schools and favoring an abortion ban.

In the concluding month of the campaign, the Reagan-Bush camp ran advertisements in over two dozen Catholic diocesan newspapers. The ads included a large picture of Reagan shaking hands with John Paul II and cited the candidate's support for tuition tax credits, an abortion ban, anti-pornography laws, and school prayer.

Many Catholic papers refused the campaign message because editors thought the photo exploited the pope politically. But a highly placed Vatican official assured Americans that the ad raised no problems.

In what amounted to an endorsement of Reagan, Archbishop John Foley, head of the Vatican office for social communications, said, "While it would be unfortunate and unfair for any political leader to exploit the connection with a public figure, especially a religious figure, with whose goals he or she would be unsympathetic, it is not surprising that a political leader will emphasize a connection with a popular public figure with whose ideas and ideals he or she is in fundamental agreement."

Ironically, the Catholic vote for the Mondale-Ferraro ticket seemed to increase in areas where the Catholic bishops tried to make abortion the central issue. In Iowa, for instance, where the state's hierarchy has repeatedly tried to force Catholics to vote for antiabortion politicians, the Democrats ran stronger this time than in 1980. Mondale carried heavily Catholic Dubuque by 2,600 votes, compared to Carter's 39-vote margin.

But the harassment of Catholic vice-presidential candidate Geraldine Ferraro on the abortion issue clearly helped detract from positive effects an urban Catholic running mate might have had on the Democratic ticket. Archbishop O'Connor and several others in the hierarchy never relented in their criticism.

On the other hand, Detroit Bishop Gumbleton and two dozen other bishops urged Catholics to give greater consideration to the nuclear arms race as a "pro-life" issue. And Cardinal Joseph Bernardin of Chicago opposed "single-issue" politics, in favor of a "consistent ethic" of life issues. But their moderating rhetoric failed to remove the religious cloud hovering over Ferraro.

For her part, the Democratic vice-presidential candidate never wavered in her support for church-state separation.

The three-term congresswoman vowed to quit public office if her public duty ever conflicted with her religious beliefs. Asked what that meant, Ferraro explained, "If my church were to say to me, 'Because you are not supporting our position on, say abortion, we will remove you, we will excommunicate you,' I'd quit my job."

The statement went unchallenged in the news media. Catholic officials said formal excommunication is extremely rare, and almost never results from disagreement with church teaching on a moral question. Some observers, however, thought Ferraro's position raised as many questions as it answered. Such statements at the least resurrected old Protestant concerns about the independence of Catholic officeholders from the church hierarchy. Did Ferraro really mean to imply that she would grant the church hierarchy the power to decide whether she remained in public office?

Though fundamentalists and Catholics moved to Reagan, there was one gaping hole in the patchwork of religious groups supporting the reelection of the president. Jewish voters turned overwhelmingly against the nationwide tide, and actually gave Mondale a landslide vote of 70 percent. That's nearly 25 percentage points better than President Carter did among Jews in 1980.

The most logical explanation for this dramatic shift seemed to be President Reagan's alliance with fundamentalist Christians and his emphasis on religious issues like school prayer. Jews have been persecuted by majority religions throughout history, and they know, probably better than most religious groups in America, the importance of the separation of church and state.

Jews have historically voted Democratic, and when Reagan won 40 percent of the Jewish vote in 1980, that was considered a strong showing for a Republican. But the fact that Mondale did so much better than Carter did, in spite of all the trends in Reagan's favor, indicates that the church-state debate disturbed Jewish voters. One election-day poll by the American Jewish Committee said three-fourths of Jewish voters who switched from Reagan in 1980 to Mondale in 1984 cited church-state separation as the reason for their change.

Besides Jews, the only other voters that seemed to move toward the Democrats this year were the "unchurched," or those not affiliated with any religious group. They awarded Mondale about 15 percent more than they gave Carter in 1980. The unchurched gave Reagan about 6 percent more this year than in 1980, when John Anderson drew almost 20 percent of their vote. (This group is hard to locate and define precisely, and its impact on the election seems to have been minimal. In states where church attendance and membership are low—Nevada, Oregon, Washington, Colorado, West Virginia—there was no significant loss of support for Reagan. He carried those states with ease.)

For the most part, candidate Reagan did not suffer for all his controversial religious appeals over the previous four years. He may have offended Jews and the unchurched, but the vast majority of religious voters still supported him strongly, either because of—or in spite of—his religious crusade.

Many Presbyterians, Episcopalians, Methodists, and other voters who have long supported the Republican party, but who were thought by some observers to be unhappy with the Reagan administration's social and religious policies, gave him overwhelming support. Reagan improved on his 1980 showing among mainline Protestants, drawing almost 65 percent of their votes. In Yankee Protestant towns throughout New England and in midwestern and far western counties settled by New England Protestants, Reagan had little problem winning 3 to 2 or 2 to 1 margins. Lutheran voters, concentrated in the Midwest and mostly middle income, have occasionally voted Democratic, but gave Reagan comfortable majorities that year as well as in 1980.

Seventh-day Adventist voters, who might have been expected to register dissent from Reagan's policies on church and state, especially the ambassadorship to the Vatican, stuck with the president. Reagan piled up 75 percent of the vote in Loma Linda, California; 78 percent in College Place, Washington; 71 percent in Berrien Springs, Michigan; and 78 percent in Keene, Texas—all identifiable Adventist communities. In each instance, Reagan improved his showing over 1980.

Similarly, Reagan still won a 3 to 2 majority at Principia College in Elsah, Illinois, the nation's only Christian Science college.

Other traditionally Republican religious groups remained firmly committed to the Reagan candidacy. Heavily Mormon counties in Utah gave 85 percent to 90 percent of the vote to Reagan. The counties surrounding Brigham Young University voted five to one for the president. Dutch Reformed towns in Iowa and Michigan gave Reagan a whopping 80 percent of the vote.

Despite the Reagan landslide, the president did not find his religious agenda any easier to press in Congress. All nine incumbent senators—five Democrats and four Republicans—who voted against Reagan's school prayer amendment were returned to office.

The one big victory for the Christian Right came in North Carolina, where Sen. Jesse Helms survived a strong challenge from Gov. Jim Hunt. Religion was a major factor in the campaign—Jerry Falwell was one of Helms's biggest boosters—and a massive effort was made to register fundamentalist voters. Helms painted himself as "the Christian candidate" and claimed his victory was "a signal through the world that North Carolina is a conservative, God-fearing state . . . a state where people believe in school prayer and they want to restore it."[4]

Helms also promised to work hard for tougher restrictions on abortion.

Helms won with just 52.6 percent of the vote, and many analysts credited his victory to Reagan's coattails and strong support by Jerry Falwell. Reagan and Falwell also proved helpful to several Moral Majority–backed candidates for the House of Representatives in North Carolina and Texas.

Elsewhere, however, Reagan and Falwell came up short.

In Virginia's Sixth Congressional District, where Falwell's headquarters is located, the Moral Majority–backed candidate was defeated by a moderate Democrat and Unitarian, James Olin. Garland even trailed in the city of Lynchburg, despite Falwell's endorsement. After the election, Falwell denied that Garland's loss was a loss for him. He claimed that he had only spoken in favor of Garland publicly. Because he had not traveled the district for Garland as he had for Helms in North Carolina, Falwell said he took no responsibility for Garland's defeat. Garland's advertisements and campaign literature, however, emphasized his connection to Falwell.

In California, John Paul Stark used the Campus Crusade for Christ as his political base in an attempt to defeat liberal Democrat George E. Brown for Congress. But Brown countered Stark's appeal with the Campus Crusade and other fundamentalists by making the rounds of mainline churches in the district and emphasizing the social gospel. Brown won.

The Jewish vote seemed particularly important in Illinois, where incumbent Sen. Charles Percy, a Republican, offended Jewish constituents by his support for school prayer. (Faced with a right-wing primary opponent, Percy even flew back to Washington from campaigning to vote for the Reagan school prayer measure.) When asked at a candidates' forum if a prayer amendment would put pressure on Jews and other minority religions, Percy said, "Yes, it does, but they might as well, I suppose, live in the real world."[5]

Percy received hisses from the predominantly Jewish audience, and his opponent, Rep. Paul Simon, quickly accused him of insensitivity. Simon won the race, 51 percent to 49 percent, with strong Jewish support.

In Michigan, a Republican congressman raised the religious issue against a Jewish Democrat, urging pastors in a letter to "send another Christian to Congress." Rep. Mark D. Siljander wrote letters to fundamentalist ministers opposing the reelection of the Democratic incumbent, Rep. Howard E. Wolpe, from his neighboring district.

In his letter, Siljander said the election of "liberals like Howard Wolpe" was one reason "the minority viewpoint of evolution is taught to our children in the public schools." By defeating Wolpe, fundamentalist voters could help return creationism to public school classrooms.

Wolpe, who pointed out that creationism had not been discussed in the campaign, said he believed he was singled out because he was Jewish. "I didn't know religious tests were part of running for office."[6] Despite the religious issue, Wolpe won reelection.

In Tennessee, Christian Right alchemist Ed McAteer struck out badly in his independent run for the Senate slot left vacant by retiring majority leader Howard Baker. Showing surprising political naivete, the former Religious Roundtable chief drew far-right support away from the Republican candidate. Democrat Albert Gore won easily.

McAteer, a member of the Rev. Adrian Rogers's Belleview Baptist Church, won his pastor's endorsement, but only 5 percent of the vote. Rogers, a former president of the Southern Baptist Convention, was a leading light of the fundamentalist bloc that has pressed for the Christian Right agenda both within his denomination and in Congress.

Moral Majority activists were disappointed in Alabama, where incumbent Democrat Howell Heflin easily defeated Christian Right activist Albert Lee Smith, a former congressman.

The evangelical realignment toward the Democrats in 1976 and then toward the Republicans in 1980 and 1984 can be seen by looking at those states that experienced the greatest change in their voting patterns between elections.

In 1976 all ten states where Jimmy Carter made the strongest gains in voter support compared to George McGovern were in the evangelical base region. All were Deep South, except for Oklahoma, and Baptists were influential in all of them. A combination of Southern pride and Baptist voting strength clearly impacted favorably on the Carter vote.

In 1980 the pattern was not quite so clear, since only five of the ten states where Ronald Reagan received his greatest increase in support compared to Gerald Ford were in the evangelical South (Arkansas, Florida, Georgia, Oklahoma, and Texas). The two Mormon strongholds of Utah and Idaho ranked fifth and tenth respectively. Joining them were North and South Dakota, both Lutheran and Catholic in character. The Dakotas are below average in evangelical strength, but they are relatively conservative states. Nevada, the least formally religious state, recorded Reagan's third highest rise in voter support, showing that Reagan appealed to both religious conservatives and Western libertarians.

In 1984 nine of the ten states where Reagan's support increased the most over 1980 were evangelical and Southern, including the Border states of Kentucky and Delaware. Without Carter at the head of the ticket, the Democratic vote plummeted. The only nonevangelical state on Reagan's top ten was Maine, which remained something of an anomaly. Economic factors were paramount in Maine, and, though the Down East state may be the most conservative and Protestant state in New England, it is far less so than states in the South and Midwest.

Arkansas and Georgia were the only states that appeared on the top ten swing states in all three elections. Arkansas had the second highest gain for Carter in 1976 but four years later recorded the highest decline in Carter support and increase in Reagan support in the nation. In 1984 it had the fourth greatest increase in Reagan strength. Georgia responded largely to the candidacy of its former governor, giving him an incredible 42-point gain over McGovern in 1976. Without Carter in 1984, the Mondale vote collapsed, and Reagan's greatest national gain was recorded in the Peach State. But even with Carter running for reelection in 1980, Georgia gave Reagan his eighth highest gain.

The evangelical states were pacesetters in the national voter shifts during the Carter-Reagan terms of office. In 1976 Carter's gains over McGovern exceeded his national gain in every evangelical state except Indiana. In 1980 Reagan's gains were greater than his national increase in every evangelical state except Delaware, Maryland, and Mississippi. In 1984 his national percentage gain in voter support was exceeded in all the evangelical states except Indiana and Kansas. The below-average voter changes in Indiana are probably due to that state's great political stability. (See table 5.4.)

Table 5.4

Evangelicals and Political Realignments, 1976–1984
Ten States Where Carter and Reagan Made
Their Greatest Gains in Voter Support

Rank	Carter 1976	Reagan 1980	Reagan 1984
1	GA	AR	GA
2	AR	ND	SC
3	MS	NV	MS
4	AL	OK	AR
5	SC	UT	NC
6	NC	SD	AL
7	TN	FL	KY
8	FL	GA	ME
9	OK	TX	DE
10	LA	ID	LA

1988

Republican George Bush won the presidential election with the votes of about 80 percent of born-again white Protestants, according to ABC and CBS News exit polling data. He won 60 percent of the mainline Protestants, but failed to win among other religious groups.

The Catholic vote was more divided than in any election since 1956, but Democrat Michael S. Dukakis appeared to have won 52 percent to 54 percent of the strategically important Catholic bloc. The CBS exit poll showed a slight majority for Bush among Catholics, but a survey of more than 100 heavily Catholic counties showed that Dukakis won more than 60 of them.

While Bush's Catholic support was impressive, he ran about 8 to 10 percentage points behind President Reagan's 1984 support.

Dukakis won 71 percent of Jewish votes and about two-thirds of those of other religions and those who said they were not members of a particular church.

Bush's landslide among evangelical Protestants kept Ohio, Pennsylvania, Illinois, and Missouri in the Republican column. It also accounted for his strong showing in the South.

Mainline Protestants, who made up about 35 percent of all voters, went for Bush by a 3-to-2 ratio. This showing was instrumental in the Republican ticket's victory in states such as Indiana, Connecticut, Vermont, and Michigan.

The Catholic vote, which was about 30 percent of the electorate, was something of a surprise. Dukakis won a majority among Catholics everywhere except the South.

The Catholic vote contributed to Dukakis's victories in Wisconsin, New York, Massachusetts, and Rhode Island and to his close showing in Pennsylvania, New Mexico, Illinois, and Connecticut.

In some respects the Catholic vote for Dukakis was impressive because the Bush campaign had engaged in an elaborate and well-organized effort to win these votes. Bush campaigned heavily in Catholic areas, appeared at three Catholic schools, attended mass with Philadelphia's retired Cardinal John Kroll, and spoke at a rally at the University of Notre Dame on All Saints' Day.

The Dukakis-Bentsen ticket did well among those outside the white Christian mainstream. But there remains a solid core of about 30 percent of Jews who have supported Republican candidates since President Nixon ran for reelection in 1972.

The 8 percent of the electorate that has no religious affiliation and the 6 percent that adheres to other religions went better than 2 to 1 for Dukakis. This may have been the key to the Massachusetts governor's victories in Washington State, Oregon, and Hawaii.

The election results indicate that the gap between Protestant and Catholic voting preferences had widened. Although Catholics now have a higher income and education than Protestants, they were 13 percent less likely to vote for Bush, a difference that resembles the Eisenhower and Nixon eras rather than the Ford and Reagan elections. The Dukakis candidacy struck a responsive chord with the social justice tradition among Catholic voters.

The longstanding marriage of white Protestants to the GOP has endured. It may be significant that Bush and Vice President-elect Dan Quayle were the most quintessentially white Protestant candidates since Herbert Hoover was elected president in 1928—ironically, the last time the Republicans won three straight elections.

Evangelicals seem to be less willing to vote for candidates outside that religious tradition. Dukakis's multicultural image—a Greek Orthodox Christian who attended a Quaker college and married a Jew in a Unitarian ceremony—may have appealed to religious liberals, but it turned off evangelicals.

The 1988 American National Election Study found that 70 percent of all evangelicals voted for Bush. (This is lower than the 80 percent reported by the CBS–*New York Times* poll, but that poll defined evangelicals so narrowly that only 9 percent of voters placed themselves in the category. The CBS poll was probably restricted to fundamentalists, who are generally to the right of evangelicals.)

There were some denominational variances in the National Election Study, ranging from 80 percent support for Bush among the Dutch Reformed voters to 61 percent among those belonging to the Church of Christ. This reflects the traditional GOP/Democratic cleavage between these two groups. The nondenominational evangelicals, who often attend large megachurches or Bible churches, gave Bush 76 percent, and the independent Baptists gave Bush 75 percent. The Southern Baptist support level for Bush was 68 percent, while Pentecostals gave the president 65 percent. (Mainline Protestants gave 64 percent of their ballots to Bush. This was the second straight election in which evangelicals exceeded mainliners in their support for a Republican presidential candidate.)[7]

Denominational differences also appeared in the Republican presidential primaries in the spring of 1988. Pat Robertson received the support of 23 percent of the evangelicals but only 4 percent of mainline Protestants on the all-important "Super Tuesday" primaries, where evangelicals cast 40 percent–50 percent of the total vote. Even among evangelicals, Bush beat Robertson better than 2 to 1, winning 48 percent. Bob Dole did better among mainline Protestants, receiving 29 percent of their support compared to 16 percent of evangelicals.[8] Three sociologists from Ball State University studied the support for Pat Robertson's presidential candidacy in Muncie, Indiana. They found that his support "came from those who watched the '700 Club,' who were social traditionalists or political conservatives, and who were less well educated."[9] Their interpretation minimized the religious factor somewhat, concluding, "The Christian Right, in general, and Pat Robertson, in particular, have not won widespread support for significant cultural and structural reasons. By and large, Americans do not want as public officials the kind of person who epitomizes Christian Right values and attitudes."[10]

A study of the 1988 Republican primary in South Carolina found that Pat Robertson polled much higher among his fellow charismatics and Pentecostals than he did among mainstream evangelicals and Baptists. He had virtually no support among nonevangelical Protestants, Catholics, or Jews.

At the state party convention, Robertson's delegates were religiously distinct: 61 percent were charismatic in theology, 35 percent were members of nondenominational churches, and 18 percent were members of pentecostal churches.[11]

Robertson's third-place finish in religiously conservative South Carolina essentially ended his quixotic campaign. He only secured 19 percent of the primary vote, while Dole won 21 percent and Bush won a commanding 49 percent. Robertson did best in Spartanburg and Greenville, both fundamentalist bastions, and in Oconee County, a Blue Ridge Mountain area in the state's far northwest corner.

In the 1988 general election, Michael Dukakis's secularity, his Greek Orthodox cultural and religious background, and his wife's Judaism were distinct disadvantages in evangelical America. H. J. Bissinger, a Pulitzer Prize–winning investigative reporter for the *Chicago Tribune*, spent 1988 reporting on life in the West Texas towns of Midland and Odessa. His book *Friday Night Lights* has become a classic of contemporary reportage, and though it concentrates mainly on the region's obsession with sports, primarily Friday night high school football, it includes much pungent social and political commentary.

Bissinger described the local Religious Right, a group called Odessans for Decency, which lobbied for school prayer and promised to obliterate abortion, pornography, and homosexuality. The group evolved into the Christian Voting Bloc, an organization dedicated to electing only candidates who espoused Christian values. The leader, Joe Seay, sent out endorsements of approved candidates and took credit for driving an adult bookstore out of Odessa, preventing a cable television station from offering racy programs in the community, and stopping an Australian rock group from holding a concert in Odessa. The group praised a state district judge's decision in 1988 to give a murderer a light sentence because his victims were homosexuals.

Democratic presidential candidate Michael Dukakis became the brunt of local Christian Right antagonism. Writes Bissinger,

> As election day neared in Odessa, the antagonism toward Dukakis and all that he represented became more and more venomous. . . . During the election season a so-called Michael Dukakis fact sheet started making the rounds in Odessa. The pamphlet, drawn up by a group called the League of Prayer in Montgomery, Alabama, and handed out at a local doctor's office, brutally condemned Dukakis as a pro-choice, pro-homosexual advocate of sodomy who was soft on defense and soft on criminals and who sought "to rid America of its Godly heritage." The pamphlet described him as a "card-carrying member of the ACLU," which it said was the equivalent of being "against everything moral, ethical, righteous, holy, Christian, Godly and patriotic."[12]

George Bush was still a hero to West Texans even though, as Bissinger notes, "the economy of Midland-Odessa had fallen apart during the Reagan-Bush administration, and it was hard to think of any other single area of the country that had suffered as much."[13] A rise in unemployment and bankruptcies and a decline in oil prices made the economy awful, but conservative religious values kept the voters faithful to the GOP because, as Bissinger explains, "liberalism had come to be perceived not as a political belief but as something unpatriotic and anti-American, something that threatened the very soul of the hardworking whites who had built this country and made it great."[14]

Not surprisingly, Bush won 74 percent of the votes in the Midland-Odessa area, where 67 percent of adults are church members—well above the state and national average, according to the Glenmary study. About 54 percent of all adults are members of evangelical churches, and they cast their ballots for Bush.

1992

Issues involving church and state, religious freedom, conscience and values continued to play a role in the formation of public opinion and political party strategy. Both the 1992 candidates and the party platforms suggested strong differences of opinion on these issues, perhaps reflecting the constituencies within the parties and their perception of voter loyalties.

While domestic economic issues captured most of the attention of the Democratic platform, the party pledged itself to maintain abortion rights and to protect public education.

On abortion the platform proclaimed,

Choice. Democrats stand behind the right of every woman to choose, consistent with *Roe* v. *Wade,* regardless of ability to pay, and support a national law to protect that right. It is a fundamental constitutional liberty that individual Americans—not government—can best take responsibility for making the most difficult and intensely personal decisions regarding reproduction. The goal of our nation must be to make abortion less necessary, not more difficult or more dangerous. We pledge to support contraceptive research, family planning, comprehensive family life education, and policies that support healthy childbearing and enable parents to care most effectively for their children.

On a related issue the Democrats said, "Explosive population growth must be controlled by working closely with other industrialized and developing nations and private organizations to fund greater family-planning efforts."

On education, the Democrats said they "oppose the Bush Administration's efforts to bankrupt the public school system—the bedrock of democracy—through private school vouchers."[15]

Governor Bill Clinton, the Democratic nominee, was comfortable with these positions. In a major address to the National Education Association shortly before the July convention, Clinton told the nation's public school teachers that he was "unalterably opposed" to aiding private and parochial schools.

Both Clinton and his running mate, Tennessee Senator Al Gore, supported freedom of conscience on abortion, though their positions have evolved in recent years. Both Clinton, as governor of Arkansas, and Gore, while in the U.S. House and Senate, expressed reservations about federal funding of abortions under Medicaid and supported parental notification. Clinton supported amendments to an Arkansas law that made it easier to bypass parents and receive permission from a judge in certain cases. Both Clinton and Gore favored the inclusion of abortion services in any future national medical insurance programs, and Gore voted for Medicaid-funded abortions in 1988. Gore also said on June 16: "The decision to have an abortion is an intensely personal one, and I do not believe that the federal government should participate in the decision."

Both Clinton and Gore are Southern Baptists, which is the largest Protestant denomination in America. Both appear to identify with its moderate to liberal wing, as did former Presidents Jimmy Carter and Harry Truman. Clinton attended Immanuel Baptist Church in Little Rock, while his wife Hillary attended that city's First United Methodist Church. Clinton said his family's life had been enriched by attending different churches.

Clinton, a graduate of Georgetown University, won a Rhodes Scholarship to Oxford and received his law degree at Yale. Many of Georgetown's Jesuit professors remembered Clinton as a serious young man who thought about moral and ethical issues in public policy.

Gore attended Episcopal-related St. Alban's School and Harvard, where he serves as a member of the Board of Trustees. He studied theology at Vanderbilt while he was a reporter for a local newspaper.

Clinton's acceptance speech called for a "New Covenant" between government and the American people, a use of religious imagery that pleased some scholars but offended the Religious Right. Television evangelist Pat Robertson said Clinton's idealistic appeal "bordered on blasphemy" because Clinton supports freedom of choice on abortion. The redoubtable Rev. Jerry Falwell accused the Arkansas governor of "misquoting and manipulating Holy Scripture for political purposes."

The Clinton-Gore campaign was beset by anti-abortion demonstrators. Operation Rescue's militant leader Randall Terry and three supporters tried to hand a fetus to Clinton in New York during the convention. An extremist group called the Pro-Life Action Network promised to "hound Clinton at every whistle-stop," according to its director, Joseph M. Scheidler. During the campaign Terry announced that it was a sin for Christians to vote for Clinton.

For twelve years successive Republican administrations promoted a distinctive religious agenda and advocated church-state policies sharply at variance with the Democrats. Though unsuccessful even at the height of President Reagan's popularity, the GOP stood foursquare for a constitutional ban on abortion, a constitutional amendment authorizing government-sponsored prayer in public schools, and public tax subsidy of denominational and other private elementary and secondary schools. The party continued to advocate those policies, despite dissent within its ranks and declining public support for such policies.

The party platform called for the abolition of legal abortion in all cases except those required to save a woman's life. The platform committee, meeting in Houston in August, even rejected amendments permitting abortion in the case of rape or incest. Despite vigorous pro-choice lobbying by many active and committed Republicans, the party machinery—and the president and vice president—slammed shut the doors of compromise. The GOP remained the anti-choice party and its links with anti-abortion crusaders were firm. Chants of "four more years" reverberated through the air at the National Right to Life Convention in Washington in June. Bush's reelection was the top priority of America's anti-choice voters, who were aware that the Republican platform reaffirmed its call for the appointment of anti-choice judges at all levels of the judiciary. The Bush administration had also given legal and moral support to Operation Rescue's tactics aimed at closing abortion clinics and intimidating medical personnel.

The GOP hoped that the one-issue anti-abortion voters would outnumber pro-choice voters. This appears to have been the case in 1980, 1984, and 1988, when the anti-choice minority voted for Reagan and Bush in larger numbers than pro-choice voters supported the Democrats. But in 1990 and 1991 pro-choice voters, angered and frightened by the intimidation and the drift in the U.S. Supreme Court, made a crucial difference in many elections. Surveys throughout the summer of 1992 indicated that voters who felt strongly about the abortion issue favored Clinton over Bush by a 3 to 2 margin. The party's 1964 conservative standard-bearer Barry Goldwater denounced his party's anti-abortion position and said it would cost them the election.

While George Bush appeared uncomfortable with the abortion issue, Dan Quayle was quite happy to raise the issue among zealots and activists. The vice president told delegates to the National Right to Life Convention in June, "We shall carry the day. By honoring God in all things, you keep the pro-life movement oriented to the Author of Life."

Quayle was also willing to promote fundamentalist counterattacks within America's mainline churches, in one of which (Presbyterian) he is active. In a July 1991 address to the Good News Convocation in Washington, Quayle told Methodist conservatives who were trying to reshape their denomination, "It's not easy being in the minority, but a determined minority can turn itself into a majority." Quayle also claimed that the contentious and highly visible movement "has been a blessing not only to the United Methodist Church but to the nation as well."

President Bush, a lifelong Episcopalian, had cultivated ties to the Religious Right and had spoken to enthusiastic delegates of the Southern Baptist Convention, where a fundamentalist faction seized control during the 1980s. During his vice presidency Bush assured a group of fundamentalist and evangelical churchmen that he shared their religious views.

The Bush reelection campaign targeted parochial school patrons in its quest for votes, and Bush delivered a hard-hitting address at Archbishop Regan High School in Philadelphia on July 21. Bush, flanked by Cardinal Anthony Bevilacqua, told an audience of carefully selected parents, students, and guests that he "would clearly take this case to the American people this fall." Bush seemed, however, uninformed about the specifics of his own voucher plan. He told one questioner that a $1000 voucher would go to any student in any private or church-related school, regardless of family income. The voucher proposal then before Congress excluded families with incomes over $40,000.

Cardinal Bevilacqua told the president, "We want a fair share for our Catholic school parents." Most of those invited to hear the president were activists who had lobbied unsuccessfully for a parochial school voucher program in Pennsylvania. The ambitious voucher scheme was defeated by Pennsylvania legislators in 1991.

Bush reminded his audience that parochiaid was "an issue on which I have a distinct difference with my opponent. If you believe in this, you ought to vote not only for me but for members of the U.S. Congress whose support will be necessary to pass this legislation."

There was a sense of *déjà vu* in this Bush campaign stop. Just twenty years before, President Richard Nixon spoke in Philadelphia to the National Catholic Educational Association and promised tax support for church schools.

While most voters, legislators, and courts have opposed such proposals, the Republican Party apparently saw the issue as a potential vote-getter. On the day of Bush's address, Philadelphia Rep. Thomas M. Foglietta denounced the plan and reminded voters, "Most of Philadelphia's children are not in parochial school." The Jewish Community Relations Council also reaffirmed its opposition.

On a related issue Bush escalated his rhetoric at an appearance at the Three Saints Russian Orthodox Church in Garfield, New Jersey: "The Democrats want public schools to hand out birth-control pills and devices to teenaged kids. The family is under siege." Bush reiterated these themes before a Knights of Columbus audience attended by New York's Cardinal John O'Connor. At that event Bush also criticized the Supreme Court's decision on high school graduation prayers and called for a constitutional amendment authorizing school-sponsored prayer.

The Republican platform was largely shaped and dictated by the party's increasingly powerful and strident Religious Right. More than three hundred convention delegates were members of Pat Robertson's Christian Coalition, the most visible Religious Right organization. Nearly 42 percent of delegates surveyed by the *Washington Post* called themselves "born-again," and delegations from Iowa to Washington State were top-heavy with religious conservatives who had, in many instances, ousted religious moderates in bitter intraparty strife. One prominent drafter of the platform's "family values" planks was Keith Butler, a Detroit city councilman and pastor of the Word of Faith Christian Center.

The platform, seasoned with quotes from the King James Version of the Bible (the Protestant version demanded by evangelicals on the platform committee), called for a constitutional amendment banning all abortions except those few necessary to save a woman's life. It also opposed all public funding for the procedure and called for "abstinence education" in public schools. The party opposed birth-control services in public schools and urged an increase in adoptions "through significant tax credits, insurance reforms and legal reforms." The party also endorsed legislation to make the Fourteenth Amendment applicable to "unborn children."

The Republican establishment slammed the door shut on millions of pro-choice Republicans. All amendments to the harsh anti-abortion position were defeated by the platform committee, and supporters of choice were unable to mount a floor fight on the subject despite polls showing a significant number of delegates wanted the Barbara Bush solution—no party position on abortion. However, even pro-choice delegations from California, Vermont, and New Jersey refused to act on this crucial issue because they did not want a divisive floor fight to endanger Bush's reelection campaign.

On education the Republicans endorsed a $1,000 per child tuition credit to encourage attendance at parochial and private schools. The party endorsed school prayer and prayer at "commencements or other occasions," and pledged "strong enforcement of the equal access" law allowing religious groups to organize activities in public schools. The platform affirmed, "We must not remain neutral toward religion itself or the values religion supports." The platform, while claiming that "America must remain neutral toward particular religions," proclaimed itself to be "mindful of our country's Judeo-Christian heritage." Presumably, this excludes millions of Americans who adhere to different religious heritages.

The Republicans pledged themselves to oppose civil rights protections for gay Americans and laws allowing gays to adopt children or provide foster care, and to uphold the ban on homosexuals in the military "as a matter of good order and discipline." On the AIDS issue the party urged education stressing "marital fidelity and abstinence."

On related family policies, the Republicans said that welfare "taxes families to subsidize illegitimacy." The foster-care system should be overhauled to "promote marital stability." "Republicans recognize the importance of having fathers and mothers in the home. The two-parent family still provides the best environment of stability, discipline, responsibility, and character," said the party's official 1992 statement of principles.

Finally, the GOP waded into the sensitive area of arts and media, which they called "promoting cultural values." The statement charged that "elements within the media, the entertainment industry, academia and the Democratic Party are waging a guerrilla war against American values. They deny personal responsibility, disparage traditional morality, denigrate religion, and promote hostility toward the family's way of life." Government, the Republicans said, "has a responsibility to insure that it promotes common moral values. . . . We therefore condemn the use of public funds to subsidize obscenity and blasphemy masquerading as art."

In an aside, Republicans lectured the nation that "no artist has an inherent right to claim taxpayer support for his or her private vision of art if that vision mocks the moral and spiritual basis on which our society is founded."

The entire Republican campaign document was suffused by a kind of evangelical Protestant cultural nationalism that presupposes that certain inherent values are superior to others and that the government is somehow responsible for fostering individual morality. While the Republican party historically has always tended toward the politics of moralism, this document went further than any previous platform in enunciating a specific vision of family life and societal values. It was ironic that an increasingly pluralistic society would be addressed in such a manner by the ruling party, which condemned changes in society over which it presided for most of the two prior decades.

This campaign effort was highlighted by the appearance of President Bush at a gathering of the extreme-right Religious Roundtable in Dallas on August 21. The *New York Times* concluded that "the preachers and ideological spokesmen of the religious right . . . anointed President Bush as their champion in a battle between good and evil." Speakers urged clergy to organize their congregations on behalf of the Republican ticket, even though such efforts could jeopardize their tax-exempt status.

Speaker after speaker castigated those on the Democratic ticket as friends of pornography who would let "a sea of homosexuals and lesbians" into the White House. Retired Army general Daniel Graham, a former Reagan advisor, claimed that "atheists and agnostics and their trained-seal scientists" invented environmental threats to advance their schemes for "world government." Numerous Baptist preachers denounced their co-religionists Clinton and Gore. The Rev. Donald F. Wildmon, president of the American Family Association, warned the audience, "If Bill Clinton goes to the White House, he'll take his friends the homosexuals, the abortionists and the pornographers." Patrick Buchanan, the *enfant terrible* of the Far Right, told listeners that the Los Angeles rioters "came out of public schools where God and the Ten Commandments and the Bible were long ago expelled." Buchanan reiterated his convention charge that the United States is "engaged in a religious war, a battle over America's soul."

Bush pounded these themes in appearances in Alabama and Georgia, both evangelical strongholds. He did everything but get converted at a tent revival meeting in his quest for votes. He phoned National Association of Evangelicals President Don Argue on August 5 and emphasized his opposition to homosexuality. Argue told supporters the president "identifies with our biblical view against homosexuality." Bush recorded greetings for a Harvest Crusade evangelism rally in Orange County, California.

Meanwhile, Vice President Quayle, called "the Christian Coalition's docile mascot" by columnist Mary McGrory, appeared at the "God and Country" rally mounted by TV evangelist Pat Robertson in Houston. Quayle promised that he would "never give up" his fight for "traditional family values" and against the "cultural elites." Wife Marilyn Quayle expressed concerns that the Clintons attend different churches. Robertson told viewers that the Clintons "were out to destroy the traditional family."[16]

Bush attacked the Democrats for not mentioning God in the Democratic platform. However, previous Republican platforms generally did not do so either. The first Republican document in 1856 did not invoke the blessings of a deity. Neither did the great convention of 1860 that nominated Abraham Lincoln. In fact, from 1856 through 1944, Republican platforms only mentioned God once: in 1876, platform writers used the oblique phrase "in the economy of Providence" to explain the Republican abolition of slavery.

It was not until 1948 that Republicans began to insist on specific religious invocations. Since then, only the 1972 platform, on which Richard Nixon and Spiro Agnew ran for reelection, omitted any references to a deity.

As one might expect from the party of Thomas Jefferson, the Democrats refused religious invocations in thirty-one of their thirty-five platforms since 1856. Only in 1948 and 1952, during the era of the Cold War, McCarthyism, and the Korean War, did the Democrats join the Republicans in considerable religious rhetoric. Brief references, such as "on God's earth," appeared in 1960 and 1924.[17]

Education and religion were major factors in shaping how voters responded to the issues and personalities of the 1992 presidential race. Bill Clinton was only the second Democrat since polling began to win among college-educated voters, a high-status, influential, and historically Republican-leaning group (since education and income are almost directly correlated in terms of status and economic achievement). Clinton won 44 percent-39 percent over Bush (with 16 percent for Perot) among all college-educated voters and was relatively stronger among women than men. Among voters with advanced degrees Clinton won decisively 49 percent-36 percent (15 percent for Perot), a margin that may have exceeded Johnson's 1964 margin over Goldwater—the only other Democrat to win among this growing portion of the electorate. College-educated voters are religiously diverse and generally hold liberal positions on all of the cultural flashpoint issues—abortion, school prayer, tax aid for nonpublic schools, gay rights, sex education, tolerance for alternative lifestyles, censorship of books and films, religious tolerance, and opposition to religious-based political appeals. The well-educated voters in every religious community reject the belief that the Bible is literally true or inerrant, and are opposed to the Religious Right's attempt to impose a narrow or unitary moral vision on society. They were incensed at the religious intolerance at the Republican convention in August and were opposed to the sectarian slant to the GOP's platform positions on numerous "family values" positions. So were many voters who are not college graduates, but the defection from the Bush ticket by so many former supporters in the high-education, high-income echelons is a warning signal that Republican leaders will ignore to their peril. These issues also affected the highest-income voters—those making above $75,000 annually—who only gave Bush 48 percent support this time compared to 68 percent four years ago.

Upscale voters may have reacted against Bush's "Know Nothing" campaign, his sneers at Clinton's Oxford education. (Bush did the same in 1988, lampooning Michael Dukakis's Harvard and Swarthmore education, as if Bush's prep school and Yale degrees were greatly different.) Bush's ignorance of history, as when he condemned the Democratic platform for omitting references to God, is evident as *most Republican and Democratic platforms* before 1948 did not claim divine blessings for their political positions.

Republicans in Congress have been far more likely than Democrats to cut education and library spending and to attack the National Endowments for the Arts and Humanities and public television. The Republican platform's endorsement of a "common moral vision" in art and culture was considered inappropriate by voters.

The cultural/religious divide in this election looks at first blush quite simple: frequent church attendees versus casual attendees, and white Protestants versus everyone else. Here is what the Voter Research and Surveys exit polling data showed: Among the 40 percent of voters who attend church weekly—in whatever tradition—Bush won 47 percent , Clinton 38 percent, Perot 15 percent. Among the 60 percent who attend occasionally or not at all, Clinton won 47 percent, Bush 31 percent, Perot 22 percent. The difference was especially significant among Bush voters. Nearly half of weekly churchgoers supported Bush while less than a third of the less observant did so.

The old Republican/white Protestant nexus remained partially intact, though defections from moderate, liberal, mainline and "cultural" Protestants reduced Bush's support level. All white Protestants (49 percent of voters) gave Bush 46 percent, Clinton 33 percent, and Perot 21 percent. All others (51 percent) went for Clinton heavily, giving him 53 percent, Bush 30 percent, Perot 17 percent.

While the GOP has always received more support from white Protestants than from any other segment of the electorate, its support is now concentrated among more intensely involved, conservative Protestants of moderate income and education who reside in the South.

The intimations of a cultural war perceived at the GOP convention can be seen in how voters responded to major issues. The results show that the issues emphasized by the Republicans did not engage the concerns of the average voter. Indeed, the vast majority of voters were concerned about the economy, with the environment and education well behind: 43 percent of voters cited the economy as the paramount issue, and Clinton defeated Bush decisively among this group. Clinton also won a clear majority of the three-candidate vote among voters concerned about the environment, health care, jobs, and education. Bush won among voters concerned about taxes and foreign policy, and Perot tied Clinton among voters concerned about the budget deficit.

Where did that leave Bush? He won two-thirds of so-called family values voters, but they were only 15 percent of all voters. (Of Bush's voters 27 percent cited "family values" as a factor in their votes compared to only 8 percent of Clinton's and 9 percent of Perot's voters.) Bush beat Clinton 54 percent to 38 percent among voters who cited abortion as a major concern, suggesting that anti-choice activists are still more likely than pro-choicers to let that issue affect their presidential vote. Still, only a third of voters listed abortion as top priority. Bush won among the tiny segment of voters (12 percent) who raised the issue of marital fidelity. The Republicans emphasized issues that were of peripheral concern to most voters, and the repeatedly negative tone of the Bush campaign offended many. Fully 30 percent of voters said Bush's attacks on Clinton were "unfair" compared to 9 percent of those who thought Clinton's attacks were unfair.

Clues to the cultural war's voting impact are spread throughout the voter profiles that emerged from this election. Women went decisively for Clinton by 11 points, especially working women (12 percent margin) and single mothers (20 percent margin). Only homemakers gave Bush the edge. While Bush's support went up as voter income increased, he won only 48 percent of those whose income exceeded $75,000. He won 23 percent among those whose family income was under $15,000. But this 25-point difference pales when compared to religious differences, where 50 points separated Bush's support from top (evangelicals and fundamentalists) to bottom (Jews). Unmarried voters gave Clinton 49 percent, Bush 33 percent, Perot 18 percent, while married voters split evenly. Even among the quarter of the electorate who said their family's financial situation had improved, only 62 percent voted for Bush. (In 1984 voters who felt that way gave 86 percent to Reagan.) Obviously, something other than economic self-interest was at work in this election. In all of the above categories, Clinton did well among culturally liberal and tolerant voters who rejected the Republican embrace of Religious Right extremism.

Voter profiles showed that Clinton and Perot voters were closer to each other on family-morality issues than either was to Bush. Fully 28 percent of Bush's voters were white evangelicals and fundamentalists, compared to 14 percent of Perot's and 9 percent of Clinton's. Even among the Bush coalition, only a fourth singled out family-values issues as decisive to their vote.

Clinton trounced Bush among Jews, black Protestants, Catholics, religious liberals, and religiously nonaffiliated voters. The Clinton/Gore ticket made sharp inroads among the historically Republican mainline Protestants in the West and North. The Bush/Quayle ticket won among evangelical and fundamentalist white Protestants, especially in the Deep South, and among

Mormons. One of the more intriguing patterns of this unusual election was Bush's victory among white Southern Baptists, the religious affiliation of both Governor Clinton and Senator Gore. Clinton did not do nearly as well among his fellow Baptists and among white Southerners generally as Jimmy Carter did in 1976.

Clinton triumphed in all twelve of the nation's most heavily Catholic states—from New Mexico to Massachusetts—the first Democratic sweep of these states since Lyndon Johnson in 1964. Four years earlier Catholics were almost evenly divided. Clinton's emphasis on economic issues and social justice played well among Catholic voters; Bush's emphasis on family values and character did not. Clinton made a major policy address on family values and religious tolerance at the University of Notre Dame, while the Bush campaign played up several issues (parochiaid, abortion) thought to be of specific appeal to Catholic voters. Bush also made two campaign appearances at the side of Philadelphia's Cardinal Anthony Bevilacqua. But the strategy failed as Catholics voted 44 percent to 36 percent for Clinton, with 20 percent for Perot.

While Clinton's Catholic triumph represented a return home for Catholic voters, his margin was the same as Carter's in 1976 and a good deal less than that of Humphrey, Kennedy, and Truman. Hispanic voters, who are 70 percent Catholic, favored Clinton 62 percent to 25 percent, with about 14 percent for Perot. Hispanic support was extremely important in moving New Mexico to the Democratic column for the first time since 1964. Cajun Catholics in southern Louisiana helped carry that state for Clinton. The trend-setting French Catholics have gone for every winner since 1956 (except 1968). This time they gave Clinton 48 percent, Bush 39 percent, Perot 13 percent.

Even in Cardinal Bevilacqua's bailiwick, Catholics went for Clinton. Delaware County, a significantly Catholic Philadelphia suburb, went Democratic for the first time since 1964, as did St. Louis County, Missouri; Baltimore County, Maryland; and Middlesex County, New Jersey—which have a high percentage of Catholic voters. Clinton even carried Manchester, New Hampshire. Clinton did well among all Catholic ethnic subgroups. Among Catholics of French descent in New England, Clinton ran strongly, with Perot second and Bush a poor third.

Mainline Protestants, a mainstay of the Republican party since 1856, were far less likely to support Bush than any previous Republican president. These voters, economic moderates but social-issue liberals, may have reacted against the extremism perceived at the Republican convention in August and the party's embrace of Religious Right platform positions. Clinton's victories in Vermont, Connecticut, Maine, New Hampshire, Ohio, Michigan, and

Iowa—where many of these voters reside—were telltale signs of disapproval of recent trends in Republican politics.

Vermont, a state with many mainline and Catholic voters, went Democratic for only the second time in 160 years. The Green Mountain State, which may be the nation's most tolerant state, and whose Congressional representatives have steadfastly opposed Religious Right positions, gave Bush only 31 percent of its votes—lower than Barry Goldwater's 1964 showing and indeed the worst Republican showing in history.

Mainline Protestants, who almost always give 60 percent to 70 percent vote support to Republican presidential candidates, gave Bush just 38 percent nationwide. Clinton won slightly over 38 percent and Perot won 24 percent. "Yankee Protestants" all over New England deserted their party in droves as Clinton carried Cape Cod, Nantucket, Wellesley, and scores of similar communities.

Bush won decisively among the 17 percent of the electorate that called itself "white born-again Christian": 61 percent of these voters compared to Clinton's 23 percent and Perot's 15 percent. While Bush was down from the 81 percent he had won in 1988, his strong showing among these voters saved a number of southern states and possibly Kansas for the GOP. Bush carried such religiously conservative cities as Greenville, South Carolina; Lubbock, Texas; and Bakersfield, California.

Bush's three strongest states were Mississippi, South Carolina, and Alabama, all heavily Baptist states. In these states white Baptists and other Protestants, for a variety of racial, cultural, and religious reasons, have deserted Democratic presidential candidates, and even a Baptist governor of Arkansas could not bring them back. The more religiously homogeneous regions of the Protestant South (North Carolina, parts of Florida, Georgia, Texas, and Louisiana) also favored the Bush/Quayle ticket.

In ninety-six heavily Southern Baptist counties in eleven Southern states, Bush won 46 percent to Clinton's 40 percent and Perot's 14 percent. In suburban areas of the south, Bush appears to have won 55 percent of Baptists.

Bush also won 45 percent in heavily Mormon Utah, which had been his banner state with 67 percent in 1988. Independent Ross Perot cut into the Mormon vote here and ran second statewide. The heaviest Mormon counties in Utah and Idaho gave Bush 55 percent, Perot 27 percent, and Clinton 18 percent. Bush won his biggest margin in the county that includes Brigham Young University.

Bush could take comfort among one small evangelical subgroup, the fiercely conservative Dutch Reformed voters in rural Michigan and Iowa, who gave him 61 percent of their votes compared to 22 percent for Clinton and 17 percent for Perot.

Another predominantly midwestern religious group, the Lutherans, favored Clinton with 40 percent to Bush's 35 percent and Perot's 25 percent. Lutherans split almost evenly in 1988, and the high Perot support was something of a surprise in this election, though previous independents like LaFollette and Anderson had run strongly among Lutheran voters.

Anger at the Republican party's capitulation to the Religious Right fueled Jewish defections to Clinton, who swept 78 percent of the Jewish vote while Bush won 12 percent and Perot 10 percent. Bush won at least 30 percent of the Jewish vote in 1988. The Jewish landslide for Clinton helped to swing Westchester, Rockland, and Nassau counties, New York; Broward County, Florida; and Westport, Connecticut, to the Democratic column. Jewish and mainline Protestant defections pushed Bucks and Montgomery counties, Pennsylvania, to the Democrats for the first time since 1964.

Religiously pluralistic large suburbs throughout the nation deserted the GOP. Clinton carried seventeen of the nation's twenty-six largest suburban counties. He did especially well in counties where a majority of voters are college educated and religiously diverse, e.g., Howard and Montgomery counties, Maryland; and Arlington and Alexandria, Virginia. Clinton may also have benefited from voter anger at the Religious Right's takeover of the Republican party in San Diego, California. This large population center, which remained loyal to Barry Goldwater in 1964, went for Clinton.

Finally, the 10 percent to 12 percent of the electorate who are religiously nonaffiliated or who adhere to religions outside the Judeo-Christian mainstream rejected Bush as they had in 1988. These voters were instrumental in the Clinton sweeps of California, Washington, Oregon, Hawaii, and Nevada. Nevada, which has the lowest percentage of church members of any state, gave Clinton an upset victory. Religiously nonaffiliated voters gave Clinton 65 percent, Perot 20 percent, and Bush only 15 percent support.

Counties in Arizona, New Mexico, North Dakota, South Dakota, and Wisconsin where Native Americans form the majority of the population went for Clinton by a landslide of 62 percent to 27 percent for Bush and 11 percent for Perot. The Republican vote has steadily declined in these areas since 1984. (Reagan won a majority in 1980.)

Clinton won a greater landslide than Lyndon Johnson in 1964 in San Francisco and its suburbs, especially in Marin County—all strongholds of religious diversity. Clinton won heavily in such religiously liberal areas as Pitkin County, Colorado; Brookline, Massachusetts; and Provincetown, Massachusetts. Clinton also won impressive majorities in almost every county where universities and colleges are the dominant cultural influence. Even in southern states carried by Bush, Clinton won 2 to 1 in religiously and culturally diverse towns like Chapel Hill, North Carolina; Charlottesville and Williamsburg, Virginia; and Gainesville, Florida.

John Green and his colleagues, using the 1992 American National Election Survey data from the University of Michigan, arrived at three conclusions: (1) religious voting blocs were very important in 1992, despite the enormous impact of economic distress; (2) George Bush gained more votes than he lost on social issues, but these gains were dwarfed by his losses from the economy; and (3) Christian Right activists may have helped mobilize their constituency for the Republican ticket."[18]

This interpretation is questionable at some points and disregards precinct and county data that lead to a different set of conclusions. Exit polls are themselves limiting because they only ask certain questions. No exit poll in 1992 specifically asked voters if their presidential vote had been affected by their view of the Republican Right on the issue planks in the Republican platform that were aimed at winning the Religious Right vote. The questions only asked if "family values" and "abortion" were issues for the individual voter. Thus, analysts must occasionally use inferences and interpolations of trends from the raw vote totals that correlate with religious or other influences to supplement the limitations of the exit poll data.

Based on another study of the data, Green and colleagues divided America up into five religious blocs: Evangelical Protestants (25 percent), Roman Catholics (24 percent), Mainline Protestants (20 percent), Other Religious Traditions (16 percent), and Seculars (15 percent). They say that all groups have been growing except for the mainline Protestants, who were once "the culturally dominant religious tradition" (45). They say, "Characterized by a willingness to accommodate orthodox Protestant beliefs to the modern world, this group has declined in influence and size in recent decades" (45).

These scholars have added the nonpracticing or only occasionally practicing Protestants and Catholics to the religiously nonaffiliated, thus expanding the secular category to 15 percent of the adult population, double the percentage usually found in Gallup polls and network exit polls. While there is some logic to grouping people this way, it may not be truly accurate. Many people stoutly resist the "no religion" category in polls, reserving to themselves the right of classification even if they decline to participate actively in religious services. The Green approach also tends to increase the Republican vote among seculars, since many lapsed or semi-lapsed people are prosperous, well-educated Republican-leaners. Thus, the Green interpretation of the National Election Study shows a lower Clinton vote and a higher Bush vote in the secular category than the exit polls.

Still, the basic contours remain. Clinton received his greatest support from other (Jewish, black Protestant, Eastern Orthodox), secular, and Catholic voters. Bush's greatest support was received among evangelicals, followed by mainline Protestants.

Church attendance and level of commitment also affected voters' choices. Write Green and his colleagues, "An analysis of church attendance and other measures of religious commitment showed that Perot voters were drawn from the least committed members of each religious tradition, and that Clinton voters had lower levels of religious commitment than Bush voters" (52).

Bush won 70 percent of highly committed evangelicals, compared to 56 percent of all of them. Among Catholics the highly committed favored Bush 40 percent–39 percent while all Catholics opted for Clinton 40 percent to 33 percent. Evangelicals accounted for 38 percent of the Bush vote, but only 20 percent of the Perot vote and 18 percent of the Clinton vote. "Secular and other" religious traditions accounted for 39 percent of Clinton's vote, 25 percent of Perot's vote, and only 16 percent of Bush's vote. The Republicans remain the white Protestant party. Bush received 62 percent of his vote from white Protestants while Clinton's vote was only 35 percent white Protestant. Of the Perot vote 46 percent came from white Protestants.

The Republicans are obviously dependent on the evangelicals, and evangelicals may demand more concessions from party leaders as a reward for their support. Even though Green does not believe that Bush's defeat came from an anti–Religious Right backlash, he warns that "religious conservatives could well present the GOP with serious problems" because "social-issue conservatism is simply not strong enough to be the sole basis for winning elections" (63).

As to the overall meaning of the 1992 election, Green and colleagues have this to say: "The enduring religious underpinnings of electoral coalitions strongly suggest that culture is the foundation of American politics, and that rival sets of beliefs, world views and lifestyles set the bounds of consensus and conflict. . . . While both cultural and economic factors clearly influence election returns, the former represent long-term influences and the latter short-term factors" (46). (See tables 5.6 through 5.9.)

Clyde Wilcox of Georgetown University, a specialist on the Religious Right, disagrees with Green's claims that religious conservatives were at least slightly helpful to Bush in 1992. He says, "I find that the total effect of abortion, Christian Right figures, and the Republican Convention was a loss of 2 percent for the Republicans."[19]

The University of Oklahoma's Allen D. Hertzke also argues that the Catholic vote for Clinton was critical. He says, "In 1992 Bush dropped from 50 percent to 33 percent of the Catholic vote, while Clinton and the Democ-

Table 5.5

The Religious Factor and the 1992 Presidential Electoral Vote

Religious Character of State	Electoral Votes Clinton	Electoral Votes Bush	% Clinton
High evangelical	76	134	36.2
Low evangelical	294	34	89.6
	370	168	66.9

Table 5.6

Cultural Voting in New England 1992

Typology	% Bush	% Clinton	% Perot	Rank Order Bush	Clinton	Perot
Upper Income Republican Suburbs	46.2	36.2	17.6	1	6	4
Republican Small Towns	42.3	35.0	22.7	2	7	2T
Upper Income Liberal Suburbs	29.0	58.8	11.2	3	3	7
French Catholic Towns	24.1	46.7	29.2	4	5	1
Democratic Blue-Collar Towns	23.3	54.0	22.7	5	4	2T
College Towns	20.9	62.8	16.3	6	2	5
Liberal Towns	19.1	67.9	13.0	7	1	6
% Difference Between Highest and Lowest Typology	27.1	32.9	18.0			

Table 5.7

Economic Voting in New England 1992

Income Level	% Bush	% Clinton	% Perot	Rank Bush	Clinton	Perot
Upper	38.9	45.8	15.3	1	3	3
Middle	26.4	57.0	16.6	2	1	2
Lower	23.5	52.7	23.8	3	2	1
% Difference between best and worst support level	15.4	11.2	8.5			

Table 5.8.

Changes in New England Voting Patterns 1976 and 1992

Typology	% Change in Democratic Vote, 1976 & 1992
Upper Income Republican Suburbs	+ 9.5
Republican Small Towns	+11.0
Upper Income Liberal Suburbs	+16.7
French Catholic Towns	− 9.9
Democratic Blue-Collar Towns	− 1.7
College Towns	+12.9
Liberal Towns	+ 8.9

Table 5.9

Support for Third Party Candidates in New England, 1980 and 1992

Typology	% Perot 1992	% Anderson 1980	Rank Order Perot	Anderson
French Catholic Towns	29.2	10.8	1	7
Republican Small Towns	22.7	14.0	2T	5
Democratic Blue-Collar Towns	22.7	12.5	2T	6
Upper Income Republican Suburbs	17.6	14.1	4	4
College Towns	16.3	26.6	5	1
Liberal Towns	13.0	19.8	6	2
Upper Income Liberal Suburbs	11.2	18.3	7	3

rats retained a much higher percentage, going from 50 to 45 percent. I think that Clinton's appeal to Catholics was an important part of his success."[20]

Regardless of interpretation, it remains clear that Bush's base vote was reduced to evangelical white Protestants. Bush defeated Clinton in the nineteen most evangelical states by 134 electoral votes to Clinton's 76. But in the thirty-one states where evangelicals are a smaller percentage of the population, Clinton won 90 percent of the electoral votes, securing 294 to Bush's 34. (See table 5.5.)

Notes

1. Beryl F. McClerren, "The Southern Baptist State Newspapers and the Religious Issue During the Presidential Campaigns of 1928 and 1960." Ph.D. diss., Southern Illinois University, 1963.

2. Finlay Lewis, "Religion is the X Factor in Election," *Minneapolis Tribune*, October 10, 1976.

3. Haynes Johnson, "Too Much Religion?" *Washington Post,* October 7, 1976.

4. Quoted in Albert J. Menendez, "Religion at the Polls, 1984," *Church & State* 37 (December 1984): 12.

5. Ibid.

6. Ibid.

7. James L. Guth and John C. Green, *The Bible and the Ballot Box: Religion and Politics in the 1988 Election* (Boulder, Colo.: Westview Press, 1991), p. 147.

8. Ibid., p. 145.

9. Stephen D. Johnson, Joseph B. Tamney, and Ronald Burton, "Pat Robertson: Who Supported His Candidacy for President?" *Journal for the Scientific Study of Religion* 28 (1989): 387–99 at 397.

10. Ibid., p. 397.

11. Tod A. Baker, et al., "Preachers and Politics," in Guth and Green, *Bible and the Ballot Box*, pp. 94–112.

12. H. G. Bissinger, *Friday Night Lights* (New York: HarperCollins, 1990), pp. 189–90.

13. Ibid., p. 187.

14. Ibid., p. 189.

15. *Voice of Reason* 42: 1, 4.

16. "Church, State and the Presidency," *Voice of Reason* 42 (Summer 1992): 1, 4–9; and "Culture Wars, Round One," *Voice of Reason* 43 (Fall 1992): 4–7.

17. See Donald Bruce Johnson, *National Party Platforms 1840-1976* (Urbana: University of Illinois Press, 1978).

18. John C. Green, James L. Guth, Lyman A. Kellstedt, and Corwin E. Smidt, "Murphy Brown Revisited: The Social Issues in the 1992 Election" in *Disciples and Democracy: Religious Conservatives and the Future of American Politics,* ed. Michael Cromartie (Grand Rapids: Eerdmans, 1994), pp. 43–67. Additional page references to this work appear in parentheses following the cited material.

19. Michael Cromartie, ed., *Disciples of Democracy: Religious Conservatives and the Future of American Politics* (Grand Rapids, Mich.: Eerdmans, 1994), p. 75.

20. Ibid., p. 69.

6

Evangelicals, Republicans, and the 1994 Elections

The unexpected Republican triumph in the 1994 congressional elections, which gave them control of both the House and the Senate for the first and only time since Dwight Eisenhower's 1952 election, was energized by the changing patterns of religious voting. Four specialists on religion as a factor in politics concluded unequivocally, "The 1994 campaign marked evangelical Protestantism's arrival as a force in national politics. It has produced several organizations supported by aroused activists; it has sparked the shift of evangelical voters from the Democratic to the Republican camp and their mobilization into fuller electoral participation; and it has earned growing representation in the Republican Party."[1]

These scholars are well known in the field and have participated in seminars and in the Religion and Politics Caucus of the American Political Science Association. John C. Green is director of the Ray C. Bliss Institute for Applied Politics at the University of Akron. James L. Guth is professor of political science at Furman University and is an expert on the political attitudes of Southern Baptist clergy. Lyman A. Kellstedt is professor of political science at Wheaton College, and Corwin E. Smidt is professor of political science at Calvin College. Wheaton and Calvin are sometimes referred to as the Harvard and Yale of the evangelical world.

Continuing their analysis, the scholars observed, "Thus, while evangelicals are not yet a political monolith, they constitute a substantial Republican voting bloc. If the past few elections are any guide, this bloc now includes at least three-fifths of the voters in this large religious tradition. And partisan identification has followed the vote. For the first time ever, a majority of evangelicals identify themselves as Republicans, and only one-third identify themselves as Democrats."

Focusing on the Religious Right's co-option of evangelical partisanship through its "informal web of activists," they say that the "Christian Right probably mobilized 4 million activists and reached 50 million voters." "All this activity pushed in one direction: for the Republicans. This exclusivism reflects not only the movement's natural affinity for GOP conservatism but also its new institutionalized role in Republican politics."

The Christian Right was largely responsible for the evangelical voter shift in the South.

> The Christian Right is strongest in the South, West and Midwest, where evangelical Protestants abound, but particularly Baptists, Pentecostals, and the new wave of nondenominational churches. In fact, the simple propor- tion of "born again" white voters in a state's electorate is a very good pre- dictor of movement strength. Conversely, the Christian Right is weak where the voting public is dominated by mainline Protestants, Catholics and adherents of other traditions. The Christian Right flourishes where voters identify themselves as conservatives and are pro-life, opposed to gay rights and attached to "traditional family values." Not surprisingly, the movement also thrives where religion is most politicized—in states where citizens report that their faith is "very important" to political choices. . . . Not unex- pectedly, the Christian Right was most active in 1994 GOP campaigns where it is most influential, most notably in North Carolina, Georgia, Ten- nessee, Oklahoma, Washington, Oregon, and Arizona, and to a slightly lesser extent in South Carolina, Florida, Texas, Iowa, Minnesota, Califor- nia, Kansas, and Indiana.

This movement impacted unfavorably on areas of traditional Democra- tic voter preference. "The movement's overall impact is best illustrated in the races for the U.S. House of Representatives. The Christian Right entered at least 120 House races, one-third of all contested elections—more races than ever before. Candidates backed by the Christian Right won 55 percent of these campaigns—also a record. . . . Was the role of the Christian Right deci- sive? It appears so. In races with heavy Christian Right involvement, 30 Republican victories were won by margins of 5 percent of the vote or less— close enough for Christian Right help to have made the difference."

These shifting fortunes of political partisanship took their toll on the Democrats. The Republican victory margin, 230 to 204 in the House, was clearly impacted by the Religious Right. "Almost three-quarters of all Democratic open seats won by the GOP went to candidates backed by the Christian Right, while almost one-half of the defeated Democratic incumbents lost to such candidates."

Evangelical identifiers and churchgoers were also elected to Congress in record numbers, as might be expected. A study by the Kuyper Institute found that more than one-fourth of the newly elected freshmen were affiliated with strongly evangelical churches or even with nondenominational fundamentalist churches. Green and his colleagues write, "The 1994 election was probably the first in modern history in which the proportion of evangelicals among new House members matched the proportion in the voting population."

The Christian Right mobilization and get-out-the-vote efforts appear to have been effective. The percentage of the total vote cast by evangelicals increased over 1992. According to Green and his colleagues, 75 percent of evangelicals who were contacted by Religious Right activists voted, compared to 54 percent who were not contacted (presumably, this is a percentage of registered voters, not of all evangelicals, since only 38 percent of voters cast their ballots in the congressional elections). The Republicans ran 20 percentage points stronger among those evangelicals who were contacted than among those who were not. "Christian Right campaign efforts not only increased turnout among evangelicals already disposed toward the GOP, but may also have switched some votes into the Republican column." Evangelical voters constituted 26 percent of those who voted in the 1994 elections, a record high. They even exceeded the Catholics, who were 24 percent of voters.

The news gets worse for the Democrats. Younger evangelical voters are the most Republican-oriented of all, especially those who reside in the South. And those evangelicals who consider themselves political conservatives outnumber political liberals by a 5-to-1 margin, which is still well above the 70 percent Republican congressional margin in 1994. (Thirty percent of evangelicals voted Democratic but only 16 percent call themselves liberals.)

Green and his fellow specialists are probably right when they say, "Probably no Republican candidate can win the presidency without massive evangelical support." But this is true only if voters of other religious traditions do not identify an evangelical threat to their well being and security in the community. This impact could also be diminished over time if evangelicals become so safely Republican that they are ignored by the party leadership except at election time and are taken for granted between elections when legislative policies are formulated and enacted.

Voters who are historically closer to the mainstream, i.e., the political center, may in the long run be more likely to influence policy and to determine the outcome of close elections, especially if both parties attempt to

Table 6.1

**Religion and the Congressional Vote
Results (%) for 1992 and 1994**

Religious Tradition	1994 GOP House	1992 GOP House	GOP Gain '92–'94	1994 % of Public	1994 % GOP Voters	1994 %Dem Voters
Evangelical						
Regular attender	72	60	+12	14	23	11
Less than regular	59	41	+18	12	11	7
Mainline						
Regular attender	60	60	0	6	9	7
Less than regular	63	45	+18	10	15	10
Catholic						
Regular attender	56	42	+14	11	14	13
Less than regular	46	36	+10	13	10	12
Black Protestant						
Regular attender	22	9	+13	5	2	9
Less than regular	5	14	– 9	6	0	8
Jewish	31	24	+ 7	2	2	4
Secular	43	36	+ 7	15	8	13
All Others	48	35	+13	4	5	7

Source: 1992 and 1994 National Election Studies, *Christian Century* (July 5–12, 1995): 678.

Note: Figures are rounded off to the nearest full percentage point.

---

appeal to them. Catholic voters, for example, have tended to support the winning presidential candidate in most elections since 1932.

Other voters were also instrumental in the 1994 GOP win. The Perot centrists, one-fifth of the electorate, voted 2-to-1 Republican, giving Republicans a 51-to-19 victory over the Democrats in the seventy House districts where Perot ran strongest in 1992. These relatively secular, economic-issue voters have an agenda quite different from that of the Religious Right, and the Republican leadership may have to choose between the two groups at some future date, possibly sooner than they wish. Even secular voters in the West trended Republican in 1994, for reasons unrelated to religious value issues. Even Green and his colleagues admitted, "Though it is clear that the Christian Right played a major role in the election, it was only one factor contributing to the dramatic GOP gains. . . . The Christian Right was just part of a much larger, unusually energized, and united conservative coalition which was able to lavish its resources on the typically small midterm electorate." (See table 6.1.)

The national network exit polls in 1994 also include data that are helpful to this study. A combination of religious, cultural, and economic factors fueled the Republican triumph on November 8. In the Northeast, where Catholics outnumber Protestants, and Jews and mainline Protestants are influential, the Republicans gained only three seats. In heavily Roman Catholic New England they gained none at all.

In the bastion of evangelical Protestantism, the GOP gained nineteen seats and reached a historic high. In the eleven states of the Old Confederacy, Republicans won sixty-four seats and the Democrats sixty-one—a feat never achieved since the artificial Republican majorities of the Reconstruction days and military occupation after the Civil War. (Democrats had a 77–48 majority going into the 1994 elections.) For the first time in history, Republicans outnumber Democrats in the congressional delegations of Georgia, North Carolina, South Carolina, and Tennessee. They expanded their lead in Florida to 15–8. In the Border South, the GOP won 17–16, with major victories in Oklahoma and Kentucky, both heavily Baptist-fundamentalist in complexion. Thus, in the "Cultural South" the Republicans won eighty-one seats and the Democrats seventy-seven, a political tidal wave of monumental proportions.

But the sweep also engulfed the Midwest, with its large Lutheran, Methodist, and Catholic communities. The GOP gained four House seats in Ohio and three in Indiana. For the first time in memory, all five House seats in Iowa are Republican-held, despite the easy Clinton and Dukakis victories there.

In the largely secular West, the Republicans rebounded on the strength of the unpopularity of President Clinton and Interior Secretary Bruce Babbit. A political earthquake hit Washington State, a largely secular state that supported Clinton and Dukakis. Republicans gained six seats in the Evergreen State, which shifted from 8-to-1 Democrat to 7-to-2 Republican. The most prominent casualty was Speaker of the House Tom Foley, who became the first Speaker to lose his seat since the U.S. Civil War.

Religion is only one factor in voting behavior, but it has become increasingly prominent in recent years as politicians now realize that many voters make political decisions as a result of their religious values and convictions.

The 1994 voting showed strong Republican trends all across the religious spectrum. The nonreligious or secular voters (7 percent of all) showed the largest trend (9 percent) toward the GOP since 1992. They still voted 63 percent–37 percent Democratic, but the Republicans gained 9 points and ran considerably better than George Bush, who received just 15 percent of the religiously nonaffiliated vote two years before. These voters—largely young, male and living on the coasts—are generally liberal on social and cultural issues and oppose attempts to weaken the wall of separation between church and state. Their shift to the Republicans was surprising.

A large and influential swing vote is the Roman Catholic community (30 percent of 1994 voters said they were Catholic, according to exit polls). They moved 8 points in the Republican direction, favoring GOP congressional candidates by 52 percent to 48 percent, according to some exit polls. The Mitofsky International exit poll showed Catholics still voted 52 percent to 48 percent Democratic. Regardless of which poll is correct, Catholics cast a record high vote for Republican congressional candidates. Even when Nixon won a majority of Catholic votes in 1972 and Reagan in 1984, Catholic voters still gave the Democrats a majority of their congressional vote. The last two times the Republicans won Congress, in 1952 and 1946, Catholics were still solidly Democratic. This GOP shift among voters who are frequently barometers of national politics, and who tend to be moderate to liberal in their political views, may be the most disturbing trend for the Democrats to emerge from this midterm vote. Catholics remain more liberal on most issues than white Protestants, but they have defected in large numbers to the GOP, just two years after giving Bill Clinton a solid 8-10 point margin over George Bush. Clinton carried all twelve of the nation's most heavily Catholic states.

Does this presage a permanent swing to the right, and is it the first victory for a long-discussed Catholic-evangelical alliance? Some think so, but others point out that there remain sharp cultural and historical differences between the average Catholic and the average evangelical Protestant voter.

How much is this swing due to specifically Roman Catholic issues or perceptions of discontent? Articles have appeared in the *Baltimore Sun* and elsewhere suggesting that some Catholics have grown displeased with the Clinton administration's policies, mainly on symbolic issues like the Cairo World Population Conference and the controversial statements attributed to Surgeon General Joycelyn Elders. Some observers suggest, however, that the overall Catholic vote change was due primarily to the high Perot vote (20 percent) among Catholics in 1992. Perot voters went 2-to-1 Republican in this congressional balloting, and that shift explains much of the Catholic defections.

White Protestants remain the largest voting bloc (41 percent–45 percent) and the most Republican (66 percent). Nothing has changed here. The GOP gained about 9 points among its historic base group. Evangelicals and fundamentalists are a major part (probably a majority) of the broad white Protestant community, and they voted overwhelmingly (76 percent) Republican. Even in Virginia, they gave 60 percent to defeated Republican candidate Ollie North, and the self-defined fundamentalists gave him even more. White Protestants include many mainline church members, who tend to be liberal on church-state and cultural issues, moderate to conservative on economic issues, and historically Republican. They seem to have shifted somewhat to the Republicans.

Voters who say their religious tradition is something other than Protestant, Catholic, or Jewish remained Democratic, but Republicans registered small gains.

That leaves the Democrats their most loyal religious constituencies, Jews and black Protestants. Despite tensions between these historically Democratic voting groups, both remained staunchly Democratic. Fully 88 percent of blacks and 78 percent of Jews cast Democratic ballots for Congress.

This election's Republican revolt was fueled by reported dissatisfaction with President Clinton's performance thus far (only 44 percent of voters approved), slightly higher turnout (38.7 percent compared to 36.5 percent in 1990), disappointment among middle-income voters, a solid 16-point Republican gain among the one-fifth of voters who favored Ross Perot for president two years before, and regional factors.

The Clinton factor can be seen in this data: In the Northeast, where 52 percent of voters approved of Clinton's job performance, the Republicans gained only three seats in the House. In the South, where only 39 percent of voters approved of the president's record, the Republicans gained nineteen seats. The West had a similar Republican gain and low job-approval ratings for Mr. Clinton.

Turnout was higher among the energized and unhappy voters, especially among Republicans and conservatives in rural and suburban areas. Vote turnout in Democratic city and minority areas was low. Turnout plunged in cities such as Philadelphia and Baltimore.

Republicans registered disproportionate gains among voters with middle-to-lower middle incomes and high school educations or those with some college training. Democrats did best, and minimized their losses, among the least well educated and the best educated, and among the poorest and wealthiest voters. The Perot factor was paramount. The largest single GOP gain in the various subgroups comprising the electorate came from those who supported Perot. (Polls show many continue to support him in 1996.)

The Republican character of this year's voter rebellion was symbolized by the fact that not one incumbent Republican governor, senator, or representative was defeated.

The question on everyone's mind is, How did the Religious Right do in the 1994 elections? The answer is reasonably well, whether as a direct or indirect influence. The Christian Coalition claims to have distributed 33 million voter guides, mostly in churches, throughout the nation. These voter guides, while they stopped short of actually endorsing candidates, selected issues important to televangelist Pat Robertson's organization and rated candidates accordingly.

Many victorious Republican candidates courted Religious Right support and ran campaigns closely identified with Religious Right pet causes. In Florida Joe Scarborough won the First Congressional District in the troubled Pensacola area by adopting hard-line anti-abortion and Christian conservative positions. Another Religious Rightist, Dave Weldon, won the Cape Canaveral area on a similar campaign platform. He defeated pro-choice Democrat Sue Munsey, who had been a Republican. Both districts had been Democratic.

Helen Chenoweth ousted a Democrat in Idaho's First District. Jon Christensen in Nebraska, Steve Largent in Oklahoma, and Andrea Seastrand in California were winners who are closely identified with the Religious Right. Steve Stockman, who ousted forty-two-year veteran Jack Brooks in Texas, raised most of his funds in the conservative churches of East Texas. Linda Smith, who upset Jolene Unsoeld in Washington's Third District, was the favorite of grassroots Christian activists. The political neophyte, who never attended college, is a member of the Assembly of God church, which is a major participant in the Christian Coalition and in anti-abortion crusades. Conservative Christian activists also helped elect Todd Tiahrt over longtime Democratic incumbent Dan Glickman in the Fourth District of Kansas.

Many of the fifty-two seats gained by the GOP in the House are more sympathetic to Religious Right positions on school prayer, abortion, and private school vouchers.

David Beasley, a Democrat-turned-Republican, won the South Carolina governorship on a frankly religious platform, discussing his conversion to fundamentalist Christianity as often as he outlined his plans for governing the Palmetto State. Beasley defeated a moderate GOP Congressman from Charleston, Arthur Ravenel, who is of French Huguenot and Episcopalian background, in a bitter primary before defeating Democratic Lt. Gov. Nick Theodore in November. The South Carolina result was predictable. The state has the highest percentage of voters who call themselves born-again Christians, and is the most Protestant and least Catholic state in the Union.

Many of the newly elected Republican senators ran with Religious Right support, including Mike Devine in Ohio, James Inhofe in Oklahoma, and Rick Santorum in Pennsylvania. This may understate the depth of their strength, however, since several Republicans who succeeded Republicans are far more supportive of the Religious Right than their predecessors. Rod Grams in Minnesota is an ultraconservative Lutheran who succeeded David Durenberger, a

Catholic who increasingly opposed religious conservatives during the latter days of his term of office. In Missouri ex-Governor John Ashcroft, a member of the Assembly of God church, whose favorite pastime is gospel hymn singing, is a fierce foe of abortion rights. Ashcroft replaces John Danforth, a moderate and an ordained Episcopal priest who played a prominent role in the Senate fight against school prayer in 1984. Of the newly elected Republican senators only Olympia Snowe of Maine, who is Greek Orthodox in faith, can be counted upon to oppose the religious conservatives.

On the other hand, many darlings of the Religious Right went down to defeat. Chuck Robb, a staunch liberal on church-state issues, defeated Oliver North, an extremist of the Far Right and a Catholic-turned-fundamentalist, in the bitterly fought Virginia Senate race. Dianne Feinstein edged out Michael Huffington in California, though religious issues were relatively minor in that race. Representative Vic Fazio, a California Democrat who forthrightly blasted the Religious Right's agenda for America, survived a tough race with a Republican conservative who emphasized religious issues. In the Maryland governor's race, archconservative Ellen Sauerbrey, who opposed abortion rights, promoted vouchers for private and parochial schools, and received active Christian Right support, narrowly lost to liberal Democrat Parris Glendening, a Catholic who favors abortion rights and supports public education. And Senator Ted Kennedy was decisively reelected in Massachusetts. These Democratic triumphs were few and far between, however, in an election that may have altered the political landscape for years to come.

Many observers saw this election as a comeback for the Religious Right. Commented the late Arthur Kropp, president of People for the American Way, "The Religious Right came out of the election stronger than they came in. They were critical to a lot of victories. This was not just a wake-up call but a fire alarm for mainstream America."[2]

Kropp also predicted that the Republicans would be forced to accede to many Religious Right demands. "Precinct by precinct, Religious Right activists were the single largest organized group doing the tedious chores of voter registration and get out the vote activities. That is a huge political debt Republican leaders can be expected to repay with interest," he observed.

The Religious Right cannot win elections on its own, however, especially if candidates are seen as intolerant or exclusive. Political analyst Robert D. Holsworth of Virginia Commonwealth University in Richmond said, "It is difficult for candidates of the Religious Right to win elections, but support of the Religious Right is essential." Thus, the Republican dilemma is to find ways to court these voters without offending the values and sensibilities of others.

The long-range impact of this election on public policy may be devastating to those who cherish a religiously pluralistic society protected by a wall of separation between church and state. Abortion, school prayer, vouchers, religious activities in public schools, and censorship laws are likely to be affected. Warned Kate Michelman, president of the National Abortion and Reproductive Rights Action League (NARAL), "Led by the Christian Coalition, the Radical Right organized furiously and exploited pro-choice complacency. As a result, the most fundamental rights and freedoms of American women will be endangered for years to come. The 104th Congress could well be the most anti-woman, anti-choice Congress in our history." Michelman's analysis concludes that at least forty House members and five senators who supported freedom of choice were replaced by anti-choice members.

Michelman's analysis is supported by exit polling data, which found a wider voting gap between men and women than in any recent election: 54 percent of women voted Democratic for Congress, but only 44 percent of men did so. In states like Massachusetts and Maryland the difference was 12-18 points.

While the Religious Right is clearly stronger now than before the November 8 elections, it is by no means invincible. Much depends on the nature of the electorate, the character of the candidates, and the tenor of the campaign. People for the American Way's analysis concluded that about 60 percent of candidates closely identified with or backed by the Religious Right were victorious. But 40 percent were not. In the latter category were the contenders in the Senate race in the Old Dominion, where the well-financed ($20 million) candidacy of convicted felon and right-wing zealot Ollie North failed to dislodge Democratic incumbent Chuck Robb.

The defeat of an anti-abortion proposal in Wyoming, rejection of a measure mandating religious studies in public schools in Utah, and passage by Oregon voters of an initiative allowing doctors to assist gravely ill persons to end their suffering were exceptions to the national swing to the right. Voters showed that on some issues the conservative shift of the electorate was not absolute. Voters, especially in the West, perhaps, are still wary of religious group involvement in political life. Here are the details.

Abortion

Wyoming's generally libertarian, conservative voting public soundly rejected by 61 percent to 39 percent Proposition 2, which would have prohibited abortion in all cases except rape, incest, or danger to the mother's life.

Republican Senator Alan Simpson, the assistant GOP leader in the Senate, was one of the leaders of the pro-choice camp. Reflecting on the decisive outcome, pro-choice leader Lorna Johnson observed, "It's a very conservative electorate here. But Wyoming people cherish their privacy and sense of liberty, and they saw that this initiative attacked their basic freedoms by having government intrude into their most personal, private decisions."

Religion in Public Schools

Despite almost no organized opposition, Utah's conservative, largely Mormon voters turned down Proposition 3, which would have "insured nonsectarian study of religion in public schools." Voters said no by 53 percent to 47 percent.

Doctor-Assisted Suicide

Oregonians made their state the first in the nation to approve a measure exempting from prosecution physicians who assist terminally ill patients who wish to end their suffering. Patients must make this request three times before physicians are allowed to prescribe life-ending drugs. Measure 16 passed by a 52-percent-to-48-percent margin.

The Oregon campaign was fierce. Religion became a central issue. In terms of its politicoreligious context, Oregon is the most likely state in which this kind of proposal could be approved. Oregon is the most secular state in the union. Fully 17 percent of Oregonians say they have no religious affiliation, the highest of any state. Only a third of citizens are members of religious groups. About half the state's residents profess a religious identification but are not affiliated with specific congregations.

But the opposition, often emotional, has defeated similar proposals in other states, notably Washington and California, neighboring Pacific Coast states that share Oregon's secularity and pluralism. Church groups went all out to defeat Measure 16. The Roman Catholic Church took the lead, even to the point of including an in-pew collection of funds from those parishioners who attended church services on September 25. This collection was highly controversial among Catholics, however, many of whom denounced it as inappropriate politicking in a captive religious setting. Mary LaBarre, director of pastoral studies at the Catholic-affiliated University of Portland, said it was not the Church's business to be collecting for a political campaign in church. One pastor of a Portland parish told the *National Catholic Reporter* that the action violated separation of church and state. Many Catholics must have agreed. The special collection netted $276,748 from 13,000 contributors. Since there are 300,000 Catholics in Oregon, this represents less than a dollar per member. (And only 4 percent of Catholics contributed anything.)

Still, the national Church was heavily involved in the Oregon campaign. The National Conference of Catholic Bishops' Secretariat for Pro-Life Activities donated $100,000 to the political action committee opposing Measure 16. "This really is a national battle," observed Richard Doerflinger, a staff person at the Secretariat.

Peggy Wehmeyer, ABC News religion specialist, reported that Protestant and Jewish groups joined the Catholic effort, making the opposition to the proposal almost exclusively religious. But in secular Oregon, the religious group efforts fell a little short.

Under the proposed and now-approved law, an adult resident of Oregon will be able to request a lethal dose of drugs after two physicians have determined that the patient has six months or fewer to live.

After three requests, each witnessed by two people, and a fifteen-day waiting period, the attending physician will be allowed to prescribe a fatal dose with immunity from prosecution.

These safeguards apparently made the Oregon law more acceptable to voters than ones rejected earlier in Washington and California, though the Oregon decision is awaiting a court ruling before it can be implemented.

Gay Rights

Voters in Oregon and Idaho also turned down measures promoted by religious conservatives that aimed at denying civil rights to gays and lesbians. The ultraconservative Oregon Citizens Alliance rewrote an anti–gay rights proposal rejected by the voters in 1992, limiting its scope somewhat. The Oregon measure, defeated by 54 percent to 46 percent, would have prohibited laws banning discrimination against gays and would have barred discussion of homosexuality in public elementary schools.

The Idaho measure was identical in language and was also rejected 51 percent-49 percent in one of America's most conservative, and second most heavily Mormon, states.

Censorship

Voters in Oregon and Colorado soundly rejected proposed constitutional amendments initiated by the Religious Right. Both dealt with censorship of allegedly obscene or sexually explicit printed or visual matter and would have affected bookshops and libraries. The proposals—Ballot Measure 19 in Oregon and Amendment 16 in Colorado—were designed to give local governments the power to adopt censorship laws.

Publishers, authors, and book people took an active interest in defeating the proposals, couched as they were in the language of "child pornography and family values." (The Oregon measure was placed on the ballot by the Christian Coalition, and the Colorado proposal by Focus on the Family, the two largest Religious Right lobbies in the nation.) Opposition was spearheaded by the Oregon Coalition for Free Expression and Colorado Citizens Against Censorship. Oregonians turned down the proposal by 54 percent to 46 percent, while Coloradans did so by an overwhelming 63 percent to 37 percent.

Oren Teicher, president of the American Booksellers Association's Foundation for Free Expression, was exultant. "I found it amazing that in such a conservative year both initiatives met with resounding defeats," he said.

Gambling

Gambling used to be considered a church-state issue, or at least one of those "sin" issues that divided Protestants and Catholics, with the former taking a militantly negative position against all forms of gambling. In the past thirty years, however, the increasing popularity of state lotteries, which were promoted as ways to raise state revenue and keep taxes lower, has made the issue less contentious from a religious perspective. (Even Protestant Iowa allows casino gambling on riverboats, and Missouri allows some forms of horse racing.)

In 1994 Florida voters, who approved a state lottery in 1986, turned down casino gambling by a 3-to-2 margin. Wyomingites rejected slot machines, black jack, and poker, but Missourians approved legalization of slot machines on riverboat casinos. New Mexicans approved a statewide lottery and video gambling. Rhode Island voters made the state casino law an amendment to the state constitution by a 2-to-1 margin.

In the above-mentioned states, religion, education, and place of residence still affect voter opinions on the gambling issue. Rural Baptist and Methodist areas are still more likely to oppose gambling schemes than areas where voters adhere to other religious traditions. Rural areas are far more opposed to gambling than are cities or suburbs, as are jurisdictions where education and income are low.

Notes

1. John C. Green, James L. Guth, Lyman A. Kellstedt, and Corwin E. Smidt, "Evangelical Realignment: The Political Power of the Christian Right," *Christian Century* 112 (July 5–12, 1995): 676–79. Quotes appearing on pp. 175–79 come from this source.

2. "The 1994 Elections," *Voice of Reason* 51 (Fall 1994): 4–8. Quotes on pp. 183–87 come from this source.

7

Case Studies of
Evangelical Political Involvement,
1993-1994

Since Clinton was elected, a number of elections reflect the increasing political activity of the Religious Right and of conservative evangelicals generally.

Here are descriptions of a number of them, which may serve as case studies of evangelical political involvement.

The 1993 Lieutenant Governor's Race in Virginia

The 1993 elections in Virginia saw the emergence of a full-fledged Religious Right figure in the person of Michael Farris, the GOP nominee for lieutenant governor. Farris is the director of the Home Schooling Legal Defense Association and had served as Moral Majority director in Washington State in the 1980s before joining Concerned Women for America's Washington, D.C., staff.

After defeating a moderate Republican, Bobbie Kilberg, who happened to be a Jewish woman and a New York native, in the convention, which was dominated by Religious Right activists, Farris was soon plunged into the real world of hard-ball politics. His opponent, the incumbent Don Beyer, and other Democrats began to raise the issues of Farris's long record of contempt for public education and his support for fundamentalist assaults on public school textbooks and academic programs.

As lead attorney for a group of fundamentalist parents in Hawkins County, Tennessee, during the 1980s, Farris had publicly labeled public schools "godless" and had encouraged Christians to remove their children from these citadels of Satan. Farris represented parents who wanted their children to read alternative books in reading classes, objecting to the assigned selections because the readers were inclusive, multicultural, and favorably depicted religions other than Christianity. (They objected to *The Diary of Anne Frank* because it portrayed Jews favorably.) Some elements in the campaign wanted to remove all textbooks that were deemed objectionable to conservative religious groups. This case, the *Mozert* case, resulted in a defeat for fundamentalist forces, and the emotions generated by the controversy reverberated around Farris. After the U.S. Supreme Court refused to hear a challenge to the federal appeals court's decision in *Mozert*, Farris declaimed, "It's time for every born-again Christian in America to take their children out of public schools, and the quicker the better."[1] In an address to the 1987 Convention of Concerned Women for America, Farris, an ordained Baptist minister with a law degree from a Catholic university, had said, "It is very, very dangerous to have the machinery called public schools. In fact, I believe that public schools are per se unconstitutional."[2]

In a book written two years before he sought public office, Farris wrote, "For a growing number of people it is a violation of their religious conscience to have their children attend the public schools. The activities in the public schools are so godless, and in many cases, anti-God, that it is a violation of the Christian faith to participate in such schools in any way."[3]

Farris also evinced a wistful nostalgia for an earlier era of U.S. life when conservative Protestants dominated the nation. In a 1992 book he wrote that "the founding fathers of this country believed that the principles of God's word should be used in our nation and employed the Word of God in the public arena."[4] In the same book he expressed admiration for early state constitutions that mandated religious tests and restricted public office to white Protestants.

This led one writer to ask, "Does Michael Farris support Article VI of the Constitution? If so, how does that square with his approval of pre-constitutional religious tests for public office? And does Michael Farris, who would be a heartbeat away from the office once held by Madison and Jefferson, support religious freedom for all? Or Christians only?"[5]

The Democrats bore down on these issues and infuriated religious and political conservatives. The Republicans went on the offensive and accused the Democrats of stirring up religious bigotry. Ralph Reed, executive director of the Virginia-based Christian Coalition, called a press conference and said, "Never before in the history of Virginia have voters been subjected to such a vicious campaign of lies, distortions and religious bigotry."[6]

Republican National Committee Chairman Haley Barbour accused the Democrats of "shrill, bigoted attacks" because "the left wants to minimalize Christian conservatives and demonize them."[7] Barbour released $15,000 of Republican National Committee funds to the Farris campaign. Nationally prominent conservatives like William Bennett compared Farris to John F. Kennedy, as did Farris himself in a public debate, accusing Beyer of "religious bigotry, making fun of my faith. I thought that had ended with Jack Kennedy."[8] Syndicated columnist Cal Thomas said Farris "has been the subject of bigoted attacks simply because he is open about his faith and seeks to apply it."[9]

Farris agreed with Thomas on one point. "I will bring my religion into politics," he told listeners during the only televised debate between the two candidates.[10] The opponents clashed over several religion-based issues, including abortion, aid to private religious schools, censorship of public school textbooks, teen pregnancy, and distribution of birth-control devices in public schools. The same issues divided the two candidates for governor, Republican George Allen and Democrat Mary Sue Terry.

The comparison of Farris with John F. Kennedy was patently absurd. Farris promised that he would apply his religious principles to public office. Kennedy promised that he would not, implying that it would violate the Constitution to do so. Farris's Baptist religious community had never been the subject of exclusionary political campaigns or formal legal discrimination as were Roman Catholics throughout U.S. history. Religious test acts were directed primarily at Catholics during the eighteenth and early nineteenth centuries. Fundamentalists and Baptists were the most prominent religious groups involved in the defamatory movements aimed at preventing Kennedy in 1960 and Governor Smith in 1928 from achieving the presidency. For them to sanctimoniously claim victimhood and martyrdom status today is a profound misreading of history and an attempt to claim for themselves a historical status that is unwarranted.

The press also had a field day with another extraneous issue: the religious affiliations of the candidates and their wives. While Republicans howled about religious bigotry, it was the Democratic candidates whose religious affiliations became a minor issue. It was revealed that Lt. Gov. Beyer, a 1968 graduate of Gonzaga High School in Washington, D.C.—the alma mater of Patrick Buchanan and William Bennett—had switched from the Roman Catholic Church to the Episcopal Church after his divorce and remarriage. His second wife also shifted from Catholic to Episcopalian. Democratic gubernatorial nominee Mary Sue Terry, a lifelong Baptist, had quietly become an Episcopalian. Republican candidate George Allen was a nominal Presbyterian who often attended his second wife's Baptist church, the church she joined after renouncing Catholicism. This religious switching, now common in American life, was potentially more of a vote-loser than Farris's status as a devout Baptist. As it turned out, there was little if any denominational impact on the shape of the vote. Religious voting has become more sophisticated.

Farris lost his bid to become Virginia's lieutenant governor, but he won almost 46 percent of the 1.7 million votes cast. Farris's vote followed traditional Republican patterns and was greatest in rural and small town areas.

As can be seen from table 7.4, the Republican vote tends to rise as the size of the community becomes smaller. Both Allen and Farris did best in small-town, rural, and exurban Virginia. Allen did well in large and medium suburbs, though Farris lost and Allen barely carried Virginia's large and medium size cities, which Farris lost rather heavily. Farris won by 20,000 votes outside of urban and suburban areas but lost by 173,000 in the seventeen large population centers, particularly in Northern Virginia, the Richmond area, and the Greater Norfolk area. This is a pattern that is increasingly true for Republican candidates. George Bush had the same pattern in Virginia and in most other states. If only nonurban Virginia had voted, Farris would have won.

The decline in support for Michael Farris as compared to Republican gubernatorial winner George Allen is the focus of this study since it is those voters who supported the Republican candidates for governor and for attorney general but who refused to vote for Farris who may have been most susceptible to the religious issues. Farris's decline was somewhat greater in the suburbs than elsewhere, but it varied from region to region where other factors were more important.

Farris won his strongest showing statewide, as expected, among traditional Republican voting groups, particularly those in small-town and rural areas. Farris won nearly 60 percent of the votes in those counties that are prewar Republican, that is, those that voted Republican before World War II. Many of these are the old Shenandoah Valley counties, where many people are of German descent and have been Republican for generations. Farris won 54 percent in postwar Republican counties, those counties that went Republican for Thomas Dewey in 1948 and have stayed with the GOP since then. Farris did, however, run about 15 points behind Allen in the postwar Republican counties. Farris also won majorities, unexpectedly so, among low-income miners in the southwestern part of the state, in counties with high Baptist and Methodist church memberships, and in counties that supported George Wallace in 1968.

Farris declined significantly in counties where there was big support for Ross Perot in 1992. Farris won 49 percent in these counties compared to almost 64 percent for Allen. The factor of church membership, though, is very mixed. Farris actually lost 51 percent to 49 percent in those counties that have the highest church membership. The pattern is mixed, even by religious group and by region of the state. Farris lost 14 percentage points in high-income counties near Washington, D.C., where voters could be considered moderate rather than liberal or conservative. These swing counties gave Allen 53 percent and Farris 39 percent. Farris did poorly in areas that have large numbers of college students, a high black population, and white liberal professionals with high incomes and high education. And while Farris carried the Shenandoah Valley, he ran 15 points behind Allen there. Farris's most impressive victory came in the Virginia Mountains, where he won 53.6 percent. This area of the state had voted for Bill Clinton for president a year before. It was in these culturally conservative populist areas that the GOP trend was strongest. (See table 7.5.)

Farris lost, but Allen won, in high-income, well-educated counties like James City County, a suburb of Williamsburg that has many Episcopalian and Catholic voters; Albemarle County, the fashionable area surrounding Charlottesville; and Fairfax County, one of the nation's premier elite counties in terms of per capita income and percentage of college-educated residents. Farris also failed to carry Lynchburg, the home base of Jerry Falwell, or Chesapeake-Virginia Beach, the center of the Pat Robertson empire. The Christian Coalition had a million voter guides distributed by friendly churches.

Exit polls showed that 77 percent of evangelicals voted for Allen and 69 percent voted for Farris. About one-third of Virginia's electorate called itself evangelical. Only 18 percent of Catholics supported Farris even though Beyer had switched from Catholic to Episcopalian.[11]

The Republicans continued to press the religious issue after the election, probably to solidify their support among evangelicals. Congressional leaders from the GOP called on President Clinton "to denounce this type of religious intolerance."[12]

The outcome of the 1993 elections in Virginia suggests that candidates too closely identified with the Religious Right will lose, but those who agree with some Religious Right positions and use the Religious Right as one ally in a broad-based coalition can win. (See tables 7.1 through 7.6 and map 7.1.)

The 1994 Virginia U.S. Senate Race

The controversial ex-Marine Oliver North captured the GOP nomination for the U.S. Senate in a contentious party convention dominated by Christian

Map 7.1. Virginia

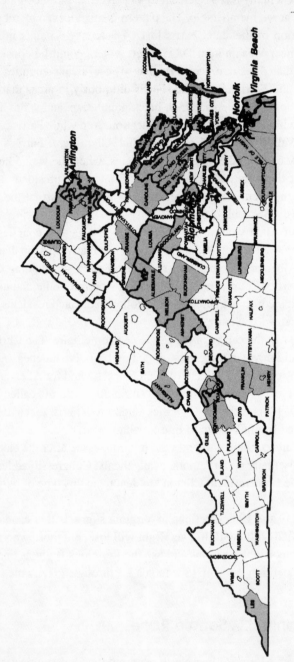

1993: Supported Allen for governor but rejected Farris for lieutenant governor

Table 7.1

Anti-Farris Voting in Greater Richmond

County/City	% of Precincts Supporting Allen, not Farris	% of Precincts giving Allen 20% over Farris
Richmond	23.9	9.9
Henrico	39.1	28.7
Chesterfield	17.2	20.7
Hanover	24.0	8.0

Table 7.2

**Farris Decline among Absentee and
Republican Upper-Income Voters Greater Than among All Voters**

County	% Farris Decline All Voters	% Farris Decline Absentee Voters	Highest Allen Precincts
Richmond	−12.2	−18.3	−26.8
Henrico	−18.0	−21.3	−23.1
Chesterfield	−17.0	−19.0	−20.0
Hanover	−18.0	−21.2	−18.9

Table 7.3

High Anti-Farris Voting in Upper-Income Precincts

Precinct	Location	% Allen	% Farris	% Farris Decline
106	Richmond	79.3	46.4	−32.9
(Mooreland)	Henrico	81.0	50.7	−30.3
102	Richmond	74.7	47.7	−27.0
105	Richmond	66.4	40.1	−26.3
103	Richmond	68.1	42.9	−25.2
Salisbury	Chesterfield	78.5	53.5	−25.0
104	Richmond	68.5	43.5	−25.0
Tuckahoe	Henrico	76.2	51.5	−24.7
Canterbury	Henrico	78.2	53.5	−24.7
Smoketree	Chesterfield	76.2	51.7	−24.5

Table 7.4

Size of Community

	Allen	Farris	Farris Decline
Large and medium cities[1]	50.4	37.8	−12.6
Large and medium suburbs[2]	57.6	42.8	−14.8
Small towns, rural, exurbs	63.7	51.3	−12.4

1. Alexandria, Chesapeake, Hampton, Newport News, Norfolk, Portsmouth, Richmond, Roanoke, Virginia Beach.
2. Arlington, Chesterfield, Fairfax, Hanover, Henrico, Loudon, Prince William, Roanoke County.

Table 7.5

1993 Vote among Cultural Subgroups

	% Allen	% Farris	% Farris Decline
White liberal elite	37.2	26.2	−11.0
High Wallace	61.0	50.3	−10.7
High Perot	63.5	49.0	−14.5
Low-income white populist	61.4	52.2	− 9.2
College towns	45.9	34.7	−11.2
Postwar Republican	68.8	54.2	−14.6
Prewar Republican	71.5	59.7	−11.8
High government employees	64.5	50.3	−14.2
High manufacturing	58.6	49.7	− 8.9
High-income "moderate"	53.2	39.3	−13.9
High black population	40.6	29.5	−11.1
High church membership	62.1	48.7	−13.4
High Baptist and Methodist	63.1	51.0	−12.1
Shenandoah Valley	66.9	52.1	−14.8
Southwest Mountains	62.7	53.6	− 9.1

Table 7.6

A Comparison of Pro-Farris and Anti-Farris Counties

Counties	% Church Members	% White Baptist or Methodist	Per Capita Income	% College Educated
Pro Farris[1]	46.3	30.2	7,942	7.2
Anti-Farris[2]	52.3	28.9	11,156	14.0
Statewide	47.9	21.0	11,894	19.1

1. Counties where Farris ran 1%–9% behind Allen.
2. Counties where Farris ran 17%–24% behind Allen.

Right and pro-gun ownership activists. Even with a favorable constituency, North only defeated former Reagan Office of Management and Budget director Jim Miller by 55 percent to 45 percent. Most observers believe North would have lost a primary open to all voters. Caucuses and tightly controlled conventions tend to favor highly organized candidates with committed supporters who espouse an ideological bent.

Rozell and Wilcox studied the North and Miller delegates and found that they represented radically different visions of society, especially on social and cultural issues. Among North delegates 42 percent called themselves born again, a term of religious definition held by only 10 percent of Miller delegates. Thirty-six percent of North's delegates were members of evangelical, fundamentalist, or pentecostal churches, while only 10 percent of Miller's delegates were. On the other hand, 54 percent of Miller supporters compared to 29 percent of North supporters were members of mainline Protestant churches. (Interestingly, about 20 percent of both candidates' delegates were Catholic, compared to 5 percent of all Virginians.)

North delegates were much more religious than Miller's, since 68 percent of North's delegates attended church weekly or more often, compared to 43 percent of Miller's delegates. Of Miller's supporters, 34 percent rarely or never attended church compared to 15 percent of North delegates. Half of North delegates watched religious television programs, compared to 21 percent of Miller's, and 67 percent of North delegates said the Bible was literally true and inerrant, compared to 37 percent of Miller delegates.[13]

While both groups were conservative on economic and foreign policy questions, North delegates were much more conservative on social issues. A majority of North delegates favored a ban on all abortions, mandatory teaching of creationism in schools, encouragement of home schooling, and mandatory death penalties for all murderers. A majority of Miller delegates were opposed. Among North delegates 75 percent supported banning gay teachers from public schools, compared to 53 percent of Miller delegates. On free trade, North supporters were early Buchananites: only 46 percent supported free trade, compared to 73 percent of Miller delegates.

On some issues a segment of North delegates favored extremist positions: 30 percent said AIDS is God's punishment to gays, 26 percent believed known homosexuals should be jailed, and 38 percent thought government should regulate pornography. Almost no Miller delegates held such positions (119).

With a convention dominated by North supporters, delegates passed resolutions favoring a constitutional amendment to prohibit abortion, supported "voluntary" prayer in schools, denounced the state's public school sex education program, and called on the state to "interpose" itself against the federal government. (Shades of the states rights and segregationist crusades of the 1950s.)

In the general election against incumbent Democratic Senator Charles Robb, North hardly toned down his Far Right agenda. He was the hero of the Far Right, of both its secular and religious divisions. Wrote Rozell and Wilcox, "North's campaign emphasized his religious convictions and experiences. North made numerous appearances throughout the campaign before evangelical church congregations. . . . North declared every word in the Bible literally true" (122–23). North's campaign solidified his support from all kinds of conservative Christians. "Although North had his strongest ties to charismatic Christianity, he received strong support from fundamentalists like Farris" (123).

The connections continued right down to the wire. "North was a professed born-again Christian who attended a charismatic church and was unapologetic about openly expressing his faith. On the Sunday before the election, Christian Right groups, including the Christian Coalition, passed out over a million voter guides throughout the state" (124).

Chuck Robb had personal problems, stemming from charges of drug use and adultery, as well as a bitter intraparty feud with former Democratic Governor Douglas Wilder, who was running as an independent and threatened to siphon off black votes from Robb. Moderate and some conservative Republicans, including the state's other senator, John Warner, supported an independent candidate, Marshall Coleman, a former Republican attorney general who had lost two previous races for governor.

Virginia is a paradox. The state that nurtured the largest number of the Founding Fathers, including early presidents like George Washington, Thomas Jefferson, and James Madison, Virginia was also the intellectual and political capital of the Confederacy and is now home to an extraordinary number of religious and political conservatives. Jerry Falwell, Pat Robertson, Pat Buchanan, Richard Viguerie, the Rutherford Institute's John Whitehead, Supreme Court Justices Clarence Thomas and William Rehnquist, and conservative guru Os Guinness all call Virginia home. The state is politically conservative, having supported the Republican presidential candidate in ten of the past eleven elections.

But the state is also religiously moderate, even somewhat pluralistic. Its largest churches, Baptists and Methodists, are relatively moderate. Substantial numbers of Episcopalians reside in the Tidewater and in the Hunt Country, while Presbyterians are strong in the Lexington area. The Catholic and Jewish communities are growing, especially in the affluent and politically liberal Northern Virginia suburbs of Washington, D.C. The Shenandoah Valley has many Lutheran, Mennonite, and Brethren churches. The state has been noted for a high degree of religious harmony and a relative absence of religious strife. The Ku Klux Klan and the Know Nothings drew little support in the state. Religious right–backed candidate Mike Farris was defeated in the 1993 race for lieutenant governor while his Republican running mates were successful.

Still, the Christian Coalition is headquartered in the state, as is the now-tottering empire of Jerry Falwell. Ollie North, the retired Marine Corps colonel who won the Republican nomination in a convention dominated by Christian Coalition activists, pushed religious themes such as abortion restrictions, school prayer, and "personal morality" and confined his religious campaigning to evangelical and fundamentalist churches. The Christian Coalition voting scorecards clearly implied that North was right on the issues that concerned them. But North's refusal to campaign in black areas, and his endorsement of flying the Confederate flag doomed his candidacy among African-Americans, who gave incumbent Republican Governor George Allen almost 20 percent of their votes in 1993. Former Governor Douglas Wilder abruptly ended his feud with Senator Robb, terminated his independent campaign, and endorsed Robb. Moderate Republicans, including some conservatives and officials in the Reagan and Bush administrations, openly opposed North. Most backed the independent campaign of moderate Republican Marshall Coleman, though some endorsed Robb, whose votes are strongly pro–church/state separation.

Robb's 46 percent-to-43 percent victory over North (with 11 percent for Coleman) indicated sharp divisions among Virginia's voters, who turned out in high numbers. Robb won 90 percent of black voters, as well as majorities among the college educated. Robb won large majorities in the D.C.-oriented Northern Virginia suburbs, in the Norfolk metro area, and in college towns

like Charlottesville and Williamsburg. Even Republican-leaning Montgomery County, where Virginia Tech is the largest employer, voted for Robb.

North, however, swept the rural areas, carrying seventy-four of the
state's ninety-five counties. North won heavily in the Southside counties
where George Wallace ran well in 1968. He won the conservative and heavily Baptist Richmond suburbs and the traditionally Republican Shenandoah
Valley. The culturally conservative but economically liberal Southwest was
split, with coal-mining counties like Buchanan and Dickenson, which have
low church memberships and strong unions, supporting Robb. But some one-
time Democratic counties defected. Tazewell County, a blue-collar mining
area that supported Dukakis and Clinton, bolted to North. In general, Robb's
vote was below Democratic expectations in the Southwest, where low education and religious conservatism are realigning voters to the GOP.

Robb's victory in Jerry Falwell's hometown of Lynchburg and in the
Christian Coalition's home base in Chesapeake must have been highly satisfying to the Robb campaign, suggesting as it does that not all voters identify
with the Religious Right even in their bailiwicks.

North did show surprising strength in the outlying suburbs of Washington, in Prince William and Loudon Counties, for example, where the population is young and family-oriented and where Perot did best in 1992. North
captured a majority in this region.

Two results in Northern Virginia typify the kind of political realignment,
rooted in education, income, and perhaps religion, that modern America is
experiencing. Falls Church is one of America's wealthiest and best-educated
jurisdictions. A majority of voters are college-educated and affluent. In 1976
Gerald Ford carried the town. But Robb crushed North by 3 to 1 in this election, and Bill Clinton won heavily two years before. Manassas Park is a blue-
collar town, where only 12 percent of voters are college-educated. The town
voted 2-to-1 for Jimmy Carter in 1976, but it went 2-to-1 for North over
Robb. In 1992 it supported George Bush. The results in Falls Church and
Manassas Park symbolize the cutting edge of U.S. politics today, and strongly
suggest that cultural politics may soon surmount economic-based voting.

A comparison of the 1994 senate race and the 1992 presidential vote is
revealing. Eleven counties supported Republican George Bush but refused to
support Oliver North. The most important in terms of size was Fairfax County,
which Bush carried by 10,000 votes but North lost by 46,000 votes. Here is
where moderate political conservatives, religious moderates, and high-status
voters defected to Robb or to Coleman, who received 39,000 ballots, or 13
percent of the total, in Fairfax. Albemarle County, surrounding Charlottesville, and James City County, a suburb of Williamsburg, were other high-

income, highly educated areas supporting Bush and Robb. But so did Jerry Falwell's home of Lynchburg and the blue-collar towns of Newport News and Chesapeake. North also dropped 10 points behind Bush in Republican Virginia Beach and 7 points behind in Democratic Norfolk and Portsmouth.

But North carried five counties in the Virginia Mountains and in the Shenandoah Valley that had gone for Clinton. The mountains are populist country with many fundamentalists and gun-control opponents. In the twenty-county area in the state's far southwest, North won by 3 percentage points while Bush had lost them by 5 points to Clinton. In the more evangelical and moderately conservative Valley, both North and Bush won by similar margins of 13-14 points. (See map 7.2.)

The 1994 Pennsylvania Governor's Race

The 1994 election for governor of Pennsylvania involved a spirited campaign by a Johnstown housewife, Peggy Luksik, who ran as an anti-abortion, social conservative independent. Running as the standard-bearer of the Constitution Party, she secured almost 13 percent of the statewide vote, winning 450,000 voters to her banner. The moderately conservative congressman from the Erie area, Tom Ridge, was the successful Republican candidate with 45 percent of the vote, while the moderately liberal Democratic candidate, Lieutenant Governor Mark Singel, won 40 percent. (For purposes of this analysis, the 2 percent of the votes cast for Libertarians and the Patriot Party will not be considered.)

Luksik ran for governor primarily because both major party candidates were pro-choice on abortion rights, or as pro-choice as one can be in Pennsylvania, the most socially conservative state north of the Mason-Dixon line.

Another startling fact about the 1994 elections was that all three candidates for governor and both U.S. Senate candidates, incumbent Democrat Harris Wofford and Republican Rick Santorum, were Roman Catholics. The very conservative Santorum, who narrowly defeated liberal Senator Wofford, is of Italian-American ancestry, and he became not only the first Italian-American elected to the U.S. Senate from Pennsylvania, but also the first Catholic Republican senator. Tom Ridge also became the first Catholic Republican governor. This chain of events might appear unexceptional or irrelevant to some, but Pennsylvania has a long heritage of anti-Catholicism in politics. In 1910 a bogus Knights of Columbus oath was used in a congressional election to defeat a Catholic candidate. Both Al Smith and John Kennedy faced strong voter resistance in Pennsylvania during their presi-

Map 7.2. Virginia

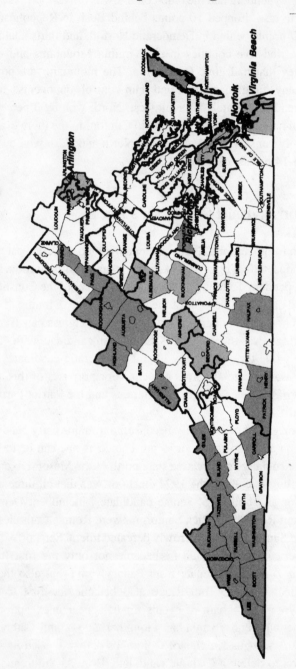

Comparative Strengths: Bush (1992) and North (1994)

■ Bush ('92 president) significantly stronger than North ('94 senator)

■ North ('94 senator) significantly stronger than Bush ('92 president)

Map 7.3. Pennsylvania

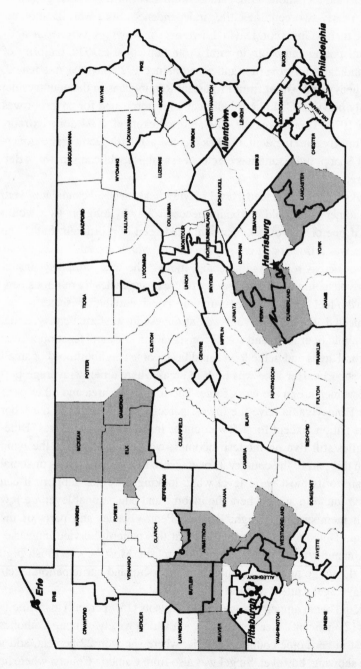

Highest support for Luksik in 1994 election for governor (18% and above)

dential campaigns. Though one of the original thirteen colonies, Pennsylvania never elected a Catholic U.S. senator until 1944 or a Catholic governor until 1958, nearly two centuries after independence. Both were Democrats and one of them, Governor David Lawrence, narrowly survived an anti-Catholic whispering campaign in rural Protestant counties. The majority of Catholic candidates for governor and senator since 1926 have been defeated, usually by heavy opposition from Protestant Republicans in the countryside. And the only previous Catholic Republican ever nominated for governor was defeated in 1970. This makes the all-Catholic tickets of 1994 quite extraordinary. (Pennsylvania, incidentally, has elected a Jewish Democratic governor, Milton Shapp, twice, and has elected a Jewish Republican senator, Arlen Specter, three times.)

The Luksik campaign faced a level playing field, since all candidates were Catholic, and her vote could not be influenced solely by religion, as it would have been if one or two of her opponents had been of a different faith. The Luksik vote was a true social conservative vote, which appealed to religious conservatives across religious lines, and, though she was ultimately unsuccessful, her vote could be a harbinger for future insurgencies by religious conservatives who feel that both parties are unresponsive to their wishes.

As expected, the Luksik vote was strongest in western Pennsylvania, where economic liberalism and social conservatism coexist. Her support was greater in rural areas and in the lower-middle-income neighborhoods of small towns and suburbs. Her vote was high in areas where a below-average percentage of women are in the work force. The Johnstown area and other parts of western Pennsylvania have the lowest percentage of women in the labor force in the nation, except for a few counties in Louisiana and Texas. Blue-collar families still live on modest incomes, with the husband as the main provider, in this part of the country. If one wishes to reduce religious or social conservatism to its most basic level when looking for voter support, it can generally be found in areas where the income and educational level are low and church membership is high. Western Pennsylvania, and parts of the Pennsylvania Dutch Country farther east, fit this pattern. Service industries and small manufacturing plants are commonplace. Most people finish high school but do not go to college. Church membership and participation levels are above average. And so was the Luksik vote.

Luksik did better among evangelical Protestants (15.7 percent) than among Catholics (12.3 percent). Her vote by religion varied widely. Among Catholics she did best in her home county, Cambria, where she won 22 percent, still a third place showing, however. Singel was also from Cambria County, where he won a majority among all voters and 53 percent among Catholics. Luksik received 17 percent in Catholic areas of Allegheny County, primarily outside of Pittsburgh, and 16 percent among Catholics in coal-mining Northumberland County. But she received 10 percent or less among Catholics everywhere else, including retiring Governor Bob Casey's home base in Scranton. In Philadelphia, Luksik's vote in Catholic neighborhoods reached only 7 percent.

Her Protestant vote also varied, reaching as high as 25 percent-30 percent in the conservative Pennsylvania Dutch regions of Lancaster, York, Cumberland, Dauphin, and Perry Counties. In fact, her support among all German-Americans (16.5 percent) was above average, probably since many of them are staunch religious conservatives. (This does represent a change of sorts, since in the past German-Americans were wary of the Prohibition movement and other crusades for moral protectionism.)

Luksik's vote was clearly more Protestant than Catholic. Her strongest precincts in the Dutch Country, in Lancaster, Dauphin, Cumberland, and York Counties, voted more heavily for Nixon in 1960 than for Eisenhower in 1956, indicating that they were largely anti-Catholic evangelicals. Even in Democratic counties, her vote was slightly more Protestant. Her strongest precincts in Beaver County gave Nixon 58 percent in 1960. Those in Westmoreland County were 54 percent for Nixon and in Allegheny County the Luksik strongholds had been 51 percent for Nixon. Beaver, Allegheny, and Westmoreland Counties had all gone for Kennedy by comfortable margins. Only in her home county (Cambria) was her vote predominantly Catholic.

Another dimension shows up in high Luksik support. She did exceptionally well among conservative Republicans, the extreme right wing of the GOP. Luksik had run for governor once before, in 1990, and nearly upset the highly favored, pro-choice moderate Barbara Hafer. Luksik carried Lancaster County against Hafer, and her supporters defected to Democrat Bob Casey in November. It is not surprising that Luksik ran so well in Lancaster County, winning over 21 percent and nearly coming second. Had it not been for Democratic votes in the more liberal city of Lancaster, Luksik would have taken second position in this legendary stronghold of Republican conservatism. As it was, she received 28 percent, a strong second, in the most Republican precincts in Lancaster County, achieving 39 percent in Conoy, a township in the northwest corner.

Statewide, Luksik won 23.3 percent support in those Republican precincts that supported George Bush by the widest margins in 1992. The right-wing tilt to her support can also be gleaned from the 23.8 percent she received in precincts that gave high support to the Libertarian Party candidate for the U.S. Senate in 1992.

Luksik received 18.5 percent of the votes in precincts populated by

"Casey Democrats," swing voters who supported Ronald Reagan and George Bush for president but who backed Robert Casey for governor in both 1986 and 1990. These precincts still went for Bush 45 percent-31 percent over Clinton, with a surprisingly large 24 percent for Perot. They backed Republican Ridge by a 20-point margin in 1994, but nearly one in five opted for the anti-abortion protest candidate.

Luksik won above-average support in areas that might be labeled "populist" because of their socioeconomic status (lower middle income) and high support for Ross Perot in the 1992 presidential race. Luksik received 15 percent in precincts carried by Perot, 17 percent in "Democrat-Populist" precincts that went for Clinton with Perot second, and 15 percent in "Republican-Populist" precincts where Bush ran first and Perot second. All three sets of Perot-oriented voters trended Republican for governor and senator in 1994. Ridge defeated Singel by one percentage point in the Democratic-Populist precincts, where George Bush ran a poor third.

The income shape of the Luksik coalition showed her greatest strength in the middle-income range (15 percent), followed by low income (13 percent), upper-middle income (11 percent), and upper income (7 percent). This comports with what researchers have generally found to be true about the social appeal of religious conservatism. It appeals most to voters in the lower- to lower-middle-income ranges, and least to those in the upper-income levels, where cultural liberalism is dominant.

This finding is confirmed by a portrait of the Luksik support in the suburbs. In conservative suburbs, which are middle income, Luksik won 16 percent of the votes. But in the high-income suburbs, where moderate Republicans are still popular, she won 9 percent. In the polyglot Philadelphia suburbs, her vote was highest in middle-income and Protestant areas, lowest in upper income and Jewish communities. She received 15 percent in middle-income suburbs, 13 percent in the lower-middle-income areas, 11 percent in upper middle, and 7 percent in upper-income suburbs. Her religious support varied from 15 percent in heavily Protestant areas, to 14 percent in Catholic communities, and 7 percent in Jewish suburbs.

In addition to the Jewish areas, Luksik's lowest support came from "Yankee Protestants" (8 percent), who are mostly mainline or nonevangelical but strongly Republican; academic precincts (8 percent), where there is little support for religious or social conservatism; liberal elite areas (6 percent), where voters have high incomes and high educations and where pro-choice sentiment on the abortion issue is pronounced; and black voters (2 percent), who respond negatively to right wing campaigns.

Finally, Luksik carried a dozen towns, including Catholic strongholds like

Table 7.7

Statewide Support for Peggy Luksik in 1994 Pennsylvania Governor's Race

Statewide: 12.8%

Type of Precinct	% Luksik
Libertarian strongholds	23.8
Bush Republicans	23.3
Casey Democrats	18.5
Democrat-Populist	17.4
German-American	16.5
Conservative suburbs	15.8
Evangelical Protestant	15.7
Low-income Protestant	15.2
Perot supporters	15.2
Republican-Populist	15.0
Middle income	15.0
Low income	13.1
Catholic	12.3
Upper-middle Income	11.3
Staunch Republican suburbs	10.6
Moderate Republican suburbs	9.0
Yankee Protestants	7.9
Academia	7.8
Upper income	7.1
Jewish	6.4
Liberal elite	5.6
African-American	1.7

Summit in Butler County and Johnsonburg in Elk County, and conservative Protestant towns like Concord and Muddycreek in Butler County, and Shippen in Cameron County. In 1960 Kennedy edged Nixon 51 percent to 49 percent in these precincts, with religion being the decisive issue. In 1992 Clinton and Bush took 36 percent each, and Perot received a surprisingly high 28 percent. In the 1994 Senate race, Republican Rick Santorum won 62 percent to 38 percent against Senator Harris Wofford, a distinct Republican trend. These towns are almost evenly divided between Protestants and Catholics.

Old enemies seemed to have joined hands in the Luksik crusade. In 1960 her strongholds in Lancaster, York, Perry, Cumberland, and Dauphin Counties were intensely anti-Catholic, where John F. Kennedy ran about 10 percentage points weaker than Adlai Stevenson. But she also did well in a string

Table 7.8

Support for Luksik in Philadelphia Suburbs

Income	% Luksik
Middle	14.9
Lower middle	12.5
Upper middle	10.9
Upper	7.0

Religion	
Pennsylvania Dutch Protestant*	14.9
Protestant	14.7
Catholic	13.9
Jewish	6.8

*"Pennsylvania Dutch" Protestants are those who live in the historically German-American rural exurbs of Bucks and Montgomery Counties. Historically Democratic, they went for Eisenhower in the 1950s and have remained Republican, though Ross Perot did well among them in 1992.

---

of rural Catholic towns that liked Kennedy. In Elk County, for example, Luksik ran strongly in Johnsonburg and Fox, which supported Kennedy, and in Millstone, a Protestant village that supported Stevenson in 1956 and Nixon in 1960. (See tables 7.7 and 7.8.)

The 1994 South Carolina Governor's Race

The Palmetto State is rapidly becoming the most Republican state in Dixie. It was the second-strongest state for George Bush in 1992, has elected a string of Republican governors, and became the first Southern state since Reconstruction to elect a GOP state house in 1994. Its venerable patriarch, 93-year-old Senator Strom Thurmond, signaled the GOP trend when he changed his party affiliation in 1964.

South Carolina is also one of the most religious states in the Union, almost entirely Protestant, evangelical, and churchgoing. An incredible 90 percent of South Carolinians identify themselves as Protestants, compared to fewer than 7 percent who are Catholic, Jewish, or Mormon, and 3 percent who are religiously unaffiliated. Almost 62 percent are Baptists or Methodists.[14] About 62 percent of the state's residents are church members, according to the Glenmary Research Center, but this percentage does not

include some of the smaller denominations.[15] A poll conducted in July 1995 by the *Charlotte Observer* found that 62 percent of South Carolinians attended church every Sunday and 81 percent said they belonged to a church. On average, South Carolinians were 10 percent more religious than North Carolinians.[16] Polls taken during elections consistently show that 55 percent to 60 percent of South Carolinians, blacks as well as whites, call themselves born-again Christians.[17]

Religious activism is strong. The Christian Coalition had a precinct organization in 1,000 of the state's 1,900 precincts in 1994.[18] Clergy routinely endorse candidates from the pulpit.

The state has been transformed during the past three decades from one of America's poorest to one virtually in the middle rank in terms of education and income. While the textile industry has steadily declined since the 1970s, jobs are plentiful in the manufacturing sector, especially in the Greenville-Spartanburg area, where sparkling new plants produce BMW and Fuji cars. The state ranks high in foreign investment, and the state's popular GOP governor, Carroll Campbell (1987–1995), lobbied aggressively to bring these industries to the state. South Carolina is pro-business and anti-union, ranking near the bottom of the country in percentage of jobs held by union workers. Tourism has become a major industry, owing to the state's scenic beauty, traditional charm, history, and heritage.

Still, problems of poverty and race remain, as nearly 30 percent of South Carolinians are black, and, although race relations have improved, the parties are sharply divided by race. In the 1994 primaries, for example, 44 percent of Democratic voters were black but only 1 percent of Republican primary voters were African-American. Almost one in six residents lives in mobile homes, and the highway accident death rate is one of the country's highest. The violent crime rate is also high in the state, and five South Carolina metropolitan areas are in the top fifty in violent crime rate. Sumter ranks eighteenth and Columbia twenty-fifth.[19]

Religion remains an important factor in South Carolina culture and political life. Kevin Lewis observes, "In the South Carolina way of life, the evangelical concern for personal salvation to the relative exclusion of concern for social justice lies at the heart of the dominant religious ethos."[20] This factor, says Lewis, clearly has social and political implications. "South Carolinians encounter, deal with, and talk about religion and its effects daily. Reticence concerning one's guiding convictions and values may be an ingredient of the air breathed elsewhere, but not in South Carolina, where, by tradition long established, especially in the dominant evangelical communities, South Carolinians wear their religion on their sleeves. Elsewhere, religion may have

overtaken sex and death as socially taboo topics of conversation, but not in this state, where prominent media coverage of religious news seems out of proportion to most newcomers to the state" (182). It was, after all, the Columbia *State* that broke the story of Republican National Chairman Lee Atwater's death-bed conversion to Christianity.

The political effects of religious commitment are numerous. Says Lewis, "South Carolina has remained committed for longer than most states to blue laws controlling sale of alcohol on Sundays; closing hours for establishments selling beer, wine and alcohol; limited conduct of commercial business on Sunday; and betting. The conservative religious lobby has successfully prevented the coming of racetracks and with them the advent of large-scale betting on horses. South Carolinians have resisted the institution of a state lottery to raise funds for the state treasury. . . . The religious lobby has ensured that religious institutions should enjoy exemption from state taxes on property" (188). However, times are changing. Religious publications, including Bibles, are now taxed, and sale of alcoholic beverages is permitted on Sundays in certain counties, mainly the Low Country resort areas.

But Lewis says that the religious conservative lobby "remains vocal in an ongoing, still to be resolved debate over the legitimacy and usefulness of prayer in public schools" (188). Some areas still allow formal prayers, despite constitutional prohibitions. "State secondary schools in more rural communities where the population is selectively homogeneous more easily maintain the custom of public prayer and more easily permit prayers conducted in the language of the dominant evangelical Protestants" (191).

This context makes the 1994 governor's race and its outcome explicable. A leading Republican contender, state legislator David M. Beasley, was a prominent convert to evangelical Christianity who ran on a "pro family platform" stressing opposition to abortion, gay schoolteachers, and a state lottery. Beasley, a scion of a prominent family, was politically precocious: he was elected as a Democrat to the state legislature as a 20-year-old junior at Clemson University. Seven years later, after listening to Alexander Scourby's reading of the New Testament, Beasley was converted at an independent fundamentalist church. He later became a Southern Baptist and a Republican and changed from a partying bachelor to a happily married husband and father.

Beasley, who emphasized his religious conversion and published tapes of it, announced his candidacy for governor. His Up Country residence and staunch religiousness made him controversial. His two opponents were from the more religiously pluralistic Low Country, Charleston Congressman Arthur Ravenel, whose family heritage was Episcopalian but who had joined the French Huguenot Church, and Tommy Hartnett, a former congressman

and a member of the state's tiny Catholic minority. Beasley appealed to supporters of Pat Robertson, who won a fifth of the 1988 presidential primary
vote, to activists from fundamentalist Bob Jones University (BJU), and to his
fellow Southern Baptists. This religious appeal to one segment of the state's
increasingly diverse religious community created a fissure in the GOP ranks.

Beasley worked the religious voters. Writes Furman University political
scientist James L. Guth, "He [Beasley] traveled to a myriad of conservative
churches to recount his religious conversion in a stump speech that was distributed via audio tape and religious TV stations all over the state. Although
he spoke frequently in pentecostal and charismatic churches, he also cultivated the BJU crowd. But his main focus was on congregations and pastors
of his own new denomination, the South Carolina Baptist Convention. Rec-
ognizing the importance of the Southern Baptist vote, Beasley worked hard
at getting the word of his own membership out among Baptist churches."[21]

Beasley led in thirty-seven of the forty-six counties, especially in ones
with many Baptists and pentecostals. Ravenel ran second and made the
runoff, while Hartnett ran third and was eliminated. The First Impressions
Research exit poll found Beasley won 66 percent of the Baptist vote, a small
majority among Methodists, and a plurality of Presbyterians. Ravenel won
among Episcopalians and Lutherans and split the Catholic vote with Hartnett.
The church attendance factor was again significant: 61 percent of weekly
churchgoers supported Beasley compared to 43 percent of those who attended occasionally. Only a tiny percentage of those who rarely or never
attended worship services voted for Beasley. He also won 75 percent of
charismatics, 67 percent of evangelicals, 66 percent of fundamentalists, and
43 percent of mainline Christians.[22]

In the Republican runoff on August 23, the lines hardened. Ravenel told
a statewide television audience that the campaign was a struggle for the soul
of the GOP. "I don't believe the people of South Carolina are going to permit South Carolina to become an arm of Pat Robertson's political empire."[23]
Beasley called this "Christian-bashing" and retorted that Christian groups
"had as much right as any group" to participate in politics.[24] Hartnett
endorsed Ravenel rather half-heartedly but predicted a Beasley victory. The
Christian Coalition went to work and distributed a half million fliers at
churches or by mail, though only one-third of evangelical churches permitted the activity.[25] The Christian Coalition rated Beasley "right" on all ten
issues that interested them, while Ravenel was right on only four issues.
David Yearrick, pastor of Hampton Park Baptist Church in Greenville, commented that "Arthur Ravenel or any Republican doesn't have a ghost of a
chance without the Christians."[26] Guth agrees. "Given the religious composi-

tion of South Carolina, Ravenel's strategy of attacking the Christian Coalition seemed doomed from the outset."[27]

Beasley won easily, securing 58 percent of the votes to Ravenel's 42 percent. Religious differences in the runoff would prove to be much stronger than in the November election against the Democratic nominee, Lt. Gov. Nick Theodore, who barely defeated Charleston's popular Mayor Joe Riley in the Democratic runoff. In the GOP race, Beasley won 73 percent in the ten most Baptist counties but only 26 percent in Beaufort, Berkeley, and Charleston counties, where many voters are Episcopalian, Presbyterian, Methodist, Lutheran, and Catholic. Beasley rolled up 79 percent in Greenville County, noted for its heavy concentration of independent fundamentalists as well as Baptists. However, Beasley also carried the Lutheran stronghold in Newberry County and the religiously diverse Columbia area.

Sharp religious and cultural differences persisted, as expected, in the general election. Says Guth, "Most of the issues that dominated the campaign had strong religious or moral overtones."[28] Beasley opposed a state lottery, supported consideration of vouchers for private schools and prayer for public schools, and was resolutely anti-abortion, though he had admitted in a statewide debate that he would support his daughter's decision to have an abortion if that were her choice. Beasley promised a pro-business and pro-family administration. Theodore took the opposite positions on all these issues.

The Christian Coalition, the American Family Association, and the Palmetto Family Council (associated with James Dobson's Focus on the Family group in Colorado) vigorously supported Beasley. Mainline Protestant and Catholic leaders warned about identifying Christianity with partisan political agendas.

Beasley won on election day by 3 percentage points, almost identical to Carroll Campbell's 1986 victory, but a few points behind the 8-point margin of George Bush in 1992. Religion was an important factor in voter decisions since the exit polls showed 70 percent of white born-again Christians, who are themselves a majority of all voters, supported Beasley. He did less well among mainline Protestants and Catholics, but received a high enough level of support from them to offset his poor 5 percent showing among blacks. The black turnout was low, which helped Beasley, and his low black support was normal for South Carolina Republicans. He won 54 percent in the ten heaviest Baptist counties and just under 50 percent in the Charleston-Beaufort area. Voters returned to their roots, since there are Baptist Democrats and Episcopalian Republicans who stuck by their party's candidates, despite the religious tensions of the campaigns.

In comparison with Campbell's 1986 vote and Bush's 1992 vote,

Table 7.9

County Character	Beasley vs. Bush	Beasley vs. Campbell
Wallace strongholds	–4.3	+4.9
Perot strongholds	–2.2	+3.0
Big three metropolitan	–6.5	–6.5
Black majority	+0.5	+0.1
High Southern Baptist	–2.6	+2.7
High income	–5.0	–5.0
High education	–4.9	–4.5
Statewide	–2.7	–0.3

Beasley's showing was quite mixed. He ran weaker than Bush in all types of counties, including Baptist ones, except in the black majority counties, where low black turnout was significant. In comparison with Campbell's first win in 1986, Beasley gained 3 percent in Baptist counties and 3 percent-5 percent in strongholds of Ross Perot in 1992 and George Wallace in 1968, suggesting perhaps a populist tinge to the Beasley vote. In rural areas, Beasley ran rather well, carrying five counties (Lancaster, Chesterfield, Darlington, Calhoun, and Edgefield) that had gone for Clinton for president but losing 5 counties that supported Bush (Charleston, Sumter, Laurens, Union, and Cherokee). (See maps 7.4–7.6 and table 7.9.) He ran stronger than Bush in seventeen counties, mainly those in tobacco country and in the "Olde English District" that borders North Carolina, as well as the Aiken area. He ran stronger than Campbell in those same jurisdictions.

Beasley's primary weakness came in metropolitan areas, where "sophistication" and religious pluralism predominate. The big three counties (Greenville, Charleston, Richland [Columbia]), gave a 28,000-vote majority for Bush, and an 18,000-vote majority for Campbell. But Beasley lost by 10,000 votes. He ran 6.5 percent weaker than Bush and Campbell. In high-income, well-educated counties, he ran 5 points weaker than Bush and Campbell.

Precinct returns confirm the general countywide pattern of voter choice. Beasley ran consistently weaker than Bush in high income locales, carrying them by 20 points compared to Bush's 31-point margin.

Beasley even lost some normally Republican towns like Sullivans Island and Folly Beach near Charleston. He carried Republican precincts in Greenville County by only 16 points, compared to Bush's 41-point edge, though the hometown status of the Democratic candidate may have been a factor.

In Ross Perot's strongest precincts, where the maverick won 22 percent of the 1992 presidential vote, Beasley's margin was 9 points compared to

Map 7.4. South Carolina

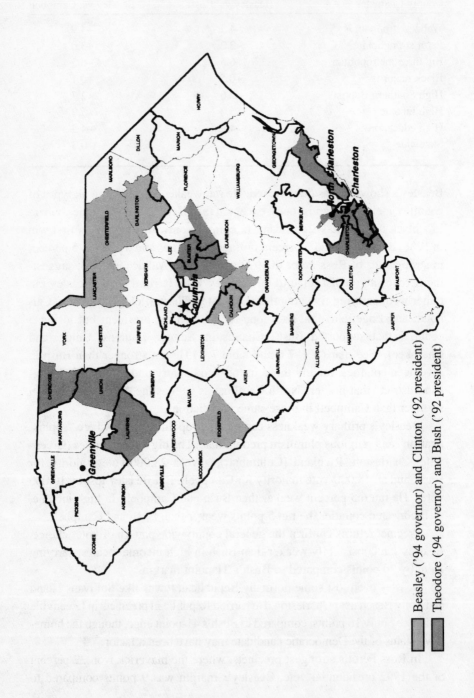

Beasley ('94 governor) and Clinton ('92 president)

Theodore ('94 governor) and Bush ('92 president)

Map 7.5. South Carolina

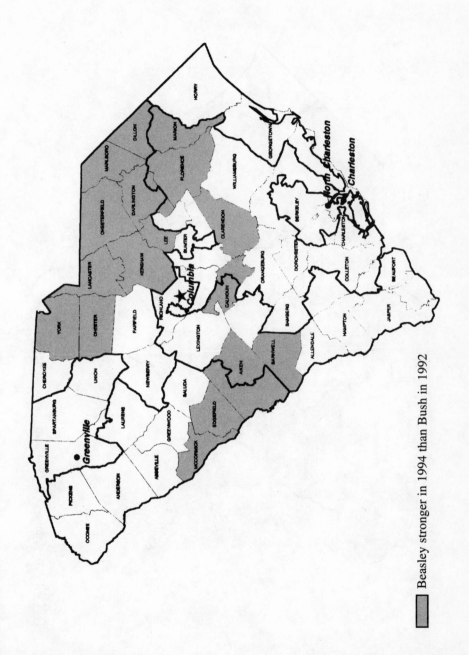

Beasley stronger in 1994 than Bush in 1992

Map 7.6. South Carolina

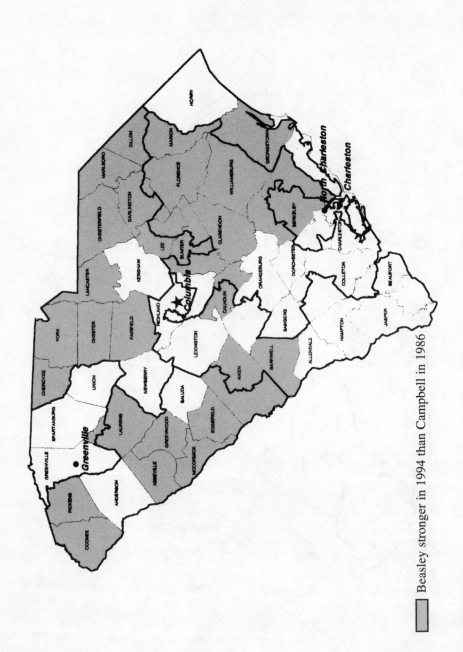

Beasley stronger in 1994 than Campbell in 1986

Table 7.10

Beasley's Weaknesses in Upper-Income Precincts

Precinct	County	Percentage Points Victory Margin Bush	Beasley
Forest Acres	Richland	36.8	5.4
Mt. Pleasant	Charleston	36.8	20.6
Isle of Palms	Charleston	32.3	14.4
Mauldin	Greenville	29.2	6.6
North Myrtle Beach	Horry	15.4	4.6
Springdale	Lexington	49.0	31.4
Deer Park	Charleston	33.0	21.2
James Island	Charleston	23.6	7.6
Zion Hill	Spartanburg	37.3	9.4
Columbia[1]	Richland	33.8	10.2

1. Wards 15, 16, 17, 24, 25, 27.

Bush's 16 points. The decline was very severe in a number of fashionable precincts like Forest Acres near Columbia, where Bush won by 37 points and Beasley by 5. The same was true in Charleston-area communities like Mt. Pleasant, Isle of Palms, Deer Park, and James Island. (See table 7.10.)

Beasley may have lost some old-line GOP voters. In a number of precincts that started voting Republican in the Eisenhower-Nixon era, for example, Beasley won by 22 points, Bush by 37. (Back in 1976, Gerald Ford carried these precincts by 43 points, despite Jimmy Carter's landslide in the state.)

But Beasley clearly showed unusual strength at the other end of the socioeconomic spectrum. Among white working class Democrats, where Jimmy Carter won an incredible 84 percent-16 percent victory in 1976, Beasley won by 7 points. Bush eked out a 3-point victory in 1992. These precincts are the bastions of the Baptist and Pentecostal blue-collar voters, and the long-range Democratic declines are one of the major factors in GOP victories throughout Dixie.

Even in Greenville County, seven white Democratic blue-collar precincts that gave Carter 74 percent in 1976 voted 51 percent to 49 percent for Beasley, even in the home county of the Democratic nominee.

Social conservatism in Greenville County helps explain the Beasley vote. A county referendum allowing a video lottery passed 54 percent to 46 percent. In the top ten pro-lottery precincts, Beasley received 20 percent, but in the top-ten anti-lottery precincts he won 71 percent.

Race played a major factor as always in South Carolina politics. Voters favored Clinton 94 percent-4 percent and Theodore 95 percent-5 percent in the all-black precincts. White voters in the black majority counties are staunch Republicans, even favoring Gerald Ford over Jimmy Carter 66 percent to 34 percent in 1976. Beasley won these white voters by 37 points and Bush had won by 41 points.

James Guth summarized the general election's religious factor in this way:

> The results suggest that Beasley benefitted from a united Christian conservative effort. Although the BJU fundamentalists, the Christian Coalition, and Southern Baptists might not worship together, they certainly combined behind the Republican ticket. The Christian Right clearly mobilized a new, hard-core Republican constituency: of the 20 percent of white voters who said they were part of the "religious right" in the Voter News Service exit poll, 80 percent voted for Beasley and for other Republican candidates. He won equally strong support from those who said family values were an important issue or that religion influenced their vote. Overall, Beasley won 70 percent among white born-again Christians, who constitute a majority of the state's population.[29]

Guth adds, "Thus, after twenty years of religious reshuffling, the GOP has become the party of united conservative Protestantism, attracting fundamentalists, charismatics, pentecostals, and conservative Southern Baptists in a powerful alignment, adding these elements to its traditional mainline Protestant base."[30]

Beasley showed that his sectarian campaign was not an accident but a carefully calculated political strategy. Shortly after his election, he made a surprise appearance at the South Carolina Baptist Convention's annual meeting, where he received a standing ovation.

The 1994 South Carolina results confirm what Clemson University professor of religion Charles H. Lippy wrote: "South Carolina will remain a bastion of Protestantism, with those of an evangelical cast exerting dominant influence."[31]

Notes

1. Quoted in Stephen Bates, *Battleground* (New York: Poseidon Press, 1993), p. 301.

2. Ibid., p. 306.

3. Michael Farris, *Constitutional Law for Christian Students* (Paeonian Springs, Va.: Home Schooling Legal Defense Association, 1991), p. 212.

4. Michael Farris, *Where Do I Draw the Line?* (Minneapolis: Bethany House, 1992), p. 26.

5. Frederick Clarkson, "Only Christians Need Apply: Religious Freedom and Michael Farris," *The Freedom Writer* (August 1993): 4–6.

6. Anna Barron Bilingsley, "From Pews to Polls," *Richmond Times-Dispatch,* November 4, 1993.

7. Ralph Z. Hallow, "GOP Sends Money to Virginia," *Washington Times,* October 22, 1993.

8. Donald P. Baker, "Lt. Gov. Beyer and Foe Stand in Firm Opposition," *Washington Post*, September 29, 1993.

9. Cal Thomas, "Religious Bigotry in the Land of Jefferson," *Washington Times*, October 31, 1993.

10. "Religion Center Stage in Candidates' Debates," *Washington Times*, October 13, 1993.

11. Mark J. Rozell and Clyde Wilcox, *Second Coming: The New Christian Right in Virginia Politics* (Baltimore: Johns Hopkins University Press, 1996), p. 136.

12. "Religious Bigotry Alleged." *Christianity Today* (December 13, 1993): 66–67.

13. Mark J. Rozell and Clyde Wilcox, "Virginia: God, Guns and Oliver North," in *God at the Grass Roots: The Christian Right in the 1994 Elections,* eds. Mark J. Rozell and Clyde Wilcox (Lanham, Md.: Rowman and Littlefield, 1995), p. 117. Additional page references to this work appear in parentheses following the cited material.

14. Barry A. Kosmin and Seymour P. Lachman, *One Nation Under God: Religion in Contemporary American Society* (New York: Harmony Books, 1993), p. 89.

15. Martin Bradley et al., *Churches and Church Membership in the United States, 1990* (Atlanta: Glenmary Research Center, 1992), pp. 343–49.

16. Ken Garfield, "Faith Takes Priority," *Charlotte Observer*, August 6, 1995.

17. July 1994 Mason-Dixon South Carolina Poll.

18. Bill McAllister, "Religious Right's Latest Star is Rising in the South," *Washington Post,* August 22, 1994.

19. *American Demographics*, August 1995, p. 25 (FBI Data for 1994).

20. Kevin Lewis, "Religion Addresses the Public Order," in *Religion in South Carolina,* ed. Charles H. Lippy (Columbia: University of South Carolina Press, 1993), p. 194.

21. James L. Guth, "South Carolina: The Christian Right Wins One," in *God at the Grass Roots,* ed. Mark J. Rozell and Clyde Wilcox (Lanham, Md.: Rowman and Littlefield, 1995), p. 137.

22. Ibid., p. 138.

23. McAllister, "Religious Right's Latest Star is Rising in the South."

24. Guth, "South Carolina," p. 139.

25. Ibid.

26. McAllister, "Religious Right's Latest Star is Rising in the South."

27. Guth, "South Carolina," p. 139.

28. Ibid., p. 140.

29. Ibid., p. 141.

30. Ibid., p. 142.

31. Charles H. Lippy, ed., *Religion in South Carolina* (Columbia: University of South Carolina Press, 1993), p. 202.

8

Evangelicals and Congress

Just over a decade ago, one of the most imaginative and insightful studies of religion's influence on politics was published, *Religion on Capitol Hill*, written by Peter Benson and Dorothy Williams, associates of an independent Minneapolis-based research group, the Search Institute. It suggested new ways of looking at religion's impact on political life.

The authors concluded, "Membership in a particular denomination does not accurately predict the type of religionist one is.[1] . . . Knowing a legislator's denomination may tell you something about the type of message delivered to members by that church, but it does not tell how the message is received and translated into the legislator's understandings and religious attitudes" (138).

Other conclusions, based on personal interviews and surveys conducted by the authors with eighty members of the Ninety-sixth Congress, are also significant. "There is a clear symmetry between what one believes and values religiously and what one believes and values politically" (153), they say.

They found that religious beliefs had a moderate influence on the voting behavior of 56 percent of the Congress members they interviewed, a major influence on 24 percent, a minor influence on 19 percent, and no influence on only 1 percent (143). No differences were discernible by political philosophy or party affiliation.

Another important finding was that "evangelical Christians in Congress are not a united voting bloc" (188). Continuing, they say, "Evangelicals spread across the political spectrum. On political orientation measures about

40 percent of evangelicals tilt to the liberal side and 60 percent are more at home on the conservative side. The heaviest concentrations of evangelicals are at the extreme ends of the political continua. There are very few evangelicals who take a moderate political position" (175).

Since this research was based on the Congress of 1979 to 1981, it just began to notice the rise of the Religious Right. The authors did find "a trend for more evangelicals to be conservative" (175), but were unsure of this significance. They said, "The ties between religious belief and political orientation are much more complex than the New Christian Right would have us believe. Sincerely religious people can be political conservatives, moderates, or liberals" (182).

In their analysis of those members who supported the Religious Right, they concluded, "In sum, the religion of the New Christian Right appears to place minimal emphasis on reaching out to people, but instead is maximally devoted to promoting and governing the interests and welfare of the self" (180). In addition to a vigorous individualism, the religious conservatives tended to emphasize "nation-building religion," which approved America's allegedly unique role in divine destiny.

Explaining this in more detail, they write, "The New Christian Right declares that abortion and homosexuality are violations of God's higher law. This political movement justifies government coercion in these moral matters by appealing to claims about God's will. Further, the New Christian Right sees expansion of the federal government into social programs based on the principle of taxing the 'haves' to aid the 'have-nots' as unnecessary (and ungodly) violations of individual liberty. . . . [T]he greater the adherence to the two beliefs about God's intent for America, the greater the likelihood that a member votes against abortion, against civil liberties for homosexuals, and against government spending for social programs" (98).

The Search Institute study helps to place in context both previous and more recent studies of religious influences on congressional voting. Congress is, after all, the premier American legislative body, whose decisions affect all Americans, and most of America's major religious groups maintain visible and relatively effective lobbies in Washington.[2]

Studies published earlier than 1982 stressed denominational affiliation as the key dividing line between members. A 1944 study by Madge McKinney concluded that in states where one religious tradition is dominant "a candidate's religious background is more important to the success of his election than is the party which he represents."[3]

A study by John Fenton of Catholic members of Congress in 1958–59 found that they were slightly more liberal than their colleagues on most issues. He also found that religion served as an important factor on issues such as civil rights, labor-management relations, foreign aid, and federal aid to parochial schools.[4]

A doctoral dissertation by John Warner, published in 1968, studied the religious factor in congressional voting during the Eighty-ninth Congress (1965–67) and reached this conclusion: "It appears that religious affiliation and party affiliation are strongly related, and that together the two are related to voting. Religious affiliation appears to be a factor in party affiliation and therefore a factor in the voting behavior of the members of Congress."[5] Warner found that, in terms of their support for issues emphasized by the "Conservative Coalition" of Republicans and Southern Democrats, Baptists were the most conservative religious group, followed by Presbyterians and Methodists. Most of these groups are the bedrock of evangelicalism. The most consistently liberal groups were Jews, Roman Catholics, and Unitarians. The United Church of Christ and Episcopalian members varied, depending on their party affiliations and whether they were in the House or Senate. (Episcopalian Democrats equaled the liberalism of Jews, Catholics, and Unitarians.) Lutherans and Mormons in the House were liberal, but Mormon senators were conservative. The Congress Warner studied was the most Democratic and liberal one since World War II, having been elected during the Lyndon Johnson landslide of 1964. There were 363 Democrats and 172 Republicans in Congress, the postwar Democratic high point. Much has changed since then.

Warner found that religion affected many of the votes cast in Congress during the Great Society years, though regionalism helped to influence or modify the religious factor. For example, "Support for foreign aid came primarily from the Jews and the Catholics" (306). On labor legislation, Jews, Unitarians, Catholics, and Lutherans were the most pro-labor, while Mormons, Methodists, and Baptists were the most pro-management. On support for poverty programs the same orientation was found. On civil liberties questions, Unitarians were the most liberal, while Presbyterians, Methodists, Baptists, and Lutherans were the most conservative. Support for expanding the role of the federal government in economic and social life was greatest among Jews, Catholics, and Unitarians, and most opposed by Baptists.

The South was the most conservative region, which undoubtedly affected the votes of Baptist members, who were strongest in the region, and among whom Southern representation was the highest. However, Warner's study revealed that, even when looking only at Southern members, Baptists were the most conservative in their voting behavior. Baptists were 51 percent more conservative than liberal, far higher than any other religious group.

Table 8.1

Percentage of Conservative Votes in the Ninety-fourth Congress

Religion	% Voting Conservative
Mormon	74.3
Baptist	70.8
Lutheran	67.5
Presbyterian	65.0
Methodist	63.3
Episcopal	53.0
Roman Catholic	35.3
United Church of Christ	34.9
"Protestant" (nondenominational)	26.1
Unitarian Universalist	25.8
Jewish	23.3
Average for all	50.8

Only Southern Catholics leaned to the liberal side in their lack of support for the Conservative Coalition (228).

On the issue of civil rights, the religion factor was pronounced. Among House members from the South, 86 percent of Southern Baptists opposed the Voting Rights Act of 1965 compared to only 33 percent of Catholics. Most other Southern Protestants also opposed the Voting Rights Act: 68 percent of Presbyterians, 67 percent of Episcopalians, 64 percent of Methodists, and 57 percent of the smaller sectarian groups (329).

A study of the Ninety-fourth Congress (1975–77) tended to substantiate these findings. Using ratings compiled by Americans for Democratic Action, a liberal activist group, it discovered that Jews, Unitarians, "Protestants" without denominational attachments, Roman Catholics, and United Church of Christ members were the most liberal. Episcopalians were the closest to the national average. The most conservative voting behavior was found among Mormons, Baptists, Lutherans, Presbyterians, and Methodists.[6] (See table 8.1.)

This study also looked at religious influences on congressional voting during the 1960s and early 1970s on four issues upon which there had been considerable disagreement among the churches: parochial school aid, immigration reform, abortion law, and school prayer amendments. Conservatives and liberals within the religious communities differed widely on these issues, and this is reflected in the way that the members voted on the key proposals.

On February 4, 1960, Senator Wayne Morse (D-Oreg.) proposed an amendment to the School Assistance Act of 1960, which would have made $75 million in loans at low interest available to private and parochial schools for school construction. It was defeated 49-37. An analysis by religion reveals widespread and durable divisions.

As expected, all Roman Catholics except John F. Kennedy favored the amendment. They would be the primary beneficiaries. Kennedy was an announced presidential candidate then, and he had opposed any public aid to parochial schools. All Lutheran and United Church of Christ members, and three of the four Unitarians favored the amendment. The United Church of Christ unanimity is quite surprising, as they have no private schools and are not notably pro-Catholic. Presbyterians divided 5-4 against the amendment. Mormons and Disciples of Christ were solidly against. The main opposition stemmed from Methodists (88 percent), Baptists (86 percent), and Episcopalians (70 percent), all three of whose leadership had generally opposed parochial school aid. Baptists and Methodists were especially vigorous in their opposition.

Revision of America's immigration laws would not seem to have had much of a religious connotation, but it did. Roman Catholics, Jews, Lutherans, and Eastern Orthodox Christians are overwhelmingly descended from the 50 million European immigrants who came to these shores since 1820. Their leadership strongly supported open immigration and rejected as bigoted the immigration restrictionism passed by Congress in the early 1920s. Many Protestants, on the other hand, had supported moves to cut off immigration, especially from Catholic and Jewish parts of Europe. They supported the national origins system established in 1924, based on the number of immigrants in the United States in the 1890 census. This census did not reflect the enormous influx from eastern and southern Europe after 1890. Much of this attitude was found among the indigenous and Anglo-Saxon-based Protestants in the Methodist, Baptist, evangelical traditions. Few of their members were immigrants or descendants of immigrants who arrived after 1890.

In 1965 Congress finally approved a long-delayed revision of the immigration laws, which eliminated the national origins quota system and its implication of inherent superiority for Northern Europeans. President John F. Kennedy was unable to pass this measure that was dear to his heart, but he wrote a book, *A Nation of Immigrants*, published posthumously, to promote the reform. President Lyndon B. Johnson gave strong support to a bill promoted as fair, equitable, and progressive. In 1965 it passed the House 318 to 95 and the Senate 76 to 18. Nearly 78 percent of Congress members supported the change.

Religious differences were noticeable. Every Lutheran, Unitarian, and

Jewish member of Congress voted for the bill, as did 97 percent of Catholics. While 88 percent of United Church of Christ and 86 percent of Episcopalians supported it, Presbyterians and Methodists were less likely than average to favor the reform, Presbyterians by 70 percent and Methodists by 62 percent.

Baptists were the only major religious group to oppose the measure, doing so by 60 percent-40 percent. Baptists were almost three times more likely than other religious groups to reject a nondiscriminatory immigration law. Lawrence B. Davis argued in his *Immigrants, Baptists, and the Protestant Mind in America* that Protestants, after supporting open immigration before 1880, feared that the Roman Catholic Church was using liberal immigration laws as an instrument of political policy to achieve cultural dominance. Protestants had also grown disillusioned by their inability to convert a significant number of the Catholic immigrants. Baptists tended to be the most sympathetic to this viewpoint.

The abortion law controversy came to floor votes in Congress during the early 1970s. Though several restrictive anti-abortion amendments to the U.S. Constitution were proposed, none reached a floor vote. One key vote, revealing perhaps a general orientation toward abortion, was taken in the U.S. Senate on April 10, 1975. Senator Dewey Bartlett (R-Okla.) proposed an amendment to bar use of Social Security funds covering Medicaid to pay for abortions. Senator Jacob Javits (R-N.Y.) moved to table the amendment and his motion carried 54-36.

Members from most religious traditions voted to kill the Bartlett amendment. United Church of Christ members voted 4 to 1, Unitarians 3 to 1, and Jews 2 to 1 against Bartlett. Presbyterians (67 percent), Episcopalians (64 percent), and Methodists (60 percent) cast pro-choice majorities. Roman Catholic senators rejected their hierarchy's anti-abortion posture, voting 8 to 7 against Bartlett. Only Baptists (5 to 3) and Mormons (2 to 1) voted for the anti-abortion position. There were several other abortion votes in the House and Senate in the mid-1970s and the religious divisions reflected in the Bartlett vote were replicated.

The prayer amendment votes of 1966 and 1971 reveal a classical culture-religion dichotomy. The powerful Protestant Establishment churches that once favored religious exercises in public schools generally adopted resolutions against a constitutional amendment designed to overrule the Supreme Court's 1962–63 prohibitions on mandatory prayer and Bible readings. But their membership in Congress generally rejected their appeals and cast decisive majorities in the affirmative, though both amendments failed to obtain the required two-thirds majority. An amendment proposed by Republican Senator Everett Dirksen of Illinois passed the Senate 49 to 37 in 1966. An amendment proposed by Ohio Republican Congressman Chalmers Wylie

Table 8.2

Prayer Amendment Votes*
(1966 Dirksen and 1971 Wylie Amendments)

Religion	% Yes
Lutheran	82.8
Baptist	72.3
Methodist	70.9
Presbyterian	70.4
Episcopal	53.6
"Protestant" (nondenominational)	53.1
Roman Catholic	48.6
United Church of Christ	43.5
Unitarian Universalist	30.0
Mormon	28.6
Jewish	15.4
Average for All	59.2

*Source: Albert J. Menendez, *Religion at the Polls* (Philadelphia: Westminster Press, 1977), p. 222.

cleared the House by a 240 to 162 vote in 1971. Baptists, Methodists, Presbyterians, Lutherans, and Disciples of Christ members were solidly supportive. Jews, Unitarians, Mormons, United Church of Christ, a slim majority of Roman Catholics, and about half of Episcopalians blocked the proposed constitutional change. Members from some of the smaller churches—Quaker, Christian Scientists, Eastern Orthodox, Adventists, and the Church of Christ—voted 15 to 5 for the amendments.

Republicans were twice as likely to favor prayer amendments as Democrats (84 percent-42 percent). Ideological conservatives voted 94 percent in favor, while only 56 percent of the moderates and 30 percent of the liberals supported it. Members from the South (78 percent) and the Midwest (58 percent) were the most likely supporters, while those from New England (46 percent) and the Pacific Coast (30 percent) were more opposed. (See table 8.2.)

Some religious factors were discernible in the 1978 votes in the House and Senate on a proposal to extend tuition tax credits to parochial and private school patrons.

After vigorous debate that lasted several months, the House approved the tuition tax credit plan for parochial schools by 209 to 194. This close vote revealed distinctive religious, political, and regional differences. Catholics

Table 8.3

House Vote on Tuition Tax Credits—June 1, 1978

	Total		Democrats		Republicans	
	%	%	%	%	%	%
By Religion	For	Against	For	Against	For	Against
Catholic	74.8	25.2	70.6	29.4	90.0	9.1
Protestant	43.2	56.8	25.5	74.5	70.8	29.2
Jewish	45.5	54.5	33.3	66.7	100.0	0.0
Subgroups						
Baptist	28.9	71.1	22.6	77.4	57.1	42.9
Episcopalian	50.0	50.0	29.2	70.8	77.8	22.2
Lutheran	58.3	41.7	33.3	66.7	66.7	33.3
Methodist	35.1	64.9	25.0	75.0	52.4	47.6
Presbyterian	54.2	45.8	30.8	69.2	81.8	18.2
Unitarian Universalist	14.3	85.7	0.0	100.0	100.0	0.0
United Church of Christ	33.3	66.7	10.0	90.0	80.0	20.0

	% For	% Against
All Democrats	40.4	59.6
All Republicans	75.2	24.8
Total	51.9	48.1

voted 3-1 for tax credits, while only 43 percent of Protestants and 45 percent of Jews were supportive.

Among Democrats 70 percent of Catholics were favorable, but only 33 percent of Jews and 25 percent of Protestants were supportive. Although only 40 percent of all Democrats favored tax credits, 75 percent of all Republicans did so.

Among Republicans all Jews and 90 percent of Catholics were in favor, but Protestant support dropped to 70 percent. Among the individual Protestant subgroups, Lutherans and Presbyterians were the most supportive, as were half of Episcopalians. Only about a third of Methodists and United Church of Christ members voted for vouchers. Only 29 percent of Baptists and 14 percent of Unitarian Universalists cast favorable votes.

Representatives from states with above-average concentrations of parochial school students and powerful church school lobbies voted 71 percent for tax credits. The Ohio and Pennsylvania delegations were overwhelmingly favorable, even though legislation adopted by those states had been declared unconstitutional by the U.S. Supreme Court in the early 1970s.

Even in those nine states where voters opposed parochiaid in state referenda between 1966 and 1976, a solid 60 percent of their House members nodded assent to the tax credit proposal. (See table 8.3.)

The Senate rejected tax credits later in 1978 on a 56-to-41 vote. Catholic opposition was much stronger in the upper chamber, led by Maine's Ed Muskie, Missouri's Tom Eagleton, and Massachusetts's Ted Kennedy. Catholic support dropped to 57 percent in the Senate, compared to 41 percent of Protestants and 40 percent of Jews. Baptists and Methodists were the most likely to be opposed in the Senate vote.

In some respects this vote was the last gasp for Catholic particularism on church-state issues. Votes during the 1980s and 1990s on this and other related issues show an increasing Catholic liberalism and support for church-state separation. Signs abound that evangelicals are moving in a conservative direction on the issue of tax support for parochial schools, joining their already high support for conservative positions on school prayer and abortion restrictions.

However, one vote in 1990 suggested that Catholic members still see partnership between religious and governmental organizations in the social welfare field as acceptable in certain circumstances.

Child Care 1990

The issue of child care, which passed the House and Senate in 1990, evoked serious religious differences. Representative Don Edwards (D-Calif.) sponsored an amendment to bar use of federal funds for sectarian worship or instruction and to prohibit religious discrimination in hiring child care workers. The Edwards amendment was rejected by the House on a 297 to 125 vote.

An analysis of the vote indicates some significant partisan, regional, and religious differences. Northern Democrats favored the Edwards amendment by 57 percent, but Southern Democrats gave it only 20 percent support. Republicans gave only 6 percent support compared to 45 percent among all Democrats.

Only the California and New York delegations narrowly favored Edwards. These states are traditional strongholds of church-state separation and members from those states have voted against school prayer amendments in the past. Delegates from Rhode Island (both Republicans), Alaska, (also a Republican), and Oregon also favored the amendment.

There were eighteen states where every House member opposed the Edwards amendment. These states are the bastion of evangelical influence.

Members from Alabama, Arkansas, Delaware, Kentucky, Louisiana, Mississippi, North Carolina, South Carolina, and West Virginia were unanimously opposed to Edwards, as were the Mormon-flavored delegations from Utah and Idaho. All members from Wyoming, Kansas, Nevada, New Hampshire, North Dakota, South Dakota, and Vermont also voted in the negative.

Religious differences over Edwards were among the most significant in many years. All four religiously nonaffiliated members voted in favor of the anti-discrimination amendment, as did two-thirds of Jews. But only 27 percent of Protestants and 24 percent of Catholics favored the amendment.

It was among the Democrats that cultural and religious divisions were most intense. Seventy-six percent of Jewish Democrats favored Edwards, showing their historic concern for church-state separation. Protestant Democrats were 46 percent in favor, but there were sharp differences by region. Only 20 percent of Southern Democrat Protestants favored the proposal, but a majority of Protestant Democrats from the North and West were supportive. Edwards was strongly supported by black Protestant Democratic members.

Unitarians voted 4 to 3 for Edwards, but party lines were important because Unitarian Republicans voted no while Unitarian Democrats voted 4 to 1 in favor. Mormons, probably the most conservative religious group in Congress, voted 7 to 1 against Edwards. All seven Mormon Republicans opposed it, while the one Mormon Democrat, Udall of Arizona, voted for it.

Catholic Democrats, who have opposed school prayer amendments and were lukewarm on equal access and other church-state compromises, were apparently influenced by the U.S. Catholic Conference (USCC), which opposed the Edwards amendment. Catholic Democrats voted 54 to 25 against Edwards, despite the fact that two Catholic Democrats, Pat Williams of Montana and George Miller of California, were leaders in the fight for Edwards. Catholic Democrats in states like Illinois, Ohio, Pennsylvania, Indiana, New Jersey, and Massachusetts defected from their normal liberal positions in large numbers on this vote, though Joseph Kennedy, son of Robert Kennedy and the occupant of President John F. Kennedy's old congressional seat in Massachusetts, voted yes, following the Kennedy tradition of support for church-state separation.

Another significant aspect of the vote was the near-total Republican opposition. Only 11 of 171 Republicans voted for it. While 8 percent of Catholic Republicans and 6 percent of Protestant Republicans favored it, none of the Jewish Republicans did so. Even Bill Green of Manhattan, a Jewish Republican liberal who usually favored separation, voted no. Not one Southern Republican voted for Edwards, showing again that the South is a stronghold of religious conformity and conservatism. Two Catholic Republicans who did vote yes were Claudine Schneider of Rhode Island and Connie Morella of Maryland.

For the first time since the 1978 tuition tax credit vote, Catholic members were more conservative and less supportive of church-state separation than Protestants, even though the difference was statistically small. Extensive interviews with officials of religious and educational organizations in Washington emphasized the role of the U.S. Catholic Conference in shepherding the child care bill through Congress. The USCC was the most influential player in pressuring Congress to approve vouchers and grants for church-related day care. It shaped the phraseology and advanced the arguments that weakened the church-state position. A *Congressional Quarterly* reporter said the USCC "cut a deal but reneged when they initially agreed to accept language limiting vouchers but then demanded the change months later. The USCC saw the child care bill as a wedge to lead eventually to substantial aid to church-related schools."[7]

In 1984 Congress overwhelmingly approved the Equal Access Act, which granted more leeway for formal religious group involvement in public schools, a project dear to the heart of evangelicals, who had long complained that religious activities were being expunged from the classroom. Baptists, Methodists, and evangelicals were strongly in favor of the proposal, since they are likely to be the primary beneficiaries. Only the Jewish and black Protestant members were opposed.

Abortion remained a contentious religiopolitical issue in Congress. In a study of abortion-related votes from 1976 to 1980, Charles Fimian concluded that "the religion of the individual member was found to exert a stronger influence on abortion voting than does the religious composition of the representative's constituency."[8] Fimian summarized his findings in the following chart:[9]

Constituency Religion Characteristics	Member's Religion	Tendency to Vote Anti-Abortion
Large percentage Anti-Abortion	Anti-Abortion	Very Strong
Large percentage Anti-Abortion	Not Anti-Abortion	Strong
Small percentage Anti-Abortion	Anti-Abortion	Strong
Small Percentage Anti-Abortion	Not Anti-Abortion	Weak

Political philosophy and party membership were also important variables. The members' conservative or liberal leanings, some of which are rooted in religion, were more important than Democratic or Republican allegiance in congressional votes relating to the public financing of abortion, according to the Fimian study.

Mary Eccles, in a study of the Hyde amendment vote in 1977, concluded that religion and race were the factors that best predicted a member's vote.[10]

Maris Vinovskis studied three House votes on abortion in 1976 and weighed the effect of eleven personal and constituency-related variables on those votes. He found that the member's religion was second only to the congressperson's position on the general liberal-conservative spectrum insofar as abortion votes were concerned.[11]

A sociological study of religion's effect on abortion reform votes in the Nevada legislature is not directly relevant to this study, but its observations, written before *Roe* v. *Wade*, tend to confirm the other findings. Its authors, James Richardson and Sandi Fox, concluded that "religious affiliation is a fairly good predictor of voting behavior on abortion reform legislation."[12] Catholics and Mormons were the conservative and anti-abortion groups in the late 1960s, they observed.

School prayer returned to center stage in the winter and spring of 1984 when President Ronald Reagan proposed an amendment to the Constitution to "restore" so-called voluntary prayer in U.S. public schools. It passed the Senate on a 56 to 44 vote, but that was eleven votes short of the required two-thirds majority. Evangelical and fundamentalist lobbies vigorously supported the proposal, while the moderate-to-liberal mainline churches saw it as a threat to religious liberty and pluralism, as did the Jewish community. The Catholic Church remained neutral.

Republicans and conservatives were overwhelmingly supportive, while Democrats and liberals were opposed. The strong evangelical states were the most likely to support the school prayer amendment, as they were in previous votes. Jews, Unitarians, Catholics, Episcopalians, and members of the United Church of Christ voted no. Lutherans, Baptists, Methodists, and Presbyterians were favorable. Mormons switched sides from the 1960s and 1970s and favored it, possibly because of their admiration for Reagan, who won his greatest support of all fifty states in Utah.

The Reagan prayer amendment received almost total support from Southern and Border state senators, who favored it 28-6. Democrats were 15-4 in favor and Republicans 13-2 in favor in this region. Most of the opposition came from Delaware, Maryland, and Missouri, whose senators were Episcopalian, Catholic, and Greek Orthodox. The vote in the eleven states of the Old Confederacy was 21-1 in support of school prayer. Only Dale Bumpers of Arkansas voted no. Outside the South the vote was 38-28 against the school prayer amendment.

Thus, at the height of Ronald Reagan's popularity, his supporters could muster only 56 percent support. The Southern tilt shows how different this region is from the rest of the nation on many religious issues. Over 82 percent of Southern and Border state senators (95.5 percent in the Old South) supported school prayer, while only 42 percent did so in the North and West. High-evangelical states were 81.6 percent in favor; low-evangelical states, only 40.3 percent favorable.

The religious and regional differences overshadowed partisan ones. It is true that Republicans were more supportive (67.3 percent) than Democrats (42.2 percent), but the 25-point spread between the parties was less than the 41-point difference between strongly evangelical and less evangelical regions.

The differences among Democrats was due almost entirely to religion and region. Ninety-one percent of Democrats from the Old South voted for school prayer, compared to 62.5 percent of Border state Democrats and only 15 percent of Democrats from the North and West.

Among Republicans, 87 percent of those from the South and Border states were favorable, compared to 60 percent in the North and West.

Senator Jesse Helms, an ultraconservative Baptist from North Carolina, sponsored a "sense of the Senate" resolution favoring school prayer on January 23, 1992. It was soundly defeated 55 to 38, with 68 percent of Republicans and 21 percent of Democrats supporting Helms. As was true on the Reagan prayer amendment vote eight years before, Episcopalian Republicans defected and opposed school prayer. Southern Protestant Democrats supported the measure, probably because of the intense support from the folks back home. Southern and Border state Senators voted 21-12 for the Helms resolution while those from the North and West voted 43-17 against it. Fully 64 percent of the Southern region senators supported Helms while only 28 percent of those in the rest of the nation did so. Senators from the heaviest evangelical states voted 62 percent in favor, while only 27 percent of those from the less evangelical states did so. The religion factor was critical to this school prayer vote, even more so than on other church-state issues. All 8 Jewish senators opposed Helms, as did 61 percent of Catholics.

Helms tried again with a school prayer rider to a federal election bill introduced on July 27, 1994. It was again defeated 53-47, but on this occasion support rose from 41 percent to 47 percent. This time Republican support for Helms rose to almost 80 percent while Democratic support, mostly Baptists and Methodists from the South, stayed at 21 percent. Support among Southerners and Border state senators was a solid 68 percent, while only 36 percent of those from the North or West supported Helms. Representatives from the strongest evangelical states voted 68.4 percent yes; those from states where evangelicalism is weaker gave only half as much support, 33.9 percent.

This sharp division on school prayer legislation remains, after thirty years of recorded votes.

The issue of vouchers to aid private and parochial schools perdures as a national issue. A test vote on July 27, 1994, came on a proposal by Republican Senator Robert Dole of Kansas to establish a voucher demonstration project. It was defeated 53 to 45. On this issue party differences are even stronger than on school prayer or abortion. More than seven out of eight Republicans (88.4 percent) favored vouchers while only one out of eight Democrats (12.7 percent) cast a favorable vote. Ideology and regionalism exceeded religious differences. Conservatives were overwhelmingly favorable. Liberals were opposed.

Amazingly, 58 percent of Southerners voted yes, a departure from the previous opposition found in earlier votes. Now that Protestant private schools are flourishing in the region—and parochiaid is no longer seen as a Catholic issue—the area's representatives apparently have no problem in supporting aid. Baptist and Methodist senators from South Carolina, Arkansas, and Mississippi voted yes. Democrats like Sam Nunn of Georgia also supported vouchers. Only 40 percent of senators from the North and West supported vouchers.

Senators from the strongest evangelical states favored vouchers by 62 percent to 38 percent, while only 36 percent of those from less evangelical regions did so.

The religious affiliation breakdown produced a remarkable switching of sides between Catholics and Protestants. Jewish opposition was a predictably strong, 8-1. But Catholic senators voted 13-9 against the voucher proposal, while Protestants voted 35-30 in favor of it. Compared to votes of thirty years ago, this represents a dramatic change of opinion within the religious community, reflecting as it does greater Catholic concern for public schools and a greater Protestant support for private and religious education.

Two years before this vote, Senator Orrin Hatch had proposed a voucher scheme that was rejected 57 to 36. While opposition was higher (61 percent compared to 54 percent on the Dole proposal), the basic contours of the 1994 vote were reflected then. Support in high-evangelical states was 44.4 percent compared to 35.1 percent in low-evangelical states. Protestant support was 40 percent and Catholic support was 44 percent.

Thus, the greatest increase in support for vouchers between 1992 and 1994 came from Protestant members, and from those representing the strongholds of evangelicalism. Some of this is also due to the newly elected Republicans from that region.

Even symbolic issues dealing with the free exercise of religion are influenced by the religious beliefs of the Congress member and/or of the constituents. In 1987 Congress overruled a U.S. Supreme Court decision the previous year that allowed the military to forbid the wearing of religious apparel by its personnel. The case arose when an air force captain was disciplined in 1981 for wearing his yarmulke. Congress approved an amendment to the defense authorization bill sponsored by New Jersey Democrat Frank Lautenberg, who is Jewish.

An analysis of the Senate vote on the measure yields interesting—and sometimes surprising—results. The Lautenberg amendment was favored by 75 percent of Democrats but only 35 percent of Republicans. It won majority support in all regions except the South, where only 38 percent of senators favored it. The South is considered relatively more pro-defense than other regions, and it has a lower Jewish population than the rest of the nation.

Concern for the views of Jewish constituents was apparently an important factor in the vote. All fifteen voting senators from New York, New Jersey, Maryland, Pennsylvania, Florida, California, Illinois, and Massachusetts—where most of America's Jews reside—supported the measure.

This was a more significant factor than the senators' religious affiliations per se, because Roman Catholics supported the "yarmulke bill" (as it was called) more strongly than Jews or Protestants. Fully 79 percent of Catholics and 72 percent of Jews favored the amendment, compared to 49 percent of Protestants and others.

The usually conservative and pro-military Mormons favored the bill 2 to 1, while usually liberal Unitarians opposed it 2 to 1. Episcopalians, who usually lean to the liberal side of social and religious issues, voted 10 to 8 against the yarmulke bill. Methodists were the most likely among Protestants to support it; Lutherans, the least.

Interestingly, most of the Senate's prominent evangelical Protestants, including Hatfield of Oregon and Armstrong of Colorado, voted no.

Many state delegations were split. All six Southern Republicans were opposed. In New Hampshire and Nevada, Jewish senators were opposed while non-Jewish senators were in favor.

The abortion controversy continued to be important in several congressional votes in the 1990s, though some new trends were apparent.

Abortion-related votes in the One Hundred and Third Congress (1993–1995) reaffirm the religious and political patterns that have prevailed for over a decade. Democrats of all religious traditions are primarily pro-choice, while Republicans of all religious persuasions are mostly anti-choice or pro-restrictions of various kinds.

Parental Notification

This was true in the House vote on March 25, 1993, on the subject of parental notification, supposedly one of the more popular ways to restrict abortion availability. The House rejected, by 243 to 179, a motion by Virginia Republican Thomas Bliley, a Catholic, to order that federally funded family planning clinics had to notify parents forty-eight hours in advance of an abortion performed on a minor. Fully 83.5 percent of Democrats opposed the Bliley amendment to the family planning bill while 80.2 percent of Republicans supported it.

Most members followed their party's philosophical predilection. Catholic and Baptist Democrats opposed the parental notification requirement while half of Jewish Republicans favored it. But the really interesting votes were cast by the dissenters from their party's majority.

One out of six Democrats supported the motion. A disproportionate number (18 of 41, or 43.9 percent) were Catholics, while 53.7 percent were Protestant and 2.4 percent were Mormon. Both Southern conservative Protestants and a sprinkling of northern Catholic liberal Democrats were the most likely to defect on this issue. Three of the four Mississippi Democrats and 2 out of 3 West Virginia Democrats bolted, as did 3 of 6 Minnesota Democrats (2 of them Lutheran), 4 of 10 in Illinois, 4 of 11 in Pennsylvania, and 7 of 21 in Texas. The only Mormon Democrat from Utah joined the defectors.

The conservative/liberal dichotomy is sharp. The defecting Mississippi Democrats averaged only a 13 percent liberal voting record in 1991 as measured by Americans for Democratic Action (ADA). The Texans averaged 21 percent and the Louisianans 15 percent. But the New York defectors averaged 88 percent liberal, while the Minnesotans averaged 67 percent, Illinois 56 percent, Ohio 60 percent, and Pennsylvania 50 percent. Such staunch Catholic liberals as Dale Kildee of Michigan, James Oberstar of Minnesota, and Michael McNulty and John LaFalce of New York defected on this issue. The Rev. Floyd Flake, a New York pastor of the African Methodist Episcopal church, had a 100 percent liberal voting record from the ADA in 1991.

In general, the Catholic Democrats who voted for parental notification were somewhat more liberal than Protestant Democratic defectors. The Catholics had an average ADA rating of 56.7 percent compared to the Protestants' 40.5 percent.

On the other side of the aisle were the Republican pro-choice defectors, the 20 percent of GOP House members who voted against the parental notification requirement. Almost 68 percent of those were Protestant, 21 percent were Catholic, 6 percent Jewish, and 6 percent Eastern Orthodox. They were much less likely to be Catholic than the Democratic dissenters. Geographically, they were scattered throughout the North and West, with New York and Ohio contributing four, and Pennsylvania and California three. Both New Mexico Republicans, one Catholic and one Jewish, opposed parental notification. Only three of the thirty-four Republican defectors were from the South. Two were Episcopalians from Florida, while the third was Congress's lone French Huguenot member, Arthur Ravenel of Charleston, South Carolina.

While Catholic Republican pro-choicers were somewhat underrepresented, the fact that there are any shows how widespread pro-choice sentiment is today.

Since the anti-abortion coalition in Congress and the nation tends to be heavily dominated by evangelical and Catholic Republicans, the defection of seven Republican Catholic House members is significant, especially since several are conservatives who rarely depart from Republican orthodoxy.

One expects Connie Morella, the most liberal Republican House member from a highly literate and affluent Maryland suburb of the nation's capital, to vote on the liberal side of most issues. She was one of three House Republicans to oppose the Gulf War. But moderately conservative Tom Ridge from Erie, Pennsylvania,[13] and Scott Klug of Madison, Wisconsin, would not appear to be prime defection material. Neither would moderately conservative Susan Molinari from heavily Italian Catholic, conservative Staten Island, New York. Joe Skeen of New Mexico undoubtedly cast a conscience vote on this issue, since his ADA liberal rating in 1991 was 0. (The same is true for George Gekas, a Greek Orthodox Republican from Pennsylvania with a 5 percent ADA rating.)

Most of the Republican defectors lean to the conservative side, though. The two Jews had an average ADA rating of 40 percent, the Catholics 31.7 percent, the Protestants 26.3 percent, and the two Eastern Orthodox members 20 percent.

Both sets of dissenters had overall philosophical characteristics somewhat at variance with their respective party. Pro-parental-notification Democrats were more conservative than all Democrats. Catholic dissenters were 16 percent less liberal than all Catholics, Protestants 20 percent less so, and Mormons 10 percent less liberal. Catholic Democrats were more liberal than Protestant Democrats.

Among Republicans the reverse was true. Anti-parental-notification Republicans were more liberal than all Republicans. Among Catholics the difference was 15 percent, among Protestants 14 percent, and among Jews 13 percent. There was no difference among the small Eastern Orthodox bloc. Jewish and Catholic Republicans were less conservative than Protestant Republicans. (See tables 8.4 and 8.5.)

Table 8.4

Overall Liberal Ratings—U.S. House of Representatives (1991 ADA)

Religion	All Democrats % Liberal	Anti-Choice Dissenters[1]
Protestant	60.8%	40.5%
Catholic	72.6%	56.7%
Jewish	81.5%	—
None	93.0%	—
Mormon	35.0%	25.0%
Eastern Orthodox	—	—

Religion	All Republicans % Liberal	Pro-Choice Dissenters[1]
Protestant	12.7	26.3
Catholic	16.9	31.7
Jewish	27.5	40.0
Mormon	3.3	—
Eastern Orthodox	20.0	20.0

1. Dissenters on the parental notification amendment.

Table 8.5

Dissenters by Religion

	Protestant	Catholic	Jewish	Others[1]
Anti-Choice Democrats	53.7%	43.9%	—	2.4%
All Democrats	55.6%	30.0%	10.1%	4.3%
Pro-Choice Republicans	67.6%	20.6%	5.9%	5.9%
All Republicans	68.8%	22.7%	2.8%	5.7%

1. "Others" includes Mormons, Eastern Orthodox, and Nonaffiliated.

Fetal Tissue Research

On March 11, 1993 the House voted 250-161 for the Waxman amendment adding ethical safeguards to the National Institutes of Health (NIH) authorization bill to regulate and allow fetal tissue research. Of the Democrats 85.4 percent voted yes, while 74.1 percent of Republicans voted no.

This analysis looks at the dissenters: the one out of seven Democrats (14.6 percent) and the one in four Republicans (25.9 percent) who voted against their party's general abortion position.

On this issue 18 of the 35 anti-choice Democrats were Catholics (51.4 percent), 16 were Protestants (45.7 percent), and 1 was a Mormon (2.9 percent). Since Catholics were about 31 percent of all House Democrats, this is a fairly high differential. Both Catholic and Protestant anti-choice dissenters were more conservative than their Democratic pro-choice colleagues. Catholic defectors had an average ADA rating of 52.9 percent, while Protestants had a 41.2 percent liberal rating.

On the Republican side of the aisle, there was virtually no difference between pro-choice defectors and all Republicans. The forty-four defectors were 68.1 percent Protestant, 22.7 percent Catholic, 4.6 percent Jewish, and 4.6 percent Eastern Orthodox. The six Mormon Republicans were solidly anti-choice, and not one of them defected. Among Republican dissenters there was something of a regional factor. All 3 Connecticut Republicans, 3 out of 4 in Maryland, and 4 out of 6 in New Jersey favored fetal tissue research. Fully half (22 of the 44) of the defecting Republicans were from the Northeast.

Pro-fetal research Republicans were slightly more liberal than all Republicans, even though they included such staunch conservatives as Jerry Lewis and Clay Shaw of Florida. Jewish defectors had a 40 percent liberal rating, Catholics 31.7 percent, Protestants 22.9 percent, and Eastern Orthodox 30 percent.

The Gag Rule

The House in March 1993 voted overwhelmingly 273 to 149 to restore family planning counseling and referral services in clinics that receive federal funding under Title X. The bill codified President Clinton's reversal of the "gag rule" implemented previously by Republican administrations, which prohibited doctors from discussing abortion as part of counseling procedures.

Almost 30 percent of Republicans defected to the pro-choice side while only 11.2 percent of Democrats remained adamantly in favor of the gag rule. Overall, 88.8 percent of the Democrats and 29.7 percent Republicans favored the Clinton administration's policy.

Only twenty-eight Democrats opposed their president on this issue, and these may represent the hardcore anti-abortion members. Philosophically, they were even more conservative than those who opposed fetal research and supported parental notification. The Catholic pro-gag-rule Democrats had a 49 percent liberal rating, and the Protestants recorded only 36.2 percent on the liberal scale. Fifteen of the twenty-eight were from the South or the Border South, the evangelical heartland. Three of the four Texans were of Hispanic descent (two Catholic, one Methodist), and both representatives from

Cajun Louisiana (one Catholic, one Methodist) remained adamant. West Virginia, Utah, and Mississippi remained anti-abortion strongholds.

But a number of prominent "right to life" Democrats supported the president on the gag rule, including Mazzoli of Kentucky, Penny of Minnesota, Manton of New York, Kanjorski of Pennsylvania, and Applegate of Ohio.

The religious breakdown of the dissenters was predictable: 50 percent Protestant, 46.4 percent Catholic, and 3.6 percent Mormon.

It is significant that no Democrats of the Jewish and Greek Orthodox faiths, or those who are religiously nonaffiliated, have joined the anti-choice dissenters on any of the major abortion-related votes.

The Republican pro-choice, anti-gag-rule dissenters rose to fifty-one, or almost three out of ten in the GOP ranks.

All of the Republican representatives from Connecticut, New Mexico, Washington, Delaware, Maine, New Hampshire, and Rhode Island opposed the gag rule, as did a majority of Republicans from New Jersey, Maryland, and New York.

Republicans in the South and California remained strongly anti-choice. But even in the South a few dissenting votes were cast. Two Florida Episcopalian freshmen, Fowler and Miller, frequently dissented from Republican orthodoxy on abortion, as did Arthur Ravenel[14] of South Carolina, the House's only French Huguenot member. The Huguenots have traditionally placed a high premium on the sanctity of individual conscience and have looked askance at government efforts to enforce morality. The gag rule issue even brought forth a rare dissent from a Texas Republican, Lamar Smith, a conservative and a Christian Scientist.

The religious breakdown of Republican dissenters on the gag rule was similar to other key abortion issues: 64.7 percent Protestant, 23.5 percent Catholic, 5.9 percent Jewish, 5.9 percent Eastern Orthodox. The strong Catholic pro-choice contingent remains noteworthy, and may be the most significant new trend in abortion voting in Congress. And five of the thirteen pro-choice Catholic Republicans were newly elected in 1992.

The pro-choice dissenters were a bit more liberal than all Republicans. The liberal rating for Jewish dissenters was 33.3 percent, for Catholics 31.4 percent, for Protestants 24.4 percent, and for Eastern Orthodox 21.7 percent.

Abortion is an issue that stands on its own, however. *The anti-choice Democrats have a higher liberal rating for all religious groups than pro-choice Republicans.* This is true for economic and foreign policy questions. So the abortion issue is very much a conscience issue that often causes members of Congress to cross the aisle, as it were, and join those with whom they have little or nothing in common on other issues.

Table 8.6

**Senate Vote on Welfare Reform Amendment
Denying Funds to Unwed Mothers
HR 4, September 13, 1995**

| | % For Amendment | | |
Religious Character of State	All Members	Republicans	Democrats
High evangelical	39.5	60.9	6.7
Low evangelical	14.5	29.0	0
Percent difference	25.0	31.9	6.7

One additional trend was noticeable in these abortion votes. The large freshman class elected in 1992 was decidedly pro-choice. While one out of four pro-choice Republicans (25 percent) is newly elected, only one of seven anti-choice Democrats (14.3 percent) is a new member.

There are also some significant denominational differences.

Episcopalians are strongly pro-choice. Eight of the fifty-one anti-gag-rule Republicans are Episcopalians, but only one of twenty-eight pro-gag-rule Democrats belongs to the Episcopal Church. (Of course, all the other Episcopalian Democrats are pro-choice and the remaining Episcopalian Republicans are anti-choice, but the dissenters often signal the fault lines of the movement within communities as far as voting behavior is concerned.)

A new line of inquiry has presented itself in the present Congress elected in 1994, the most conservative one in a half century and one in which evangelicals are playing a major role. A consideration of key votes on abortion and gay rights reveals the strong influence on voting decisions that is brought to bear by the percentage of evangelicals in the population. This may have become a more significant factor than the religion of the member. The pro-choice euphoria of 1993–95 has been replaced by a new wave of anti-choice voting behavior.

An amendment to the welfare reform bill denying funds to unwed mothers was defeated overwhelmingly 76-24 in the Senate on September 13, 1995, after having earlier passed the more conservative House. The only majority support came from Republican senators who represented heavily evangelical states. This measure, regarded as punitive and mean-spirited by the U.S. Catholic Conference and the mainline Protestant churches, was supported by many evangelical lobbies. Republicans from nonevangelical states refused to support the amendment, as did every Democrat except Robert Byrd, a Baptist from West Virginia. (See table 8.6.)

Table 8.7
Senate Vote on Federal Funding for Prison Abortions
HR 2076, September 29, 1995

Religious Character of State	% Anti-Abortion		
	All Members	Republicans	Democrats
High evangelical	77.8	100.0	42.9
Low evangelical	40.0	70.0	10.0
Percent difference	37.8	30.0	32.9

A vote denying federal funding for military abortions passed the Senate on September 29, 1995. Its support was twice as high in strongly evangelical states as in other states. Among Democrats there was four times greater support in high evangelical states. Every Republican senator from an above-average evangelical state voted yes, while 90 percent of Democrats from below-average evangelical states voted no. (See table 8.7.)

In November 1995 both the House and Senate considered a bill (HR 1868) prohibiting U.S. assistance to family planning organizations that perform abortions or provide abortion counseling. The ban, enacted in 1984 during the Reagan administration, was repealed by President Clinton in 1993. This bill would have reimposed the ban.

The differences in the religious character of the states were pronounced in the Senate, where members from states with high evangelical populations were twice as likely to support the ban as those from states with lower evangelical populations. Every Democrat from low evangelical states voted no. The Senate voted 55 percent to 45 percent against the measure two weeks after the House had approved it 56 percent to 44 percent.

The House vote showed a smaller difference, of about 12 points, between high-evangelical and low-evangelical states. (See tables 8.8 and 8.9.)

On November 1, 1995 (All Saints Day, appropriately), conservatives in the House won two major victories dealing with abortion and gay rights. House Resolution (HR) 1833, which passed 288-139, outlawed a specific late-term abortion procedure. The other resolution, HR 2546, revoked a District of Columbia law allowing city employees to buy health insurance for same-sex domestic partners; it was approved 249-172.

Members from strongly evangelical states were anti-abortion and anti-gay rights, but the difference was decidedly greater on the gay rights question (24 percent) than on abortion procedures (12 percent). Many Catholics and moderate Protestants supported the ban on partial-birth abortions but

Table 8.8

Senate Family-Planning Vote, HR 1868, November 15, 1995

Religious Character of State	% Anti-Abortion		
	All Members	% Republicans	% Democrats
High evangelical	64.9	90.9	26.7
Low evangelical	32.8	66.7	0
Percent difference	32.1	24.2	26.7

Table 8.9

House Family-Planning Vote, HR 1868, November 1, 1995

Religious Character of State	% Anti-Abortion		
	All Members	Republicans	Democrats
High evangelical	63.7	93.5	26.7
Low evangelical	51.6	78.5	20.7
Percent difference	12.1	15.0	6.0

Table 8.10

Abortion and Gay Rights Votes, HR 1833 and HR 2546, November 1, 1995

Religious Character of State	All Members		Republicans		Democrats	
	% Anti-Abortion	% Anti-Gay Rights	% Anti-Abortion	% Anti-Gay Rights	% Anti-Abortion	% Anti-Gay Rights
High evangelical	74.7	73.7	97.8	94.6	46.8	47.3
Low evangelical	62.6	49.6	90.5	81.8	31.1	12.1
Percent difference	12.1	24.1	7.3	12.8	15.7	35.2

also supported the gay health-insurance law. In fact, a majority of representatives in less evangelical states supported the gay rights position while almost three-quarters of those from strongly evangelical states supported an anti-gay-rights posture. (See table 8.10.) The most significant differences were observed among Democrats. Democratic members from high-evangelical states were four times more likely to adopt an anti-gay-rights position

Table 8.11

Senate Vote on Partial-Birth Abortions, HR 1833, December 7, 1995

	% Anti-Abortion		
Religious Character of State	All Members	Republicans	Democrats
High evangelical	71.1	95.7	33.3
Low evangelical	45.0	76.7	13.3
Percent difference	26.1	19.0	20.0

Table 8.12

Senate Vote on Flag Desecration, Constitutional Amendment SJR31, December 12, 1995

	% in Favor		
Religious Character of State	All Members	Republicans	Democrats
High evangelical	81.6	94.7	60.0
Low evangelical	52.5	91.2	16.1
Percent difference	29.1	3.5	43.9

than Democrats from less evangelical states. Political party differences were enormous, as 87 percent of Republicans but only 26 percent of Democrats supported the anti-gay-rights position: a 61-point difference.

In the Senate the partial-birth abortion procedure ban passed 54-44. This 55 percent support was a good deal lower than the 67 percent support in the House. The Southern and Border states carried the day, with 70.6 percent support compared to 46.9 percent support in the North and West. All nineteen Republicans from the South-Border voted yes. Senators from the highly evangelical states were 71 percent supportive compared to 45 percent in the less evangelical states.

The religious character of the senator's state proved more significant than the member's religion. Some votes were easy to predict. All three Mormons voted yes, while all eight Jews and the one nonaffiliated senator (Campbell of Colorado) voted no. The Eastern Orthodox senators voted 2 to 1 no. Catholics were 55 percent favorable, and Protestants were 62 percent supportive. (See table 8.11.)

A Senate vote on December 12 on a constitutional amendment to prohibit desecration of the American flag can be considered a key vote on patriotism (or ultranationalistic patriotism) and civil liberties. The amendment passed 63-36 but fell four votes short of the required two-thirds majority.

Table 8.13

Percentage of Conservative Votes, 1994

Religious Character of State	Economic Issues		Social Issues		Foreign Policy Issue	
	Demo-crat	Repub-lican	Demo-crat	Repub-lican	Demo-crat	Repub-lican
High evangelical	27.3	68.6	37.6	73.7	33.7	72.9
Low evangelical	18.9	73.0	21.6	71.3	20.5	73.4
Difference	+ 8.4	− 4.4	+16.0	+ 2.4	+13.2	− 0.5

This vote again shows how different the South is from the rest of the nation, and how flag-waving emotionalism transcends more rational concerns for civil liberties in areas where evangelicalism predominates. Nearly 80 percent of the senators from the South and Border voted yes, including 95 percent of the Republicans (all except Mitch McConnell of Kentucky) and 60 percent of the Democrats. In the rest of the country only 55 percent supported the amendment.

In the highly evangelical states, 81.6 percent voted yes; in the less evangelical states, only 52.5 percent did so.

There was more division in the Democratic ranks than in the GOP camp, where support was nearly unanimous. Even Oregon Republican Mark Hatfield, a prominent evangelical and critic of civil religion, voted yes. Only one in six Democrats (16.1 percent) from states with few evangelicals voted yes, compared to three out of five (60 percent) Democrats in the evangelical bastions. Both the South and the Republican Party have a highly developed civil religion and a passionate regard for symbolic expressions of patriotic sentiment. (See table 8.12.)

One additional religious influence can be isolated and studied: the percentage of congresspersons who have attended church-related colleges. In the House one-fourth (25.7 percent) of members were undergraduates at church colleges, while one-eighth (12.6 percent) attended church-related graduate schools. In the Senate it was 16 percent for undergraduate study, and 7 percent for graduate degrees. On the undergraduate level 64 percent of those who went to church colleges chose one of their denomination. Only 42 percent of those who went to church-related graduate schools chose one belonging to their faith group. (Interestingly, 6 Protestant congressmen attended Catholic colleges, seven Catholics attended Protestant colleges, and 2 Jews attended Catholic colleges.)

Table 8.14

Congressional Religious Affiliations

Religious Group	Members in the 104th Congress	Changes since the 103rd Congress
Roman Catholic	148	+7
Baptist	68	+4
Methodist	63	–6
Presbyterian	60	+3
Episcopal	49	–1
Jewish	33	–9
Unspecified Protestant	23	+2
Lutheran	21	–1
Mormon	13	+2
United Church of Christ	12	–2
"Christian"	6	+5
Christian Science	5	+1
Eastern Orthodox	5	n.c.
Unitarian Universalist	5	–2
No Affiliation	5	–2
Assembly of God	3	+3
African Methodist Episcopal	3	–1
Disciples of Christ	2	n.c.
Seventh-day Adventist	2	n.c.
Church of Christ	2	–3
Christian Reformed	2	n.c.
United Brethren in Christ	1	+1
Christian Church	1	n.c.
Christian and Missionary Alliance	1	+1
Pan African Orthodox	1	n.c.
Church of the Nazarene	1	+1

On several key votes, church college attendance brings an additional conservative influence on members' voting. Catholics who graduated from Catholic colleges are more anti-abortion than Catholics who attended secular colleges, and they are more anti-abortion than all other members of Congress. Protestants who attended church colleges support school prayer to a higher degree than other Protestants or members of other religious traditions.

The trends in congressional religious affiliation are also factors to consider. Since the 1960s Catholics, Jews, and Mormons have steadily gained

Table 8.15

Party Breakdown by Religion

Religious Group	Democrat	Republican
Roman Catholic	83	65
Baptist	32	36
Methodist	28	35
Presbyterian	22	38
Episcopal	17	32
Jewish[1]	27	5
"Protestant" (nondenominational)	6	17
Lutheran	9	12
Mormon	2	11
United Church of Christ	7	5
"Christian" (not designated)	1	5
Unitarian Universalist	2	3
Christian Science	0	5
Eastern Orthodox	1	4
No Affiliation	5	0
All Others	9	10
Total	251	283

1. One Jewish member is Independent.

representation, though this leveled off in the 1990s. Methodists, Presbyterians, Episcopalians, and United Church of Christ members have declined, reflecting perhaps their declining membership in the nation as a whole. (See tables 8.14 and 8.15.)

Many organizations rate the members of Congress on their votes cast on certain issues during each session. Most are special interest lobbies with relatively limited concerns. Some are multipurpose conservative or liberal ideological organizations that take positions on a host of issues. Some of the best-known of these are the conservative Americans for Constitutional Action and the liberal Americans for Democratic Action. These ratings have been consulted for this study.

But the *National Journal* has devised an ingenious formula that probes the different kinds of conservatism or liberalism that can be discerned from congressional votes. Some members are liberal on issues dealing with economic security, for example, but are conservatively oriented on foreign policy or sociocultural issues. Rather than classifying them as "moderate" when they might more accurately be defined as economic-issue liberals and social-issue conservatives, or some variation thereof, these ratings, which appear in the *Almanac of American Politics* every two years, represent a broader approach to the way members vote. Therefore, the following analysis is based on the 1994 ratings for Congress members, the most recent year available. Each member is rated by economic, social, and foreign policy votes. I have arranged them by party, religious affiliation of the individual member, and the predominant religious character of the state—primarily looking for differences in voting behavior for representatives from states with a high or above-average percentage of evangelicals, compared to those states with a low or below-average evangelical population.

The findings add significantly to our knowledge of how religion affects, and is affected by, party affiliation, regionalism, and type of issue. The 1994 votes occurred during the last Democratic-controlled Congress, during the second year of the Clinton presidency. When available, data from 1995 and 1996 will undoubtedly show an even more conservative domination of legislative voting patterns.

The findings are clear on several points. Republicans in every state are more conservative than Democrats on all three types of issues, economic, social, and foreign policy. But the differences are greatest for the social issues in the states with a high evangelical population, and especially for the Democrats representing those states. (See table 8.13.) Support for social-issue conservatism is 10 points higher than for economic conservatism among Democrats representing high evangelical states. And, conservative votes are 16 points more likely to be cast on social issues among Democrats in highly evangelical states than among Democrats from states with lower evangelical populations. For Republicans the difference is 5 points more conservative. Clearly the percentage of evangelicals in the state's population creates a tendency for their congressional representatives to cast more conservative votes on social issues than on economic or foreign policy issues.

For Republicans the difference is less, since between two-thirds and three-fourths of all votes cast by Republicans on all kinds of issues in both high evangelical and low evangelical states are conservative votes. Still, it is mildly significant that the highest percentage of conservative votes cast is the social issue voting by Republicans from strongly evangelical states. Also, only on social issues are Republicans from strongly evangelical states more conservative than Republicans from less evangelical states. On economic issues, by contrast, Republicans from highly evangelical states were 4 percent less conservative in their votes than Republicans from states with smaller evangelical populations. Next, let us look at the voting patterns for each major religious group.

This study is a replication of one I completed on the 1984 Congress. At that time I ranked the religious groups by degree of conservative voting on social, economic, and foreign policy issues. For some groups, there was a predictable result. Jews and Unitarians were the two least conservative groups on all three types of issues, while Mormons and Lutherans were the most conservative on all of them. The most significant difference came among Catholics, who proved to be the third most conservative religious community on social issues (which include abortion, school prayer, gun control, and crime control) but the third least conservative on economic and foreign policy questions. Members of the United Church of Christ and nondenominational Protestants lean to the liberal side, especially on social issues. Episcopalians were centrists, though somewhat more liberal on social issues and less so on economic issues, which would seem to accord with studies showing that high status groups tend toward economic conservatism, but that their high educational level correlates positively with social and cultural liberalism. Methodists, Presbyterians, and Baptists lean to the conservative side, though Baptists were less so on economic issues. The Eastern Orthodox members divided along by party lines, leaning to the less conservative side because of the Democratic predominance in their ranks.

The 1994 results revealed both continuities and changes. Two findings from 1984 have not changed: Mormons are the most conservative and Jews the least conservative religious group in Congress. They are also the most and least Republican, respectively, in the congressional makeup. (See table 8.16.)

"Nondenominational" Protestants, however, have moved from being relatively liberal to the second most conservative group. There may be a number of evangelicals in this amorphous category, which is the least satisfying definitionally. In the past, observers tended to think that the Protestant category was a catch-all for those who lacked strong commitments or attachments to any religious community. Most of those who listed their religion as merely Protestant, which is a very minimal statement considering the number and variety of Protestant groups that exist in the United States, were Democrats and liberals. Even in 1994, the small number of nondenominational Protestant Democrats was the least conservative of all Democrats. But in the 1993–95 Congress, three-fourths were Republicans, and their overall conservative rating was high.

Methodists and Lutherans ranked third and fourth in conservative support, which was higher than their Republican ranking. Quite a few Methodist Democrats were moderate or conservative Democrats from the South. Presbyterians ranked fifth in conservative ranking and fourth in Republican ranking. Episcopalians were less conservative than they were Republican, ranking sixth in conservative voting but third in Republicanism.

The least conservative and Republican groups were Baptists, United

Table 8.16

Republican-Conservative Ranking 1994 Congressional Votes
by Major Religions[1]

Rank	% Republican	Rank	% Conservative
Mormon	81.8	Mormon	74.3
"Protestant"	76.5	"Protestant"	58.0
Episcopalian	60.0	Methodist	57.8
Presbyterian	54.3	Lutheran	55.7
Methodist	50.9	Presbyterian	53.1
Lutheran	50.0	Episcopalian	52.6
Baptist	42.6	Baptist	48.5
United Church of Christ	41.7	United Church of Christ	45.1
Catholic	36.9	Catholic	42.1
Jewish	12.1	Jewish	25.6

1. Religions which had at least 10 members in Congress in 1994.

Table 8.17

Racial and Political Differences among Baptists
1994 Congressional Voting Patterns

	% Conservative			
	Economic	Social	Foreign	All
Black Democrats	2.7	14.5	15.8	11.0
White Democrats	38.0	53.2	44.0	44.8
White Republicans[1]	74.8	81.5	79.5	78.6

1. There was only one black Republican, Gary Franks of Connecticut, in the 1994 Congress, which does not give enough of a sample to be meaningful.

Church of Christ members, Catholics, and Jews. Compared to 1984, Lutherans, Baptists, and Catholics were less conservative.

Baptists have a strong racial division that has made their overall conservative index appear lower. One-third of the Baptist members elected in 1992 were African-Americans, seventeen of them Democrats, and one Republican. A majority of Baptist Democrats in Congress are members of the Congressional Black Caucus, and they are the most liberal single group in Congress. (See table 8.17.) Only 11 percent of their votes on all issues are conservative, compared to 45 percent of the votes of white Baptist Democrats and 79 per-

Table 8.18

The "Social Issue" Effect by Religion
(All Members, All Parties, Major Religions)

Religion	% More Conservative on Social than on Economic Issues
Baptist	+10.3
Mormon	+ 8.5
Catholic	+ 4.4
Methodist	+ 3.4
Presbyterian	+ 2.5
Lutheran	+ 1.9
Episcopalian	0
Jewish	– 0.4
"Protestant" (Nondenominational)	– 0.5
United Church of Christ	– 2.2

cent of the votes of white Baptist Republicans. The changing racial configuration explains the decline in Baptist conservative ranking from second or third to seventh. White Baptist Republicans, however, are the second most conservative voting group in Congress, and the election of many new Baptist Republicans in 1994 will undoubtedly influence future Baptist rankings.

Only 42 percent of Catholic votes were conservative, making them a good deal less conservative than all Protestants. Jewish Democrats were the second least conservative Democrats, and Jewish Republicans were the least conservative Republican group.

Social issues clearly have a religious component. Baptists and Mormons of both parties are more likely to cast conservative votes on social and cultural issues than on economic issues. (See table 8.18.) Baptists are 10 percent more conservative on social than on economic issues, and Mormons are 8 percent more conservative. Catholics, Methodists, Presbyterians, and Lutherans are slightly more conservative. Episcopalians, Jews, "Protestants," and, especially, members of the United Church of Christ are no more or even less likely to favor social-issue conservatism.

When one breaks voting down into the smallest and most discrete components, it seems clear that Democrats are more susceptible to social issue differentials than Republicans, though Democrats of all religious persuasions are less conservative on social and economic issues. Still, Democrats who belong to Eastern Orthodox churches, Mormons, "other Christian" (often

Table 8.19

Social Issues Gains and Losses
All Religions by Party

Religion	Party	% Gain
Gains		
Eastern Orthodox	Democrat	+19.0
Mormon	Democrat	+16.0
"Other Christian"	Democrat	+13.6
Baptist	Democrat	+13.4
Nonaffiliated	Democrat	+ 9.0
Methodist	Democrat	+ 7.4
Eastern Orthodox	Republican	+ 7.0
Mormon	Republican	+ 6.9
Baptist	Republican	+ 6.2
Catholic	Democrat	+ 6.1
Losses		
Unitarian Universalist	Republican	–24.0
United Church of Christ	Republican	–12.8
Jewish	Republican	– 6.5
"Protestant"	Democrat	– 3.3
Episcopalian	Republican	– 2.1

small evangelical bodies), Baptists, Methodists, and Catholics are more conservative on social issues than on economic issues. (See table 8.19.) Surprisingly, this is also true for religiously nonaffiliated Democrats. On the other hand, Unitarian Universalist Republicans are 24 percent less conservative on social issues than on economic issues. Unitarian Universalist (UU) Republicans are the only subgroup among Republicans to take a liberal position on social issues. On economic and foreign policy issues, UU Republicans are conservative. Republicans who belong to the United Church of Christ, Jewish, and Episcopalian traditions are less conservative on social than on economic questions, as are "Protestant" Democrats. (See table 8.20.)

Congressional Religious Membership Trends

Though the 1994 elections represented a major shift toward the Republican party, the religious preferences of members of Congress changed much less.

Table 8.20

Percentage Conservative Votes by Issue and Religion[1]

Religion	Party	Economic	Social	Foreign	All
	Democrat	20.7	26.8	22.5	23.3
Catholic	Republican	73.0	74.6	75.1	74.2
	All	40.0	44.4	41.9	42.1
	Democrat	18.6	32.0	28.5	26.4
Baptist	Republican	74.8	81.0	79.5	78.4
	All	42.6	52.9	50.2	48.5
	Democrat	33.8	41.2	39.6	38.2
Methodist	Republican	76.0	75.7	78.7	76.8
	All	55.3	58.7	59.5	57.8
	Democrat	24.3	27.8	22.2	24.8
Presbyterian	Republican	75.8	77.4	77.6	76.9
	All	52.3	54.8	52.3	53.1
	Democrat	23.5	26.6	30.1	26.8
Episcopalian	Republican	70.5	68.4	70.4	69.8
	All	51.7	51.7	54.3	52.6
	Democrat	21.0	21.3	20.1	20.8
Jewish	Republican	65.8	59.3	64.5	63.2
	All[2]	25.8	25.4	25.6	25.6
	Democrat	39.2	40.6	31.6	37.1
Lutheran	Republican	74.2	76.6	72.2	74.3
	All	56.7	58.6	51.9	55.7
	Democrat	9.3	6.0	0	5.1
Nondenominational Protestant	Republican	74.0	74.4	74.3	74.2
	All	58.8	58.3	56.8	58.0
	Democrat	25.0	30.3	28.9	28.0
United Church of Christ	Republican	76.2	63.4	67.4	69.0
	All	46.3	44.1	44.9	45.1
	Democrat	36.0	52.0	43.0	43.7
Mormon	Republican	76.7	83.6	83.0	81.1
	All	69.3	77.8	75.7	74.3
	Democrat	20.0	20.0	20.0	20.0
Unitarian Universalist	Republican	63.7	39.7	64.0	55.8
	All	42.2	27.8	42.4	37.5
	Democrat	0	19.0	6.0	8.3
Eastern Orthodox	Republican	66.3	73.3	79.7	73.1
	All	49.8	59.8	61.3	57.0
No Affiliation	Democrat	7.3	16.3	22.5	15.3
Other Christians	Democrat	16.1	29.7	27.3	24.4
	Republican	77.0	75.8	73.7	75.5
	All	48.2	53.9	51.7	51.3

1. Religious groups with ten or more members in Congress.
2. Including Independent Bernard Sanders of Vermont.

In general terms, it was a good year for Baptists, generic or unspecified Protestants, and Roman Catholics. It was not a good year for Episcopalians, Jews, and Methodists. Catholics, the largest group by far, increased their membership by seven. Some small religious groups received representation for the first time in a number of years.

Catholics maintained their unusual ability to withstand landslides for either party. Catholics have done well in Democratic landslide years like 1964 and in Republican landslide years like 1972, 1984, and now 1994. In the past, Catholics were likely to gain representation during Democratic years like 1958 and to decline somewhat during Republican triumphs. There are 148 Catholics in this Congress, compared to 141 in the previous one.

But U.S. Catholics, whose positions generally lie close to the center, are now prominent in both parties, thus strengthening their role as swing voters in U.S. elections. For generations Catholics were underrepresented in Congress. In 1962, for example, there were only ninety-nine Catholics elected to Congress—18 percent of the members—though Catholics were 22 percent of the population. During the 1980s, the Catholic representation was 25 percent-27 percent, which reflects the general Catholic population, or is perhaps slightly above it. ("Official" Catholic data show 22 percent of Americans are members of Catholic parishes, but preference polls and surveys generally show 25 percent-28 percent Catholic. Exit polls conducted in 1994 found 30 percent of those who voted were Catholic.)

The 1994 results show a sharp rise in Catholic Republicans, from forty-nine to sixty-five, with a corresponding decline in Catholic Democrats, from ninety-two to eighty-three.

Baptists have moved into second place, with sixty-eight members elected to the One Hundred Fourth Congress. In the past Baptists have generally placed fourth or fifth. This reflects two demographic and political changes since 1990. One is the increase in black congressional representation, mandated by reapportionment and court rulings before the 1992 election. There are thirty-nine African-American congresspersons, and twenty are Baptist. The other is the rise of the Religious Right, which is significantly Baptist in most areas. Many white Southern Baptist Republicans elected in the 1990s represent the right wing of the religious and political spectra in the United States.

Baptists were long underrepresented in Congress. They are America's second largest religious community, though sharply divided by race and politics. Some surveys show 20 percent of U.S. citizens are Baptists, while official membership is around 12 percent of U.S. adults. Their growing membership in Congress now reflects these trends.

Methodists have declined significantly in congressional representation, from 102 in 1962 to 69 in 1992 and 63 in 1994. This may to some extent reflect their declining national membership. For many decades Methodists were the largest religious group in Congress, until Catholics moved well ahead in the mid- and late 1960s. Methodism has often been regarded as the middle road in theology, income, and politics, and Methodists generally split their votes between the parties. Even in geography, Methodists are strongest in the upper South states (Maryland, Delaware, West Virginia, Virginia) and in the lower North (Iowa, Nebraska, Kansas). They are also strong in the Texas and Louisiana delegations.

Presbyterians rank fourth with sixty members, a small gain from 1992. Almost two thirds are Republicans. Presbyterians are well represented throughout the nation in terms of congressional members.

Episcopalians have always been the most overrepresented religious group in Congress (along with Unitarians), owing perhaps to their historic role in the formation of the Constitution, the Declaration of Independence, and their prominence in the upper echelons of U.S. life. For many years they were first in the U.S. Senate and generally third or fourth in the whole Congress. From 1981 to 1983 they were in second place in the entire Congress. In 1994 they dropped to fifth place, with forty-nine members, and there are now fewer Episcopalians in Congress than there have been in over thirty years. The fact that 1994 was a Republican year only underscores the Episcopalian decline in politics, which may also reflect their membership losses since 1965. This decline is also affected by the large number of liberal Episcopalian Democrats who were defeated in 1994. Of all groups, Episcopalian Republicans were the least favorable to the Religious Right agenda under President Reagan, and Episcopalian Republican senators were the most likely to oppose their party's policies on abortion, school prayer, and aid to church schools. The new Republican majority in Congress has far fewer Episcopalian members than during the Reagan, Nixon, and Eisenhower years.

Jews were underrepresented in U.S. political life until the 1980s, when their congressional representation soared, topping forty during the late 1980s and early 1990s. There were ten Jewish senators elected in 1992, an all-time record. Total Jewish representation was forty-two, or 8 percent, compared to 2 percent of the population. The 1994 elections reduced the Jewish membership to thirty-three. Since most Jews are liberal or moderate Democrats, this change is not unexpected.

The number of "Protestants" who have no traditional denominational attachments has increased but the character of this group has changed considerably. In the past, most were Democrats and liberals on church-state matters.

Now, the majority are Republicans. A number of the newly elected call themselves "Christian" or "Nondemoninational Christian," which could reflect the rise of nondenominational, parachurch groups on the conservative side of U.S. religious life.

Lutherans remain the most underrepresented religious group in political life. There are twenty-one Lutherans in the new Congress, down from twenty-two in the old. But America's nine million Lutherans have far fewer representatives than Presbyterians or Episcopalians, who have fewer members.

There are thirteen Mormons in the One Hundred Fourth Congress, a gain of two. All but two are Republicans. The entire Utah delegation belongs to the Church of Jesus Christ of Latter Day Saints, as do four California Republicans.

The United Church of Christ, which once had twenty-five or thirty members in Congress, now has only a dozen. This liberal church was once predominantly Republican in membership, but its members in Congress have moved toward the Democrats since the 1970s, and Democrats still outnumber Republicans 7-5 in the UCC ranks.

Another highly influential group, the Unitarians, have been reduced to only five members. Even among this liberal faith group, Republicans outnumber Democrats 3-2, though Unitarian Republicans belong to the moderate wing of their party.

All five Christian Scientists in the new Congress are Republicans, including two from Virginia. The five religiously nonaffiliated members are Democrats, though one, Senator Ben Campbell of Colorado, joined the Republicans in 1995.

The conservative Republican ranks are now joined by three Assembly of God members, a group that once frowned on politics but is often considered a reliable ally of the Religious Right. The Church of the Nazarene is also represented for the first time in years, being the denomination of Jim Bunn, the Republican winner in Oregon's Fifth District. Republican Jon Christensen of Nebraska's Second District, whose campaign was closely allied to Christian conservatives, is a member of the Christian and Missionary Alliance Church, which has 270,000 U.S. members.

The smallest religious body to have one of its members elected to Congress is the United Brethren in Christ, a faith group with 25,749 members, with its headquarters in Dan Quayle's hometown of Huntington, Indiana. Representative Mark Souder, the Republican victor in Indiana's Fourth District, belongs to this church.

The changes in religious affiliations in Congress may reflect the changing configuration of U.S. religious life, the increased or decreased activity of some religious groups in politics, the decline of prejudice against certain communities, and/or their increasing acceptability to the electorate. These changes—which are relatively small from election to election—become meaningful only when they foreshadow long-range and substantial movements over a longer period of time.

Notes

1. Peter L. Benson and Dorothy L. Williams, *Religion on Capitol Hill* (San Francisco: Harper & Row, 1982), p. 137. Additional page references to this work appear in parentheses following the cited material.

2. See Allen D. Hertzke, *Representing God in Washington* (Knoxville: University of Tennessee Press, 1988).

3. Madge M. McKinney, "Religion and Elections," *Public Opinion Quarterly* 8 (Spring 1944): 110–14.

4. John H. Fenton, *The Catholic Vote* (New Orleans: Hauser Press, 1960).

5. John Robert Warner, Jr., "Religious Affiliation as a Factor in the Voting Records of Members of the Eighty-ninth Congress" (Ph.D. diss., Boston University, 1968), p. 261. Additional page references to this work appear in parentheses following the cited material.

6. Albert J. Menendez, *Religion at the Polls* (Philadelphia: Westminster Press, 1977), p. 149.

7. "Child Care, Congress, and Sectarian Special Interests," *Voice of Reason* 34 (Summer 1990): 10–12.

8. Charles Fimian, "The Effects of Religion on Abortion Policy-Making: A Study of Voting Behavior in the U.S. Congress, 1976–1980" (Ph.D. diss., Arizona State University, 1983), p. 360.

9. Ibid., p. 252.

10. Mary Eisner Eccles, "Abortion: How Members Voted in 1977," *CQ Weekly Report* 36 (February 4, 1978): 258–67.

11. Maris A. Vinovskis, "The Politics of Abortion in the House of Representatives in 1976," *Michigan Law Review* 77 (August 1977): 1790–1827.

12. James T. Richardson and Sandie Wightman Fox, "Religious Affiliation as a Predictor of Voting Behavior in Abortion Reform Legislation," *Journal for the Scientific Study of Religion* 11 (September 1972): 347–59.

13. Ridge was elected governor of Pennsylvania in 1994.

14. Ravenel lost the GOP nomination for South Carolina governor in 1994.

9

A Catholic-Evangelical Alliance: Pros and Cons

Pros

If there is any one thing that makes Republican party strategists and culture war conservatives salivate with the prospects of unending electoral triumphs, it is the development of a permanent political alliance between Catholics and evangelicals. The Christian Coalition's executive director, Ralph Reed, explains this hope: "The future of American politics lies in the growing strength of evangelicals and their Roman Catholic allies. If these two core constituencies—evangelicals comprising the swing vote in the South, Catholics holding sway in the North—can cooperate on issues and support like-minded candidates, they can determine the outcome of almost any election in the nation. No longer burdened by the past, Roman Catholics, evangelicals, Greek Orthodox, and many religious conservatives from the mainline denominations are forging a new alliance that promises to be among the most powerful and important in the modern political era."[1]

There have already been a number of political contests in recent decades where a majority of evangelicals and Catholics have supported the same candidate, often the conservative Republican one. There have even been a few races where Catholic Republicans have triumphed in evangelical states. War hero Jeremiah Denton won in Alabama in 1980, as did Don Nickles in Oklahoma. Tommy Hartnett won a congressional seat in the South Carolina Low Country during the 1980s. Bob Martinez, who won the Florida governorship in 1986 only to lose it in 1990, won considerable evangelical support because

258

of his anti-abortion policies. In 1990 Martinez won a majority of Baptist and evangelical voters, while losing among most other groups.

Oklahoma is an unlikely state for Catholics, especially Catholic Republicans, to win strong statewide support, but that in fact has happened. Dewey Bartlett, a Princeton-educated Tulsa business executive, won the governorship in 1966 and later was elected to the U.S. Senate. Frank Keating, the present governor, won in 1994. Don Nickles has won three U.S. Senate races, in 1980, 1986, and 1992. All are Catholic Republicans from the state that had the highest anti-Smith and anti-Kennedy voting in the nation, and where anti-Catholic discrimination and prejudice were rife, even to the point of job discrimination and social antipathy. Catholics were routinely fired from civil service jobs during the 1920s and 1930s. The "bone dry" law passed in the early 1920s and was supported by Baptists and evangelicals despite its onerous provisions. It was so strict a prohibitionist measure that even sacramental or communion wine was outlawed, thereby effectively prohibiting the celebration of the Mass in Oklahoma until the state supreme court voided the measure.[2] Episcopalians, Lutherans, Jews, and some other religious groups also protested the law's refusal to exempt religious organizations from the act's enforcement provisions.

Don Nickles, in particular, has proved popular among the state's conservative Protestants, primarily because he campaigns in their churches and supports the most extreme conservative social positions. Even Nickles, however, may have lost some votes because of his Catholicism. In 1980 there were eleven counties that supported Reagan for president but opposed Nickles. These counties were more anti-Kennedy in 1960 (he ran 8 percentage points behind Stevenson) than the state as a whole (Kennedy ran 4 points weaker than Stevenson). Even in 1992 Nickles lost five of these counties.

One example of Catholic and evangelical support for a political candidate can be seen in Pennsylvania, in the support given to Robert Casey, a moderate Catholic Democrat, in his 1986 and 1990 campaigns for governor. Casey's policies on education, civil rights, and women and children's health programs evinced an overall concern for the disadvantaged and the underdog, a classic liberal Democratic posture. He was also viewed as a man of integrity with a warm and successful family life. But his strenuous and unyielding opposition to abortion, and his repeated attempts to limit the procedure legislatively and legally, made his term of office controversial. Polling data and precinct data show that he both gained and lost votes from those highly committed on the abortion issue. He probably gained more than he lost, because Pennsylvania is usually seen as a pro-life state. His support should be viewed somewhat cautiously as a paradigm of Catholic-evangeli-

cal political unity, because his overall record as governor was far more liberal than that which usually animates evangelical voters nationally.

The Casey story begins in 1986, when the former state auditor, who had
lost three previous bids for the governorship, won the party's nomination to
oppose Republican William Scranton, the state's lieutenant governor and son
of a popular governor of the 1960s. Casey was an economic liberal and a
social conservative, while Scranton was an economic conservative and a
social liberal. This made for an unusual political mix, with the probability of
much switching by voters who were more accustomed to supporting either
solid liberals or unswerving conservatives.

Casey won his close election (51 percent to 49 percent), one of the few
Democratic statewide victories in the previous two decades—by putting
together an interesting coalition of Catholics and rural evangelical Protestants. These traditional opponents in Pennsylvania political life liked Casey
a great deal better than recent Democratic presidential candidates. Casey won
69 percent of the votes of Catholics in heavily Catholic key precincts, from
the inner cities of Scranton and Johnstown to rural areas in Elk County. He
also won 57 percent in Philadelphia, where a majority of Catholics voted for
Reagan and Bush in the three previous presidential elections.

He was able to win 86 percent of the black vote statewide, which is
always Democratic—even though he did not do as well as Dukakis and Mondale. He also won 57 percent of the Jewish vote in Philadelphia, and large
margins (79 percent) among working class labor union voters, both Catholic
and Protestant.

Casey's 69 percent of the Catholic vote outside the suburbs was most
impressive. It compared to 59 percent for Dukakis and 57 percent for Mondale, though it still failed to reach the 77 percent won by John F. Kennedy in
1960. Casey was particularly attractive to Catholic voters who are economic
liberals but social conservatives and those who share Casey's opposition to
abortion. The abortion issue, as can be seen from election results, is at least
implicitly the single most important issue since it helped Casey among conservative Catholics and Protestants but cost him votes among liberal suburbanites, students, and academic faculty, and at least some Jewish and black
voters. Consequently, the race was extremely close.

The Catholic vote was particularly favorable to Casey in Luzerne County
and in his home of Lackawanna County as well as in Cambria and in the
ever-Democratic vote in Greater Pittsburgh (Allegheny County). Elk County
was perhaps the most impressive since Casey won 62 percent in the heavily
Catholic precincts in this normally Republican county. These same precincts
gave only 40 percent for Dukakis and 32 percent for Mondale. Casey even

exceeded John Kennedy's vote in Elk County. Rural Catholic conservatives who are usually Republican seemed to like Casey's social conservatism.

In the Pittsburgh area Casey was not as popular as Dukakis, running 7 percentage points behind him in the city of Pittsburgh and 3 percent behind in the suburbs. Consequently, Pittsburgh Catholics gave Casey 1 percent less than they had given Dukakis, but Pittsburgh Catholics are overwhelmingly Democratic, voting 78 percent for Dukakis and 77 percent for Casey. This compares to Philadelphia Catholics who have been moving in a conservative Republican direction since the mid-1960s. Philadelphia Catholics, for example, gave only 46 percent to Dukakis and 47 percent for Mondale, a dramatic contrast to their co-religionists in Pittsburgh.

Not all religious groups, however, respond the same way, nor do all voters within a religious group. There are considerable differences according to economic status, educational attainment, and residency. A look at the Catholic vote in the Philadelphia suburbs, for example, suggested a continuing Republican preference. Casey only gained 2-4 percentage points over Dukakis in substantially Catholic neighborhoods in four Philadelphia suburban counties (Bucks, Chester, Delaware, and Montgomery). Even in many precincts that had gone for Kennedy in 1960, Casey was unable to win a majority. He won 41 percent, for example, in heavily Catholic parts of Delaware County compared to Kennedy's 51 percent and Dukakis's 37 percent. The Catholic vote in the suburbs has moved toward the Republicans and has become somewhat indistinguishable from the Protestant middle and upper class in recent years. Catholic voters in the suburbs are more prosperous and better educated, which has tended to increase the Republican vote. But Catholic voters in the suburbs are also more likely to be pro-choice on the abortion question and far more likely to disagree with church leadership than Catholic voters in rural and small-town areas. So these factors reinforced each other in keeping the Casey vote somewhat low among Catholic suburbanites. Still, he did somewhat better than recent Democratic presidential candidates.

Perhaps the most significant statewide result, though, was Casey's good showing among evangelical and conservative Protestants in the rural counties of Pennsylvania. These voters, who have been strongly Republican in most areas since the Civil War, have always reacted negatively to Catholic candidates. Even in areas like York and Berks counties, where many Protestant rural voters were traditional Democrats, Kennedy lost badly in 1960. Statewide only 33 percent of evangelical conservative Protestants voted for Kennedy, compared to 45 percent who voted for Stevenson in 1956. In recent years Mondale, Dukakis, Humphrey, and McGovern have all done poorly among rural Protestant voters. But Casey won a remarkable 46 percent throughout these counties compared to Dukakis's 35 percent and Mondale's 32 percent. In some counties Casey gained as much as 20 percentage points over Dukakis in the heavily Protestant precincts. It is worth noting that statewide Casey's biggest gains over Dukakis tended to come in either heavily Catholic counties or in heavily conservative Protestant counties.

In many instances the swing was amazing. Some of the most anti-Catholic precincts that turned most strongly against Kennedy in 1960 showed some of the largest and most impressive gains for Casey. It is probable the abortion issue and other questions of morality and family life issues have brought conservative Catholics and Protestants together during the past twenty years. Casey's more modest economic background was also perhaps more impressive in these small-town areas than the Republican candidate's upper-class demeanor.

Upper-income voters, who are concentrated in the Philadelphia and Pittsburgh suburbs, are and always have been Republican. But they are less Republican than they used to be, just as much of the Democratic working class and the Catholic middle class is less Democratic than it used to be. Eisenhower and Dewey won more than 80 percent of the statewide vote in upper-income, mostly Protestant areas. But Humphrey and McGovern did better than Kennedy, who had done better than Stevenson in these precincts. Mondale and Dukakis won a respectable 25 percent to 30 percent, particularly in some precincts in the Pittsburgh and Philadelphia suburbs. Dukakis won about 30 percent of the statewide upper-income vote. Casey was expected to run into some trouble here because in the past Catholic candidates, particularly those of Irish descent and running on the Democratic ticket, have not done particularly well with upper-income Protestant voters. If there is anti-Catholicism here, it's probably more of the social snobbery type rather than theological or cultural. Kennedy did do very poorly in some of these precincts in 1960 but he also did respectably in others. Casey did not suffer the losses that were expected here, as he was down about 1 percent in upper-income areas in Montgomery and Delaware counties compared to Dukakis and was down about 3 percent to 4 percent in Chester and Bucks counties. In the Pittsburgh suburbs, however, Casey did experience a 7 percentage point loss and in some very wealthy towns like Mt. Lebanon Township and Ben Avon Heights, he dropped more than 10 percent behind Dukakis. Casey also dropped 8 points in the Montgomery County suburb of Bryn Athyn, which is also a Swedenborgian community. Statewide, Casey won 29 percent and Dukakis 31 percent of the upper-income vote.

Casey did run into one major hurdle in the campaign. For want of a better term, this is the liberal elite, or the well-educated, prosperous suburban voter who is concerned about abortion, women's rights, environmental issues, and a whole host of liberal concerns. This segment of the electorate, which also includes university, student, and faculty communities, turned against Casey in large numbers. It is among these voters that the cultural clash over abortion is most intense and where candidates opposing abortion, whether Democrat or Republican, will lose votes.

In the city of Philadelphia Casey's vote plunged 30 percentage points or more in the liberal upper-income districts of the city known as "Center City," "Society Hill," and "Chestnut Hill." These areas, which liked McGovern and Dukakis, are culturally similar to inner-city bohemian districts all over the country. These Philadelphia neighborhoods resemble Washington's George-town, New York's Greenwich Village, Boston's Beacon Hill, Chicago's North Shore, and San Francisco's Nob Hill, where high-income but well-educated voters favor the Democratic presidential candidates and liberal causes generally. Casey lost these precincts that have gone Democratic for president since the 1960s. Similar results came in Pittsburgh's Ward Fourteen and Ward Seven, where Casey dropped nearly 25 percentage points. These are upper-middle-class liberal areas with many Jewish voters. They also favored Dukakis by large majorities. Ward Fourteen of Pittsburgh gave Dukakis 70 percent and Casey only 45 percent, for example. A comparable community was New Hope, an artsy-craftsy town in Bucks County where many artists and actors reside, and where Casey dropped 20 percentage points. In several other liberal suburbs of Philadelphia, Casey ran more than 10 points behind Dukakis.

"Liberal elite" voters are the most difficult to classify since they are the most unpredictable and least loyal to any political party. Well educated, well read, and well-to-do, they are committed political activists, cause oriented and media conscious, highly susceptible to fashionable movements of the moment. They are dedicated to such causes as abortion rights, environmental concerns, feminism, public television, opposition to censorship, civil liberty, and separation of church and state.

Their primary religious culture is secular, though there are likely to be liberal Protestants, Jews, Unitarians, Quakers, and even liberal Catholics in this newly emergent classification. They are united in opposition to religious authoritarianism. They are more individualist than communal.

Liberal elite voters are likely to be found in gentrified inner-city areas and close-in suburbs, but they avoid rural and small-town areas and exurbs. They represent a growing "new class" of voters virtually unknown to political analysts before, say, 1970. They come from many ethnic and cultural groups, though a considerable number come from Republican upper-class backgrounds. They are clearly an intriguing and volatile sector of the electorate.

Dukakis won about 70,000 votes in ten key liberal-elite voting districts while Casey received just 30,000.

Casey dropped 34 points in Swarthmore, a university town dominated by Swarthmore College. Swarthmore has had one of the most significant political shifts of any town in the state. Historically a Protestant Republican town with a large Quaker influence, Swarthmore gave less than 10 percent of its 1948 presidential vote to Harry Truman. It gave 17 percent to Stevenson and 23 percent to Kennedy and has begun to move in a Democratic direction ever since. George McGovern won 47 percent there, better than Humphrey's 39 percent. Walter Mondale was the first Democrat to win a majority in Swarthmore since Lyndon Johnson, and Mondale did better! In 1988 Swarthmore alumnus Michael Dukakis swept 65 percent of the town's vote, but in 1986, Casey won only 31 percent. Casey's views on abortion were undoubtedly responsible for pushing his vote back to the levels that Democrats won thirty years ago in Swarthmore.

Casey also lost heavily in other university towns, running 11 points behind Dukakis at State College, in Centre County, which is the Pennsylvania State University area. He dropped 11 points at West Chester State University precincts in Chester County and 20 points in Ward Twenty-seven in Philadelphia, dominated by the University of Pennsylvania students and faculty. But even in conservative towns like Millersville in Lancaster County and Slippery Rock in Butler County, Casey ran 7 or 8 points behind Dukakis. In Lower Oxford Township in Chester County, which is dominated by Lincoln University, a black college, Casey lost the town that had gone for Dukakis and Mondale. When it comes to abortion and other issues of lifestyle, a conservative candidate cannot win in university areas, even if he is running on the Democratic ticket whose candidates routinely carry these areas in presidential races.

Another segment of the population is the white working class, a labor-union-oriented vote particularly associated with steel mills and heavy unionization and traditionally Democratic. These voters are concentrated in the western part of the state in Allegheny, Cambria, Lawrence, Westmoreland, and Washington counties—with some in the eastern counties near Scranton—and have remained loyal Democratic bastions. Every Democratic presidential candidate from Roosevelt to Dukakis—except George McGovern—has won 70 percent or more of the votes of the white working class. Casey won a strong 79 percent, a slight improvement over Dukakis's 76 percent. These voters—Catholics and Protestants both—can be counted on to remain

Democrats. While a significant number are Catholic, there are also large numbers of Presbyterians and Methodists of Scots-Irish descent, particularly in some of the counties surrounding Pittsburgh. They are economic liberals and social conservatives and they have not defected from Democratic candidates, regardless of religious or cultural issues. Their impact on the statewide electorate is declining, however, since the percentage of the vote that is still white working class and labor oriented has declined considerably since 1948. The children and grandchildren of many of these voters who poured out to support Truman and Roosevelt are now in the upper middle class.

An important voting group is the state's large German-American community, comprising one of seven voters statewide. In nine counties voters of German ancestry make up between a third and almost half of the electorate. Casey did well with this group, winning over 38 percent, a gain of almost 6 points over Dukakis. These voters are heavily Protestant, mostly Lutheran, Mennonite, Methodist, or United Church of Christ. They are moderate to conservative in religion rather than evangelical and historically Republican. Casey ran 6 to 12 points ahead of Dukakis in all of the German counties except Lancaster, a large, prosperous, and adamantly Republican bailiwick. In 1960 Kennedy ran even with Stevenson among all German-Americans, but was weaker in the more rural areas. This is another Protestant group historically antagonistic to Catholic candidates that trended toward Casey.

The turnout of these cultural groups also affected a very close election. Groups that liked Casey better than Dukakis had a relatively high turnout, while those who disliked him had a relatively low turnout. In a 51-percent-to-49-percent election, this could have been the deciding factor.

The Protestant-Catholic conflict that culminated in the intense religious voting of 1960 had many elements. Many Protestants feared the Catholic Church, disliked its theology and worship, saw Catholic values as a threat to their own, and were wary that Catholic public officials would seek to advance Catholicism in many ways. Much of this sentiment was based on ignorance or misinformation, but it was real to many voters. Other elements included a traditional rural distrust of cities, which were heavily Catholic, and historic fears that religious liberty for Protestants would be diminished by Catholic public officials at such high levels as president or governor. The rivalries and conflict brought from Europe by various ethnic groups were handed down from generation to generation in the conservative churches and close-knit community character of small-town Pennsylvania. Thus, prejudice, cultural rivalry, ethnic misunderstanding, social conflict, and clashes over lifestyle, education, and values produced a Catholic-Protestant cold war that erupted into disruptive and harmful religious voting in 1958 and 1960.

Table 9.1

1988 and 1986 Elections by Type of Voter

	% Casey	% Dukakis	% Difference	% Kennedy 1960	% Kennedy loss or gain[1]
Catholic	68.6	58.6	+10.0	77.2	+19.0
Rural Protestant	46.2	35.5	+10.7	32.9	−12.0
Upper Income	28.9	30.5	− 1.6	3.2	+ 6.6
Lower-Income White	78.6	76.1	+ 2.5	79.9	+10.3
Black	85.8	94.8	− 9.0	81.2	+ 8.8
Student-Faculty	40.7	55.4	−14.7	36.6	+ 8.0
German-American	38.3	32.8	+ 5.5	36.7	+ .2
Liberal Elite	37.1	60.1	−23.0	44.3	+10.0
Jewish	57.8	65.3	− 7.5	77.5	+ 7.0

1. Kennedy's loss or gain compares his percentage of the vote to that of Stevenson in 1956.

The 1986 returns suggested that this conflict has almost completely vanished in Pennsylvania. Nearly three decades of closer ecumenical contacts have created a mostly harmonious interfaith climate. Differences of opinion still exist, but they are usually expressed with civility and respect, rather than with suspicion and recrimination.

The abortion rights issue, however, has threatened this new harmony and has created a new cultural conflict. The culture conflict over abortion transcends religious lines. It is a lifestyle issue, an issue affected more by income and education than by religious affiliation.

Those who oppose abortion, its legalization and its availability, tend to be the more conservative members of all religious communities and somewhat more likely to attend worship services regularly. They are older, less wealthy, and less well educated than those who favor the legalization and widespread availability of abortion as an option. The pro-choice segment of the electorate represents religious liberals and progressives in each faith group, as well as the more secular and humanistic sector of the elite intelligentsia. Hence the old Protestant-Catholic clash, which deeply affected the candidacies of David Lawrence in 1958 and John F. Kennedy in 1960, evaporated in most areas of the state when Robert Casey was the Democratic candidate in 1986. An old culture conflict had died but a new one has replaced it, one with the same intensity and ability to shift voter sentiment.

Governor Casey was reelected in 1990 by the largest margin (68 percent

Table 9.2

Top Ten Casey Gains by County*

County	% Gain	Character
1. Wayne	18.5	Rural Protestant
2. Wyoming	17.5	Rural Protestant
3. Montour	16.8	Rural Protestant
4. Lackawanna	15.6	Catholic, Casey home county
5. Columbia	15.0	Rural Protestant
6. Northumberland	14.9	Small Town—Mixed Protestant/Catholic
7. Elk	14.4	Catholic Rural
8. Luzerne	14.2	Catholic Urban
9. Fulton	14.2	Rural Protestant
10. Potter	13.8	Rural Protestant

*The gain refers to Casey's percentage of the vote in 1986 compared to Dukakis's percentage of the vote in 1988.

to 32 percent) of any gubernatorial candidate since 1926. He carried every county except high-income, Republican-leaning and socially liberal Montgomery County, where he just missed by a relative handful of votes.

Casey won an extraordinary Republican crossover vote, some of it no doubt related to his conservative policies on abortion. He was the first Democrat ever to carry rock-ribbed Republican Lancaster County for governor. He not only carried it but also received 73 percent of the ballots cast, sweeping every precinct. In the northern and eastern Mennonite rural areas, called Amish Country by tourism promoters, Casey received a mind-boggling 78 percent. Most Democrats are fortunate to win 20 percent of the votes in Amish Country. Casey received a majority of the county's Republican vote.

Casey's social conservatism was the major factor, since his Republican opponent, Barbara Hafer, made her pro-choice position on abortion the centerpiece of her campaign, despite her conservatism on other issues. Women candidates have fared poorly in Pennsylvania politics. The state ranks in the bottom ten, along with much of the South, in the percentage of its state legislators who are women. Few members of Congress from the Keystone State have been women. Genevieve Blatt, a liberal Democrat, failed to win a U.S. Senate seat in 1964 even though Lyndon Johnson was winning a 65 percent landslide in the presidential race. Lynn Yeakel failed to oust Republican Senator Arlen Specter in 1992, even though Democrat Bill Clinton easily won the state for president.

Table 9.3

Casey's 1990 Triumphs among Protestant Republicans

County	Town	% Casey 1990	% Kennedy 1960	% Casey Stronger
Huntingdon	Birmingham	78.1	10.1	68.1
Lancaster	Earl	77.9	11.9	66.0
Bedford	Lincoln	72.1	6.5	65.6
Schuykill	Eldred	72.6	8.1	64.5
Lancaster	Rapho	79.4	16.0	63.4
Snyder	Center	75.8	13.0	62.8
Lancaster	Clay	74.9	12.7	62.2
Jefferson	Polk	70.7	8.7	62.0
Lebanon	South Annville	74.4	12.8	61.6
Lancaster	Leacock	71.7	10.8	60.9
York	East Prospect	76.2	15.9	60.3
Lancaster	Akron	73.1	14.1	59.0
Snyder	West Perry	74.9	16.2	58.7
Lebanon	North Annville	75.0	17.0	58.0
Dauphin	Conewago	72.0	14.2	57.8
Lancaster	East Earl	72.6	15.0	57.6
Lancaster	Paradise	71.6	14.0	57.6
Wyoming	Braintrim	71.6	14.4	57.2
Lancaster	West Donegal	69.9	13.1	56.8
Northumberland	Upper Mahanoy	72.2	15.4	56.8

Casey won a record Protestant evangelical vote, 69 percent, a phenomenal figure for a Democrat. He won decisively among Appalachian Protestant Republicans, who had opposed Al Smith and John Kennedy by enormous margins. Casey was the first Catholic Democrat in history to win majorities from Appalachian evangelicals, Scotch-Irish Presbyterians, and the Mennonite, Brethren, Moravian, and Schwenkfelder voters in the Dutch Country. He defeated his Lutheran opponent by 2-to-1 margins in Lutheran Republican precincts in Berks and York Counties.

Casey won a majority among all religious groups, including 80 percent of fellow Catholics and 52 percent among the pro-choice Jewish community, which was below the Democratic norm, revealing that the abortion issue cuts both ways. Casey also won narrowly in academic areas, though he still failed to carry State College and Swarthmore. He won a small majority among high-income voters, but he still lost 57 percent to 43 percent in liberal-elite precincts.

Casey's greatest 1990 gains came from Protestant evangelical Republicans, especially from those in German-American areas and in the traditional towns and villages of the Pennsylvania Dutch Country. Casey's vote soared from 38.3 percent to 68.7 percent in the German counties. In a startling departure from historical political traditions, an Irish Catholic Democrat took almost seven out of ten votes from German Protestant Republicans.

Casey's extraordinary appeal to Protestant Republicans can be visualized in table 9.3, which depicts twenty towns where Casey's percentage of the vote total was 57 to 68 percentage points higher than that of Kennedy in 1960. In the tiny Huntington County hamlet of Birmingham, Casey received 78 percent of the ballots cast for governor in 1990, while Kennedy won only 10 percent of the presidential vote in 1960. In Earl Township, deep in the heart of the Amish Country in Lancaster County, Casey received 78 percent and Kennedy 12 percent. There were several dozen communities that responded in like fashion. Eight of the top twenty pro-Casey towns were in Lancaster County. Most of the others were in German-American counties.

Casey, who once contemplated challenging President Clinton for renomination in 1996 but bowed out because of his health, is an intriguing political figure, not only for his political successes but because of his blend of conservatism and liberalism. In an address in Baltimore on October 21, 1994, Casey reiterated his support for free health insurance for poor children and low-cost insurance for the children of the working poor, family and medical leave programs, drug treatment and nutrition programs for women and children, and an expanded scholarship program for needy youth. He chided conservatives, "Many conservatives seem to close their eyes to the common good and social responsibility as I view it. I am talking about our obligation to the less fortunate, to the poor, to the sick, to the unemployed, to the homeless, to all of those people in our society who perhaps need a helping hand."[3] He said there was a "cosmic importance to the protection of human life."[4] Abortion, he said, "can have no legitimate place in American life because it is inconsistent with our national character."[5] He claimed the issue was "the most compelling and far-reaching civil rights issue of our time."[6]

Pennsylvania's Catholic bishops were in the forefront of the anti-abortion movement and were joined by many evangelical Protestants. Evangelical historian Randall Balmer sees an inconsistency in this evangelical position on the abortion issue. He writes, "It strikes me as an odd issue to serve as a rallying point for evangelical political activists. There is nothing in the Bible that explicitly condemns abortion, and the pro-life position does not appear to arise out of any abstract devotion to the sanctity of human life. Many pro-life evangelicals, for instance, also favor capital punishment, and the majority of evangelicals have seldom shied away from the exercise of military force."[7]

The 1996 primaries indicate that there already exists a tentative Catholic-evangelical alliance but one that is limited to the extreme right of the political spectrum. And since a much larger percentage of evangelicals than of Catholics supports the right, the alliance can hardly be said to fulfill the requirements of a full-scale entente.

Pat Buchanan's presidential campaign of 1996 reveals some of this voter movement. Buchanan received a much higher level of support among evangelical and fundamentalist Protestants than among Catholics or mainline Protestants. The national exit polls established by CBS, NBC, ABC, CNN, and AP included a new and somewhat vague religious category called "other Christian" in addition to Protestant and Catholic. (Jews, other religions, and no religion were the other choices offered.) This will make direct comparisons with 1992 and earlier data more difficult, but it does pinpoint some of the most recent voting trends.

In every state Buchanan's greatest support came from those who called themselves supporters of the Religious Right, and those who wanted more governmental restrictions on abortion.

Buchanan's voter appeal to religious conservatives is evident from the pivotal South Carolina primary on April 2, 1996, which probably saved Bob Dole's political life. Despite Dole's easy victory, by 45 percent to 30 percent for Buchanan, and 13 percent for Forbes and 11 percent for Alexander, Buchanan showed impressive strength in the Baptist and evangelical counties. He carried Cherokee County, the most heavily Southern Baptist county in the state. In the ten strongest Baptist counties, he narrowly lost to Dole by 4 percentage points.

Buchanan won convincingly, 42 percent to 36 percent for Dole, in Anderson County, where religious fundamentalism has transformed a Democratic stronghold into a Republican redoubt. As the *Washington Post*'s William Booth wrote, "Much of the politics of Anderson County begins in the big churches. The minister of Siloam Baptist, for example, with 2,000 congregants, has been arrested for marching against abortion. The candidates all work the churches and the Christian Coalition distributed more than 50,000 voting cards during the 1994 election."[8] Anderson County's Democratic state legislator, C. D. Chamblee, switched to the Republicans after the 1994 election, helping to give the GOP control of the South Carolina State House for the first time since Reconstruction.

Buchanan also came within two hundred votes of defeating Dole in nearby Spartanburg County, which shares a similar religious configuration.

William Booth attributed the Republicanization of South Carolina to the "awesome power of the Christian right in a deeply religious region."[9]

Buchanan did not do nearly so well in the metropolitan, high-income, or highly educated counties in South Carolina—or elsewhere. In the South Carolina Perot strongholds, Forbes did unusually well, as he did in New York and Colorado. And, despite Buchanan's neo-Confederate rhetoric, white voters in rural black-majority counties gave Dole his strongest statewide margin, 51 percent to Buchanan's 29 percent.

Conservative Roman Catholic Buchanan, who stressed religious and cultural conservatism as well as economic populism, opposition to immigration, and a hardline "America First" isolationism, appealed to many Protestant conservatives. He defeated Dole 2-1 in Dutch Reformed Sioux County, Iowa, and won convincingly in Berlin, New Hampshire, a French Catholic blue-collar town that has experienced economic difficulties in recent years. Throughout the short-lived primary season of 1996, Buchanan's candidacy was disproportionately welcomed by conservative Protestants. He also received the endorsement of the ultraconservative Catholic weekly newspaper, *The Wanderer*, which had endorsed Buchanan's old boss, Richard Nixon, rather than John Kennedy in 1960.

Cons

As this book has repeatedly highlighted, America's evangelical and Catholic communities have little in common politically, socially, or culturally, not to mention religiously. In the past they have usually moved in opposite political directions, often in response to perceptions about the motives and objectives of each other.

Catholics remain far more committed to governmental solutions to solving economic and social problems. They see government as morally neutral, as an acceptable mode within which grievances can be resolved and social justice can be achieved. The "preferential option for the poor" undergirds and is embedded in Catholic social philosophy. Catholics are communitarian, by and large, and believe that gaps between the haves and have nots need to be addressed by government. They are realists; they know from long historical experience that private church-run charities, however noble in concept and beneficent in practice, cannot cope with the massive degree of social dislocation and despair found in modern society.

Catholic economic philosophy has always steered a moderate course between the Scylla of unrestrained capitalism and the Charybdis of state socialism. Catholic social philosophy prefers a mixed economy, with substantial contributions to the common good from the mediating structures external to government. Catholics often see partnerships where others see conflict when problems needing resolution are addressed.

A vote in the House of Representatives on the minimum-wage issue on May 23, 1996, exemplifies the gulf in Catholic and Protestant attitudes on economic questions.

Of the forty-three Republicans who broke with their party to support President Clinton's proposal to increase the minimum wage, twenty were Catholic, twenty were Protestant and three were Jewish. This means that 46.5 percent of pro-minimum-wage Republicans were Catholics, but only 24.8 percent of all Republicans are Catholic. On the other hand, only two evangelical Republicans—Dunn of Oregon and Stockman of Texas—voted in the affirmative. Of the seven Democrats who voted against the president, six were Southern Protestant evangelicals and one was a Mormon from Utah. Three of the four Jewish Republicans in the House voted for the minimum wage bill.

Thus, on this key economic issue, which reflects the historic Catholic commitment to the concept of a "just wage," 34.5 percent of Catholic Republicans but only 12 percent of Protestant Republicans voted yes.

Of all House members voting, 70 percent of Catholics supported the minimum-wage bill compared to only 44 percent of Protestants. All Jews except one (96 percent) voted yes but all ten Mormons voted no. The four religiously nonaffiliated members voted yes and the two of Greek Orthodox faith voted no.

Members from states with a small percentage of evangelical citizens were twice as likely to support a minimum-wage increase as were those from states with a high percentage. Among white evangelicals, the vast majority were opposed.

In regard to education, Catholics have grown fond of public education at the very time when other groups have soured on it. Nearly three-fourths of U.S. Catholic children are educated in public schools, a sharp increase during the past three decades. While Catholics probably want more involvement in and contributions from religious communities in education, they are generally unwilling to see public school life disrupted by religious strife and factionalism.

As a result, Catholics are still more likely than are evangelicals to vote Democratic for president and for Congress, and to support moderately liberal legislative initiatives. Catholics are far less likely to own guns than are evangelicals (and other Protestants, too) and are more likely to support gun control and bans on assault weapons. They are more sympathetic to civil rights legislation and are more supportive of a welcoming immigration policy than are white Protestant evangelicals.

These differences can be discerned in elections. In Louisiana 68 percent of born-again Christians voted for David Duke for governor in 1991; only 52 percent of white Catholics did so. Of the eighteen parishes (counties) carried by Duke, all but two were populated by white Baptists. In North Carolina, white Baptists and evangelicals reelected Senator Jesse Helms in his blatantly racist campaign in 1990. A majority of Catholics voted for his African-American Democratic opponent, Harvey Gantt. These differences over racial posture are clear and distinct. It is no surprise, also, that Catholic schools have far higher percentages of minority enrollments than evangelical or fundamentalist schools. Catholics, unlike many evangelicals, are also far more tolerant and respectful of religious traditions that differ from their own.

Catholics consistently vote Democratic by 20–30 more percentage points than do evangelicals. On most political issues they are at least 20 points more liberal. In California the *Los Angeles Times* exit poll in 1994 found that 69 percent of Protestants and only 49 percent of Catholics supported Proposition 187, which curtailed government and educational services for illegal immigrants.

Kosmin and Lachman have noted these differences: "Polling data show that Catholics remain more likely than white Protestants to support an expanded role for government. This is in keeping with the stance of their church, which has never endorsed laissez-faire capitalism and has frequently advocated a communitarian view of society. This gap is particularly reflected among the middle class. National Opinion Research Center data for the 1980s show that 34 percent of Catholic college graduates believe that government should do more to improve society, whereas only 16 percent of white Protestant college graduates hold that opinion."[10]

Evangelicals tend to see government as inherently evil and coercive, a behemoth that needs to be permanently restrained—except in areas of national defense and, ironically, personal morality. Evangelicals are individualists, both in social philosophy and in religious matters. Their solutions, such as they are, to social problems posit a much-reduced governmental role, and an enhancement of voluntary self-help groups, free enterprise, and church-oriented charities, which they honestly believe will end social disorders on a more permanent basis than governmentally oriented proposals. This is the gist of Marvin Olasky's proposals, which are widely popular among evangelicals in particular and social conservatives generally. Olasky favors a central role for religious organizations and individuals, even to the point of encouraging religious conversion (to evangelical Christianity).

This individualism has made evangelicals, unlike Catholics, relatively unfavorable to trade unions and the union movement. Evangelicals also tend to have an uncritical regard for capitalism and, with some exceptions, like Senator Mark Hatfield of Oregon, an unswerving kind of my-country-right-or-wrong nationalism. Evangelicals to a large extent invented and shaped American civil religion, and they often see America as a nation uniquely blessed by God and deserving of uncritical praise, especially for its foreign policy. This blend of American exceptionalism and naivete tends to push evangelicals further to the political right.

Catholics are likely to be the losers in any alliance with evangelicals. Two evenly sized groups with such different cultures and divergent historical memories will not coexist as equals for long. There will be inevitable clashes over the spoils of victory.

No one can predict the future, of course, but the past offers some guidance for future projections. The intensity of past evangelical dislike of Catholics and Catholicism and the reality of lukewarm, grudging mutual regard do not augur well for the development of a permanent political alliance. One or the other will inevitably seek domination.

Evangelicals are likely to dominate the public schools, owing to their generously financed and well-staffed parachurch organizations specializing in school proselytism. This is almost a certainty if school prayer or religious equality amendments ever become the law of the land.

Even in today's somewhat restrictive environment, evangelicals are aggressive in their public-school outreach programs. They show little or no respect for those who adhere to other religious traditions. America's schools may be the primary battleground, where religious strife and rancor will add a new (and certainly unhelpful) element to an already cloudy and unpredictable educational future.

The half of America that is neither evangelical nor Catholic will rejoice. The creation of political power blocs based on religion will not advance the cause of democracy, political justice, or fairness; nor will it enhance the harmonious mutuality among religions that has become the genius of American pluralism.

Catholic Answers in San Diego was established to counteract the new fundamentalist and evangelical attacks. Its leaders include Karl Keating, author of *Catholicism and Fundamentalism*, and Patrick Madrid, who edited a volume of convert stories, *Surprised by Truth*, in June 1994.

A number of prominent evangelicals, including the witty Boston College philosophy professor Peter Kreeft, and Thomas Howard, author of *Evangelical is Not Enough*, explored reasons for their conversions to Catholicism in

Table 9.4

Attitudinal Differences between Protestants and Catholics from Barna Reports

Religious Beliefs with Possible Political Implications	Protestant	Catholic	From Barna Report
AGREE STRONGLY THAT			
The Bible is totally accurate in all of its teachings	48	24	VA 317
Must tell others about your religion	36	16	VA 318
OPTIMISM			
America is doing better than 5 years ago	38	54	VA 189
Strongly agree that the future will be better	25	47	B93–94, 248
America's children have a bright future	40	55	VA 229
AGREE STRONGLY THAT			
Homosexuality is immoral	53	36	B93–94, 268
Christianity has all the answers	80	63	B92–93
Churchgoing is a manmade requirement, not a biblical one	42	61	B92–93, 261
All good people will go to heaven	30	65	B92–93, 262
Watch religious television	60	36	B92–93, 283
Listen to religious music on radio	59	22	B92–93, 288
Do not tell others about my religious beliefs	40	70	B93–94, 176
All religions teach similar lessons about life	52	76	B93–94, 207
Religious views have greatest impact on life	52	34	B93–94, 247

Reports:

VA—George Barna, *Virtual America: The Barna Report 1994–1995* (Ventura, Calif.: Regal Books, 1994).

B93–94—George Barna, *Absolute Confusion: The Barna Report 1993–1994* (Ventura, Calif.: Regal Books, 1993).

B92–93—George Barna, *The Barna Report 1992–1993* (Ventura, Calif.: Regal Books, 1992).

Robert Baram's *Spiritual Journeys*, published in 1988 by the Daughters of St. Paul in Boston.

Thomas Howard's decision to enter the Catholic Church in 1985 was a cause célèbre, because Howard was considered evangelicalism's most distinguished writer as well as a popular professor of literature at Gordon College in Wenham, Massachusetts.

Howard first became an Episcopalian, as have many of the evangelical intellectuals who described their spiritual aeneids in a book called *Evangelicals on the Canterbury Trail* (edited by Robert Webber and published by Word in 1985). But Howard was convinced that Roman Catholicism was where he wanted to be religiously.

It was not he who made his change of religious allegiance a public event, but news of his decision spread like wildfire throughout the evangelical community. *Christianity Today*, often considered the foremost evangelical magazine, made his conversion a major story in its May 17, 1985, issue. Howard, whose siblings include one pastor and four missionaries, apparently did not intend that his change of religious allegiance become front-page news, but *Christianity Today* treated it as such. In a response typical, it seems, of the intellectual insecurity of many evangelicals, the journal accompanied its "special report" with a snide and critical condemnation of Catholicism by John P. Woodbridge.[11]

Howard resigned, or was forced to resign, from Gordon College after a fifteen-year career as an English professor who was popular with students and faculty. He had written a number of books that were widely read and admired. However, the faculty senate at Gordon determined that Roman Catholic doctrine is incompatible with the college's statement of faith, which all faculty are required to sign. Therefore, no Catholic, however competent, would be allowed to teach there. Howard accepted the ruling but said the report's criticism of Catholic beliefs resulted from a misunderstanding of Catholic doctrine.[12]

Although Gordon College found it impossible to retain Thomas Howard, America's most prestigious Catholic university, Notre Dame, is known for its religiously diverse faculty. Numerous Protestants and evangelicals hold major teaching positions at this symbolic outpost of American Catholic academia. According to Kevin Coyne, "In 1970, 66 percent of the faculty were Catholic; today (1992) it was 58 percent; and only 42 percent of the new professors hired this year were Catholic."[13] James F. White, a Methodist, is a professor of liturgical studies and author of several books on the history of Christian worship. A prominent Southern Baptist, Tom Morris, teaches in the philosophy department. Evangelicals such as Nathan Hatch hold important positions in the theology and history departments. Long-time professor of history Gerhart Niemeyer is an Episcopalian.

This contrast between Gordon and Notre Dame symbolically expresses the wide gap in tolerance between evangelicals and Catholics that constitutes one of the major barriers to the development of any permanent political alliance between these two powerful and very different religious cultures and religious worldviews.

Christianity Today has frequently expressed the ambivalence of many evangelicals toward the Catholic Church. In the late 1950s, it published numerous anti-Catholic tirades, warning of a potential takeover of the nation's political system by Catholic politicians subservient to the Vatican. On the eve of the opening of the Second Vatican Council in October 1962, this preeminent journal of evangelical opinion published the spiritual autobiography of a Spanish Catholic priest who became an evangelical. Since then, *Christianity Today* has waxed and waned in its tolerant attitudes toward Rome. While friendly at some times, it is still more likely to be hostile and suspicious. Attacks on Catholic doctrine are frequent. In the early 1980s the magazine raised questions about the Catholic percentage of students at West Point and Annapolis, an article worthy of yesteryear's nativism and bigotry. In 1985 then-editor Kenneth Kantzer gave some faint praise to Pope John Paul II's conservative policies but still concluded, "He is, when all is said and done, a traditional Roman Catholic in doctrine and ethics. Like his predecessors—only with more enthusiasm and greater skills of communication—he stands for all those things that have, since the days of Luther and before, divided a biblically rooted evangelicalism from a Roman Catholicism based partly on biblical revelation and partly on human tradition. . . . Rome is still Rome, and Pope John Paul II is simply its most effective voice."[14]

John E. Tropman, a professor of social policy at the University of Michigan, published a seminal work filled with important insights about how religious values become articulated in social and political thought. Called *The Catholic Ethic in American Society,* Tropman's work argues that a uniquely Catholic ethic runs parallel to the historically dominant Protestant ethic that has long influenced American culture.

Tropman says that the Catholic ethic is far more accepting of human inadequacy and takes an inclusive view toward the disadvantaged. He writes, "The Catholic ethic is a sharing ethic because it supports the idea that the human condition, ever beset with problems as it is, will always require help. The provision of that help is part of the basic framework of the Catholic ethic. . . . If there is any judgmental tilt within the Catholic ethic, it is toward the poor and toward a suspicion of great accumulation."[15] In contrast, the Protestant ethic, he says, "is oriented heavily to work, wealth and achievement" (xiii). "The Catholic ethic," he continues, "is suspicious of those who have much and supportive of those who have little" (7).

Some of these core values have definite political implications. Tropman argues, "The support for progressive social welfare policies that has devel-

oped in the Catholic ethic may owe much to the way the structure of the
Catholic Church itself has accustomed church followers to the uses of a need-
meeting bureaucracy. . . . In some ways the Catholic Church apparatus and
its operation and purpose are parallel to the welfare state, making the func-
tions of the welfare state familiar and acceptable to Catholics" (149). Tropman's analysis suggests that the Protestant ethic values achievement, individualism, individualistic capitalism, and is person focused. "The Protestant
ethic sees resources as scarce, is suspicious of the poor and nonachievers, has
a this-worldly orientation, and is often judgmental and given to exclusion.
The Catholic ethic values sharing and communalism, is family and community focused, emphasizes forgiveness and acceptance, is sympathetic to the
poor and suspicious of achievers. It is also otherworldly in orientation and
sees abundant resources in this world" (186).

In conclusion, he says, "In naming the Catholic concern for the poor a
culture of sharing, I wanted to convey the Catholic belief that the disadvantaged have some claim on our resources; sharing implies that there is a community involved in the procuring and development of resources and that all
are entitled to enjoy them, though perhaps not in equal amounts. Thus, the
Catholic ethic is a sharing ethic, supporting a culture of sharing throughout
the population that it touches" (203).

The Tropman thesis is one further warning that a full-scale, permanent
Catholic-Evangelical alliance is unlikely to occur because it is doomed from
the start by coherent philosophical differences about the core visions of
reality.

Keith A. Fournier, who calls himself an evangelical Catholic, is an attorney and a graduate of the Franciscan University of Steubenville, Ohio. He is
also the executive director of Pat Robertson's American Center for Law and
Justice (ACLJ). Fournier reveals that Catholics "constitute six of the twenty-
six full-time ACLJ lawyers in America, and an increasing number of Roman
Catholics are becoming part of the ACLJ's financial support base along with
thousands of evangelical Protestants."[16]

Fournier encourages evangelical-Catholic cooperation and has endorsed
the "Evangelicals and Catholics Together" (ECT) statement, a product of a
consultation that began in September 1992 and was officially released in
1994. While dealing primarily with theology and evangelism and encouraging Catholics and evangelicals to work together as fellow Christians and to
quit trying to raid each other's constituency, ECT also waded firmly into the
waters of politics and public life.

One Catholic participant, scholar Avery Dulles, commented favorably,
"In resisting moral evils and in working to preserve the Christian heritage of

our nation against militant secularism, evangelicals and Catholics can find common ground."[17]

The political bias of ECT is quite conservative when it addresses "the right ordering of society" (xxiii). Abortion is called "the leading edge of an encroaching culture of death" (xxv). In addition, "Abortion on demand must be recognized as a massive attack on the dignity, rights and needs of women. . . . That the unborn child has a right to protection, including the protection of law, is a moral statement supported by moral reason and biblical truth" (xxv).

The ECT declaration repeats a charge often advanced by religious conservatives. "Religion, which was privileged and foundational in our legal order, has in recent years been penalized and made marginal" (xxiv). The statement criticizes sexual and cultural permissiveness, claiming, "We reject the claim that . . . tolerance requires the promotion of moral equivalence between the normative and the deviant" (xxv).

The document also supports "parental choice in education," denounces "sexual depravity and antireligious bigotry in the entertainment media," endorses "a vibrant market economy" and commends "a renewed appreciation of Western culture" (xxvi–xxvii).

The "Evangelicals and Catholics Together" statement should be viewed in the context of ecumenical relationships that have developed since World War II. First of all, it needs to be stressed that this is a very unexceptional, even routine and slightly dated, document. Ecumenical dialogues between Catholics and Protestants go back to the Robert McAfee Brown–Gustave Weigel conversations of the 1950s. Most Protestant, Eastern Orthodox, Anglican, and Old Catholic churches sent official observers to the Second Vatican Council, which met from 1962 to 1965. Then there have been any number of formal dialogues and consultations between the Roman Catholic Church and other Christians at the highest institutional and intellectual levels for the past thirty years.

Therefore, a 1994 statement by evangelicals and Catholics represents a belated, if welcome, attempt to moderate hostilities and bring the evangelical-Catholic cold war to an end. But it is hardly new or earth-shattering in its implications.

Also, the signers, however well meaning, were not those in top leadership echelons of their respective faith traditions. They were at best mid-management types, without formal credentials allowing them to speak for their religious bodies.

A Protestant backlash denounced ECT as soon as it was released in the spring of 1994. The virulent, vituperative, and fear-ridden reactions from many evangelicals can only be interpreted as typical of a separationist siege mentality representative of fundamentalists and conservative evangelicals. The intensity of their rejection of the statement, and the power of these critics to force many evangelical signers to retract their signatures of accord or to submit modifications, shows how durable and unyielding is traditional anti-Catholicism among many conservative Protestants. Significantly, the denunciations were not aimed at the political or economic statements but contended that Catholics were not fellow Christians but adherents of a false religion and that the Protestant signatories were traitors to the Reformation and betrayers of the Gospel.

This unreconstructed animosity was widespread and even forced such prominent evangelical signers of ECT as Chuck Colson, J. I. Packer, Bill Bright, and Kent Hill to issue a mild disclaimer on January 19, 1995, saying that their original signature "does not imply acceptance of Roman Catholic doctrinal distinctives or endorsement of the Roman Catholic church system."[18]

Other evangelical signers were forced to recant their signatures by pressure from the grassroots. John H. White, president of Geneva College and past president of the National Association of Evangelicals, was forced to withdraw his name by his denomination, the Reformed Presbyterian Church of North America.

Richard D. Land, executive director of the Southern Baptist Christian Life Commission, came under fire from his denomination's foreign mission board, which claimed that ECT was "harmful to Southern Baptist work of global witness and missionary outreach."[19] Land "privately regrets signing" ECT,[20] according to Geisler and MacKenzie.

Dave Hunt condemned evangelical signers in harsh language. "The document overturns the Reformation and does incalculable damage to the cause of Christ and represents the most devastating blow against the gospel in at least a thousand years."[21] *Tabletalk*, the monthly magazine of the Ligonier Ministries, stated that "Catholics, if they believe the doctrines of their church, are not Christians."[22]

Since ECT, attacks from the Protestant Far Right have mounted. John F. MacArthur, pastor of the Grace Community Church in Sun Valley, California, claims ECT "compromises and obfuscates essential evangelical truths,"[23] says that evangelical and Catholic differences of opinion about the doctrine of justification are not just an honest disagreement but "damning heresy" (138), and accuses "the evangelical drafters of the document of either downplaying, compromising or relinquishing all the key evangelical distinctives" (149).

To MacArthur, "The Reformation was not a tragedy but a glorious victory for Christianity" (148), and asks, "Are we ready to concede that the thousands of martyrs who gave their lives to oppose the tyranny and false doctrine of Rome all died for an unworthy cause?" (149). MacArthur denounces those who "make peace with enemies of the Gospel" (149). He demands that evangelicals convert Catholics to save them from Hell, where they will all go "until they abandon their blind faith in the Roman Catholic system" (151). Like most professional Catholic-haters, MacArthur loves to regale his readers with horror tales of the Inquisition (201–207) and the "guilt of the Church" (205–207), saying, "The Roman Catholic Church is culpable not merely for the atrocities, corruption and moral abuses that have been perpetrated in her name but primarily for her doctrine" (207). MacArthur even dedicates his screed to "Marcel Cotnoir, missionary, pastor, friend, who for many years has fought the battle for truth against the Roman system and is seeing the Gospel triumph."

Harvest House Publishers in Eugene, Oregon, has made anti-Catholicism into a cottage industry. They published Tony Coffey's *Once a Catholic* in 1993, a rather simplistic, superficial memoir of an ex-priest who now lives in the Republic of Ireland, trying to convert papists to fundamentalism. His book gives little indication of how successful his efforts have been over two decades, but it does indicate that there is plenty of religious freedom in Ireland—something American fundamentalists have often misrepresented to their American audiences.

In 1995 Harvest House issued *The Gospel According to Rome* by ex-Catholic James G. McCarthy, founder and director of Good News for Catholics, Inc. McCarthy follows in a long line of professional ex-Catholics who make a living out of religious animosity and interfaith conflict.

Warning liberal Catholics that their reformist impulses are doomed to failure, McCarthy says, "Far from admitting error, the Roman Catholic Church has shamelessly opposed its critics, staining its hands with their blood down through the centuries."[24] All Catholics must leave their apostate church, he says, and become evangelical Protestants. "What about your Catholic family and friends? The best thing you can do for them is to leave the Roman Catholic Church yourself and become part of a strong, biblically based church" (313). Catholics are deluded and are not "consciously aware that they are serving Satan's purposes" (315). All Catholics are doomed to hell and perdition. "Having believed a false gospel, they remain in their sins. Consequently, but for a great outpouring of the Holy Spirit in these last days, the vast majority of Roman Catholics alive on earth today, clergy and laity alike, will die in their sins" (315).

McCarthy denounces interfaith cooperation at all levels and says ecumenism must be resisted. "Such ecumenical compromise must be opposed. There is no room in biblical Christianity for unity or cooperation with Rome and its false gospel" (320).

A 1995 book by evangelical television personality John Ankerberg and his sidekick John Weldon attacks, distorts and misrepresents Catholicism and regards Catholics as ignorant dupes. Though they are uninformed outsiders, they take it upon themselves to categorize Catholics into ten categories of belief, including "pagan, syncretistic, eclectic, lapsed and apostate." "Nominal, modernist and cultural Roman Catholics comprise millions of persons and possibly the majority of American Catholics. . . . Like many liberal Protestants, they remain Catholics primarily because of social convenience, religious needs, or perhaps personal guilt, rather than because of personal conviction concerning Rome's authority."[25]

Ankerberg and Weldon claim that because Catholicism "is unregenerate and therefore rejects the truth" (188), its religious system "increases sin and pride" (216). They then cite unsubstantiated claims that "one-third of the 57,000 Roman Catholic priests could be HIV infected and up to 3,000 priests are pedophiles" (216).

They firmly say that Catholics are "not genuine brothers and sisters in Christ with Protestants" (270) and that Catholics must leave their church and join an evangelical church to avoid hell and damnation (241).

Completely ignoring the Second Vatican Council's Declaration on Religious Liberty in 1965, Ankerberg and Weldon write, "Wherever Catholicism has been the dominant religion in a given nation, Evangelicals seem to have suffered for it. . . . Hasn't Roman Catholicism persecuted Evangelicals throughout history, while Evangelical sins in this regard have been almost nonexistent by comparison?" (262, 263). Ankerberg and Weldon seem to have no knowledge of Cromwell, the Elizabeth persecutions in England, or the Ku Klux Klan. They claim that Catholics today "engage in physical persecution, suppression and killing of evangelical Christians" (262, 263).

Ankerberg and Weldon revel in such charges that "throughout history hundreds of thousands of Protestants died at the hands of Catholics" (265) without even acknowledging that Catholics also died at Protestant hands during the Thirty Years War and on other occasions. Ankerberg and Weldon say that Protestant leaders are traitors who "don't want to hear any negative reminders of the millions tortured and slain by the Church to which they now pay homage, or the fact that Rome has a false gospel of sacramental works" (265).

It is significant that this book includes "A Personal Word" (12–13) of endorsement from D. James Kennedy, the Florida Presbyterian pastor and Religious Right activist who claims to favor Catholic-Protestant cooperation.

Harvest House also published another volume by Ankerberg and Weldon entitled *The Facts on Roman Catholicism*.

John Armstrong edited a half-hearted attempt at ecumenism and understanding, but in common with most books published by the evangelical side, this one also sideswipes the papal enemy whenever possible. One contributor to the anthology, ex-Catholic turned evangelical William Webster, solemnly affirms, "The gospel promulgated by the Church of Rome is a perversion of the Gospel of Grace. . . . I appeal to Roman Catholics to come out because the Church of Rome is moving farther and farther away from the truth. The Church has historically demonstrated a terrible resistance to correction and reform. We have seen a continued and progressive departure from the truth and a hardening of the Roman Church theologically against the Gospel. On the other hand, there is a disturbing trend developing, a growing tolerance of pagan religions in the name of unity and peace."[26] Webster went on to denounce Pope John Paul II for praying for peace in Assisi, Italy, in 1986 with representatives of other world religions (except fundamentalist Protestantism, of course).

The hoary canard that the pope individually, or the Catholic Church corporately, is the Antichrist receives a new dose of support in Dave Hunt's *A Woman Rides the Beast: The Roman Catholic Church and the Last Days*. Denouncing as evil ecumenism and agreements toward world peace and understanding, Hunt claims that "the Vatican qualifies uniquely as the woman astride the beast in Revelation 17."[27] But the "alliance will be between the world ruler (the Antichrist) and the Vatican" (470). "A pope will not be the Antichrist, but will be his right-hand man, the false prophet of Revelation" (465).

In Hunt's phantasmagoric world, all is evil, traitors are everywhere, and doom is just around the corner. "The world is being prepared for the one who rides the beast, and even evangelical leaders and their flocks are being deceived (461). . . . Uncompromising Christians will be put to death for standing in the way of unity and peace" (469).

Hunt believes the Virgin Mary, or a pseudo-Mary, will also be involved in these nefarious doings. "Faith in Catholicism's Mary, supported by her thousands of apparitions, prepares the way as perhaps nothing else could for a world religion, a New World order, and the reign of Antichrist (465). . . . Catholicism's Mary has taken the place of Christ as the one through whom peace will come, and the present pope and his Church support this heresy. That the woman is astride the beast seems to indicate that this pseudo-Mary of the apparitions will play a key role in the false peace by which Antichrist shall destroy many" (460).

Hunt considers Catholicism a vile, evil, and depraved religion. Claiming that the Catholic Church caused the Holocaust and supported Nazism, he writes, "The Roman Catholic Church has been the greatest persecutor of both

Jews and Christians the world has ever seen, and has martyred far more Christians than even pagan Rome or Islam" (262).

Hunt charges that "through its media dominance, Rome projects an image that makes the truth difficult to believe and adeptly covers her real intentions with sweet words and hides her true character behind beautiful art and moving manifestations of piety" (390).

He claims there is "widespread sexual promiscuity among priests" (390), that "every shade of New Age, occult and mystical belief permeates Catholic schools" (420), and that "Catholic retreat centers around the world mix Christianity with Hinduism, Buddhism and all manner of New Age beliefs and practices" (421). He denounces the pope and Mother Teresa for counseling tolerance toward other world religions, asking, "How can one respect beliefs that lead people to hell? Far from asking us to respect pagan beliefs, the Bible condemns them" (418).

Hunt's 540-page tirade is reminiscent of the kind of books routinely issued by evangelical presses. The fact that it was published in 1994, not 1894 or 1844, is significant and perhaps symptomatic of a resuscitation of warfare (intellectual, so far) between some evangelicals and Catholics.

Hunt's identification of the papacy with the Antichrist prophecies goes back to the Reformation-era polemics when it was common among Protestant controversialists. As late as 1961, shortly after John F. Kennedy's election, J. Dwight Pentecost wrote, "Romanism is the great harlot. According to Revelation 17, this politico-religious system is going to move behind the scenes to cause nations to federate. When this alliance takes place, Rome will be in control, dominating, dictating and directing. . . . In our country, we have elevated to our nation's highest office one whose primary allegiance must be to one who resides across the ocean."[28]

Even Hal Lindsey's bestseller, *The Late Great Planet Earth,* stopped just short of making a Vatican-Antichrist connection. He also thought the World Council of Churches and liberal Judaism would be part of an apostate world religion. Paul Boyer says the tradition of labeling the Vatican the Antichrist "remained alive in postwar prophecy belief but the Vatican faded after 1945 as a target of Antichrist watchers."[29]

Conservative Catholics have not totally turned the other cheek in this new paper war over conversion and doctrine. Ignatius Press in San Francisco published Scott and Beverly Hahn's *Rome is Home* in 1993, a hard-hitting conversion memoir of an evangelical Presbyterian minister who became a Roman Catholic and now teaches at the Franciscan University of Steubenville. In 1995 the same press issued David B. Currie's *Born Fundamentalist, Born Again Catholic*, another odyssey of an evangelical convert to Rome.

Currie makes an interesting point in his book: "Evangelicals may desire Catholic cooperation on political or moral issues, but they do not consider Catholics to be Christian brethren."[30]

Beneath the surface of this idyllic panorama of amity lies a very different reality. There has been a backlash of anti-Catholic prejudice slowly developing and now emerging in the open among some evangelicals and fundamentalists. This intense animosity threatens to undo the concord advocated by many conservative leaders in both communities.

In some respects this trend should not be at all surprising. For centuries evangelicals have kept up a guerrilla war against Catholics, especially at the ground level of interfaith communication. Evangelical publishers have published literally thousands of anti-Catholic books, tracts, and pamphlets throughout American history. Ray Billington details in a fascinating way some of this sordid literary output before the Civil War in his *The Protestant Crusade.*

The policy continued unabated throughout the twentieth century. Some individuals made a living out of anti-Catholic propaganda during the first three decades of the century. William Lloyd Garrison, a self-styled anti-papal propagandist, established a flourishing anti-Catholic enterprise called The Railsplitter Press in the tiny town of Milan, Illinois. *The Menace* magazine was a highly successful Catholic-baiter read by millions during its heyday, when it was published in an obscure village in the Missouri Ozarks. Organizations devoted to the conversion of Catholics to evangelicalism were found even in the Northeast: Christ's Mission, variously ensconced in Oyster Bay, New York, and Hackensack, New Jersey, until the 1980s; The Convert, located in the gritty blue-collar town of Clairton, Pennsylvania; and The Conversion Centre, still operating out of Havertown, Pennsylvania. These groups specialized in conversion efforts and anti-Catholic lectures and publications, and brought forth much ill will. Although they declined somewhat during the ecumenical climate of the 1960s and 1970s, they have begun to make a comeback.

Some fundamentalists have never changed their attitudes and convictions about Catholics and Catholicism. A Tennessee publication, *Sword of the Lord,* commented that the worst thing about the Kennedy assassination was the televising of a Roman Catholic funeral Mass on the day of the president's burial. Bob Jones University (BJU) in Greenville, South Carolina, has kept up a steady anti-Catholic barrage through its textbooks published for private schools and its close ties to the Reverend Ian Paisley's Protestant extremist theopolitical movement in Northern Ireland. When Paisley was denied a visa during Ronald Reagan's first term, Dr. Bob Jones, Jr., prayed openly that God would strike dead U.S. Secretary of State Al Haig, a Catholic. The BJU Press published Bartholomew F. Brewer's *Pilgrimage from Rome* in 1982. Brewer, an ex-priest, has followed in a long line of ex-priests and nuns who make their living attacking and berating their former religion and encouraging Catholics to renounce their beliefs. Brewer now runs an outfit called Mission to Catholics International in San Diego, which is supported largely by independent Baptist and fundamentalist churches.

Similar organizations, most of which operate out of post office boxes in California, have been established to trash Catholicism and encourage Catholic conversions to evangelicalism. Among them are Christians Evangelizing Catholics, a San Jose–based group that published Bill Jackson's *A Christian's Guide to Roman Catholicism*; the Radio Bible Class in Grand Rapids, Michigan; and Jimmy Swaggart Ministries, or what's left of it, in Baton Rouge, Louisiana. Swaggart published a crude anti-Catholic book called *Catholicism and Christianity* in 1986, shortly before his penchant for prostitutes precipitated the collapse of his empire. Newspapers in Baton Rouge and elsewhere panned Swaggart's contribution to literature as barely literate, hardly more than comic-book prose, and grossly inaccurate.

Fringe groups peddling anti-Catholicism also exist, though they are something of an embarrassment to conservative Protestants. Tony Alamo's enterprises in Alma, Arkansas, specialized in blanketing towns all over the nation with anti-Catholic posters and pamphlets during the 1980s. His bizarre organization was frequently buffeted by lawsuits and bad publicity after he was unable to raise his wife, Susan, from the dead in 1982, after keeping her body unburied for many days.

A murky outfit in Chino, California, is Jack Chick Publications, which specializes in reprints of anti-Catholic "classics," and comic books detailing the Vatican's plot to destroy American Protestantism. While moderate evangelicals have condemned Chick, and *Christianity Today* exposed the group as a fraud in its March 13, 1981, issue, Chick continues to influence the lunatic fringe of fundamentalism. Allegations typical of Chick's outrageous charges can be found in his popular book, *Smokescreens,* in which he claims that "when the Vatican takes control of the United States, every pastor and his family will be shot in the head."[31]

Karl Keating studied these phenomena and concluded, "The United States boasts (if that is the proper word) hundreds of anti-Catholic organizations."[32]

The revival of anti-Catholic antipathy among fundamentalists is not surprising when fundamentalist schools are examined in terms of their teaching tools and their social dynamics. For example, the Reverend Tim LaHaye, a fundamentalist Baptist firebrand, ordered the firing of two Catholic teachers from his Christian High School in El Cajon, California, in 1981. His actions were based solely on the teachers' religious affiliation, not their professional record.[33] In Texas the Longview Christian Academy canceled a basketball game with another school after years of competition when school officials discovered their opponents were Catholics.[34] Paul F. Parsons, in his ground-breaking study, *Inside America's Christian Schools*, found that fundamentalist schools "consider Catholicism to be a form of fraudulent Christianity and abhor a variety of Catholic practices and beliefs."[35]

Textbooks published by fundamentalist Bob Jones University and Pensacola Christian College Press have singled out Catholicism for the harshest criticism.

In world history the students are only informed about the features of Catholic faith, culture, and practice that are deemed objectionable or heretical by fundamentalists. No attempt is made to understand the historical development of Christianity, or the mutations that it underwent as it emerged from Palestine to become the dominant force and culture of European civilization.

The student learns nothing about the writings of early church fathers, the rise of the papacy, the conflicts between church and state, the development of religious calendars and holy days, basilica architecture, theological controversies, the development of a cult of honor accorded to martyrs and confessors, liturgy, or church government. What is taught is essentially caricature.

Catholic practices and traditions are frequently distorted or incorrectly described. Sweeping generalizations militate against the nuanced and balanced view of history that ought to inform education that encourages students to think critically and thoughtfully.

One American history volume proclaims that "Catholicism enslaves man" and is a "corrupted system."[36]

The treatment of the Reformation in all of these books is deficient. No attention is given to the sociological, economic, cultural, geographic, or political factors that predisposed certain nations toward acceptance of Reformation theology and social organization. Students are told that God intervened directly in history to bring about this event, and no further discussion is needed. This is a grossly unacceptable way to teach students the meaning and matter of history.

There is also surprisingly little discussion of such politically influential Protestant principles as private judgment in the interpretation of the Scriptures. These texts continually tell students what certain biblical passages mean, and no dissent is encouraged.

Catholics are constantly accused of persecuting Protestants, but Protestant transgressions are never mentioned. Literature texts include many pages from John Foxe's sixteenth-century *Book of Martyrs*, a quintessential Reformation-era diatribe that most historians regard as religious propaganda masquerading as history.

Catholic contributions to literature are minimized or denied altogether. Religious bias also permeates the historical background to the literary selections and the biographical sketches of those writers selected.

Anti-Catholic prejudices permeate geography texts, since predominantly Catholic countries are depicted as little better than cesspools of pagan ignorance.

Immigrants to the United States are ignored or ridiculed in most of these textbooks. "Immigration aggravated labor unrest and made immigrants widely resented" (349). This was because "many immigrants, especially those from southeastern Europe, were Roman Catholic, a fact that aroused fear and resentment among Protestants and others who feared the potential political power of the Roman Church" (349). Keeping Catholic immigrants out of the United States through immigration restriction legislation is praised.

At least two historical events are so distorted that serious questions about the historical accuracy of fundamentalist textbooks can be raised. One is the nonsensical depiction of the French and Indian War as "a war for religious freedom," and "part of an effort to preserve biblical Protestantism in America" (92).

Another absurdity promoted in these texts is the charge that one factor in the Civil War was the South's desire to retain it's Protestant identity in the face of "unbiblical beliefs such as Unitarianism, Catholicism and Transcendentalism, which were most numerous in the Northeast" (284).

Religious bias also permeates the literature texts, which downplay and ridicule Catholic contributions to English and American literature, while showcasing and exaggerating the extent of evangelical influences.

In short, fundamentalist schoolbooks convey a message that Catholic Christianity is evil and corrupt and not really Christian at all. The same charges are leveled at Episcopalians, Eastern Orthodox, and liberal Protestants, but the anti-Catholic animus represents a preoccupation that is central to the curriculum.[37]

Pat Robertson's Christian Coalition has met resistance in its attempt to harness Catholic support. Its own internal data, claiming 1.7 million members, reveal that 16 percent are Catholic, 2 percent are Jewish, and 82 percent are Protestant. Critics have questioned the 1.7 million claim, since public records filed by the organization show far fewer paying members. Be that as it may, the coalition established a Catholic Alliance division in December 1995. Why they would seek to segregate Catholics remains highly controversial.

A conservative Catholic, William A. Donohue, president of the Catholic

League for Religious and Civil Rights, urged Catholics to be wary of the Robertson group's goals. Donohue noted that Catholics who attended the Christian Coalition's March to Victory conference in September 1995 were questioned about their faith, ridiculed, and otherwise demeaned. "It could be questioned why a Catholic Alliance is necessary in an organization called the Christian Coalition," Donohue observed. "Why is there no Lutheran Alliance or a Methodist one? But then again, maybe that's because Catholics aren't Christians."[38]

The Christian Coalition and the Rutherford Institute, both Virginia-based Religious Right groups, sponsored a lecture by Northern Ireland's anti-Catholic extremist Ian Paisley at Pat Robertson's Regent University in the fall of 1995. A Christian Yellow Pages listing in California removed from its register Catholic Answers, a Catholic missionary enterprise in San Diego, allegedly because it did not consider Catholics to be Christians. The Washington state affiliate of the Christian Coalition publicly criticized a Catholic priest for presiding at a funeral service for a state senator who died of AIDS. (This points up one of the major attitudinal differences between Catholic inclusiveness and compassion and evangelical exclusion and judgmentalism.)

Meanwhile, both Catholic officialdom and liberal Catholics have blasted the Catholic Alliance. On the official side, Bishop Howard Hubbard of Albany, New York, warned that the Catholic Alliance was "an effort to split Catholics from their bishops," that the alliance "does not speak for the bishops," and that "we should be very careful about disseminating their materials through our parishes and other church organizations."[39] The bishop noted that there were serious differences between the groups on welfare reform, capital punishment, and a host of other issues.

On December 7, 1995, nearly a hundred moderate and liberal Catholic organizations released a statement challenging and criticizing the goals of the Christian Coalition. Three bishops joined 2,000 individual Catholics in this effort. Sister Maureen Fiedler of Catholics Speak Out said forthrightly, "Pat Robertson and Ralph Reed think they can lure Catholics into their fold using a pro-life and pro-family label, but it won't work. Catholics are generally progressive on the social issues touted by the Right. They will be rightfully suspicious of the political motives driving the formation of this so-called Catholic Alliance."[40]

Will a Catholic-evangelical alliance, then, be part of America's future political landscape? The best answer is that a semblance of one could be constructed in the short term, around a very few issues, or a possibly attractive candidate. But in the long run it is unlikely to be successful because evangelicals and Catholics do not share a significant number of philosophical perspectives. They have profoundly different histories and historical memories.

The *average* evangelical or fundamentalist has little in common with the *average* Catholic, owing primarily to cultural and lifestyle differences, but also to the evangelical dislike of Catholics and Catholicism, which is strongly ingrained and impervious to reason. Evangelicals are Johnny-come-latelys to ecumenical engagement. They tend to lack the mutual respect and appreciation for other religious traditions that are essential to the kind of broad ecumenical understanding that will endure during periods of tension. They are likely to retreat to a ghetto, where their values can remain preeminent and unchallenged.

Of course, the most conservative members of both communities are already tending toward the same political direction and goal. But the majority sentiment in each community is wary of any permanent, entangling alliance that might compromise the religious integrity and distinctiveness of their own community.

Even a political victory over perceived enemies would likely lead to a battle over the spoils, a spirited battle for domination by one side or the other.

Notes

1. Ralph Reed, *Politically Incorrect: The Emerging Faith Factor in American Politics* (Dallas: Word, 1994), p. 16.

2. See Thomas Elton Brown, *Bible Belt Catholicism: A History of the Roman Catholic Church in Oklahoma, 1905–1945* (New York: United States Catholic Historical Society, 1977).

3. Robert P. Casey, "Reconciling the Faith with Public Life," in *Catholics in the Public Square*, ed. Thomas Patrick Melady (Huntington, Ind.: Our Sunday Visitor, Inc.), p. 72.

4. Ibid., p. 81.

5. Ibid., p. 80.

6. Ibid., p. 79. See also Robert P. Casey, *Fighting for Life* (Dallas: Word Publishing, 1996).

7. Randall Balmer, *Mine Eyes Have Seen the Glory: A Journey into the Evangelical Subculture in America* (New York: Oxford University Press, 1989), p. 123.

8. William Booth, "Southern Officials Switching Sides," *Washington Post*, March 16, 1995.

9. Ibid.

10. Barry A. Kosmin and Seymour P. Lachman, *One Nation Under God: Religion in Contemporary American Society* (New York: Harmony Books, 1993), p. 200.

11. "Special Report: The Conversion of Thomas Howard," *Christianity Today* 29 (May 17, 1985): 46–59.

12. "Gordon College Rules That Catholics Cannot Sign Its Faculty Statement of Faith," *Christianity Today* 29 (September 20, 1985): 38.

13. Kevin Coyne, *Domers: A Year at Notre Dame* (New York: Viking, 1995), p. 108.

14. Kenneth S. Kantzer, "A Man Under Orders," *Christianity Today* 29 (September 6, 1985): 14–15.

15. John E. Tropman, *The Catholic Ethic in American Society* (San Francisco: Jossey-Bass Publishers, 1995), p. 145. Additional page references to this work appear in parentheses following cited material.

16. Keith A. Fournier with William D. Watkins, *A House United? Evangelicals and Catholics Together* (Colorado Springs: NAV Press, 1994), p. 14.

17. Avery Dulles, "The Unity for Which We Hope," in *Evangelicals and Catholics Together,* ed. Charles Colson and Richard John Neuhaus (Dallas: Word, 1995), p. 140. Additional page references to this work appear in parentheses following cited material.

18. J. I. Packer, "Crosscurrents among Evangelicals," in Colson and Neuhaus, *Evangelicals and Catholics Together,* pp. 160–61.

19. Norman L. Geisler and Ralph E. MacKenzie, *Roman Catholics and Evangelicals* (Grand Rapids: Baker Books, 1995), p. 498.

20. Ibid.

21. Quoted in ibid., p. 494.

22. Quoted in ibid., p. 496.

23. John F. MacArthur, *Reckless Faith* (Wheaton, Ill: Crossway Books, 1994), p. 145. Additional page references to this work appear in parentheses following the cited material.

24. James G. McCarthy, *The Gospel According to Rome* (Eugene, Oreg.: Harvest House Publishers, 1995), p. 312. Additional page references to this work will be found in parentheses following the cited material.

25. John Ankerberg and John Weldon, *Protestants and Catholics: Do They Now Agree?* (Eugene, Oreg.: Harvest House, 1995), p. 247. Additional page references to this work appear in parentheses following the cited material.

26. William Webster, "Did I Really Leave the Holy Catholic Church," in *Roman Catholicism: Evangelical Protestants Analyze What Divides and Unites Us,* ed. John Armstrong, (Chicago: Moody Press, 1994), p. 287.

27. Dave Hunt, *A Woman Rides the Beast: The Roman Catholic Church and the Last Days* (Eugene, OR: Harvest House, 1994), p. 467. Additional page references to this work appear in parentheses following the cited material.

28. J. Dwight Pentecost, *Prophecy for Today* (Grand Rapids: Zondervan, 1961), pp. 187–88.

29. Paul Boyer, *When Time Shall Be No More: Prophecy Belief in Modern American Culture* (Cambridge, Mass.: Harvard University Press, 1992), p. 275.

30. David B. Currie, *Born Fundamentalist, Born Again Catholic* (San Francisco: Ignatius Press, 1995), p. 110.

31. Jack Chick, *Smokescreens* (Chino, Calif.: Chick Publications, 1983), p. 88.

32. Karl Keating, *Catholicism and Fundamentalism* (San Francisco: Ignatius Press, 1988), p. 12.

33. *Los Angeles Times*, April 30, 1981, p. 1.

34. *Arkansas Gazette*, December 31, 1983, p. 5.

35. Paul F. Parsons, *Inside America's Christian Schools* (Macon, Ga.: Mercer University Press, 1987), p. 137.

36. Glen Chambers and Gene Fisher, *United States History for Christian Schools* (Greenville, S.C.: Bob Jones University Press, 1982), p. 15. Additional page references to this work appear in parentheses following the cited material.

37. For an extensive treatment of this subject, see Albert J. Menendez, *Visions of Reality: What Fundamentalist Schools Teach* (Amherst, N.Y.: Prometheus Books, 1993), especially pp. 32–61.

38. Quoted in "Catholic Alliance Draws Hostile Fire From Right and Left," *Church & State* 49 (January 1996): 18–19.

39. Ibid.

40. Ibid.

10

A Confessional Party System
in America's Future

There is abundant evidence that the U.S. political system is being transformed by religion. Voting patterns are increasingly being determined by religious conviction and participation. The new divisions differ from those of the past, even the recent past. They are not the old Protestant versus Catholic, or Christian versus Jewish, differences. Today's cultural divisions pit the conservative or orthodox adherents in all religions against the less conservative, or modernist, members of all religions.

James Davison Hunter has studied this phenomenon and defines cultural conflict as "political and social hostility rooted in different systems of moral understanding. The end to which these hostilities tend is the domination of one cultural and moral ethos over all others."[1] Today these differing worldviews and contending visions of moral authority do not follow strict religious lines. Says Hunter, "This cleavage is so deep that it cuts across the old lines of conflict, making the distinctions that long divided Americans—those between Protestants, Catholics and Jews—virtually irrelevant."[2]

Hunter argues convincingly that "pragmatic alliances are being formed across faith traditions because of common points of vision and concern."[3] These divisions, he says, "have extended into the broader realm of public morality and have become the expedient outcome of common concerns."[4] Therefore, a fundamental realignment is developing in American public life, centered around different moral visions, concepts of authority, the nature of virtue, community, and the meaning of the American experience itself.[5]

Furthermore, there is now evidence that the intensity of religious convictions and attendance at worship services affect voters by pushing them further toward the right and increasing likely support for conservative Republican candidates. Data confirming this trend go back as far as 1960, when the University of Michigan Survey Research Center found that Kennedy lost about 1.5 million more voters than he gained because of religious voting. Among Protestants anti-Kennedy voting increased as church attendance increased. This was true of both evangelical and mainline Protestants. By the 1990s this pattern had intensified.

How much weight does religion have when voters take into account all the factors that influence their choice? It obviously varies from individual to individual, and perhaps within the religious communities. Those who are most observant and who attend churches where politically relevant messages are commonplace are undoubtedly the most susceptible to religious influences on their voting behavior. Just before the 1992 election, about 10 percent of all voters said that religion would be the determining factor in their vote, though 26 percent of regular churchgoers cited religion as the defining factor.[6] This finding shows a steady tenth or so of the population citing religion (either as values or convictions held by the candidates or the voters) as the major voting factor. In any given election, this figure could rise if religious issues are given more prominence in the platforms or campaigns.

Everett Carll Ladd adds,

> Religious conservatives are another critical group in the realignment. Historically, the "religious divide" in the United States was largely an ethnic one—separating Americans of Protestant ancestry from Roman Catholic ethnics. Today, in contrast, it is mostly between religious participants and non-participants. Not all participants are in any sense political conservatives, but Republicans do better within the religiously participating community than do Democrats. Those identifying with the "religious right" and members of the Christian Coalition are overwhelmingly Republican.[7]

National surveys are increasingly conclusive that church attendance and orthodox belief combine to increase conservative attitudes. A 1993 California Field Poll shows this to be true in the nation's largest, and frequently trend-setting, state.

The 21 percent of voters who were religious conservatives wanted abortion laws made more restrictive, were the most supportive of a constitutional amendment permitting formal prayer in public schools, endorsed the teaching of creationism in public schools, and opposed openly gay men and women's ability to serve in the armed forces. The one-quarter who are religious moderates fell right in the middle but were closer to religious liberals

Table 10.1

Religion and Politics in California

Issue	% Agreeing		
	Religious Conservatives	Religious Moderates	Religious Liberals
Abortion laws should be stricter	52	29	10
Favor constitutional amendment on school prayer	78	56	34
Gay men and women should serve in armed forces	29	42	57
Both evolution and creationism should be taught in schools	60	56	33
Gay lifestyle is acceptable	27	41	63

Source: Field Poll, appearing in the *San Francisco Chronicle*, Sept. 27, 1993, p. A18.

(called secularists in the poll, they comprised 54 percent of all Californians) on all questions excerpt creationism. (See table 10.1.)

This connection between religious conservatism and Republicanism has led, inevitably and ineluctably it seems, to increasing Religious Right domination of state Republican parties.

John F. Persinos concluded in 1994 that the Religious Right controlled the GOP in eighteen states and held a substantial influence in thirteen others. The strength of evangelicalism in the state was only one factor, but a mildly positive one. Half (50 percent) of the eighteen states dominated by the Religious Right were substantially evangelical, compared to five of thirteen (38 percent) of the states where Religious Right influence was substantial, and five of the nineteen states (26 percent) where Religious Right influence was minimal. Weak local Republican organizations in Alaska, Hawaii, Minnesota, Oregon, and Washington probably accounted for the Religious Right domination in those low-evangelical states. (See table 10.2.)

This Religious Right influence strengthens anti-censorship and anti-abortion sentiment in the party platform. Religion, once again, is a major explanation for pro- and anti-censorship opinions. An influential *Library Journal* survey on censorship in the mid-1980s discovered that Baptists and evangelicals supported maximum efforts to remove religiously, politically, or sexually objectionable material from public libraries. Jews, Catholics, Episcopalians, and the religiously nonaffiliated were vigorously opposed to censorship of any kind, while middle of the road Protestants like Methodists,

Table 10.2

Religious Right Influence in the Republican Party, 1994

Dominant Control	Substantial Control	Minimal Control
AL	AR	CO
AK	IN	CT
AZ	KS	DE
CA	KY	DC
FL	ME	IL
GA	MI	MD
HI	MS	MA
ID	MT	MO
IA	NE	NH
LA	NV	NJ
MN	OH	NM
NC	PA	NY
OK	UT	ND
OR		RI
SC		SD
TX		TN
VA		VT
WA		WV
		WI
		WY

Source: *Campaigns & Elections* (September 1994): 20–24.

Lutherans, and Presbyterians were typically in the midpoint of the attitudinal spectrum.

The abortion question is becoming murkier. The GOP governors of California, New York, and New Jersey have called on their party to scrap the call for a ban on all abortions that the party adopted in 1992. Even Ralph Reed thought this could be done in a subtle way without damaging the party's moral authority. Pat Buchanan and others have promised a punishing floor fight at the 1996 convention. However it turns out, there is indication that Republican primary voters, perhaps the most conservative voters in the nation, are less supportive of an anti-abortion plank than was previously supposed. Of the twenty-seven primary states for which there are comparative exit polling data, in only three (Mississippi, Louisiana, and Tennessee) did a majority of Republican voters want to retain a call for a constitutional amendment to outlaw abortion. Conservative Mississippians were most sup-

Table 10.3

Percent Supporting Anti-Abortion Plank in 1996 Republican Platform

State	% in Favor	State	% in Favor
MS	56	CO	37
LA	52	OR	37
TN	52	FL	36
WI	48	AZ	35
OK	46	MD	34
IA	45	ME	34
SD	45	RI	33
GA	44	NY	32
TX	44	CA	31
MI	44	MA	28
SC	43	NH	27
ND	42	VT	27
OH	42	CT	24
IL	40		

Source: *The American Enterprise* 7 (May/June 1996): 92.

portive (56 percent). But majorities opposed this even in South Carolina, Georgia, Texas, and Oklahoma. Only about half were favorable in Iowa and Wisconsin. Fewer than one-third of Republicans supported an anti-abortion plank in the party platform in New Hampshire, Connecticut, Massachusetts, Rhode Island, Vermont, New York, and California. (See table 10.3.)

An even lower percentage of GOP primary voters said they considered themselves "part of the Christian political movement known as the religious right." Again, only in Mississippi did a majority respond favorably, and only in Tennessee, Oklahoma, and Louisiana did 40 percent or more voters so describe themselves. Fewer than 25 percent of Republicans accepted this designation in New Hampshire, North Dakota, Connecticut, Massachusetts, Rhode Island, Vermont, or New York. (See table 10.4.)

This suggests more and more that the Religious Right is a kind of elite group that exerts disproportionate power over the GOP that most party voters themselves really do not support. Like some other special interest groups, the Religious Right claims more grassroots support than it actually has.

Some voters still consider a candidate's religious affiliation when casting a ballot, despite the explicit ban on religious tests in the federal Consti-

Table 10.4

Percentage of GOP Primary Voters Who Are Supportive of the Religious Right

State	% in Favor	State	% in Favor
MS	54	MD	28
TN	46	ME	27
LA	43	CA	27
OK	40	WI	27
GA	38	OH	26
TX	37	IL	25
OR	36	ND	24
SC	36	NY	19
IA	35	RI	18
FL	32	NH	17
CO	31	CT	16
SD	30	VT	16
MI	29	MA	15
AZ	29		

Source: *The American Enterprise* 7 (May/June 1996): 91.

tution and in thirty-one state constitutions. Writes Gary L. Bauer, president of the Family Research Council:

> Devout Protestants pay considerably more attention to a political candidate's religious faith than do other Americans. Forty-four percent of Protestants who attend church weekly say they "always" or "often" consider a candidate's religious faith when deciding whom to vote for. Only 22 percent of the general public say the same. Moreover, 35 percent of all devout Protestants say they would opt for a candidate "who shared your religious beliefs, but not your political beliefs," over a candidate "who shared your political beliefs, but not your religious beliefs." Only 17 percent of the general public respond similarly.[8]

America's Founding Fathers would frown on this attempt to frame political debate in terms of religious referents. It is often forgotten in the rough and tumble of political debate that when the United States adopted its written Constitution more than two centuries ago, the nation pioneered a wholly new concept: no religious tests for public office. When South Carolina's Charles Pinckney proposed on August 20, 1787, that "no religious test shall ever be required as a qualification to any office or public trust under the

United States," he probably did not foresee how revolutionary and how beneficial this would become to the American body politic. As the third clause of Article 6, it has allowed the electorate to select the best-qualified candidates, irrespective of their religious beliefs, for all political offices.

Any political efforts, therefore, that aim to Christianize or sectarianize positions of public trust are profoundly at variance with our nation's highest ideals.

Joseph Story, a Supreme Court member and a constitutional scholar often invoked by conservatives, had this to say about Article 6 in his *Commentaries on the Constitution*:

> This clause is not introduced merely for the purpose of satisfying the scruples of many respectable persons, who feel an invincible repugnance to any religious test, or affirmation. It had a higher object: to cut off for ever every pretence of any alliance between church and state in the national government. The framers of the Constitution were fully sensible of the dangers from this source, marked out in the history of other ages and countries; and not wholly unknown to our own. They knew that bigotry was unceasingly vigilant in its stratagems to secure to itself an exclusive ascendancy over the human mind; and that intolerance was ever ready to arm itself with all the terrors of the civil power to exterminate those who doubted its dogmas or resisted its infallibility. The Catholic and the Protestant had alternately waged the most ferocious and unrelenting warfare on each other. . . . The history of the parent country, too, could not fail to instruct them in the uses and the abuses of religious tests. They there found the pains and penalties of non-conformity written in no equivocal language and enforced with a stern and vindictive jealousy.[9]

One potential threat to religious tests lies in the Religious Right's emphasis on religion as an essential dividing point in political dialogue.

The Religious Right leadership has tried to make its positions more palatable to a wider audience by downplaying its more extreme rhetoric, by signaling acceptance of gradual or incremental steps toward the realization of its goals, and by endorsing certain secular postures. Ralph Reed explained this strategy in an appendix to his Christian Coalition's Contract with the American Family. He enumerated the Religious Right's priorities: "First, the government should promote and defend rather than undermine the institution of the family";[10] "our second priority is to radically downsize and re-limit government";[11] "our third priority is to replace the failed and discredited welfare state with a community—and charity—based opportunity society";[12] "the fourth and final priority of the new Congress should be to secure religious liberty and freedom of conscience for all of our citizens."[13]

This last charge is commonplace today. Many conservative evangelicals believe that they are now persecuted in the United States, that their values and their ability to influence the public square of culture, education, government, and law has somehow been restricted in recent decades (despite Republican domination of the White House during most of the era). Typical of their angry complaints are these:

- "The Supreme Court's erroneous interpretations of the Establishment Clause have institutionalized agnostic secularism as the official national creed."[14]
- "The phrase [separation of church and state] is a propaganda tool to suppress an entire segment of the population—that is, religious people."[15]
- "Modern U.S. Supreme Courts have raped the Constitution and raped the Christian faith and raped the churches."[16]
- "Just like what Nazi Germany did to the Jews, so liberal America is now doing to the evangelical Christians."[17]
- "Today the ungodly are doing their best to destroy . . . and the club they are using to beat back the idea of religious liberty is the 'wall of separation between church and state,' usually in the hands of the ACLU. Like Hitler's big lie, this false doctrine has been used to brainwash the American people and to attempt to drive Christians and the Christian faith into oblivion."[18]

Can these charges can be substantiated? If they are true, what can be done about it? If they are not true, why are people promoting them, and what is their real agenda?

How do Americans define themselves religiously? The total membership for all religious groups in the United States is 156,336,384, though the criteria for membership vary widely among religions. This figure includes 86 million Protestants, 58 million Catholics, 6 million Jews, and 4 million Eastern Orthodox Christians. There are 358,194 churches or places of worship in the United States.[19] There were 58,430 seminarians in the 215 seminaries and theological academies that belong to the Association of Theological Schools. These findings from 1992 represent an increase over the 52,194 seminarians reported in 1987.[20] According to the U.S. Census of 1990, there are more than 500,000 clergy in the United States, though not all of them are active pastors.

Religion in America is big business. Among forty-four large U.S. Protestant communions, total contributions in 1992 reached $16,647,464,955. This figure does not include Roman Catholic, Episcopalian, or Eastern Orthodox communities.[21] Other studies by Andrew Greeley have suggested that religious giving in America remains quite robust. Greeley found that America's Protestants give about 2 percent of their annual income to their churches, a figure that has remained unchanged for the last three decades. Roman Catholics have reduced their giving from about 2 percent of their income in the 1960s to 1 percent of their annual income in the 1990s.[22] Two other researchers have also found that giving to thirty-one major Protestant denominations remains at a fairly high level. John and Sylvia Ronsvalle concluded that members of the major Protestant denominations contributed 2.54 percent of their annual income to their churches in 1991, compared to 3.09 percent in 1968. This represents an annual contribution well into the billions.[23]

In 1992 there were 444 major religious periodicals published in the United States. This does not include denominational weeklies, state Baptist papers, and the many Episcopal and Catholic diocesan publications.[24]

Researchers commissioned by the Graduate School and University Center of the City University of New York conducted a national survey of religious identification over a thirteen-month period during 1989 and 1990. They found that more than five of six Americans (86.5 percent) called themselves Christians. This represents 151,668,000 out of 175 million Americans who are over eighteen years of age. The specific denominational breakdowns are broadly similar to official church membership claims, though the national survey also includes many nominal adherents. (About 1 in 7 respondents, 14.4 percent, said they were "Protestant" or "Christian" but were not associated with any specific group.)[25]

According to the *Almanac of the Christian Church*, the United States is home to 1,840 Christian radio and television stations. These are full-time stations that broadcast only viewpoints representative of conservative Protestant Christianity. Ranging from fifty-seven stations in Florida to one each in North Dakota, Rhode Island, Vermont, and Wyoming, these stations blanket the nation. There are, in contrast, almost no Catholic, Jewish, mainline Protestant, Eastern Orthodox, or other religious radio and television stations.

This does not begin to measure the extent of the near-total control of religious broadcasting exercised by one religious community. Evangelical and fundamentalist evangelists also dominate the market on commercial and network television, despite the sexual and financial scandals affecting several televangelists a few years ago. Few countervailing religious viewpoints are heard. All of the top-ten religious television programs, in terms of audience, are exemplars of conservative Protestantism.

This represents a major gain for this segment of U.S. religion, since only a handful of Catholic, Jewish, and mainline Protestant programs exist. This has been largely true since radio began in 1921. In his reference book, *Religious Radio and Television in the United States, 1921–1991*, Hal Erickson cited more than four hundred regularly scheduled radio and television programs directed at the religious community.[26] Only about seven of these programs were Catholic and three were Jewish. During the early days of television, the major networks made free time available to the major religious communities. One network, NBC, was noted for its "Frontiers of Faith" series, a weekly half-hour program that ran from 1951 to 1970. The acclaimed series provided twenty-four programs for Protestants, sixteen for Catholics, eight for Jews, and four for other religious communities. Since that time, religious programming has been purchased by the sponsoring groups and is almost completely dominated by evangelical, charismatic, and fundamentalist groups.

In the One Hundred Fourth Congress, elected in 1994, Christians number 497 of the 535 members (93 percent).[27] America's national legislature includes 331 Protestants, 148 Roman Catholics, 13 Mormons, and 5 Eastern Orthodox Christians. There are 33 Jews and 5 religiously unaffiliated members. And while the percentage of Christians in Congress is a bit lower than it was two or three decades ago, it still represents an overwhelming dominance, an even higher percentage than those who call themselves Christian in national surveys.

Christian bookselling is big business. The evangelical Protestant market share exceeds $1 billion yearly. A network of 3,400 stores that are members of the Christian Booksellers Association dots the nation.[28] *Publishers Weekly* reported that the organization's forty-fifth annual convention in Denver in June 1994 revealed that "Christian retailing is an industry rapidly approaching an annual gross of $3 billion,"[29] of which about one-third is generated by book sales.

At the behest of many conservative Christians, who complained that their authors were ignored by the general book media, *Publishers Weekly*, the bible of the book trade, now publishes weekly "religious best seller" lists.

There are also Baptist, Catholic, Episcopalian, Lutheran, Mormon, Seventh-day Adventist, and other religious bookstores throughout the United States. It should be noted that most of these specialty stores, especially those belonging to the Christian Booksellers Association, carefully screen and censor the materials carried so that only their religious teachings and culture are promoted. There is little of the variety commonly found in religion sections of the major U.S. book shops.

All kinds of religious publishing are booming, from New Age to Native American to Pentecostal. In 1994 the largest U.S. book wholesaler, Ingram

Book Company, announced a 249 percent growth in religious book sales. The Association of American Publishers reported a 59 percent increase in the religion/spirituality category between February 1992 and February 1994.[30] In June 1992, *American Bookseller* concluded that the "Religion category's expansion is indisputable."[31]

Paul Weber, chair of the political science department at the University of Louisville, has spent many years observing religious interest groups in politics. He has identified 120 religion-based lobbies in Washington, D.C., whose primary purpose is to advance a religious-oriented agenda at the federal political level. All but a handful of these groups are Christian oriented. Three of the oldest, those of the Quakers, the Methodists, and the Catholics, have been operating for three-quarters of a century.[32] The U.S. Catholic Conference also maintains affiliates in 28 states, which seek to influence state legislation and appropriations. Americans also have a fondness for religious figures and personalities. Billy Graham, Pope John Paul II, and Mother Teresa are "perennial favorites" according to Gallup polls published during the last fifteen years.[33] In the December 1992 Gallup poll, Billy Graham ranked fifth and Pope John Paul II ranked sixth in a list of the most admired men. (The pope came in first in 1980.) Mother Teresa was named the second-most-admired woman by Americans in the same poll.[34]

In a July 1992 Gallup poll devoted to honesty and ethical standards, the clergy ranked second only to pharmacists. Until 1989 they had ranked first, but scandals involving sexual misconduct and child abuse lowered their standing somewhat. Still, clergy were far more widely admired than doctors, teachers, lawyers, and many other professionals. Gallup commented, "It is evident that the clergy have never recovered from the ethical battering sustained during the Bakker and Swaggart televangelist scandals; their ratings have steadily declined since 1985."[35]

One highly controversial subject is the alleged anti-Christian bias of television and Hollywood. Those who have made this charge include the Rev. Donald Wildmon of the American Family Association in Tupelo, Mississippi, an organization that "monitors" television for sexual content and anti-religious bias, and such conservative Jewish critics as Ben Stein and Michael Medved.

While the treatment of religious issues, moral concerns, ethics, and the portrait of religious communities varies widely on U.S. commercial, cable, and public television, there is little hard evidence to substantiate any widespread anti-religious bias. There is some, to be sure—perhaps rooted in the general religious illiteracy of modern culture. But those with a historical perspective would suggest that the pendulum has swung, perhaps too sharply to satisfy some viewers, from the schmaltzy, uncritically pro-religious bias that permeated Hollywood during the 1930s and 1940s (remember *Going My Way* and *A Man Called Peter*?) to that of today. The media treat religion and religious issues somewhat more critically today, but this is true for political and other subjects as well.

A 1994 book, *Prime Time: How TV Portrays American Culture*, demolishes the myth, often propounded by the Religious Right, that American television is hostile to religion. Written by S. Robert Lichter and Linda S. Lichter of the Center for Media and Public Affairs, a conservative watchdog group in Washington, D.C., the book is a scientific survey of a thousand programs that appeared on prime-time network television from the 1950s to the 1990s. The Lichters and co-author Stanley Rothman have been cited by religious conservatives for their previous studies of religion and the media.

The authors conclude: "Clergy are a rarity on prime time, and religious themes are rarer still. When they do appear, however, the clergy are portrayed as the establishment's human face. Unlike executives, politicos, and military brass, they have always been one of television's good-guy professions. Throughout the three decades of our study, the proportion of positive clergy has always exceeded 80 percent."[36] During the 1950s and 1960s, television always portrayed clergy as "compassionate and humanitarian as well as in placing their behavior in the context of traditional religious settings. Shows from the 1950s and early 1960s dealt directly with religious themes by portraying a transcendent God whose ways surpassed human understanding but whose laws must be obeyed."[37] Portrayals of the clergy since the 1970s have tended to emphasize their roles as "either social activists or questioners of church authority."[38] The common theme remains that "only the clergy have always commanded television's respect."[39]

Several other television critics and observers echo this theme. Writes Stephen Seplow of the Knight-Ridder newspapers: "Religion, long a subject shunned by prime-time television, is emerging from its usual setting in the Sunday morning evangelical Bible Belt to become one of the frequent themes on weekly network drama series. Catholics are praying for guidance everywhere from the operating room to the squad room. Jews are seeing visions of rabbis past and are wrestling with nightmares about sins not atoned for on Yom Kippur. Protestants are berating themselves for spending too little time in church with their families."[40] He adds, "Shows with prominent religious themes, such as CBS's "Northern Exposure," have done well in the ratings. There is also an important group of TV writers who have moved into their middle years, a time for asking basic questions about mortality and the ultimate meaning of things."[41]

Quentin Schultz, who teaches a course in religion and the media at Calvin College in Grand Rapids, Michigan, observes, "Writers and producers see that religion is of interest to many Americans and provides good subject matter. They are finding that in some cases it pays off with generating an audience. So I think we're seeing a trend, not just a fad."[42]

Thomas Skill, chairperson of the Communication Department of the University of Dayton, studied prime-time religion during October and November 1990. He concluded, "There is an emphasis on religious life that takes such a positive approach that it's surprising to most hardened critics of television."[43]

There are numerous examples of programming that treat religious subjects in a shallow way and with a sympathetic tilt. Recent U.S. television programs have been saturated with angels, near-death experiences and returns from the dead, miracles, healings, and other paranormal phenomena.

Time magazine's late cultural critic William A. Henry III criticized recent television coverage for its uncritical treatment of religious subjects. Henry cites a 1993 CBS documentary which "purported to provide scientific evidence for the existence of Noah's Ark in Turkey."[44] A critic "infiltrated the research process and demonstrated that most of the testing was inadequate, suspect, or just plain fraudulent,"[45] wrote Henry. But Henry notes that no reporter from any major news media, except *Time*'s Leon Jaroff, gave attention to the critique. Henry says, "Any refutations of the Noah's Ark story were . . . certain to bring retribution from the Christian devout."[46]

Henry also draws attention to the CBS affiliate in New York that in February 1994 unveiled a "heavily hyped series on miracle cures, replete with assertions that prayer made the difference. Even when such stories are balanced, science and common sense are treated at best as just another point of view, with religious self-delusion taking center stage. Where, for contrast, were the anecdotes about regular churchgoers who kept praying and stayed paralyzed or died of cancer anyway?"[47]

At times church leaders' objections to television coverage are suspect. In 1987 the Lutheran Church-Missouri Synod raised serious objections to and deliberately tried to block the filming and televising of the CBS movie *Murder Ordained,* which dealt factually with a case of a Lutheran minister in Kansas who, together with his paramour, was convicted of murdering his wife. The minister is now serving a lengthy prison sentence. The television film was no assault on the church, but an examination of how an individual dedicated to doing good could be seduced into committing a great evil.[48]

The Lutheran Church-Missouri Synod also objected a few years later when another television program recounted the case of a man who slaughtered his family in New Jersey, changed his name, and surfaced years later in another state, remarried and quietly teaching Sunday school.[49] Why should churches object to factual examinations of the existence of evil within the religious community? Their reaction suggests an attempt to cover up scandals, rather than an honest and aggrieved appeal for impartiality and objectivity.

Church wealth is one of the most closely guarded secrets of American life. The extent of tax-exempt church property is enormous, as are stock holdings, land ventures, and types of unrelated business income. Every state and local government exempts church-owned property of various kinds from taxation, which, though constitutionally permissible, constitutes a kind of indirect subsidy.

There is also government support, directly and indirectly, for church schools under a myriad of federal and state programs. A modest estimate of governmental aid to parochial and other private religious secondary and elementary schools exceeds $1.5 billion per year. (Most forms of direct aid have been held unconstitutional.) Church-related colleges and universities receive substantial government support, and the courts have allowed assistance to all but the most pervasively sectarian ones.

Researchers and scholars have generally ignored the subject of church wealth. But about twenty years ago, two independent researchers, Martin Larson and C. Stanley Lowell, concluded that total church assets then exceeded $150 billion, in addition to $20 billion in annual income.[50] Surely it has increased substantially since that time.

The American public generously supports chaplains in the armed services, the Congress, and in many state legislatures. There are publicly paid chaplains in some public hospitals, police departments, and fire departments. Virtually all are Christian. Even though some U.S. presidents such as James Madison questioned the constitutionality of congressional chaplains, they have been a part of the congressional scene for two centuries. Protestants have completely dominated the chaplaincy corps, and the Methodists and Presbyterians have tended to monopolize the Senate chaplaincy. The same is generally true in state legislatures, and a challenge to the Nebraska practice was rejected by the U.S. Supreme Court in a 1980s case called *Marsh* v. *Chambers*.

The most ambitious and financially costly chaplaincy program is maintained by the U.S. Armed Forces for the benefit of its personnel and their dependents. As of the fall of 1994, there were 3,063 full-time chaplains assigned to the army, air force, and navy (which includes the Marines). All but 38 of them were Christians. There were 2,455 Protestants (80.2 percent), 544 Catholics (17.8 percent), 37 Jews (1.2 percent), 26 Eastern Orthodox Christians (0.8 percent), and 1 Muslim chaplain in the armed forces. Their salaries alone cost taxpayers millions per annum, and this does not include support personnel, building maintenance, and other administrative and program costs.[51]

Religious groups in the United States have long provided much of the nation's long-term health care. A recent study revealed, "Catholic hospitals constitute a full 16 percent of total U.S. hospital admissions, inpatient days, surgeries, payroll and expenses. The Catholic healthcare system also includes hundreds of health care centers and more than 1,500 specialized care institutions, such as nursing homes and drug treatment centers."[52]

These institutions—and their many Protestant and Jewish counterparts— receive a major portion of their funding from government agencies. Medicare and Medicaid are major sources of revenue. An estimated 55 percent of Catholic hospital revenue in 1990 came from government sources.[53] This is roughly true for all types of hospitals.

Between 1946 and 1974, the Hill-Burton Act granted federal financial aid for the planning, construction and improvement of hospitals. Almost 70 percent of Catholic hospitals received those grants.[54]

Despite the infusion of government money, the Catholic hospitals benefit from a "conscience clause," statutory language that allows them to refuse to provide abortion and sterilization services, or to limit or ban other services such as in vitro fertilization. These prohibitions against certain medical procedures that violate canon law are extended to patients and providers, irrespective of religious affiliation. Legal challenges to government funding of hospitals that maintain a sectarian medical code failed in the U.S. Supreme Court nearly a century ago.

One final area where conservative religion is resurgent and ascendant is in the world of sports. For decades the Fellowship of Christian Athletes and Athletes in Action, a sports ministry of Campus Crusade for Christ, have sponsored religious activities on college and high school campuses. Sports figures routinely identify themselves as evangelicals, and evangelical publishers routinely bring out biographies of evangelical sports heroes.

What's more, evangelical Protestantism dominates the market. Many professional football and baseball teams have chaplains who conduct regular worship services for players and team personnel. They are invariably Protestant and mostly evangelical. Public proclamation of their religious convictions and conversion of others are frankly stated goals. There may be other religious-faith traditions represented in professional athletics, but they are disadvantaged by the strong evangelical overtones, which one journalist called "a camaraderie based on public witness to their faith."[55]

One scholar who has studied the nexus between sports and religion has concluded, "The shift of professional sports toward religious ritual and the metamorphosis of evangelism and college sports toward televised entertainment have altered the faces of both religion and sports."[56] He added, "There are many examples of the contemporary connection of religion and sports. Protestant institutions of strong evangelical bent are notorious in their use of sports to gain converts."[57]

This brief overview of the primary role of religion in American life hardly suggests a pattern of persecution and discrimination. And even this listing of strength does not complete the picture. There are numerous informal, ceremonial aspects of religion's link to secular power. Presidential inaugurations always include clergy in central roles, informal prayer services, and the traditional attendance of the president at St. John's Episcopal Church on Lafayette Square. The Rev. Billy Graham is accorded the status of a national pastor, it seems.

The U.S. Supreme Court's opening day each October is preceded by attendance at a "Red Mass" at St. Matthew's Roman Catholic Cathedral; though attendance is voluntary, the ceremony is taking on the aura of a semi-official event. In 1994 Bishop Edward M. Egan of Connecticut asked the jurists to reject "political correctness," which he claimed muzzles the voices of those who oppose abortion and support government aid to religious education. Egan urged the jurists not to reject out of hand the political opinions of religious people. He proclaimed from the pulpit, "There is a tactic abroad in our land to characterize inappropriate thinking as exclusively religious and to refuse to allow it a fair hearing on that score. The tactic is clever, widespread and effective. It should also be frightening."[58]

The National Christmas Tree Lighting Ceremony on the Ellipse in Washington has been an annual presidential event since Coolidge was chief executive, and it has been televised since Eisenhower's term of office. The event has frequently become an occasion for presidential forays into theological reflections on the American experience, or for reminders of the role of religious faith in U.S. life. Similar Christmas and other civil religious events are repeated in state capitols and mayoral offices throughout the land. Attempts to silence religious expression are not representative of America in the 1990s, despite the irresponsible claims of some in the religious community.

Why, then, does Ralph Reed, the personable and seemingly "moderate" director of Pat Robertson's Christian Coalition charge in a recent book, "Today the First Amendment has been twisted into a weapon that billy-clubs people of faith into submission and silence"?[59] It is clear that these charges are baseless.

How people vote is a composite of many things: tradition and family upbringing, where one lives, how one earns a living and how much one earns, how much and what kind of education one has, ethnic background, and now religious beliefs, and what kind of church one attends and how often—all these influences play a role. But religion, once thought dormant or irrelevant by political researchers, is looming increasingly large in the framework of political formation, so much so that some wonder if the United States is heading toward a European-style confessional party system, where religious belief and practice determine political choice and party selection. Ironically, America may be rushing headlong to adopt what Europeans have been gradually rejecting. Virtually every European country from Spain to Ireland is moving in the direction of greater secularization and marginalization of religion as a political factor, while the United States heads in the opposite direction.

Maybe the Europeans know something we don't: that religion can be a divisive and even dangerous force when too closely linked to politics, and that religious divisions, when permanently yoked to political structures, can lead to the balkanization of nations, with grave consequences to their peace and security.

This concern is shared by a number of specialists. Based on their years of research, John Green and James Guth offer these predictions: "Mutually reinforcing connections between religion and politics, similar to those found in ethnocultural communities, could be reestablished: religious and secular leaders would articulate distinctive theological or philosophical bases for politics, mobilizing activists in religious and secular organizations for ideological combat, and evoking religious and secular identifications to mobilize voters. This would set the stage for a new kind of electoral conflict in America, strikingly reminiscent of European politics: religious supporters of 'order and tradition' struggling with secular forces of 'rights and reform' over the role of religion in public life, control of schools and curricula, sexual morality, and traditional social arrangements."[60]

There are, to be sure, a number of conservative Christians who have serious questions about the drift to a confessional party system in America. Even Michael Farris, the *enfant terrible* of the Religious Right and the home-schooling movement and cochairman of the Buchanan presidential campaign, offered some cautionary advice.

He told a Washington, D.C., audience a month after his 1993 defeat for lieutenant governor of Virginia that "using the Bible as a political trump card is inappropriate both politically and theologically."[61] Farris criticized his Christian Coalition friends for passing out the "Christian Voter Guides" at polling places on election day by saying, "I was losing votes with every one that was handed out," and adding, "We cannot afford to bring something labeled 'the Christian answer' into the secular political arena."[62]

Farris seemed to have moderated his stance, at least temporarily. He told his hearers, "We should not read too much into the founding fathers' references to America as a Christian nation; these references have more to do with culture than with government."[63]

Peter Wehner, director of policy for the conservative think tank Empower America, spoke for many in a *Washington Post* column. He said, "Passionate political activism—for example, presidential candidates calling for Christians to 'break the doors open' and 'take over the party'—is simply not a model of biblical Christianity. Christ understood the corrosive effect power can have on the church as well as on individual believers."[64]

Wehner also warned that "the political arena undermines traditional Christian virtues such as love, humility, forgiveness, forbearance, kindness, mercy and gentleness. These virtues are not the coin of the political realm—including the Christian political realm. Often when Christians organize politically, the rules that are supposed to govern their behavior individually seem not to apply to them collectively. And so we find that the fuel driving much of modern-day Christian activism is anger, bitterness, resentment. Political campaigns seem only to inflame these emotions."[65] The solution? Wehner's suggestion applies to those of many, or no, religious persuasions. "The corrective is not complete retreat from the affairs of the world; it is, rather, selective political engagement characterized by distinctively Christian attitudes."[66]

The activities of the Christian Coalition, its thinly veiled Republican partisanship, and its distribution of countless millions of supposedly nonpartisan election guides have come under fire by a number of neutral observers.

University of Virginia political scientist Larry Sabato and *Wall Street Journal* reporter Glenn Simpson have labeled the Christian Coalition's tactics as "characterized neither by Christian charity nor by adherence to the spirit of the law."[67] They charge the group's voter guides with consistent "manipulations, distortions and outright falsehoods. . . . By systematically rigging the content of its voter guides to help Republican candidates, the group had essentially donated hundreds of thousands of dollars (perhaps millions) in free advertising to the Republican Party."[68] They add, "There are also indications that Christian Coalition members coordinated their activities with Republican campaigns and sometimes even actually worked in those campaigns. . . . It is indisputable that the leaders of the Christian coalition are themselves partisan Republicans."[69]

The Christian Coalition voter guides, say Sabato and Simpson, are dishonest. "Rather than simply seeking to inform voters of where candidates stood on the issues, the guides give every appearance of having been designed with the explicit intention of influencing voting decisions in favor of Republicans."[70]

Ralph Reed admits that his movement is inextricably linked to the GOP. He writes, "Religious conservatives have invested too much blood and treasure in the hard-earned gains they have won in the Republican party since the late 1970s. To simply walk away from that union, which has endured for almost twenty years and produced several electoral landslides, will take more than a family squabble."[71]

It is precisely this political bias that is beginning to discomfit and dismay some evangelicals. *Washington Post* reporter E. J. Dionne, Jr., found that "Many Christians are wary of linking religion to political power."[72] On a visit to the prestigious First Baptist Church in Tallahassee, Florida, where the late political legend Claude Pepper maintained a lifelong membership, Dionne discovered that many religious conservatives "fear that the quest for political power is becoming a form of idolatry."[73] Many members of the Baptist Center for Ethics told Dionne that, in his words, "It's altogether wrong to harness religious convictions to any particular ideology."[74] These Baptists obviously disagree with their leadership, 82 percent of whom voted for George Bush in 1992, according to James L. Guth.

The increasing identification of Republican politics with right-wing evangelicalism is also producing a backlash from those who believe such an admixture of the sacred and secular is pernicious to the preservation of democracy. Lifelong GOP activist Tanya Melich, who was raised Baptist in Utah, wrote angrily in her book *The Republican War Against Women,* "The Republican party of my youth no longer exists."[75] Melich, who endorsed Clinton in 1992, said she has "closed the door on my birthright Republicanism, to be opened only when the deeds as well as the words of the party's leaders mean freedom for all Americans. My own war to save the Republican party from extremism is over."[76]

Melich is not alone. In about twenty counties in New England and the Yankee-settled areas of Ohio and Michigan, the Republican presidential vote has collapsed. These areas are the historic strongholds of mainline Protestant Republicanism, but the Religious Right takeover of their party has produced a mass exodus in one generation. In Maine's Hancock County, Dwight Eisenhower won 87 percent of the votes cast in 1956 while George Bush plunged to 30 percent, a third-place showing, in 1992. In Lamoille County, Vermont, Ike received 84 percent and Bush 29 percent. In Gladwin County, Michigan, Ike won 74 percent and Bush 34 percent.

Some Lutheran areas of the Midwest show similar declines in Republican support. In Decorah, Iowa, where Nixon won about 80 percent in 1960, and 85 percent in the precinct surrounding Luther College, Clinton beat Bush 44 percent to 38 percent, with 18 percent for Perot. In the solidly Lutheran village of Wittenberg, Wisconsin, Nixon received 79 percent support; Bush lost to Clinton 41 percent to 37 percent, with 22 percent for Perot. The GOP vote declined by half.

Notes

1. James Davison Hunter, *Culture Wars* (New York: Basic Books, 1991), p. 42.
2. Ibid., p. 43.
3. Ibid., p. 47.
4. Ibid.
5. See Fred Barnes, "The Orthodox Alliance," *American Enterprise* 6 (November/December 1995): 70–71.
6. Barry A. Kosmin and Seymour P. Lachman, *One Nation Under God: Religion in Contemporary American Society* (New York: Harmony Books), p. 166.
7. Everett Carll Ladd, "Thinking about the 1996 Election," *American Enterprise* 7 (January/February 1996): 87.
8. Gary L. Bauer, "Needed: A Moral Renewal," *The World and I* 11 (February 1996): 79.
9. Philip B. Kurland and Ralph Lerner, eds. *The Founders' Constitution,* vol. 4 (Chicago: University of Chicago Press, 1987), p. 646.
10. *Contract with the American Family* (Nashville: Moorings, 1995), p. 138.
11. Ibid., p. 140.
12. Ibid., p. 141.
13. Ibid., p. 142.
14. Mathew D. Staver, *Faith and Freedom* (Wheaton, Ill.: Crossway Books, 1995), p. xi.
15. John W. Whitehead, *Religious Apartheid* (Chicago: Moody Press, 1994), p. 156.
16. The Rev. Jerry Falwell, quoted in "Demagogues of the Religious Right," by Leon Wieseltier, *Philadelphia Inquirer,* July 19, 1994.
17. The Rev. Pat Robertson, ibid.
18. D. James Kennedy with Jim Nelson Black, *Character & Destiny: A Nation in Search of Its Soul* (Grand Rapids, Mich.: Zondervan Publishing House, 1994), p. 125.
19. *The World Almanac and Book of Facts, 1993* (New York: Pharos Books, 1993), pp. 717–18.
20. Kenneth B. Bedell, ed., *Yearbook of American and Canadian Churches 1994* (Nashville: Abingdon Press, 1994), p. 265.
21. Ibid., p. 262.
22. Andrew M. Greeley, *Religious Change in America* (Cambridge, Mass.: Harvard University Press, 1989).

23. John Ronsvalle and Sylvia Ronsvalle, *A Report on the State of Church Giving* (P.O. Box 2404, Champaign, IL 61825). The Ronsvalle study was cited in Bedell, *Yearbook of American and Canadian Churches 1994*, p. 12.

24. Bedell, *Yearbook of American and Canadian Churches 1994*, pp. 216–32.

25. Kosmin and Lachman, *One Nation Under God*, pp. 284–302.

26. Hal Erickson, *Religious Radio and Television in the United States, 1921–1991* (Jefferson, N.C.: McFarland and Co., 1992), p. 199.

27. *Who's Who in Congress, 1995* (Washington, D.C.: Congressional Quarterly, Inc., 1995).

28. *Encyclopedia of Associations* (Detroit: Gale Research Co., 1995).

29. *Publishers Weekly*, July 18, 1994, p. 15.

30 Phyllis A. Tickle, *Rediscovering the Sacred: Spirituality in America* (New York: Crossroad, 1995), p. 18.

31. Sandra Brawarksy, "Getting Religion," *American Bookseller* (June 1992): 22–28.

32. Paul J. Weber and W. Landis Jones, *U.S. Religious Interest Groups* (Westport, Conn.: Greenwood Press, 1994).

33. George Gallup, Jr., *The Gallup Poll: Public Opinion 1992* (Wilmington, Del.: Scholarly Resources, Inc., 1993), pp. 207–208.

34. Ibid., p. 208.

35. Ibid., p. 118.

36. S. Robert Lichter, Lynda S. Lichter, and Stanley Rothman, *Prime Time: How TV Portrays American Culture* (Washington, D.C.: Regnery Publishing Inc., 1994), pp. 389–90.

37. Ibid., p. 391.

38. Ibid., pp. 392–93.

39. Ibid., p. 412–13.

40. *Fort Worth Star-Telegram*, December 11, 1994.

41. Ibid.

42. Quoted in ibid.

43. Ibid.

44. William A. Henry III, *In Defense of Elitism* (New York: Doubleday, 1994), p. 190.

45. Ibid.

46. Ibid.

47. Ibid., p. 189.

48. Robin W. Winks, "Why Clergymen Make Poor Murderers," *TV Guide*, May 2, 1987.

49. Timothy B. Benford and James T. Johnson, *Righteous Carnage: The List Murders* (New York: Scribners, 1991).

50. Martin A. Larson and C. Stanley Lowell, *The Religious Empire* (Washington, D.C.: Robert B. Luce Co., 1976).

51. Data provided to author on September 30, 1994 by Chief of Chaplains of the Air Force, Army, and Navy.

52. *The Catholic Health Care System and National Health Care Reform* (Washington, D.C.: Catholics for a Free Choice, 1994), p. 7.

53. Ibid., p. 10.

54. Ibid., p. 10.

55. Monika Maske, "Christian Living's the Goal," *Newark Star-Ledger*, October 29, 1995. See also Kent Somers, "Holy Goals," *Arizona Republic*, August 20, 1995.

56. Robert J. Higgs, *God in the Stadium: Sports and Religion in America* (Lexington: University Press of Kentucky, 1995), pp. 307–308.

57. Ibid., p. 287.

58. Michael D. Shear, "Bishop Urges Fair Hearing for Religious Views," *Washington Post*, October 3, 1994.

59. Ralph Reed, *Politically Incorrect: The Emerging Faith Factor in American Politics* (Dallas: Word Publishing, 1994), p. 43.

60. James L. Guth and John C. Green, *The Bible and the Ballot Box: Religion and Politics in the 1988 Election* (Boulder, Colo.: Westview Press), p. 212.

61. Michael Cromartie, *Disciples and Democracy: Religious Conservatives and the Future of American Politics* (Grand Rapids, Mich.: Eerdmans, 1994), p. 96.

62. Ibid., p. 97.

63. Ibid., p. 98.

64. Peter Wehner, "A Seduction of Christianity," *Washington Post*, April 21, 1996.

65. Ibid.

66. Ibid.

67. Larry J. Sabato and Glenn R. Simpson, *Dirty Little Secrets: The Persistence of Corruption in American Politics* (New York: Times Books, 1996), p. 128.

68. Ibid., p. 139.

69. Ibid., p. 132

70. Ibid., p. 134.

71. Ralph Reed, *Active Faith: How Christians are Changing the Soul of American Politics* (New York: The Free Press, 1996), p. 248.

72. E. J. Dionne, Jr., "Hijacked Faith," *Washington Post,* May 24, 1996.

73. Ibid.

74. Ibid.

75. Tanya Melich, *The Republican War Against Women* (New York: Bantam, 1996), p. 293.

76. Ibid., p. 300.

Selected Bibliography

Abramowitz, Alan. "It's Abortion, Stupid: Policy Voting in the 1992 Presidential Election." *Journal of Politics* 57 (1995): 176–86.

Adams, James L. *The Growing Church Lobby in Washington.* Grand Rapids: Eerdmans, 1970.

Adams, William C., and Paul H. Ferber. "Measuring Legislative-Constituency Congruence: Liquor, Legislation and Linkage." *Journal of Politics* 42 (February 1980): 202–208.

Allen, James P., and Eugene Turner. *We the People: An Atlas of America's Ethnic Diversity.* New York: Macmillan, 1988.

Allinsmith, Wesley, and Beverly Allinsmith. "Religious Affiliation and Politico-Economic Attitude." *Public Opinion Quarterly* 12 (Fall 1948): 377–89.

Alto, James. A. *The Politics of Righteousness: Idaho Christian Patriotism.* Seattle: University of Washington Press, 1990.

Ammerman, Nancy. *Bible Believers: Fundamentalists in the Modern World.* New Brunswick, N.J.: Rutgers University Press, 1987.

———. *Baptist Battles.* New Brunswick, N.J.: Rutgers University Press, 1990.

———. *Southern Baptists Observed.* Knoxville: University of Tennessee Press, 1993.

Anderson, Donald. "Ascetic Protestantism and Political Preference." *Review of Religious Research* 7 (1966): 167–71.

Anderson, Jon W., and William B. Friend, eds. *The Culture of Bible Belt Catholics.* New York: Paulist Press, 1995.

Baggaley, Andrew R. "Religious Influence on Wisconsin Voting, 1928–1960." *American Political Science Review* 56 (March 1962): 66–70.

Baird, Robert. *Religion in the United States of America.* Religion in America, Ser. 1. New York: Ayer, 1969. Reprint of 1844 ed.

Baker, Robert. *The Southern Baptist Convention and Its People, 1607–1972.* Nashville: Broadman, 1974.

Baker, Ross K., Laurily K. Epstein, and Rodney D. Furth. "Matters of Life and Death: Social, Political, and Religious Correlates of Attitudes on Abortion." *American Politics Quarterly* 9 (1981): 89–102.

Baker, Tod A., Robert B. Steed, and Laurence W. Moreland, eds. *Religion and Politics in the South.* New York: Praeger, 1983.

Ball, William Bentley, ed. *In Search of a National Morality: A Manifesto for Evangelicals and Catholics.* Grand Rapids: Baker Book House, 1993.

Balmer, Randall. *Mine Eyes Have Seen the Glory.* New York: Oxford University Press, 1989.

Balz, Dan, and Ronald Brownstein. *Storming the Gates: Protest Politics and the Republican Revival.* Boston: Little, Brown, 1996.

Barkun, Michael. *Religion and the Racist Right: The Origins of the Christian Identity Movement.* Chapel Hill: University of North Carolina Press, 1994.

Barna, George. *What Americans Believe: The Barna Report.* Ventura, Calif.: Regal Books, 1991.

———. *The Barna Report 1992–1993.* Ventura, Calif.: Regal Books, 1992.

———. *Absolute Confusion: The Barna Report 1993–1994.* Ventura, Calif.: Regal Books, 1993.

———. *Virtual America: The Barna Report 1994–1995.* Ventura, Calif.: Regal Books, 1994.

Barnhart, Joe Edward. *The Southern Baptist Holy War.* Austin, Tex.: Texas Monthly Press, 1986.

Barone, Michael, and Grant Ujifosa. *The Almanac of American Politics, 1996.* Washington, D.C.: National Journal, 1995.

Bates, Stephen. *Battleground: One Mother's Crusade, the Religious Right, and Struggle for Our Schools.* New York: Henry Holt, 1993.

Bauer, Gary L. *Our Hopes and Dreams: A Vision for America.* Colorado Springs: Focus on the Family, 1996.

Beatty, Kathleen, and Oliver Walter. "Religious Preference and Practice: Reevaluating their Impact on Political Tolerance." *Public Opinion Quarterly* 48 (1984): 318–29.

———. "Fundamentalists, Evangelicals and Politics." *American Politics Quarterly* 16 (1988): 43–59.

Bennett, David H. *The Party of Fear.* New York: Vintage Books, 1995.

Bennett, William J. *The Index of Leading Cultural Indicators.* New York: Touchstone, 1994.

Benson, Peter L., and Dorothy L. Williams. *Religion on Capitol Hill.* San Francisco: Harper & Row, 1982.

Berlet, Chip, and Matthew N. Lyons. *Too Close for Comfort.* Boston: South End Press, 1995.

Birdwhistell, Ira V. "Southern Baptist Perceptions of and Responses to Roman Catholicism, 1917–1972." Ph.D. diss., Southern Baptist Theological Seminary, 1975.

Birtel, Frank T., ed. *Religion, Science and Public Policy.* New York: Crossroad, 1987.

Black, Earl, and Merle Black. *Politics and Society in the South.* Cambridge: Harvard University Press, 1987.

Blanchard, Dallas, and Terry J. Prewitt. *Religious Violence and Abortion.* Gainesville: University Press of Florida, 1993.

Blumhofer, Edith L. *Restoring the Faith: The Assemblies of God, Pentecostalism and American Culture.* Urbana: University of Illinois Press, 1993.

Bochel, J. M., and D. T. Denver. "Religion and Voting." *Political Studies* 18 (1970): 205–19.

Boles, John G., and Charles R. Wilson, eds. *Religion in the South.* Jackson: University Press of Mississippi, 1985.

Boone, Kathleen C. *The Bible Tells Them So: The Discourse of Protestant Fundamentalists.* Albany: SUNY Press, 1989.

Bradley, Martin, et al. *Churches and Church Membership in the United States, 1990.* Atlanta: Glenmary Research Center, 1992.

Brady, David W., and Kent L. Tedin. "Ladies in Pink: Religious and Political Ideology in the Anti-ERA Movement." *Social Science Quarterly* 56 (1976): 564–75.

Brewer, Earl D. C. *The Southern Appalachian Region.* Lexington: University Press of Kentucky, 1962.

Bridges, Tyler. *The Rise of David Duke.* Jackson: University Press of Mississippi, 1994.

Bromley, David G. *Falling from the Faith.* Newbury Park, Calif.: Sage Publications, 1988.

Bromley, David and Anson Shupe, eds. *New Christian Politics.* Macon, Ga.: Mercer University Press, 1984.

Bruce, Steve. *The Rise and Fall of the New Christian Right.* New York: Oxford University Press, 1988.

———. "The Inevitable Failure of the New Christian Right." *Sociology of Religion* 85 (1994): 229–42.

Bruce, Steve, et al., eds. *The Rapture of Politics: The Christian Right as the United States Approaches the Year 2000.* New Brunswick, N.J.: Transaction, 1995.

Brudney, Jeffrey, and Gary W. Copeland. "Evangelicals as a Political Force: Reagan and the 1980 Religious Vote." *Social Science Quarterly* 65 (December 1984): 1072–80.

Buell, Emmett H., and Lee Sigelman. "An Army That Meets Every Sunday? Popular Support for the Moral Majority in 1980." *Social Science Quarterly* 66 (June 1985): 427–34.

———. "A Second Look at Popular Support for the Moral Majority in 1980." *Social Science Quarterly* 68 (1987): 167–69.

Bull, Malcolm. "The Seventh-day Adventists: Heretics of American Civil Religion." *Sociological Analysis* 50 (1989): 177–87.

Bull, Malcolm, and Keith Lockhart. *Seeking Sanctuary: Seventh-day Adventism and the American Dream.* San Francisco: Harper & Row, 1989.

Burner, David. *The Politics of Provincialism: The Democratic Party in Transition, 1918–1932.* New York: Norton, 1967.

Burnham, Walter Dean. *Critical Elections and the Mainspring of American Politics.* New York: Norton, 1970.

Byrnes, Timothy. *Catholic Bishops and American Politics.* Princeton: Princeton University Press, 1991.

Byrnes, Timothy, and Mary C. Segels, eds. *The Catholic Church and the Politics of Abortion.* Boulder, Colo.: Westview, 1992.

Capps, Walter H. *The New Religious Right.* Columbia: University of South Carolina Press, 1990.

Carter, Paul A. *The Decline and Revival of the Social Gospel: Social and Political Liberalism in American Protestant Churches, 1920–1940.* Ithaca: Cornell University Press, 1954.

Carter, Stephen L. *The Culture of Disbelief.* New York: Basic Books, 1993.

Castelli, Jim. *A Plea for Common Sense: Resolving the Clash Between Religion and Politics.* San Francisco: Harper & Row, 1988.

Cavanaugh, Michael A. "Secularization and the Politics of Traditionalism." *Sociological Forum* 1 (1986): 251–83.

Chalfont, H. Paul, and Charles W. Peek. "Religious Affiliation, Religiosity, and Racial Prejudice." *Review of Religious Research* 25 (1983): 155–61.

Chidesper, David. *Patterns of Power: Religion and Politics in American Culture.* Englewood Cliffs, N.Y.: Prentice-Hall, 1988.

Christian Coalition. *Contract with the American Family.* Nashville: Moorings, 1995.

Clabaugh, Gary K. *Thunder on the Right: The Protestant Fundamentalists.* Chicago: Nelson-Hall, 1974.

Clarkson, Frederick, and Skipp Porteous. *Challenging the Christian Right.* Great Barrington, Mass.: Institute for First Amendment Studies, 1993.

Cohen, Stephen M., and Robert E. Kapsis. "Religion, Ethnicity and Party Affiliation in the United States." *Social Forces* 56 (1977): 637–53.

Colombo, Furio. *God in America: Religion and Politics in the United States.* New York: Columbia University Press, 1985.

Conover, Pamela Johnston, and Virginia Gray. *Feminism and the New Right: Conflict over the Family.* New York: Praeger, 1983.

Cook, Elizabeth Adell, Ted G. Jelen, and Clyde Wilcox. *Between Two Absolutes: Public Opinion and the Politics of Abortion.* Boulder, Colo.: Westview Press, 1992.

———. "Issue Voting in Gubernatorial Elections: Abortion and Post-Webster Politics." *Journal of Politics* 56 (1994): 187–99.

Corbett, Michael. *Political Tolerance in America.* New York: Longman, 1982.

Cox, Harvey. *Fire From Heaven.* Reading, Mass.: Addison-Wesley, 1995.

Crawford, Alan. *Thunder on the Right.* New York: Pantheon, 1980.

Crespi, Irving. "The Structural Base for Right-Wing Conservatism: The Goldwater Case." *Public Opinion Quarterly* 29 (1965): 523–43.

———. "Structural Sources of the George Wallace Constituency." *Social Science Quarterly* 52 (1971): 115–32.

Cromartie, Michael, ed. *No Longer Exiles: The Religious New Right in American Politics*. Washington, D.C.: Ethics and Public Policy Center, 1992.

———. *Disciples and Democracy: Religious Conservatives and the Future of American Politics*. Grand Rapids: Eerdmans, 1994.

Cummings, Scott, et al. "Preachers vs Teachers." *Rural Sociology* 42 (1977): 7–21.

Curry, Dean C., ed. *Evangelicals and the Bishops' Pastoral Letter*. Grand Rapids: Eerdmans, 1984.

Damaske, Frederick Hans. "Sects and Politics: The Political Attitudes and Behavior of Conservative-Evangelical and Neo-Fundamentalist Protestants." Ph.D. diss., University of Minnesota, 1970.

D'Antonio, William, et al. *American Catholic Laity in a Changing World*. Kansas City: Sheed and Ward, 1989.

Danzig, David. "The Radical Right and the Rise of the Fundamentalist Minority." *Commentary* 33 (1962): 291–98.

Davis, James A., and Tom W. Smith. *The General Social Surveys: Cumulative Codebook 1972–1990*. Chicago: NORC, 1990.

Dawidowicz, Lucy S., and Leon J. Goldstein. *Politics in a Pluralist Democracy: Studies of Voting in the 1960 Election*. New York: Institute of Human Relations Press, 1963.

DeJong, Gordon F., and Thomas R. Ford. "Religious Fundamentalism and Denominational Preference in the Southern Appalachian Region." *Journal for the Scientific Study of Religion* 5 (1965): 24–33.

Diamond, Sara. *Roads to Dominion: Right-wing Movements and Political Power in the United States*. New York: Guilford, 1995.

Dobson, Ed, and Ed Hindson, eds. *The Fundamentalist Phenomenon*. New York: Doubleday, 1981.

Dobson, James C., and Gary L. Bauer. *Children at Risk*. Dallas: Word, 1990; revised, 1994.

Donough, C. Dwight. *The Bible Belt Mystique*. Philadelphia: Westminster, 1974.

Donovan, John B. *Pat Robertson*. New York: Macmillan, 1988.

Driedger, Leo. "Doctrinal Belief: A Major Factor in the Differential Perception of Social Issues." *Sociological Quarterly* 15 (1974): 66–80.

Dudley, Roger L., and Edwin I. Hernandez. *Citizens of Two Worlds: Religion and Politics Among Seventh-day Adventists*. Berrien Springs, Mich.: Andrews University Press, 1992.

Duke, James T., and Barry L. Johnson. "Religious Affiliation and Congressional Representation." *Journal for the Scientific Study of Religion* 31 (1992): 324–29.

Duncan, Philip D., and Christine C. Lawrence. *Politics in America 1996*. Washington, D.C.: Congressional Quarterly, 1995.

Dunn, Charles W., ed. *American Political Theology*. New York: Praeger, 1984.

———. *Religion in American Politics*. Washington, D.C.: Congressional Quarterly, 1989.

Eberly, Don E. *Restoring the Good Society: A New Vision for Politics and Culture*. Grand Rapids: Baker Books, 1994.

Ebersole, Luke. *Church Lobbying in the Nation's Capitol.* New York: Macmillan, 1951.

——. "Religion and Politics." *Annals of the American Academy of Political and Social Science* 332 (November 1960): 101–11.

Eccles, Mary Eisner. "Abortion: How Members Voted in 1977." *CQ Weekly Report* 36 (February 4, 1978): 258–67.

Eckberg, Douglas L., and Alexander Nesterenko. "For and Against Evolution: Religion, Social Class, and the Symbolic Universe." *Social Science Journal* 22 (1985): 1–17.

Eighmy, John Lee. *Churches in Cultural Captivity: A History of the Social Attitudes of Southern Baptists.* Knoxville: University of Tennessee Press, 1987.

Ellison, Christopher G., and Darren E. Sherkat. "Conservative Protestantism and Support for Corporal Punishment." *American Sociological Review* 58 (1993): 131–44.

Ellison, Christopher G., and Marc A. Musick. "Southern Intolerance: A Fundamentalist Effect?" *Social Forces* 72 (1993): 379–98.

Fackre, Gabriel. *The Religious Right and Christian Faith.* Grand Rapids: Eerdmans, 1982.

Fairbanks, David. "Religious Forces and Morality Politics in the American States." *Western Political Quarterly* 30 (September 1977): 411–17.

——. "Politics, Economics, and the Public Morality: Why Some States are More 'Moral' than Others." *Policy Studies Journal* 7 (1979): 714–20.

Fenton, John H. *The Catholic Vote.* New Orleans: Hauser Press, 1960

——. "Liberal-Conservative Divisions by Sections of the United States." *Annals of the American Academy of Political and Social Science* 344 (November 1962): 122–27.

Fimian, Charles. "The Effects of Religion on Abortion Policy-making: A Study of Voting Behavior in the U.S. Congress, 1976–1980." Ph.D. diss., Arizona State University, 1984.

Finamore, Frank, and James M. Carlson. "Religiosity, Belief in a Just World and Crime Control Attitudes." *Psychological Reports* 61 (1987): 135–38.

Findlay, James. "Religion and Politics in the Sixties: The Churches and the Civil Rights Act of 1964." *Journal of American History* 77 (1990): 66–92.

Finke, Roger, and Rodney Stark. *The Churching of America, 1776–1990.* New Brunswick, N.J.: Rutgers University Press, 1992.

Flake, Carol. *Redemptorama: Culture, Politics and the New Evangelicalism.* New York: Doubleday, 1984.

Ford, Thomas R. "Religious Thought and Beliefs in the Southern Applachians." *Review of Religious Research* 3 (1961): 2–21.

Fowler, Robert Booth. *A New Engagement: Evangelical Political Thought, 1966–1976.* Grand Rapids: Eerdmans, 1982.

——. "The Feminist and Antifeminist Debate within Evangelical Protestantism." *Women and Politics* 5 (1985): 7–39.

Fowler, Robert Booth. *Religion and Politics in America.* Metuchen, N.J.: Scarecrow Press, 1985.

Fowler, Robert Booth, and Allen D. Hertzke. *Religion and Politics in America.* Boulder, Colo.: Westview, 1996.

Freeman, Donald M. "Religion and Southern Politics: A Study of the Political Behavior of Southern White Protestants." Ph.D. diss., University of North Carolina, 1962.

Freeman, Jo. "The Political Culture of Democrats and Republicans." *Political Science Quarterly* 101 (1986): 327–44.

Fuchs, Lawrence B. *John F. Kennedy and American Catholicism.* New York: Meredith, 1967.

Gallup, George, Jr., and Jim Castelli. *The American Catholic People.* New York: Doubleday, 1987.

———. *The People's Religion: American Faith in the '90s.* New York: Macmillan, 1989.

Gaustad, Edwin Scott. *Historical Atlas of Religion in America.* New York: Harper & Row, 1962.

Georgiana, Sharon Linzey. *The Moral Majority and Fundamentalism.* Lewiston, N.Y.: Edwin Mellen Press, 1989.

Gilbert, Christopher P. *The Impact of Churches on Political Behavior.* Westport, Conn: Greenwood Press, 1993.

Glantz, Oscar. "Protestant and Catholic Voting Behavior in a Metropolitan Area." *Public Opinion Quarterly* 23 (Spring 1959): 78–82.

Gold, David. "The Influence of Religious Affiliation on Voting Behavior." Ph.D. diss., University of Chicago, 1953.

Gorsuch, Richard L., and Daniel Aleshire. "Christian Faith and Ethnic Prejudice: A Review and Interpretation of Research." *Journal for the Scientific Study of Religion* 13 (1974): 281–307.

Granberg, Donald N., and James Burlison. "The Abortion Issue in the 1980 Elections." *Family Planning Perspectives* 15 (1983): 231–38.

Grasmick, Harold G. "Rural Culture and the Wallace Movement in the South." *Rural Sociology* 39 (1974): 454–70.

Grasmick, Harold G., et al. "Protestant Fundamentalism and the Retributive Doctrine of Punishment." *Criminology* 30 (1992): 21–45.

Greeley, Andrew M. "How Conservative are American Catholics?" *Political Science Quarterly* 92 (1977): 199–218.

———. *Religion: A Secular Theory.* New York: Free Press, 1982.

———. *American Catholics Since the Council.* Chicago: Thomas More Press, 1985.

———. *Religious Change in America.* Cambridge, Mass.: Harvard University Press, 1989.

———. *The Catholic Myth: The Behavior and Beliefs of American Catholics.* New York: St.Martin's, 1990.

———. "Religion and Attitudes Toward AIDS Policy." *Sociology and Social Research* 75 (1991): 126–32.

Greeley, Andrew M. "Religion and Attitudes Toward the Environment." *Journal for the Scientific Study of Religion* 32 (1993): 19–28.

Green, John C., and James L. Guth. "The Christian Right in the Republican Party: The Case of Pat Robertson's Supporters." *Journal of Politics* 50 (1988): 150–65.

———. "Politics in a New Key: Religiosity and Participation Among Political Activists." *Western Political Quarterly* 43 (1990): 153–79.

Green, John C., James L. Guth, and Kevin Hill. "Faith and Election: The Christian Right in Congressional Campaigns 1978–1988." *Journal of Politics* 55 (1993): 80–91.

Green, John C., James L. Guth, Lyman A. Kellstedt, and Corwin E. Smidt. "Uncivil Challenges: Support for Civil Liberties among Religious Activists." *Journal of Political Science* 22 (1994): 25–50.

Greenberg, Stanley B. *Middle Class Dreams.* New York: Times Books, 1995.

Greenwalt, Ken. *Religious Convictions and Political Choice.* New York: Oxford University Press, 1988.

Greer, Scott. "Catholic Voters and the Democratic Party." *Public Opinion Quarterly* 25 (Winter 1961): 611–25.

Gusfield, Joseph. *Symbolic Crusade: Status Politics and the American Temperance Movement.* Urbana: University of Illinois Press, 1963.

Guth, James L., and John C. Green. "Faith and Politics: Religion and Ideology Among Political Contributors." *American Politics Quarterly* 14 (1986): 186–99.

———. "The Moralizing Minority: Christian Right Support Among Political Contributors." *Social Science Quarterly* 67 (1987): 598–610.

———. "Politics in a New Key: Religiosity and Participation Among Political Activists." *Western Political Quarterly* 43 (1990): 153–79.

———. *The Bible and the Ballot Box: Religion and Politics in the 1988 Election.* Boulder, Colo.: Westview Press, 1991.

Hadaway, C. Kirk. "Identifying American Apostates." *Journal for the Scientific Study of Religion* 28 (1989): 201–15.

Hadaway, C. Kirk and Penny Long Marler. "All in the Family: Religious Mobility in America." *Review of Religious Research* 35 (December 1993): 97–116.

Hadden, Jeffrey K., and Anson Shupe. *Televangelism: Power and Politics on God's Frontier.* New York: Henry Holt, 1988.

Hadden, Jeffrey K., and Anson Shupe, eds. *Prophetic Religion and Politics.* New York: Paragon House, 1986.

Hammond, John L. *The Politics of Benevolence: Revival Religion and American Voting Behavior.* Norwood, N.J.: Ablex, 1979.

Hanna, Mary T. *Catholics and American Politics.* Cambridge: Harvard University Press, 1979.

Harper, Charles L., and Kevin Leicht. "Religious Awakenings and Status Politics: Sources of Support for the New Christian Right." *Sociological Analysis* 45 (1984): 339–54.

Harrell, David E. *Pat Robertson: A Personal, Religious and Political Portrait.* San Francisco: Harper & Row, 1988.

Hendricks, John S. "Religious and Political Fundamentalism." Ph.D. diss., University of Michigan, 1977.

Henriot, Peter. "The Coincidence of Political and Religious Attitudes." *Review of Religious Research* 8 (1966): 50–58.

Hertzke, Allen D. *Representing God in Washington.* Knoxville: University of Tennessee Press, 1988.

Hill, Samuel S. "Religion and Region in America." *Annals* 480 (1985): 132–41.

Hill, Samuel S., ed. *"Religion and the Solid South.* Nashville: Abingdon, 1972.

———. *Religion in the Southern States.* Macon, Ga.: Mercer University Press, 1983.

Hill, Samuel S., and Dennis E. Owen. *The New Religious Political Right in America.* Nashville: Abingdon, 1982.

Himmelstein, Jerome L. *To the Right: The Transformation of American Conservatism.* Berkeley, Calif.: University of California Press, 1990.

Himmelstein, Jerome L., and James A. McRae, Jr. "Social Conservatism, New Republicans and the 1980 Election." *Public Opinion Quarterly* 48 (1984): 592–605.

Hixson, William B., Jr. *Search for the American Right Wing.* Princeton, N.J.: Princeton University Press, 1992.

Hobson, Fred. C., Jr. *Serpent in Eden: H. L. Mencken and the South.* Chapel Hill: University of North Carolina Press, 1974.

Hoffman, Thomas J. "Religion and Politics." Ph.D. diss., University of Arizona, 1982.

Houghland, J. G., and J. A. Christenson. "Religion and Politics: The Relationship of Religious Participation to Political Efficacy and Involvement." *Sociology and Social Research* 67 (1983): 405–20.

Hunter, James D. *American Evangelicalism.* New Brunswick, N.J.: Rutgers University Press, 1983.

———. "Religion and Political Civility: The Coming Generation of American Evangelicals." *Journal for the Scientific Study of Religion* 23 (1984): 364–85.

———. "The Williamsburg Charter Survey." *Journal of Law and Religion* 8 (1990): 257–72.

———. *Evangelicalism: The Coming Generation.* Chicago: University of Chicago Press, 1987.

———. *Culture Wars.* New York: Basic Books, 1991.

Hutcheson, John D., and George A. Taylor. "Religious Variables, Political System Characteristics, and Policy Outputs in the American States." *American Journal of Political Science* 17 (1973): 414–21.

Jaffe, Frederick S., Barbara L. Lindheim, and Philip R. Lee. *Abortion Politics: Private Morality and Public Policy.* New York: McGraw-Hill, 1981.

Jeansonne, Glen. *Gerald L. K. Smith: Minister of Hate.* New Haven: Yale University Press, 1988.

Jelen, Ted. G. *The Political Mobilization of Religious Beliefs.* New York: Praeger, 1991.

Jelen, Ted. G. "The Political Consequences of Religious Group Attitudes." *Journal of Politics* 55 (1993): 178–90.

Jelen, Ted. G., ed. *Religion and Political Behavior in the United States.* New York: Praeger, 1989.

Jensen, Richard. *The Winning of the Midwest: Social and Political Conflict, 1888–1896.* Chicago: University of Chicago Press, 1971.

Johnson, Benton. "Ascetic Protestantism and Political Preference." *Public Opinion Quarterly* 26 (1962): 35–46.

———. "Ascetic Protestantism and Political Preference in the Deep South." *American Journal of Sociology* 69 (January 1964): 359–66.

Johnson, Douglas, et al. *Churches and Church Membership in the United States, 1971.* Washington, D.C.: Glenmary Research Center, 1974.

Johnson, Michael. "The New Christian Right in American Politics." *Political Science Quarterly* 53 (1982): 180–89.

Johnson, Stephen D., and Joseph B. Tamney. "The Impact of the Christian Right on the 1984 Presidential Election." *Review of Religious Research* 27 (1985): 124–33.

———. "Pat Robertson: Who Supported His Candidacy for President?" *Journal for the Scientific Study of Religion* 28 (1989): 387–99.

Johnson, Stephen D., and Joseph B. Tamney, eds. *The Political Role of Religion in the United States.* Boulder, Colo.: Westview Press, 1986.

Jorstad, Erling. *The Politics of Doomsday.* Nashville: Abingdon, 1970.

———. *Evangelicals in the White House: The Cultural Maturation of Born Again Christianity, 1960–1981.* New York: Edwin Mellen Press, 1981.

———. *The Politics of Moralism.* Minneapolis: Augsburg, 1981.

———. *Holding Fast, Pressing On.* New York: Praeger, 1990.

———. *Popular Religion in America.* Westport, Conn.: Greenwood, 1993.

Kelley, Dean M. *Why Conservative Churches are Growing.* New York: Harper & Row, 1972.

Kelley, Robert. *The Cultural Pattern in American Politics.* New York: Knopf, 1979.

Kellstedt, Lyman A., John C. Green, James L. Guth, and Corwin E. Smidt. "Religious Voting Blocs in the 1992 Election: The Year of the Evangelical?" *Sociology of Religion* 55 (1994): 307–26.

Kenski, Henry C. "The Catholic Voter in American Elections." *Election Politics* 5 (1988): 16–23.

Kersten, Lawrence K. *The Lutheran Ethic.* Detroit: Wayne State University Press, 1970.

Kiecolt, K. Jill, and Hart M. Nelsen. "The Structuring of Political Attitudes Among Liberal and Conservative Protestants." *Journal for the Scientific Study of Religion* 27 (1988): 48–59.

Killan, Lewis. *White Southerners.* New York: Random House, 1970.

Kleppner, Paul. *The Cross of Culture: A Social Analysis of Midwestern Politics, 1850–1900.* New York: The Free Press, 1970.

Kleppner, Paul. *The Third Electoral System, 1853–1892*. Chapel Hill: University of North Carolina Press, 1979.

Kluegel, James. "Denominational Mobility." *Journal for the Scientific Study of Religion* 19 (1980): 126–39.

Knoke, David. "Religious Involvement and Political Behavior." *Sociological Quarterly* 15 (1974): 51–65.

Kosmin, Barry A., and Seymour P. Lachman. *One Nation Under God: Religion in Contemporary American Society*. New York: Harmony Books, 1993.

Kraybill, Donald B. *The Riddle of Amish Culture*. Baltimore: Johns Hopkins University Press, 1989.

Krinksy, Fred. *The Politics of Religion in America*. Beverly Hills: Glencoe Press, 1968.

Lachman, Seymour P. "Barry Goldwater and the 1964 Religious Issue." *Journal of Church and State* 10 (Autumn 1968): 389–404.

Leege, David C., and Lyman A. Kellstedt, eds. *Rediscovering the Religious Factor in American Politics*. Armonk, N.Y.: M. E. Sharpe, 1993.

Lenski, Gerhard. *The Religious Factor*. New York: Doubleday, 1963.

Leonard, Bill J. *God's Last and Only Hope: The Fragmentation of the Southern Baptist Convention*. Grand Rapids: Eerdmans, 1990.

Leyburn, James G. *The Scotch-Irish: A Social History*. Chapel Hill: University of North Carolina Press, 1962.

Lichtman, Allan J. *Prejudice and the Old Politics: The Presidential Election of 1928*. Chapel Hill: University of North Carolina Press, 1979.

Liebman, Robert, and Robert Wuthnow, eds. *The New Christian Right*. New York: Aldine, 1983.

Lienesch, Michael. "Right-wing Religion: Christian Conservatism as a Political Movement." *Political Science Quarterly* 97 (Fall 1982): 403–25.

———. "The Paradoxical Politics of the Religious Right." *Soundings* 66 (Spring 1983): 70–99.

———. *Redeeming America: Piety and Politics in the New Christian Right*. Chapel Hill: University of North Carolina Press, 1993.

Lipset, Seymour Martin, ed. *Party Coalitions in the 1980s*. San Francisco: Institute for Contemporary Studies, 1981.

Lipset, Seymour Martin, and Earl Raab. *The Politics of Unreason: Right Wing Extremism in America, 1790–1977*. Chicago: University of Chicago Press, 1978.

———. "The Election and the Evangelicals." *Commentary* 71 (March 1981): 25–31.

Lotz, David W., ed. *Altered Landscape: Christianity in America 1935–1985*. Grand Rapids, Mich.: Eerdmans, 1989.

Macaluso, Theodore F., and John Wanat. "Voting Turnout and Religiosity." *Polity* 12 (1979): 158–69.

Maguire, Daniel C. *The New Subversives: Anti-Americanism of the Religious Right*. New York: Continuum, 1982.

Mansbridge, Jane J. *Why We Lost the ERA*. Chicago: University of Chicago Press, 1986.

Margolis, Michael, and Kevin Neary. "Pressure Politics Revisited: The Anti-Abortion Campaign." *Policy Studies Journal* 8 (Spring 1980): 698–716.

Marsden, George. *Fundamentalism and American Culture*. New York: Oxford University Press, 1980.

———. *Understanding Fundamentalism and Evangelicalism*. Grand Rapids: Eerdmans, 1991.

Marsden, George, ed. *Evangelicalism and Modern America*. Grand Rapids: Eerdmans, 1984.

Marty, Martin E. "Fundamentalism Redux: Faith and Fanaticism." *Saturday Review* (May 1980): 37–42.

———. "Never the Same Again: Post-Vatican II Catholic-Protestant Interactions." *Sociological Analysis* 52 (1991): 13–26.

McClosky, Herbert and Alida Brill. *Dimensions of Tolerance: What Americans Believe about Civil Liberty*. New York: Russell Sage, 1983.

McIntosh, William Alex, Letitia T. Alston, and Jon P. Alston. "The Differential Impact of Religious Preference and Church Attendance on Attitudes Toward Abortion." *Review of Religious Research* 20 (1979): 195–213.

Meinig, D. W. "The Mormon Culture Region." *Annals of the Association of American Geographers* 55 (1960): 191–220.

Melady, Thomas Patrick, ed. *Catholics in the Public Square*. Huntington, Ind.: Our Sunday Visitor, 1995.

Melich, Tanya. *The Republican War Against Women*. New York: Bantam, 1996.

Menendez, Albert J. *Religion at the Polls*. Philadelphia: Westminster Press, 1977.

———. *John F. Kennedy: Catholic and Humanist*. Amherst, N.Y.: Prometheus Books, 1979.

———. *Visions of Reality: What Fundamentalist Schools Teach*. Amherst, N.Y.: Prometheus Books, 1993.

Merton, Andrew H. *Enemies of Choice*. Boston: Beacon Press, 1981.

Meyer, Donald B. *The Protestant Search for Political Realism 1919–1941*. Berkeley: University of California Press, 1960.

Miller, Arthur H., and Martin P. Wattenberg. "Politics from the Pulpit: Religiosity and the 1980 Elections." *Public Opinion Quarterly* 48 (1984): 301–17.

Miller, Robert Moats. *American Protestantism and Social Issues 1919–1939*. Chapel Hill: University of North Carolina Press, 1958.

Moen, Matthew C. "School Prayer and the Politics of Lifestyle Concern." *Social Science Quarterly* (December 1984): 1065–71.

———. *The Christian Right and Congress*. Tuscaloosa: University of Alabama Press, 1989.

———. *The Transformation of the Christian Right*. Tuscaloosa: University of Alabama Press, 1992.

———. "From Revolution to Evolution: The Changing Nature of the Christian Right." *Sociology of Religion* 55 (1994): 345–57.

Montgomery, Kathryn C. *Target: Prime Times*. New York: Oxford University Press, 1989.

Moore, Edmund A. *A Catholic Runs for President*. New York: Ronald, 1956.

Morgan, David R., and Kenneth J. Meier. "Politics and Morality: The Effect of Religion on Referenda Voting." *Social Science Quarterly* 61 (1980): 144–48.

Moseley, James G. *A Cultural History of Religion in America*. Westport, Conn.: Greenwood Press, 1981.

Mueller, Carol. "In Search of a Constituency for the New Religious Right." *Public Opinion Quarterly* 47 (1983): 213–29.

Mueller, Carol, and Thomas Dimieri. "The Structure of Belief Systems Among Contending ERA Activists." *Social Forces* 60 (1982): 657–75.

Nelson, Michael. *The Election of 1992*. Washington, D.C.: Congressional Quarterly, 1993.

Nesmith, Bruce. *The New Republican Coalition: The Reagan Campaigns and White Evangelicals*. New York: Peter Lang, 1994.

Neuhaus, Richard John. *The Naked Public Square: Religion and Democracy in America*. Grand Rapids: Eerdmans, 1984.

———. *The Catholic Moment*. San Francisco: Harper & Row, 1987.

Neuhaus, Richard John, and Michael Cromartie, eds. *Piety and Politics: Evangelicals and Fundamentalists Confront the World*. Washington, D.C.: Ethics and Public Policy Center, 1987.

Newman, William M., and Peter L. Halvorson. "Religion and Regional Culture." *Journal for the Scientific Study of Religion* 23 (1984): 304–15.

Newport, Frank. "The Religious Switcher in the United States." *American Sociological Review* 44 (1979): 528–55.

Niebuhr, H. Richard. *The Social Sources of Denominationalism*. New York: Holt, 1929.

Noll, Mark. *The Scandal of the Evangelical Mind*. Grand Rapids: Eerdmans, 1994.

Noll, Mark A., ed. *Religion and American Politics*. New York: Oxford University Press, 1990.

Noll, Mark A., Nathan O. Hatch, and George M. Marsden. *The Search for Christian America*. Westchester, Ill.: Crossway Books, 1983.

Nordin, Virginia Davis, and William Lloyd Turner. "More Than Segregation Academies: The Growing Protestant Fundamentalist Schools." *Phi Delta Kappan* 61 (1980): 391–94.

Nunn, Clyde A., Harry J. Crockett, and J. Allen Williams. *Tolerance for Nonconformity*. San Francisco: Jossey-Bass, 1978.

Odegard, Peter H., ed. *Religion and Politics*. New Brunswick, N.J.: Rutgers University Press, 1960.

O'Donnell, John P. "Predicting Tolerance of New Religious Movements." *Journal for the Scientific Study of Religion* 32 (1993): 356–65.

Oldfield, Duane. "The Right and the Righteous: The Christian Right Confronts the Republican Party." Ph.D. diss. University of California, 1992.

Olson, Daniel, and Jackson W. Carroll. "Religiously-Based Politics: Religious Elites and the Public." *Social Forces* 70 (1992): 765–86.

Olson, John Kevin, and Ann C. Beck. "Religion and Political Realignment in the Rocky Mountain States." *Journal for the Scientific Study of Religion* 29 (1990): 198–209.

Ornstein, Norman, Andrew Kohut, and Larry McCarthy. *The People, The Press and Politics: The Times Mirror Study of the American Electorate*. Reading, Mass.: Addison-Wesley, 1988.

Orum, Anthony M. "Religion and the Rise of the Radical Right: The Case of Southern Wallace Support in 1968." *Social Science Quarterly* 51 (1970): 674–88.

Page, Ann, and Donald Clelland. "The Kanawha County Textbook Controversy: A Study of the Politics of Life Style Concerns." *Social Forces* 57 (September 1978): 265–81.

Paige, Connie. *The Right-to-Lifers*. New York: Summit, 1983.

Parenti, Michael. "Political Values and Religious Cultures: Jews, Catholics and Protestants." *Journal for the Scientific Study of Religion* 6 (1967): 259–69.

Patel, Karl, Denny Pilant, and Gary Rose. "Christian Conservatism: A Study in Alienation and Lifestyle Concerns." *Journal of Political Science* 12 (1985): 17–30.

———. "Born Again Christians in the Bible Belt." *American Politics Quarterly* 10 (1982): 255–72.

Penning, James M. "Pat Robertson and the GOP: 1988 and Beyond." *Sociology of Religion* 55 (Fall 1994) 327–44.

Persinos, John F. "Has the Christian Right Taken Over the Republican Party?" *Campaign and Elections* 15 (September 1994): 20–24.

Phillips, Kevin. *The Emerging Republican Majority*. New Rochelle, N.Y.: Arlington House, 1969.

Photiadis, John D., ed. *Religion in Appalachia*. Morgantown: West Virginia University, 1978.

Pierard, Richard V. *The Unequal Yoke: Evangelicals and Political Conservatism*. Philadelphia: Lippincott, 1970.

———. "Reagan and the Evangelicals: The Making of a Love Affair." *Christian Century* 100 (1983): 1182–85.

Poloma, Margaret M. *The Assemblies of God at the Crossroads*. Knoxville: University of Tennessee Press, 1989.

Queen, Edward L. *In the South the Baptists Are the Center of Gravity*. Brooklyn: Carlson, 1991.

Quinn, Bernard, et al. *Churches and Church Membership in the United States, 1980*. Washington, D.C.: Glenmary Research Center, 1982.

Quinney, Richard. "Political Conservatism, Alienation and Fatalism: Contingencies of Social Status and Religious Fundamentalism." *Sociometry* 27 (1964): 372–81.

Rasey, Douglas, ed. *The Emergence of David Duke and the Politics of Race*. Chapel Hill: University of North Carolina Press, 1992.

Reed, John Shelton. *One South: An Ethnic Approach to Regional Culture*. Baton Rouge: Louisiana State University Press, 1982.

——. *The Enduring South*. Chapel Hill: University of North Carolina Press, 1986.

Reed, Ralph. *Politically Incorrect: The Emerging Faith Factor in American Politics*. Dallas: Word, 1994.

Reichley, A. James. "Religion and Political Realignment." *Brookings Review* (Fall 1984): 30–36.

——. *Religion in American Public Life*. Washington, D.C.: Brookings Institution, 1985.

——. "Religion and the Future of American Politics." *Political Science Quarterly* 101 (1986): 23–47.

Reid, Melanie Sovine. "On the Study of Religion in Appalachia." *Appalachian Journal* 6 (1979): 239–44.

Reinhardt, Robert Melvin. "The Political Behavior of West Virginia Protestant Fundamentalist Sectarians." Ph.D. diss., West Virginia University, 1975.

Research and Forecasts, Inc. *The Connecticut Mutual Report on American Values in the 1980s: The Impact of Belief*. Hartford, Conn.: Connecticut Mutual Life Insurance Company, 1981.

Ribuffo, Leo. *The Old Christian Right*. Philadelphia: Temple University Press, 1983.

Richard, James T., and Barend Van Priel. "Public Support for Anti-Cult Legislation." *Journal for the Scientific Study of Religion* 23 (1984): 412–18.

Richardson, James T., and Sandie Wightman Fox. "Religious Affiliation as a Predictor of Voting Behavior on Abortion Reform Legislation." *Journal for the Scientific Study of Religion* 11 (December 1972): 347–59.

——. "Religion and Voting on Abortion Reform: A Follow Up Study." *Journal for the Scientific Study of Religion* 14 (June 1975): 159–64.

——. "Public Opinion and the Tax Evasion Trial of Reverend Moon." *Behavioral Sciences and the Law* 10 (1992): 53–63.

Rojek, Dean. "The Protestant Ethic and Political Preference." *Social Forces* 52 (1973): 168–77.

Rokeach, Milton. "Religious Values and Social Compassion." *Review of Religious Research* 11 (1969): 24–39.

Roof, Wade Clark. "Socioeconomic Differentials Among White Socioreligious Groups in the United States." *Social Forces* 58 (1979): 280–89.

——. "Multiple Religious Switching." *Journal for the Scientific Study of Religion* 28 (1989): 530–35.

Roof, Wade Clark, and William McKinney. *American Mainline Religion*. New Brunswick, N.J.: Rutgers University Press, 1987.

Roozen, David A. *The Churched and the Unchurched in America: A Comparative Profile*. Washington, D.C.: Glenmary Research Center, 1978.

——. "Church Dropouts." *Review of Religious Research* 21 (1980): 427–50.

Rosenberg, Ellen M. *The Southern Baptists: A Subculture in Transition*. Knoxville: University of Tennessee Press, 1989.

Rothenberg, Stuart and Frank Newport. *The Evangelical Voter*. Washington, D.C.: Free Congress Research and Education Foundation, 1984.

Roy, Ralph Lord. *Apostles of Discord*. Boston: Beacon Press, 1953.

Rozell, Mark J., and Clyde Wilcox. *Second Coming: The New Christian Right in Virginia Politics*. Baltimore: Johns Hopkins University Press, 1996.

Rozell, Mark J., and Clyde Wilcox, eds. *God at the Grass Roots: The Christian Right in the 1994 Elections*. Lanham, Md.: Rowman & Littlefield, 1995.

Rubin, Eva Z. *Abortion Politics and the Courts*. Westport, Conn: Greenwood, 1982.

Schultze, Quentin J. *American Evangelicals and the Mass Media*. Grand Rapids: Zondervan, 1991.

Scoble, Harry M., and Leon D. Epstein. "Religion and Wisconsin Voting in 1960." *Journal of Politics* 26 (May 1964): 380–96.

Shibley, Mark A. "The Southernization of American Religion." *Sociological Analysis* 52 (1991): 159–74.

Shortbridge, James R. "A New Regionalization of American Religion." *Journal for the Scientific Study of Religion* 16 (1977): 143–53.

Shriver, Peggy L. *The Bible Vote: Religion and the New Right*. New York: Pilgrim Press, 1981.

Shupe, Anson, and John Heineman. "Mormonism and the New Christian Right: An Emerging Coalition?" *Review of Religious Research* 27 (1985): 146–57.

Shupe, Anson, and William Stacey. *Born Again Politics and the Majority: What Social Surveys Really Show*. New York: Edwin Mellen Press, 1982.

Shurden, Walter B. *Not a Silent People: Controversies That Have Shaped Southern Baptists*. Nashville: Broadman, 1972.

Sigelman, Lee, and Stanley Presser. "Measuring Support for the New Christian Right." *Public Opinion Quarterly* 52 (1988): 325–37.

Silk, Mark. *Spiritual Politics: Religion and America Since World War II*. New York: Oxford University Press, 1988.

Simpson, John H. "Socio-moral Issues and Recent Presidential Elections." *Review of Religious Research* 27 (1985): 115–23.

———. "Status Inconsistency and Moral Issues." *Journal for the Scientific Study of Religion* 24 (1985): 1119–36.

Skerry, Peter. "The Class Conflict over Abortion." *Public Interest* 52 (Summer 1978): 69–84.

Smidt, Corwin. "Evangelicals and the 1984 Election: Continuity or Change?" *American Politics Quarterly* 15 (1987): 419–44.

———. "Evangelicals v. Fundamentalists: An Analysis of the Characteristics of Importance of Two Major Religious Movements within American Politics." *Western Political Quarterly* 41 (1988): 601–20.

———. "Evangelicals Within Contemporary American Politics." *Western Political Quarterly* 41 (1988): 601–20.

———. "Praise the Lord Politics." *Sociological Analysis* 50 (1988): 53–72.

———. *Contemporary Evangelical Political Involvement*. Lanham, Md.: University Press of America, 1989.

Smidt, Corwin, and James Penning. "A House Divided: A Comparison of Robertson and Bush Delegates to the 1988 Michigan Republican State Convention." *Polity* 23 (1990): 127–38.

Smidt, Corwin, and Paul Kellstedt. "Evangelicals in the Post-Reagan Era: An Analysis of Evangelical Voters in the 1988 Presidential Election." *Journal for the Scientific Study of Religion* 31 (1992): 330–38.

Smith, Timothy L. "Religion and Ethnicity in America." *American Historical Review* 83 (1978): 1155–85.

Soper, J. Christopher. *Evangelical Christianity in the United States and Great Britain: Religious Beliefs, Political Choices*. New York: New York University Press, 1994.

Stark, Rodney. "The Reliability of Historical United States Census Data on Religion." *Sociological Analysis* 53 (1992): 91–95.

Stark, Rodney, and Charles Glock. *American Piety: The Nature of Religious Commitment*. Berkeley, Calif.: University of California Press, 1968.

Stark, Rodney, and William S. Bainbridge. *The Future of American Religion*. Berkeley, Calif.: University of California Press, 1985.

Starr, Jerrold. "Religious Preference, Religiosity, and Opposition to War." *Sociological Analysis* 36 (1975): 323–34.

Stedman, Murray S., Jr. *Religion and Politics in America*. New York: Harcourt, Brace, and World, 1964.

Steiber, Steven R. "The Influence of the Religious Factor on Civil and Sacred Tolerance." *Social Forces* 58 (1980): 811–32.

Stellway, Richard J. "The Correspondence Between Religious Orientation and Socio-Political Liberalism and Conservatism." *Sociological Quarterly* 14 (1973): 430–39.

Stevenson, William R., Jr., ed. *Christian Political Activism at the Crossroads*. Lanham, Md.: University Press of America, 1994.

Stump, R. W. "Regional Divergence in Religious Affiliation in the United States." *Sociological Analysis* 45 (1984): 283–99.

Summers, Gene F., et al. "Ascetic Protestantism and Political Preference: A Reexamination." *Review of Religious Research* (1970): 17–25.

Sundquist, James L. *Dynamics of the Party System*. Washington, D.C.: Brookings Institution, 1973.

Sweet, Leonard I., ed. *The Evangelical Tradition in America*. Macon, Ga.: Mercer University Press, 1984.

Taft, Charles P., and Bruce L. Felknor. *Prejudice and Politics*. New York: Anti-Defamation League, 1960.

Tedin, Kent L. "Religious Preference and Pro/Anti Activism on the Equal Rights Amendment Issue." *Pacific Sociological Review* 21 (1978): 55–66.

Thompson, James J. *Tried as by Fire: Southern Baptists and the Religious Controversies of the 1920s*. Macon, Ga.: Mercer University Press, 1982.

Tinder, Glenn. *The Political Meaning of Christianity.* Baton Rouge: Louisiana State University Press, 1989.

Vinovskis, Maris A. "The Politics of Abortion in the House of Representatives in 1976." *Michigan Law Review* 77 (August 1979): 1790–1827.

Wald, Kenneth D. *Religion and Politics in the United States.* New York: St. Martins, 1987.

Wald, Kenneth D., Dennis E. Owen, and Samuel S. Hill, Jr. "Churches as Political Communities." *American Political Science Review* 82 (1988): 531–48.

———. "Evangelical Politics and Status Issues." *Journal for the Scientific Study of Religion* 28 (1989): 1–16.

———. "Political Cohesion in Churches." *Journal of Politics* 52 (1990): 197–215.

Wardin, Albert W. *Baptist Atlas.* Nashville: Broadman Press, 1980.

Warner, John Robert, Jr. "Religious Affiliation as a Factor in the Voting Records of Members of the Eighty-Ninth Congress." Ph.D. diss., Boston University, 1968.

Watt, David Harrington. *A Transforming Faith: Explorations of Twentieth Century American Evangelicalism.* New Brunswick, N.J.: Rutgers University Press, 1991.

Weaver, Mary Jo, and R. Scott Appleby, eds. *Being Right: Conservative Catholics in America.* Bloomington: Indiana University Press, 1995.

Webb, George E. *The Evolution Controversy in America.* Lexington: University Press of Kentucky, 1994.

Weller, Jack E. *Yesterday's People: Life in Contemporary Appalachia.* Lexington: University Press of Kentucky, 1965.

White, John Kenneth. *The New Politics of Old Values.* Hanover, N.H.: University Press of New England, 1988.

White, O. Kendall, Jr. "Overt and Covert Politics: The Mormon Church's Anti-ERA Campaign in Virginia." *Virginia Social Science Journal* 19 (1984): 11–16.

Wilcox, Clyde. "Evangelicals and Fundamentalists in the New Christian Right: Religious Differences in the Ohio Moral Majority." *Journal for the Scientific Study of Religion* 25 (1986): 355–63.

———. "Popular Support for the Moral Majority in 1980." *Social Science Quarterly* 68 (1987): 157–67.

———. "Political Action Committees of the New Christian Right." *Journal for the Scientific Study of Religion* 27 (1988): 60–71.

———. "Evangelicals and the Moral Majority." *Journal for the Scientific Study of Religion* 28 (1990): 400–14.

———. "Religion and Politics Among White Evangelicals." *Review of Religious Research* 32 (1990): 27–42.

———. *God's Warriors: The Christian Right in Twentieth Century America.* Baltimore: Johns Hopkins University Press, 1992.

———. "Premillenalists at the Millennium: Some Reflections on the Christian Right in the Twenty-first Century." *Sociology of Religion* 55 (1994): 243–62.

Wilcox, Clyde, et al. "Attitudes Toward Church-State Issues." *Journal of Church and State* 34 (1992): 259–77.

Wilcox, Clyde, and Leopoldo Gomez. "The Christian Right and the Pro-Life Movement." *Review of Religious Research* 31 (1990): 380–89.

Wilcox, Clyde, and Ted Jelen. "Evangelicalism and Political Tolerance." *American Politics Quarterly* 18 (1990): 25–46.

Williams, Michael. *The Shadow of the Pope.* New York: Whittlesey House, 1932.

Williamson, Rene de Visme. "Conservatism and Liberalism in American Protestantism." *Annals of the American Academy of Political and Social Science* 344 (November 1962): 85–94.

Wills, Garry. *Under God: Religion and American Politics.* New York: Simon & Schuster, 1990.

Wogaman, J. Philip, "The Churches and Legislative Advocacy." *Annals of the American Academy of Political and Social Sciences* 446 (November 1979): 52–62.

Wood, Michael, and Michael Hughes. "The Moral Basis of Moral Reform." *American Sociological Review* 49 (1984): 86–99.

Woodrum, Eric. "Moral Conservatism and the 1984 Presidential Election." *Journal for the Scientific Study of Religion* 27 (1988): 192–210.

Wust, Klaus. *The Virginia Germans.* Charlottesville: University Press of Virginia, 1969.

Wuthnow, Robert. *The Restructuring of American Religion: Society and Faith Since World War II.* Princeton: Princeton University Press, 1988.

———. *The Struggle for America's Soul.* Grand Rapids, Mich.: Eerdmans, 1989.

Yinger, J. Milton, and Stephen J. Cutler. "The Moral Majority Viewed Sociologically." *Sociological Focus* 15 (1982): 289–306.

Young, Robert. "The Protestant Heritage and the Spirit of Gun Ownership." *Journal for the Scientific Study of Religion* 28 (1989): 300–309.

Zelinsky, Wilbur. "An Approach to the Religious Geography of the United States." *Annals of the American Association of Geographers* 51 (1961): 139–93.

———. *The Cultural Geography of the United States.* Englewood Cliffs, N.J.: Prentice-Hall, 1973.

Zurcher, Louis A., Jr., and George Firkpatrick. *Citizens for Decency: Anti-Pornography Crusades as Status Defense.* Austin: University of Texas Press, 1976.

Zwier, Robert. *Born-Again Politics.* Downer's Grove, Ill.: Intervarsity Press, 1982.

Index

335